Map of Great Britain

Scotland

1 ABERDEEN CITY
2 DUNDEE CITY
3 WEST DUNBARTONSHIRE
4 EAST DUNBARTONSHIRE
5 NORTH LANARKSHIRE
6 INVERCLYDE
7 RENFREWSHIRE
8 CITY OF GLASGOW
9 EAST RENFREWSHIRE
10 CLACKMANNANSHIRE
11 CITY OF EDINBURGH

12 HARTLEPOOL
13 STOCKTON-ON-TEES
14 MIDDLESBROUGH
15 CITY OF KINGSTON UPON HULL
16 NORTH EAST LINCOLNSHIRE

England

Wales

17 NEATH PORT TALBOT
18 BRIDGEND
19 RHONDDA CYNON TAFF
20 MERTHYR TYDFIL
21 CAERPHILLY
22 BLAENAU GWENT
23 TORFAEN
24 CARDIFF
25 NEWPORT
26 SOUTH GLOUCESTERSHIRE
27 BRISTOL
28 NORTH SOMERSET
29 BATH AND NORTH EAST
   SOMERSET

HIGHLAND
MORAY
ABERDEENSHIRE
ANGUS
PERTH AND KINROSS
ARGYLL AND BUTE
STIRLING
FIFE
FALKIRK
WEST LOTHIAN
EAST LOTHIAN
NORTH AYRSHIRE
SOUTH LANARKSHIRE
SCOTTISH BORDERS
EAST AYRSHIRE
SOUTH AYRSHIRE
DUMFRIES & GALLOWAY

NORTHUMBERLAND
TYNE & WEAR
DURHAM
REDCAR AND CLEVELAND
CUMBRIA
NORTH YORKSHIRE
YORK
EAST RIDING OF YORKSHIRE
LANCASHIRE
WEST YORKSHIRE
NORTH LINCOLN
GREATER MANCHESTER
SOUTH YORKSHIRE
MERSEYSIDE

ISLE OF ANGLESEY
CONWY
FLINT
GWYNEDD
CHESHIRE
DERBY
NOTTINGHAM
LINCOLN
STAFFORD
POWYS
SHROPSHIRE
LEICESTERSHIRE
WEST MIDLANDS
NORFOLK
CEREDIGION
HEREFORD & WORCESTER
WARWICK
NORTHAMPTON
CAMBRIDGE
SUFFOLK
PEMBROKESHIRE
CARMARTHENSHIRE
MONMOUTH
BEDFORD
HERTFORD
ESSEX
GLOUCESTER
BUCKINGHAMSHIRE
VALE OF GLAMORGAN
OXFORDSHIRE
GREATER LONDON
BERKSHIRE
WILTSHIRE
HAMPSHIRE
SURREY
KENT
WEST SUSSEX
EAST SUSSEX
SOMERSET
DEVON
DORSET
CORNWALL

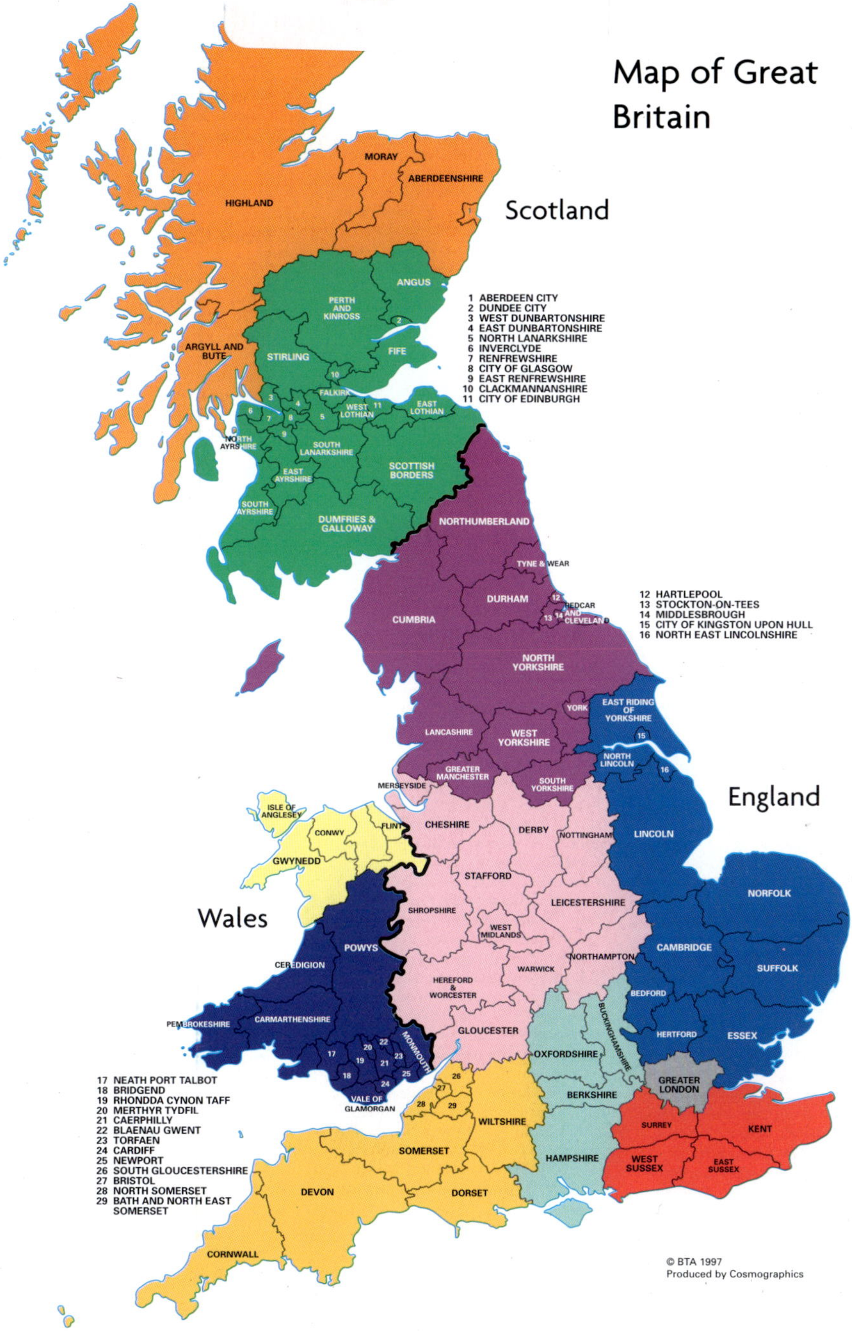

© BTA 1997
Produced by Cosmographics

1

Map Credits

Photographic Credits

Front Cover

NBC Introduction

Thank you for purchasing our 'Best of Britain' guide and NBC Discount Card.

With the increasing number of visitors from the US traveling independently we wanted to introduce a 'Best of Britain' guide that highlighted many of the best attractions, within interesting and exciting themes. Designed for independent travelers and to help you with planning and getting around, whether you are visiting for the first, 2nd, 3rd or even 4th time. There is much more to discover.

The themes offer a mixture of traditional and contemporary attractions, and are laid out to leave the choices up to you, and the 'getting around' made convenient by the guide. We also have a firm belief that, to thank you for visiting Britain, you should be made even more welcome throughout Britain than ever before. For this reason, and to enable you to spend your money on the things most important to you, we have arranged numerous offers and savings throughout your journey.

Enjoy your stay in Britain and we hope to have the privilege of seeing you again.

Acknowledgements

NBC would like to thank the BTA (with special thanks to, Lisa Davis, Julian Younger, Deirdre Livingstone, Sue Lawson and Shirley Roberts) and Tourist Boards throughout Britain for their kind help and assistance in producing the guide. Thanks to the London Tourist Board, the London Shop Associations, to London Transport, Time Out, London White Card, Global Refund, and Applause. National Express, Avis, BritRail International, Guide Friday. Best Western, Stakis and Thistle Hotels. To the National Trust, English Heritage, Treasure Houses, Cadw and Historic Scotland. To the numerous individual contributors who have kindly provided a discount or offer, and provided information and pictures to those purchasing the guide.

To Helena Frost and Derek Fawcett, Christiaan and Gemma.

Edited and Designed by Mark Hendriksen and Richard Rockwood, with thanks to Chris Pitts.

Typesetting by Richard Rockwood, William Harvey and Mark Hendriksen.

Proofreading by Kolleen Ostgaard and Helena Frost.

Printed in the UK by Reynolds Press of Coventry, England.

Published by, NBC Ltd. Great Britain.

Contents

HIG

ARGYLL AND
BUTE

NO
AYRS

W

PEMBROKESHIRE

17 NEATH PORT TALBOT
18 BRIDGEND
19 RHONDDA CYNON TAFF
20 MERTHYR TYDFIL
21 CAERPHILLY
22 BLAENAU GWENT
23 TORFAEN
24 CARDIFF
25 NEWPORT
26 SOUTH GLOUCESTERSHI
27 BRISTOL
28 NORTH SOMERSET
29 BATH AND NORTH EAST
   SOMERSET

CORN

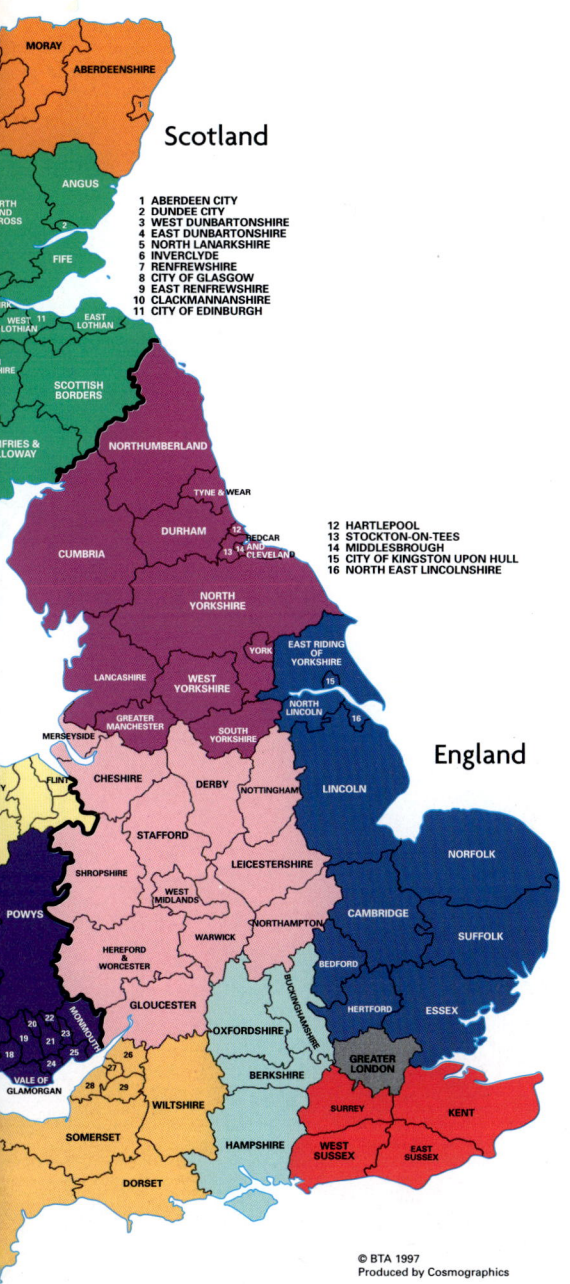

Scotland

1 ABERDEEN CITY
2 DUNDEE CITY
3 WEST DUNBARTONSHIRE
4 EAST DUNBARTONSHIRE
5 NORTH LANARKSHIRE
6 INVERCLYDE
7 RENFREWSHIRE
8 CITY OF GLASGOW
9 EAST RENFREWSHIRE
10 CLACKMANNANSHIRE
11 CITY OF EDINBURGH

12 HARTLEPOOL
13 STOCKTON-ON-TEES
14 MIDDLESBROUGH
15 CITY OF KINGSTON UPON HULL
16 NORTH EAST LINCOLNSHIRE

England

© BTA 1997
Produced by Cosmographics

Thinking of coming to Britain?

THINK

THISTLE

1ST

FOR LOCATION

Thistle Hotels has properties in key locations throughout Britain, including 24 in London alone.

Whether it be luxury in the best location in London, a Thistle Country House Hotel or modern accommodation right on the seafront promenade in Brighton, Thistle has something for everyone.

Thistle Hotels offer the perfect base to explore Britain's heritage and scenery. Plus highly individual hotels, each with a unique style and character making every experience a special one. With Thistle Hotels you can always rely on the same exceptional levels of service wherever you stay.

THISTLE HOTELS

The Park Court, London

Map of the United Kingdom showing Thistle Hotel Locations:

- Inverness
- Aberdeen
- Dunfermline
- Glasgow
- Edinburgh
- Irvine
- Newcastle-upon-Tyne
- Grasmere
- Leeds
- Haydock
- Manchester
- Liverpool
- Nottingham
- East Midlands Airport
- Birmingham
- Stratford
- Cheltenham
- Milton Keynes
- Luton
- Stevenage
- St. Albans
- **London**
- Cardiff
- Swindon
- Wallingford
- Weybridge
- Bristol
- Basingstoke
- Brands Hatch
- Gatwick/Horley
- Portsmouth
- Brighton
- Exeter
- Poole

● Thistle Hotel Locations

The Piccadilly Thistle, London

The Royal Horseguards Thistle, London

The Kensington Park Thistle, London

New Hall, A Thistle Country House

Audleys Wood Thistle, Basingstoke

Thistle Hotels is offering a special NBC rate, which may amount to as much as 15% of published rates dependant on the hotel and location plus FREE full English breakfast for every night stayed.

This offer is subject to availability and no minimum stay applies.

To make a reservation call toll free on

1-800 847 4358

and quote NBC at the time of booking or for a brochure call

1-800 295 4683

7

You'll Have A Gre
Wherever You Go

Make the most of your next trip to Great Britain with Best Western Hotels. You have a choice of over 220 fine independent hotels, set in many of the country's key business and leisure locations. All Best Western hotels in Britain are independently inspected to ensure the highest standards. Many hotels serve award-winning cuisine and there is a superb selection of hotels with top quality leisure facilities, including swimming pools, tennis, golf and much more.

Special NBC Offer

We can offer you the flexibility of touring Britain at your leisure, with the Best Western Go As You Please programme.

Book a minimum of 4 nights accommodation, pre-paid and receive accommodation vouchers that allow you the flexibility to stay at any participating Best Western hotel in Britain.*

*Ask for a Go As You Please programme brochure for a full list of participating hotels.

Best Western

Call Toll Free on 1-800 528 1234

For all Reservations, Including Go As You Please (quoting promo code EB)

at British Vacation

Best Western Oatlands Park Hotel, Weybridge

Best Western Beauport Park Hotel, Hastings

Best Western Burlington Hotel, Birmingham

Best Western Five Lakes Hotel, Maldon

Best Western Sopwell House Hotel, St Albans

Essential Information: The Best Western Go As You Please voucher programme is valid at participating hotels until 23.12.00. Each voucher is valid for a one person/one night stay, sharing a twin/double room and includes breakfast, services and local taxes. The first night's accommodation will be booked free in advance when you purchase the vouchers. Call 1-800 528 1234 for current voucher cost details. Any additional night's accommodation in this programme is subject to an additional supplement, unless it is booked less than 24 hours in advance of your stay. All additional supplements, including extra hotel and single supplements, are payable at the hotel. The offer is for a minimum purchase of 4 nights for 2 people. All reservations are subject to availability and excludes the period 23.12.99 to 3.1.00. See programme brochure for full details and hotel availability.

Stakis London Metropole - one of the five Stakis Hotels in London.

From night life to quiet life, clubs t you're sure to find the very best o

Whether you want to explore dramatic Scottish castles or dramatic London clubs, relax in sleepy village pubs or experience fine dining in cosmopolitan restaurants, discover the history of this ancient land or shop till you drop, Stakis has the answer. From major cities to lively towns to quiet

Stakis Dunkeld

...stles, shopping to island-hopping, ...takis right where you want to be.

villages, over 50 mainly 4 star Stakis Hotels throughout Britain and Ireland offer high standards of accommodation and service designed to make every guest feel special. Northern and Southern Ireland, Scotland, Wales and England - whatever your idea of a perfect vacation, Stakis can make it real.

STAKIS HOTELS
www.stakis.co.uk

How to Use The Guide London

All pages relating to London have been given a grey color band. London has been split into two sections, **Shops**, (including restaurants and services) and **Attractions**. Before each section there is useful information, and advice on the following: Attractions & Places of Interest,

in the center of London, the London maps pages 86 to 89, have a matching grid reference to enable you to quickly find an entry, and the map also indicates the nearest convenient Subway (Underground) station. The name of the nearest Underground station, corresponds to the London Underground map on pages 82,83.

How to Use, Around Britain

● Apart from London, Great Britain; England, Wales and Scotland, has been divided into 10 regions, each of which have a separate color category and chapter in the guide.
● Look at the Britain 'Color Code Map', on pages 4,5 to quickly select an area you wish to visit or to identify where you are.
● Each area begins with an 'Overview Page' and 'Area Map'. Here you will find details of the region and the list of theme trails in that area.
● Each theme trail has an introduction page with a more detailed map and reference numbers that match the main attractions.
● Each introduction page (see opposite) has the unique 'NBC

London Attractions

3. Cabaret Mechanical Theatre
A Museum of Automata, (pieces of mechanisms with concealed power to create motion). You will be pleasantly enchanted and amused by these numerous mechanical masterpieces, and there really is quite a collection. Before or after pushing numerous buttons in the main theater, you will find many amusing automated figures and game outside and around the entrance. Well worth a visit. There is a shop at the theater. Sunday open at 11.00am.

Cabaret Mechanical Theatre, 33/34 The Market, Covent Garden, London WC2E 8RE
☎ 0171 379 7961

⭐ 🗂
🕙 10-6.30pm
🖼 ✂
🎟

🚇 Covent Garden
www.cabaret.co.uk
Map ref: Page xx – E8

Penhaligon's Ltd
At Penhaligon's you will find classic scents and fine English gifts for ladies and gentlemen. By appointment to His Royal Highness the Duke of Edinburgh, and HRH Prince of Wales, this is one of England's finest perfumeries. The gift is a ladies' or gentlemen's scent library on a spend of over £20, please present your card and guide. Closed on Sundays.

41 Wellington Street, Covent Garden WC2
☎ 0171 836 2150
🕙 10-6pm
✂ (£20+)
🎟 All

🚇 Covent Garden

London Attractions and Shops

Entertainment and Nightlife, Restaurants, Shopping.
When an offer is made to NBC users the following symbol appears [*] in the listing. After each list, shops and attractions that are making a special offer are listed separately, alphabetically, together with a photo, and more detailed information.
● The simple key to the symbols, on the inside front cover, will provide the user with information at-a-glance. For all listings

South East of England

Sheerness · Margate · Herne Bay · Ramsgate · Walton-on-Thames · Woking · Canterbury · Deal · Guildford · Reigate · Sevenoaks · Dover · Tunbridge Wells · Folkestone · Crawley · Haywards Heath · Chichester · Hove · Lewes · Rye · Worthing · Brighton · Hastings · Newhaven · Eastbourne

WEST SUSSEX · EAST SUSSEX · SURREY · KENT

THE SOUTH EAST OF ENGLAND is often referred to as London's Countryside, because it's so accessible for either a day trip or short stay.
Surrey is very much a London commuter belt and very accessible to the capital. Home to Hampton Court Palace, the county is set in heathlands and the grass covered North Downs. Over a third of this whole area is designated as being 'Of Outstanding Natural Beauty'. The overall climate is temperate and Kent, known as 'The Garden of England' with its fertile soil, mild climate and regular rainfall has flourished as a fruit growing region for many years, aided by its proximity to the London markets. Importantly, with the Channel Tunnel linking Europe to the South, this is the gateway to Europe and the Continent.
Sussex, splits into East and West, where the landscapes rise and fall like waves, as with bordering Kent, this makes a good wine growing region. Here you can shop in a choice of vibrant and tranquil towns, or visit many picture-book villages, historic buildings and gardens that are all within easy reach of London. If you know or have heard of places like Brighton, Leeds Castle or Canterbury, and people like Charles Dickens,

Chaucer, (Canterbury Tales) and AA Milne, (Winnie the Pooh) then you are thinking of this part of England. But this corner of England is most famous for its landscape gardens and has ideal walking country along the 250 miles of coastline and rolling Downs, (hills) that are associated with the area, so take the opportunity to enjoy some of England's finest fresh air amongst breathtaking landscapes.

South East of England

Trail List and Page No.s
• Famous Castles and		
Canterbury Tales		100
• 1066 & The Battle of Hastings		105
• Brighton 'London by the Sea'		108
• The Body Shop and Antiques		112

Access/Getting Around
🚗 🚆 🚌 ✈ 🚇

From London
🚗 **By Road** (page ref 36,37)
The M25 London Orbital Motorway links the M4 in the west, past the M3 and M23 and M26/20 to the A2/M2 in the east.

🚆 **By Rail**
(page ref. 94,95)
A network of railway lines criss-cross the whole area but the faster services are those leading to and from London's Charing Cross, Victoria and Waterloo stations.

🚌 **By Coach**
(page ref. 96,97)
Coaches run frequently from London Victoria to most key towns in the south east, including, Canterbury, Dover, Tunbridge Wells, Hastings and Brighton.

✈ **By Air**
Gatwick Airport in West Sussex has direct flights from all parts of the world and the rest of Britain. There is a direct Rail link with London and the south east coast.

Bodiam Castle

Petworth House

Overview page, Around Britain

South East of England

Dickens, Castles and 'Canterbury Tales'

Charles Dickens spent most of his childhood in Rochester **18**, and returned there later in his life; it was the background for many scenes in 'Great Expectations' and 'Pickwick Papers', and see also, the Norman castle and cathedral **19**, side by side above the River Medway.

Canterbury **1-8**, has some fine museums and galleries, as well as the famous Cathedral. It is where Geoffrey Chaucer, (c. 1345-1400) wrote an amusing account of pilgrims' travels to the shrine of Thomas à Becket, Archbishop of Canterbury. The struggle for control of the country between church and crown led to his murder. Continuing to the east, on the tip of the coast, is Broadstairs **9**, where Dickens wrote 'Bleak House' and this house was immortalised in 'David

Copperfield'.
Keep heading south from here and you reach the Tudor-rose shaped Deal and Walmer Castles **10,11**. Continuing southerly to the port of Dover and the remarkable Roman Painted House, White Cliffs and Castle **12,13,14**. Staying on the coastline you will pass the Channel Tunnel and Eurotunnel Exhibition **17**, and can take the one third size 14 mile steam railway from Hythe **15**, or visit Port

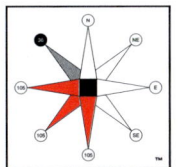

Distance from London

Dover 73miles

Lympne Wild Animal Park **7**. Towards London, Leeds Castle at Maidstone **16**, is considered as, 'one of the loveliest castles in the world'.

ℹ️ Tourist Information
Canterbury ☎ 01227 763763
Dover ☎ 01304 205108

GF Dover

Hotels
Ashford - Dover - Hythe - Rochester
Maidstone

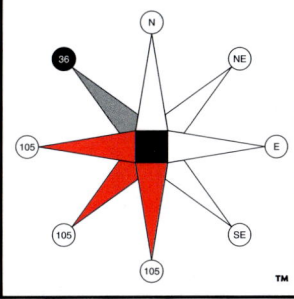

How to Use, NBCompass™

● On each of the theme pages around Britain there is an NBCompass. The compass acts like a traditional compass except that it points you to the nearest selection of attractions from your current location. This is done with a matching color and page number to where you can go next.

● At any time that you wish to return to London, follow the compass directional point with the reversed out page circle (white on black).

This enables you to plot, visit or bypass the various attractions throughout Britain, as you choose, (see above).

How to Use, NBC Card and Coupons

Your personal NBC Card, instructions and coupons are located on the inside back cover of this guide.

● Please, where applicable, read the information on each individual entry regarding use of the NBC Card.

Trail Introduction page, Around Britain

Compass' to point you to the adjoining trails.

● The page numbers and 'color bands' on the compass match the geographical perspectives, making it easy to plot, visit or bypass various attractions, as you choose. This ensures you get maximum use of your time when planning your visit, and offers you the chance to discover more of Britain.

● Each trail has details of the top sights, and additional important sights numbered and highlighted on the accompanying map. You choose what you want to see.

● With an **'easy-to-learn, easy-to-use'** key to symbols, which doubles up as a 'bookmark' on the inside front cover of the guide, you are presented with immediate and important details **'at a glance'**.

● At the beginning of this section, pages (36,37) 94 to 97, there are key maps for each method of travel, road, rail and coach (long-distance bus), which can be used for easy reference.

● On page 92 you can find information on 'Guide Friday' bus tours throughout Britain

JEWELS
of
BRITAIN

The Ultimate British Vacation

115 of the finest
hotels and 130 of t
best restaurants i
Britain.

Your passport to
client's dream
vacation in Britai

CALL
1-800-GO2-BRITA
(1-800-462-2748)
for your copies

PLANNING AND USEFUL INFORMATION

Before you plan your journey visit the BTA (British Tourist Authority) website [**www.visitbritain.com**].

BRITAIN on the internet
www.visitbritain.com

That is were you will find the best available advice and all the help you need to make your trip to Britain a resounding success.

Alternatively contact the BTA direct at:
551 Fifth Avenue
Suite 701
New York NY 10176-0799
T. 1 800 GO2 BRITAIN - Toll Free
    (212) 986 2200
Open 9-6pm Monday through Friday
625 North Michigan Avenue
Suite 1510
Chicago, IL 60611
Open 9-5pm Monday through Friday (walk in visitors only)

Before You Go
Passport and Visa/Entry
Requirements (For up to 90 days)
As an American citizen traveling to the UK **you do need:**

1. A valid passport.
(Check the expiration date!)
2. A round trip (return) air ticket.
3. Traveler's Checks
Credit Cards etc.

Check also that you are covered on medical insurance and have adequate travel insurance. In Britain the National Health Service (NHS) will only offer you free treatment in the event of an emergency.

You do not need:
1. A visa.
2. Innoculations.

Climate
The climate in Britain is, in the main, mild. None of the regions are far from the sea, and this has a moderating influence on temperatures. Summer daytime temperatures rarely exceed 86°F, but can be humid. Wintertime is more fog, frost and rain than snow.

Despite Britain's reputation, there is actually a relatively low average annual rainfall of less than 40 inches. Heavy rain is rare, but the reason why the British people talk about the weather so much is because it's rarely predictable. You should have your camera ready to take lots of pictures when the sun is shining, as it can often be shortlived. Incidentally it is also why packing an umbrella, (brolly) or light raincoat (macintosh) is a good precaution.

Rough Guide to the Average Daily Temperature
(British Meteorological Office)

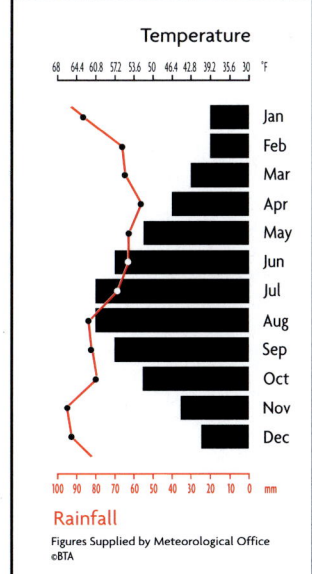

Figures Supplied by Meteorological Office
©BTA

Driving in the UK
(see pages 29,30 for more detailed information)
The good news is that when you see children or dogs in the driving seat, they are not actually driving! **Left is Right**. Don't worry, you will soon get used to driving on the 'other' side of the road. A handy tip to help you remember is to wear your watch on the other wrist.

In order to drive in Britain you will need your current driver's license. Any major car rental company will help with documentation requirements, maps, road signs, insurance, advice and answer any questions you may have. For example you can telephone the Avis Office in the US, page 93. Also, the BTA have further information on driving regulations and road signs call and ask for your 'Free' Britain map, on:
1 (800) GO 2 BRITAIN .

Fuel (gasoline is called petrol) Fuel is expensive compared to North American prices. As a general rule, supermarkets with their own gas stations charge the least, and some other gas stations have a 'Price Watch' where they match the lowest price within a local radius.

● When you are packing, check you have got your Driver's License.

Insurance
It is important to insure yourself and your belongings for the length of your stay in the UK. It is impossible to predict any unforeseen difficulties. Therefore, it is advisable to cover yourself against theft or lost property, and against illness. Your insurance adviser or travel agent will advise you of the best coverage that suits your personal requirements. Always buy your travel insurance direct from the insurance company.

Spending Money

Britain's currency is (£ - pounds) Sterling, which divides into 100 pence (p). There are no exchange controls in Britain so you can bring use it throughout Britain. British Bank Bills are in denominations of £5, £10, £20 and £50. It is best to get smaller denominations, as change is not

£5   £10

£20   £50

1p 2p 5p 10p 20p 50p £1 £2

in and take out as much cash as you like.

● The same currency is used in England, Scotland and Wales (although Scotland has different images on its currency, the denominations are the same and the currency accepted throughout Britain). Ask for 'UK Sterling' when exchanging money and you can

always available from a £50 note. Coins that are currently used are, £2, £1, 50p, 20p, 10p, 5p, 2p and 1p.

High Street Banks (open from 9.30-4.30 Monday through Friday) Lloyds, Barclays, National Westminster, Midland and Royal Bank of Scotland generally offer the most reasonable rates of exchange.

Bureaux de Change offices are located in practically every tourist area. Please be careful to check the transaction fee and minimum charges before completing any transaction. Reputable firms include; Thomas Cook, Chequepoint and American Express.

Traveler's Checks are the safest way of bringing currency into Britain. American Express, for example, do not charge a transaction fee for cashing their own traveler's checks. In some

small towns and rural areas you may need cash with you.

Credit Cards

Visa and Access/MasterCard are widely accepted. American Express and Diner's Club are also widely accepted. Check with your bank on their policy if you wish to withdraw cash on your cards in Britain.

Accommodation

Britain has an extensive range of hotels and accommodation, and whatever your budget, you will find somewhere to suit you, wherever you are in Britain. The types of accommodation from which to choose are Country House Hotels, Hotel Chains, and Bed and Breakfasts.

● Beds are not automatically big in Britain, so if you want a big bed be sure and ask for a double or king size.

Country House Hotels

The true country house hotels have some architectural or historical value, and are often furnished with antiques and fine furnishings. Often situated on extensive grounds, these are of a high standard of traditional English comfort and luxury, with a high tariff to match their exclusivity. It is worth noting that some are owned and run privately, and

Hatton Court Hotel

others may be owned by hotel chains.

Hotel Chains and Groups

There are a number of corporate hotel chains at the top end of the market in Britain, and some tend to lack individuality. However, certain groups have excellent character hotels throughout Britain. For example, Thistle Hotels, pages 6,7, Stakis Hotels, pages 10,11, Best Western pages 8,9, and Forte. Each cover most parts of Britain and are internationally recognized for their levels of service and comfort. All of these groups have booking and information desks in the US and will be happy to help with your requirements, another great option are the 'Jewels' of Britain, see page 14.

● Britain does not necessarily mirror the standard and type of service you may receive at home, so you might experience a different service from that you are used to. But, please enjoy the experience in the type of accommodation you choose, as this is part of what makes Britain so fascinating and unique.

Bed and Breakfast

Bed and Breakfast accommodation usually means that you are staying in someone's home, albeit a small house, a guest house, a farmhouse or a grand manor. It should be pointed out that this is not hotel accommodation, and the service can therefore be more intimate and interesting. Expectations

should not be so high, although one is often pleasantly surprised. It is however, an ideal chance to experience 'family life' with a range of places to stay, each with its own individual character. Many B&B's accept only cash payment, so please check if other payment methods are available.
If you want to try Bed and Breakfast accommodation whilst

Fosse Farmhouse B&B

traveling around, the local Tourist Information Centres offer a **Book-a-Bed-Ahead** service, just advise them in advance of where you are going, and they'll do the rest.

Booking by Yourself

(Making Reservations)
If you are booking any accommodation by yourself, it is advisable to write or fax requesting a brochure and rates card. When you are ready, write or fax again to arrange your stay. Quite simply you should write your name and address in the US, plus a telephone or fax number where you can be contacted, together with your arrival date, and how many of you will be staying, length of stay, room type and meal requirements, and your departure date.

National Grading & Classification Scheme

Over 17,000 establishments display an English Tourist Board crown sign at their front door (Scotland, Wales and Northern Ireland operate similar classification schemes too). All in the scheme are guaranteed to be clean, but the number of crowns displayed (1-5) gives you an indication of the number of facilities available. For example, 1 crown ensures you have at least a washbasin in your room; 4 crowns indicates each room has a color TV, radio and phone and most have a bathroom. However, only the quality gradings - Approved, Commended, Highly Commended or De Luxe - indicate the more personal, though still professional, assesment; ambience, food, the little touches that make a difference. A 5 crown hotel might only achieve an Approved grading while a 1 crown hotel could achieve a Highly Commended grading. Look out for the signs.

Finally ask for receipt of your letter and confirmation of the arrangements. See pages 6 to 11, for details on more familiar hotel groups in Britain.

Overseas Visitor Passes

The passes that should be considered before leaving the US are, the BritRail Pass (page 94), London Transport's Visitor Travelcard (page 90), and the BritExpress Coach Pass (page 96). For attractions the main passes are for National Trust and/or English

Heritage. Visitor Passes can also be pre-purchased, although their are special offers if you pick up your pass in Britain.

A coupon in the back of the guide gives you 15% off the **English Heritage** Visitor Pass and can be redeemed at any of their properties. **The National Trust** provide a comprehensive free guidebook covering all of their properties, which can be collected only by showing your NBC card when you purchase a Visitor Pass at:

The Blewcoat School Gift Shop, 23 Caxton Street, Westminster, London SW1H 0PY
(nearest tube, St James's Park).
A visit to just 2 or 3 of these properties during your visit to Britain, will easily cover the cost of a visitor pass, and you will then have the added advantage of being able to visit absolutely free. See pages 66,67,91 for information on NT and EH property opening times.

Air Travel
The least expensive airfares to Great Britain are for round-trip travel and require booking-in-advance (the earlier, the better) and a period of stay between 7 - 30 days. Be aware of cancellation charges. International flights to London arrive at either Heathrow Airport, (15 miles west of the capital and Britain's foremost airport) or Gatwick Airport, (27 miles south). Oh, and by the way do not worry about getting to the capital, transportation to London is both safe and easy from either location, (see opposite page).

Non Stop Flights
This is the best way to go. Remember that direct flights stop at least once, so make sure your flight is nonstop.

In-Flight Documentation
You will be given a Landing Card to fill in before arriving in the UK. The details are as follows:

QUESTION	DETAIL
Family Name	Rogers
Forenames	Mike
Sex	F (Female) M (Male)
Date of Birth	DD MM YY 12 12 70
Place of Birth	New York, USA
Nationality	American
Occupation	Please enter your occupation here
Address in the UK	Hotel or Address at which you are staying first
Signature	Sign you name here

Arriving in the UK
Immigration and Passport Control.
There are two check-in points marked as follows:
1. EC Passports
2. All Other Passports
Proceed to number 2. 'All Other Passports' where you will be required to show the following:
1. Landing Card
2. Passport
3. Round Trip (Return Flight) ticket

You might then be asked the following questions:
Q. How long are you going to stay?
A. Please say how many days/weeks.

Q. What is the purpose of your visit?
A. Sightseeing

Q. Do you have a return flight ticket?
A. Yes, (and please show again if required).

Baggage Claim
You will then proceed to the Baggage Claim Hall. Check your flight number on the overhead incoming flight information screens to see which gate your luggage will arrive at. Proceed to that gate and the baggage carousel. As your baggage appears take it off the carousel. Trolleys are available, and in the unlikely event that your baggage appears to be lost, take your 'baggage identification tag' to your airlines Lost and Found Counter.

Customs
The Red Channel is, 'Something to Declare'. The Green Channel is,

'Nothing to Declare'.
There are restrictions on what you can bring into the UK from outside of the EU, (European Community) so it is advisable to check the current regulations before you arrive. These are normally displayed at the duty free stores and on the airplane. No pets can be bought in without a lengthy quarantine. The penalties are severe and strictly enforced. These restrictions also apply to illegal drugs, firearms, ammunition, and vegetables, plants and fresh meats.

Traveling to London from the Airport
After passing out into the flight arrivals section, proceed by your chosen method of transportation, to where you are staying. Here are a few easy options:
From Heathrow
The Tube runs throughout London and the capital, (see pages 82,83) Heathrow is at grid reference E1.

Major UK Airports

Airport	Distance – City Center	Public Transport	Journey Time – City
Heathrow	14 miles (London)	Tube (Subway)	40 mins
Gatwick	28 miles (London)	Rail	30 mins
Stansted	37 miles (London)	Rail	45 mins
Manchester	10 miles	Rail	15 mins
Birmingham	8 miles	Bus	30 mins
Newcastle	5 miles	Metro	20 mins
Glasgow	10 miles	Bus	20 mins
Edinburgh	5 miles	Bus	15 mins

The Heathrow Express service runs every 15 minutes and takes 15 minutes, to and from Paddington station. Airbuses are available to take you downtown, but the tube where to go when you reach the end of your tube, rail, coach or taxi journey.

The rail system is the best alternative for major cities throughout Britain, although fares can sometimes be expensive if not booked in advance, (pages 94,95).

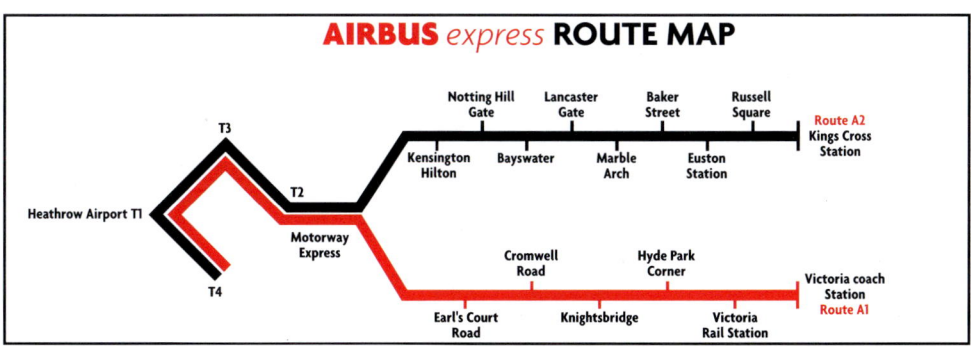

AIRBUS *express* **ROUTE MAP**

or Heathrow Express service is perhaps quickest, and easiest.

From Gatwick
There is a rail service into Victoria station, (see page 82 map ref. E4) called the Gatwick Express. From Victoria you can take the Tube throughout London. A Speedlink coach is also available, but the rail service is best.

Courtesy Buses (coaches)
From the airports to most leading airport hotels.

Taxi Cabs
Available if you want to be taken directly to where you are staying, but check the price first to avoid any unpleasant surprises.
See the London maps on pages 82 to 89, to familiarize yourself with

Traveling in Britain
As an International Gateway for air and sea traffic, traveling to Britain is easy, with a large choice of carriers from the US.
Traveling within Britain is also fairly easy, as there are extensive road networks reaching all parts of the country. Renting a car is quite often the best way to get around outside London, (page 93). London has an excellent underground rail (tube) and overground bus system which is certainly the best way to get around the capital, (pages 82,83).
Traveling around Britain can be done by coach to a large number of destinations, (pages 96,97), or by rail.

As you arrive at your chosen destinations, walking, cycling, local transport services, taxis and tour buses, (page 92), are all excellent ways of getting around, and local Tourist Information Centres have details and timetables where needed.
Britain's size makes internal air travel effective only if you are traveling a long distance. Internal air fares can be expensive unless you reserve in advance. For that reason it may be best to ask your agent to book internal flights for you to suit your schedule.
● Regarding a somewhat slower method of transport, 'walking', don't forget to look to the right first before crossing any roads.

SETTLING IN & USEFUL GENERAL INFORMATION
Introduction

Britain is made up of England, Scotland, Wales, and Northern Ireland, which is separated from the mainland by the Irish Sea. Information about Northern Ireland can be obtained from the Irish Tourist Board, telephone: **UK (0)171 493 3201**.

London is the capital of England, Edinburgh the capital of Scotland, and Cardiff the capital of Wales. Most travelers start in London, and the London Tourist Board is an extremely good source of information, with maps, phonecards, travelcards, accommodation and recommendations.

There are Tourist Information Centres at:

1. London Heathrow, Terminals 1,2 and 3

2. Heathrow Underground station concourse

3. Victoria Railway station

Forecourt*

4. Liverpool Street Underground station

*Victoria is the London linked information center from Gatwick Airport.

GREAT BRITAIN

Britain has a long and interesting history that will come to life as you spend your time traveling throughout the country. The population is around 58 million and the greatest density of population is in the Southeast and Central part of the country. Britain has a multi-cultural society, and a wide range of religions. Although Christianity is the leading religion, (Church of England and Roman Catholics) you will find Buddhist, Moslem and Jewish temples and synagogues throughout Britain.

The preservation of Britain's tradition has always been a priority, as can be seen from the diversity of architecture, the picturesque villages, historic buildings and stately homes. But Britain balances this with the needs of modern society by blending past and present throughout the country.

To give you a quick and easy timeline on the history, monarchy and some of the leading events and influential figures in Britain's history, we have combined many of these main points in the **Historical Guideline** chart, pages 21 to 24. This has two advantages:

1. an 'at-a-glance' overview of Britain's history.

2. an opportunity, when visiting places, to refer back to the period, people and events that influenced your surroundings.

As you go through Britain with the guide, there is an overview of each region, the landscape, and a focus on the counties and their attractions.

● To provide a historical 'home' reference, US Presidents are also noted.

✎Travel Notes

6 - 5000 BC	Ice Age
	Construction of Stonehenge
1800 BC	Arrival of Celtic Settlers from Europe
5 - 400 BC	**Roman Britain**
55 BC	Roman Occupation begins (Caesar)
AD 43	Claudius invades and Britain becomes part of Roman Empire
61	Boadicea rebels against Romans but is defeated
70	Romans conquer Wales and the North
122	Building of Hadrian's Wall
206	North Scotland Tribes attack Wall
410	Romans withdraw from Britain
440 - 450	Invasions of Angles and Saxons
450 - 1066	**Anglo-Saxons & Viking Kingdoms**
556	Saxons settle and set up seven Kingdoms
C.	Legendary 'King Arthur' fought Saxons
597	Rome sends St Augustine to promote Christianity
779	King Offa of Mercia, as overlord of England
851	Viking Raiders settle
871	Alfred, King of Wessex contains Viking Advances
876	York, founded by Danes
1016 - 1035	King Canute (Danish)
1035 - 1040	Harold I (son of Canute)
1040 - 1042	Hardicanute (Harold's half-brother)
1042 - 1066	Edward the Confessor
1066 - 1154	**The Middle Ages**
1066	Battle of Hastings
1066 - 1087	William the Conqueror
1086	Domesday Book (tax survey of England)
1087 - 1100	William II
1100 - 1135	Henry I (daughter marries Saxon)
1135 - 1154	Stephen, Count of Blois
1154 - 1485	**Plantagenets**
1154 - 1189	Henry II
1170	Thomas à Becket murdered in Canterbury
1189 - 1199	Richard I (Lionheart) defeats father, Henry II
1199 - 1216	King John
1215	King John signs Magna Carta at Runnymede, Crown's taxing powers restricted by wealthy Barons and sets up basic principles of English Law
1216 - 1272	Henry III
1267	Principality of Wales (title, from territorial gain)
1272 - 1307	Edward I (1277, English campaign against Wales)
1282	Battle and re-settlement of Wales by English
1296 - 1298	North England ravaged by Scots, under William Wallace
1305	Wallace executed
1307 - 1327	Edward II (married Isabel of France)
1314	Edward II defeated at Bannockburn by Robert I, King of Scotland
1327	Edward II murdered at Berkeley Castle
1327 - 1377	Edward III
1328	Scotland independent
1337 - 1377	Beginning of 100 Years War with France

1348	Black Death, plague halves Europe's population, reducing Britains to around 2.5 million
1358 - 1423	Life of Dick Whittington (Mayor of London)
1377 - 1399	👑 Richard II
1396	Treaty of Paris, peace between France and England
1399 - 1461	**House of Lancaster**
1399 - 1413	👑 Henry IV
1413 - 1422	👑 Henry V
1415	Battle of Agincourt (France) English Victory
1420	Treaty of Troyes (Henry V heir to French Throne)
1422 - 1461	👑 Henry VI
1455 - 1485	War of the Roses, between houses of York & Lancaster
1461 - 1485	**House of York**
1461 - 1483	👑 Edward IV
1465	Henry VI captured and imprisoned in Tower of London
1470	Restoration of Henry VI by Warwick
1471	Henry VI murdered by Edward IV after victory at Tewkesbury
1477	William Caxton prints first book in England
1483	👑 Edward V, and subsequent imprisonment in Tower of London
1483 - 1485	👑 Richard III (defeated by Henry Tudor in 1485)
1485 - 1603	**Tudors**
1485 - 1509	👑 Henry VII (marries Elizabeth of York) ends War of the Roses
1503	Henry VII's daughter marries James IV of Scotland
1509 - 1547	👑 Henry VIII
1535	Execution of Sir Thomas Moore (refused to acknowledge Henry VIII as head of the Church of England)
1536 - 1539	Dissolution of Monasteries
1547 - 1553	👑 Edward VI
1552 - 1618	Life of Sir Walter Raleigh (adventurer)
1564 - 1616	Life of Sir William Shakespeare
1553 - 1558	👑 Mary I
1554	Mary I marries Philip II of Spain
1558 - 1603	👑 Elizabeth I
1542 - 1567	Mary, Queen of Scots rules Scotland
1559	Mary lays claim to throne of England
1567	Mary imprisoned for 20 years by Elizabeth I
1573 - 1652	Life of Inigo Jones (architect)
1580	Elizabeth I excommunicated by the Pope
1580	Drake circumnavigates the world
1586	Plot to put Mary Queen of Scots on the throne
1587	Mary Queen of Scots executed for treason
1588	Drake (and the weather) defeat Spanish Armada
1603 - 1714	**Stuart Britain**
1603 - 1625	👑 James I (VI of Scotland)
1605	Gunpowder Plot (Guy Fawkes) to blow up Parliament
1620	Pilgrim Fathers sail from Plymouth on the 'Mayflower' and settle in New England
1632 - 1723	Life of Sir Christopher Wren (architect)
1625 - 1649	👑 Charles I
1626	Dissolution of Parliament by King
1642 - 1649	Civil War between the Royalists (Cavaliers) and the Parliamentarians (Roundheads, who win)

1492 Columbus discovers America

1607 English establish first colony in America

Historical Guideline
Kings & Queens - Famous People - Events

1642 - 1727	Life of Sir Isaac Newton (scientist)
1649	Charles I, trial and execution
1649 - 1660	**Commonwealth,** rule by Oliver Cromwell, not a King
1659 - 1695	Life of Henry Purcell (composer)
	Stuarts (Restoration)
1660 - 1685	Charles II (had mistress, Nell Gwynne)
1665 - 1667	War against Dutch
1665	Great Plague (68,000 in London died)
1666	Great Fire of London destroyed 80% of the City
1671 - 1734	Life of 'Rob Roy' (Scotland's Robin Hood)
1677	Charles II's sister marries William of Orange (Dutch)
1685 - 1688	James II
1688 - 1694	William III and Mary II
1694 - 1702	William III after death of Mary II
1702 - 1714	Queen Anne
1714 - 1837	**Georgian Britain**
1714 - 1727	George I
C.	Industrial Revolution under way
1715 - 1783	Life of Capability Brown (gardens)
1724 - 1792	Life of John Smeaton (engineer)
1727 - 1760	George II
1728 - 1779	Life of Capt. James Cook (navigator)
1728 - 1792	Life of Robert Adam (architect)
1730 - 1795	Life of Josiah Wedgwood (potter)
1745	Battle of Culloden, Bonnie Prince Charlie
1749 - 1823	Life of Edward Jenner (smallpox)
1752 - 1835	Life of John Nash (architect)
1757	First Canal completed
1759 - 1796	Life of Robert Burns (Scots poet)
1760 - 1820	George III
1760 - 1850	Life of Marie Tussaud (Tussaud's)
1769	Patent issued for Watt's Steam Engine
1770 - 1850	Life of Wordsworth (poet)
1771 - 1832	Life of Sir Walter Scott (Scots poet)
1775 - 1783	Britain loses its American colonies
1775 - 1817	Life of Jane Austen (author)
1775 - 1851	Life of Turner (landscape painter)
1788 - 1824	Life of Lord Byron (poet)
1792 - 1822	Life of Shelley (poet)
1795 - 1821	Life of John Keats (poet)
1800 - 1877	Life of Fox-Talbot (photography pioneer)
1801	Union with Ireland
1803 - 1859	Life of Robert Stephenson (engineer)
1805	Naval Victory at Trafalgar, Nelson dies
1806 - 1858	Life of Brunel (civil engineer)
1809 - 1892	Life of Tennyson (poet)
1812 - 1870	Life of Charles Dickens (author)
1815	Battle of Waterloo, defeat of Napoleon by Duke of Wellington
1816 - 1855	Life of Charlotte Brontë (author)
1819 - 1900	Life of John Ruskin (author and art critic)
1820 - 1830	George IV

Right column events:

1692 The famous witchcraft trials at Salem

1722 Samuel Adams was born in Boston

1743 Boston Tea Party

1776 Declaration of Independence

1789-1797 George Washington President

1797-1801 John Adams President

1801-1809 Thomas Jefferson President

1809-1817 James Madison President

1817-1825 James Monroe President

Historical Guideline
Kings & Queens - Famous People - Events

1820 - 1910	Life of Florence Nightingale (nurse)
1830 - 1837 ♛	William IV
1832 - 1898	Life of Lewis Carroll (Alice in Wonderland)
1833	Construction of Britain's Rail network begins
1834	Parliament outlaws slavery
1837 - 1901 ♛	**Victorian Britain**
1840	Victoria marries Prince Albert
1840 - 1928	Life of Thomas Hardy (novelist and poet)
1850 - 1894	Life of Robert Louis Stevenson (author)
1851	Great Exhibition in Hyde Park during the height of the British Empire
1854 - 1900	Life of Oscar Wilde (author and dramatist)
1863	First London railway opens (Underground)
1865	Bicycle invented
1866 - 1943	Life of Beatrix Potter (Peter Rabbit)
1866 - 1946	Life of HG Wells (author)
1881 - 1955	Life of Alexander Fleming (penicillin)
1874 - 1934	Life of AA Milne (Winnie-the-Pooh)
1882 - 1956	Life of Gustav Holst (composer)
1884	Telephones introduced
1895	First Motor Show in London
1901 - 1917	**House of Saxe-Coburg**
1901 - 1910 ♛	Edward VII
1905	First Motor Buses in London
1910 - 1936 ♛	George V (Changed name to Windsor)
1914 - 1918	First World War
1914 - 1953	Life of Dylan Thomas (Welsh poet)
1917 -	**House of Windsor**
1919	Women over 30 win right to Vote
1919	Ireland declares independence from England
1926	General Strike (in support of the striking coal miners)
1931	Depression, great unemployment
1936	Abdication of Edward VIII
	(marries American divorcee, Mrs Wallis Simpson)
1936	First scheduled Television
1936 - 1952 ♛	George VI
1939 - 1945	Second World War
1939	Winston Churchill becomes Prime Minister
1947	Independence for India and Pakistan
1949	Independence of Republic of Ireland
1952- ♛	Elizabeth II accession to throne
1959	First motorway built (M.1)
1963 - 1965	Beatles gain fame across the World
C.	Mini Skirts become fashion
1969	Prince Charles investiture in Wales
1973	England joins European Community
1976	Concorde makes first flight
1981	Prince Charles marries Lady Diana Spencer
1978- 1991	Margaret Thatcher, first woman Prime Minister
1994	Channel Tunnel opens to France (Eurotunnel)
1997	Diana, Princess of Wales dies

1825-1829	John Quincy Adams President
1829-1837	Andrew Jackson President
1837-1841	Martin van Buren President
1841	William Henry Harrison President
1841-1845	John Tyler President
1845-1849	James Polk President
1849-1850	Zachary Taylor
1850-1853	Millard Filmore President
1853-1857	Franklin Pierce President
1857-1861	James Buchanan President
1863	Gettysburg Address (Nov 19)
1861-1865	Abraham Lincoln
1865-1869	Andrew Johnson President
1869-1877	Ulysses S. Grant President
1877	Edison invented phonograph
1877-1881	Rutherford B. Hayes President
1881	James Abram Garfield
1881-1885	Chester A. Arthur President
1885	Eastman marketed first box camera
1885-1889	Grover Cleveland President
1889-1893	Benjamin Harrison President
1893-1897	Grover Cleveland President
1897-1901	William McKinley President
1901-1909	Theodore Roosevelt President
1908	Henry Ford produces first Model T
1909-1913	Howard Taft President
1913-1921	Woodrow Wilson President
1921-1923	Warren G Harding President
1923-1929	Calvin Coolidge President
1929-1933	Herbert Hoover President
1933-1945	Franklin D. Roosevelt President
1945-1953	Harry S. Truman President
1953-1961	Dwight D. Eisenhower President
1961-1963	John F. Kennedy President
1963-1969	Lyndon B. Johnson President
1969-1974	Richard M. Nixon President
1969	Apollo 11 lands on Moon
1974-1977	Gerald R. Ford President
1977-1981	Jimmy Carter President
1981-1989	Ronald Reagan President
1989-1993	George Bush President
1993-	Bill Clinton President

Holidays and Events

Britain has a number of public holidays, (referred to as 'bank holidays') during the year, and also certain key events. Many of these are listed below as an aid to your planning.

Public holidays and events will affect the number of visitors to both shops and attractions, as well as increasing the weight of traffic on the roads, trains and coaches.

E-ENGLAND, S-SCOTLAND, W- WALES

January
1st   - Holiday (**ESW**)
2nd - Holiday (**S**)
International Boat Show
1st two weeks.
25th - Burns Night (**S**)

February
The Chinese New Year, London.
in late Jan, early Feb.
Jorvik Festival, York (**E**)

March
Crufts Dog Show at
Birmingham (**E**)
St Patrick's Day, Ireland.
Good Friday Holiday (**ESW**)
late March or early April.
Easter Monday Holiday (**EW**)
late March or early April.
Clocks go forward 1 hour, end
of March. (**ESW**)

April
Easter (see March)
The Shakespeare Season
starts in Stratford. (**E**)
London Marathon

May
May Day Holiday (**ESW**)
1st Monday in May.
Well Dressing, Derby (**E**)
Chelsea Flower Show London
(mid - May).
Holiday last Monday in May (**ESW**)
Brighton Festival (**E**)
Glyndebourne Opera Festival

begins (**E**)
Highland Games (**S**)
Shakespeare Open Air Theater,
London.

June
Royal Academy Summer
Exhibition begins, London.
Bath International Festival (**E**)
Kenwood Lakeside Concerts
in London.
Trooping the color in
London. (Sat nearest 10 June)
Glasgow Jazz Festival (**S**)
Henley Regatta (**E**)
late June, early July.
Wimbledon Tennis.

July
International Eisteddfod (**W**)
Hampton Court Flower Show (**E**)
Royal Tournament, London
Cambridge Folk Festival (**E**)
Royal Welsh Show (**W**)
Promenade Concerts begin in
London.

August
Edinburgh Intl. Festival (**S**)
Holiday 1st Monday in August (**S**)
Cowes Week, Isle of Wight (**E**)
Notting Hill Carnival, London.
Beatles Festival, Liverpool (**E**)
Holiday last Monday in Aug (**EW**)

September
Blackpool Illuminations (**E**)
Intl. Sheepdog Trials (**E**)
Horse of the Year Show at
Wembley, near London.
Glyndebourne Opera Festival
ends (**E**)

October
Harvest Festivals (**ESW**)
Canterbury Festival (**E**)
Clocks go back 1 hour, end
of October (**ESW**)
31st - Halloween (**ESW**)

November
Opening of Parliament, London
end of October, early November.
London - Brighton Vintage
Car Rally 1st Sunday (**E**)

5th - Guy Fawkes (Fireworks) (**E**)
London Film Festival.
Lord Mayor's Show, London.

December
Carol Concerts (**ESW**)
Christmas Tree put up in
Trafalgar Square, London.
25th - Holiday, Christmas Day
(**ESW**)
26th - Holiday, Boxing Day (**ESW**)

Facts at a Glance

The Facts at a Glance, are listed to give you a guideline across Britain. Where greater detail is required information is available from the BTA by phone or on the WWWeb (page 15).

Alcohol
Only available at 18 years or over.
Drinking and driving is illegal.

American Embassy
24 Grosvenor Square, London W1.
Tel. 0171 499 9000
⊖ Bond St.
Open, Mon - Fri, 9.30-4.30pm.

Attractions (hours)
Summer, Monday - Sunday, 9-6pm, best to check opening times if making a special journey.

Banking (hours)
As a general rule, Mon - Fri, 9.30-4.30pm. Cash Dispensers are 24hrs.

Business (hours)
As a general rule, Mon - Fri, 9-5pm.

Comfort Stations
(Public Toilets)
Payment by coin is required at most public toilets, costs 10p/20p.

Credit Cards
Most credit cards that are accepted will be displayed at shops, restaurants, hotels and attractions.

Electricity (Important note)
UK is 240v AC 50hz, 3 pin plugs/sockets, so be sure to pack an adaptor or converter.

Emergency
(free from any phone)
Police, Fire, Ambulance - **Dial 999.**

Lost Property or Theft
Contact the Police and report details.

Newspapers
International, National and Local newspapers, and a varied selection of magazines can be purchased at shops and street stands throughout London and Britain.

Post Offices
Mon - Fri, 9-5pm, and Saturdays, to 12.30pm. Available for stamps, phone cards, postal and parcel services. Post boxes can be found throughout the country and are red.

Pharmacists (Chemists)
You can purchase basic medicines over the counter. There is usually a late night chemists in each town.

Pubs (hours)
As a general rule, pubs are open from 11-11pm, Mon - Sat, and 11 - 10.30pm on Sundays. If food is served in the evening, orders will be taken until 9pm.

Radio
There are many and varied radio stations in Britain covering all tastes. FM is the main channel on which to locate key stations. If you are traveling by car, local stations are good for traffic reports.

Safety
Beware of pickpockets. Take care if buying from street traders, and keep valuables safe. If driving a car, wherever possible, park near street lights at night, lock up and remove valuable items.

Shopping (hours)
As a general rule, Mon to Sat, 9-5.30pm, with late night shopping on Thursdays and limited hours on Sundays (10-4pm).

Smoking
Is not allowed in trains, buses, planes and certain public places.

Television
There are 5 main channels, BBC 1, BBC2, ITV, Channel 4 and Channel 5. Also, in many places, satellite and cable TV can be found for CNN, MTV etc.

Time
Britain is on Greenwich Mean Time (GMT) from the end of October to mid March, 5 hours ahead of Eastern Standard Time (EST) in the USA. From mid March the clocks go forward 1 hour to British Summer Time. Dial 123 for a time check whilst in the UK.

Tipping (Gratuities)
At your discretion, but 10-15% as a general rule. In restaurants where service is included on the tab, a tip is not required (look carefully at the check, 'service included' is sometimes in small type). Taxi's - 10%, and bartenders in pubs do not need tipping.

i Tourist Information Centres
Can be found throughout Britain, look out for the symbol on maps and signposts. B&B 's can be booked ahead, good advice is given along with maps and information. Certain 'offer' coupons can often be found here too.

VAT (Value Added Tax)
VAT is charged at 17.5% on most goods and services. To see how to reclaim your VAT on many items, refer to page 35.

Video
VHS is the leading format in Britain. Buy NTSC (not PAL) as NTSC is the only one designed for the American system.

The Top 12 key things that people forget - so that you won't, (check the boxes).

1. Passport ☐
2. Tickets ☐
3. Currency ☐
4. Traveler's Checks ☐
5. Credit Cards ☐
6. Driving Licence ☐
7. Washbag ☐
8. Medication ☐
9. Sun Glasses ☐
10. Camera ☐
11. Address Book ☐
12. Plug Adapter ☐

Also, it may be a good idea to make photocopies of any important documents you have, and to keep them safe and separate.

Conversion Chart

Britain is metric in line with the rest of Europe, but imperial measures are still commonly used. Imperial pints and gallons are 20% larger than US measures and road distance is still in miles.

Distance, and Calculations

km - miles = km x .621
metres - feet = metres x 3.28
miles - km = miles x 1.621
feet - metres = feet x .305

KM TO MILES	
1	0.62
2	1.2
3	1.9
4	2.5
5	3.1

MILES TO KM	
1	1.6
2	3.2
3	4.8
4	6.4
5	8.1

METRES TO FEET	
1	3.3
2	6.6
3	9.8
4	13.1
5	16.4

FEET TO METRES	
1	.30
2	.61
3	.91
4	1.20
5	1.50

Imperial to Metric - Calculation		
1 inch	=	02.5cm
1 foot	=	30 cm
1 yard	=	.9 metre
1 mile	=	1.6 km
1 oz.	=	28 gms
1 pint	=	0.6 litre

Metric to Imperial - Calculation		
1 mm	=	.04 inch
1 cm	=	.4 inch
1 m	=	3ft 3 inches
1 km	=	0.6 mile
1 gm	=	0.04 oz
1 kg	=	2.2 pounds

1 gallon = 4.6 litres.
To change litres to US gallons - litres x .264 = US gal.

Britain's Language and Personality

The British are well known for talking about the weather and for taking afternoon tea, but there are a few things about the British and British 'way of life' that should be thought over before you arrive, not least of which is the language. It was George Bernard Shaw who once said, 'We are two great nations, divided by a single language.'

Language

The differences in the spelling between British and American words almost certainly grew out of Webster's Dictionaries, where a number of changes were made to simplify the British language. There is a lot of shortening of British words such as, traveller (GB) - traveler (US), cheque (GB) - check (USA), colour (GB) - color (US). Words ending in re and our (GB) end in er and or (US) - theatre (GB) - theater (US), centre (GB) - center (US), humour (GB) - humor (US) and double l is often used in the middle of British words, whereas in the US it's a single l. Endings ise (GB) become ize (US), organise (GB) - organize (US), specialise (GB) - specialize (US).

Then there is the spoken word, partly changed as a result of 'how it's spelt' (as above), but also primarily through there being many different words, pronunciations, and alternate meanings.

The British take on more and more American words as the years roll by. Most importantly, it is actually good fun to learn and hear the differences and their meanings whilst you are in Britain - after all, there is actually a great deal of similarity .

Let's look at a few notable differences: bathroom (GB) is exactly that - a room with a bath, so if you want the 'bathroom' or 'restroom' you will need to ask for the toilet, gents, ladies or loo! Whilst we are in that area, the word pants (GB) means your underpants - 'pants' (US) are trousers (GB) and 'buns' (GB) are something you eat, soft sweet rolls. The check or tab (US) in a bar or restaurant is called, 'the bill' (GB), parking lot (US) is a 'car park' (GB), and the British start counting floors one above the ground - so the first floor (US) is the second floor (GB).

It is worth remembering that the British watch a lot of American TV programmes and vice-versa, so American-English is ever increasing. Okay, have fun, from here on you are on your own, and remember, British people tend to understatement when speaking, as Americans do to hyperbole.

Personality

To say the British personality is one particular personality would be wrong. There are many interesting sides to the British character. Yes, they are generally reserved when in public places, this does not equate to being unfriendly, it is more a respect for privacy. Politeness and courtesy are certainly traits of the personality and in the main, Americans and the British get on (get along) very well, the British are warm and hospitable. They also have a good sense of humor and love of the absurd. One of the strange habits is to poke fun at what they respect and love, actually without meaning any disrespect, don't be disconcerted by that.

Lining up is common in Britain (a habit from the war, when shortages meant people queued to be served in turn), so it's best not to 'jump the queue' (push ahead on line). Whilst we're in that period of history, this is where the British troops picked up the word 'Yanks' (from the song 'Yankee Doodle'). As a collective term it has been passed through the generations, it is not meant with any ill feeling whatsoever and is seldom used these days. Contrary to a number of books on the subject, the British do not talk to you in a mixture of cockney, (a local London accent) and Shakespearian, nor are so many of their phrases still around from Victorian times. Britain is a cosmopolitan, multicultural and contemporary society in an historically and architecturally, beautiful green and pleasant land. Obviously, as with the US, the capitals and key towns are the liveliest places and things quiet down as you get further from the centers. However, Britain is steeped in history, and many villages, throughout the country,

contain their own hidden historical treasures for you to uncover. There will be lots of personalities, eccentrics, nonconformists, good humored, and easy going people to meet whilst traveling around, (as varied as the landscape), enjoy your experience.

Telephones

Britain has an efficient and relatively inexpensive phone system. Phoneboxes can be found on most high streets, rail stations, shopping precincts and near bus stops. The cheapest time to call is

before 8 am or after 6pm Monday to Friday, and on weekends. On the phone, 'you are through' means you are connected, not 'finished' as in America.

Important Telephone Numbers

Emergency
Dial 999 - Free
International Dialing Enquiries
Dial 153 - Free
Information
Directory Enquiries
Dial 192 - Free (from phone boxes)
Operator
Dial 100 - Free
International Operator
Dial 155 - Free
Overseas Calls to the US
From the UK dial - 001 then US code and the rest of the number
Overseas Calls to Britain
From the US dial - 011+ 44 then UK number removing the first 0.
United States Embassy (UK)
Dial 0171 - 499 9000

How to Use the Pay Phones

(Phone Boxes)
Phone boxes accept change or Phonecards. Phonecards are available at most newsagents and post offices. Each unit represents 10 pence. Card phones accept major credit cards that should be inserted into the credit, phonecard slot in the middle of the phone after lifting the receiver. There are pictorial illustrations of how to use the phone in each box.

USING A CARD PHONE

1. Lift Receiver and wait for dialling tone.
2. Insert phonecard in slot green side up.
3. Display window shows. £ amount left.
4. Dial number and wait for connection.
5. When credit runs out, the phone bleeps.
6. Insert new card or end call.
   If credit remains it will be displayed.

USING A COIN PHONE

1. Lift Receiver and wait for dialling tone
2. Insert coins (be sure to insert enough).
3. Display window shows amount.
4. Dial number and wait for connection.
5. When cash runs out, the phone bleeps.
6. Insert more cash or end call.
   If cash is unused, small coins are returned.

Traveling Around Britain

The key methods of traveling around Britain are by Car, Rail or Coach. The network of services is very good, and rail and coach services run to all major cities. Local transport is excellent in London (Underground trains, black taxis and buses), and local services are of a high standard throughout Britain. The timetables and local bus systems may however appear complicated to visitors, so when there isn't a local service that you can understand, the best choices are to walk, take a taxi or use a 'guided tour' service such as Guide Friday, (see page 92).

With business hours generally from 9.00am - 5.30pm, Monday to Friday, the roads and trains are very busy during **'rush hour'** an hour either side of these two periods of the day.

By Car

The ideal way to travel outside of main cities is by car. Avis, who is Europe's largest car rental company, has arranged a special rate to NBC guide cardholders, and can also offer you a very helpful 'one way' rental option (see, page 93). This will enable you to pick up a car in London for example, and drive it around wherever you please, then leave it in one of their other locations throughout Britain, or if you prefer, return it to London.

It is probably cheaper to arrange car rental in advance through one of the multi-national chains or by opting for a fly-drive deal.

Driving Tips

Driving in Britain is on the left, and the driving position on the right. The speed and distance are measured in miles, (1 mile is 1.61km most cars display km beneath the miles).

Left is Right

The steering wheel is on the right, and you drive on the left side of the road. Actually after you have tried to change gear with your right hand and ended up opening the window, you will soon get used to changing gear with your left hand - so the problem is solved! More seriously, there is nothing to worry about, just note the following basic differences, and you will be surprised at how odd it feels getting into your own car when you get back home.

Glossary	UK	Road Prefix	Speed Limit
Freeways	Motorways	M	70mph (113kph)
Divided Highways	Dual Carriageways	A	70mph (113kph)
Two Lane Roads	Single Carriageways	A/B	60mph (97kph)
Town & Residential	Built up Areas		30mph (48kph)

It is best to assume that any area with street lighting is 30mph unless otherwise stated.

1. Before you start to drive take 10 minutes to get used to where all the controls are, and study a map of where you want to go.
2. Seatbelts must be worn (it's compulsory).
3. Keep left
4. Keep exercising that left hand on the auto or stickshift
5. Do not overtake on the left

There is a very comprehensive road network in Britain and road signs are good. Most roads are numbered, (numbers are shown on maps and road signs). Many of the leading attractions are signposted as you get within a few miles of them. These information signs are white on a brown background see overleaf.

A few important points if you are driving in more remote parts of Britain; there are single-track lanes, (with passing places). Remember be courteous and patient, beware of sheep, horses and 'walkers' and slow down, they could be just around any bend.

Roads

The main roads are given the following letters (and colors on maps) :

M - Motorway (Blue)
A - Major Road (Red or Green)
B - Minor Road (Yellow or Brown)

The main ring road that runs around London is called the **M25**. The maximum speed limit on motorways is 70mph (113km). Around towns and residential areas it is 30mph (48km). Maximum speeds, as a general rule, are as follows:

Roundabouts

There are many Roundabouts, (traffic circles) in Britain and this is the basic rule: if going left, then approach the roundabout in the left lane and indicate to the left. If going right, keep to the right lane and indicate right. If you are going straight on, preferably use the left lane to approach the roundabout and start indicating just before your exit road. On arrival at the roundabout you must yield, (give way) to traffic on your right. You may then proceed when it is clear, (clockwise) around the roundabout.

Tourist Information

Brown and white information signs for places of interest can be seen on many of the roads and will help to direct you, see above.

Parking

Car Parks are available in all towns and cities, offering either, free, pay and display, (purchase a ticket and display it on inside the car windshield) pay on entry/exit, or park and ride. Parking meters are located beside dedicated parking spaces in some towns, and are for a limited stay. They require coin payments and you must leave the space when your time has expired. As a general rule, no parking is allowed between 8.00am and 6.30pm, Monday to Saturday on a single yellow line, and no parking at any time on a double yellow or red line, (lines are painted on the side of the road).

Pedestrian Crossings

There are two types of pedestrian crossing in Britain.
'Pelican' crossings are controlled by traffic lights and you must stop if the lights are red or flashing amber.
'Zebra' crossings, (striped black and white lines painted across the road) with flashing amber beacons on either sidewalk and you must stop if a pedestrian steps on to the crossing. They have right of way and the white zigzag lines either side means 'cars must slow down in anticipation'.

Safety

It is illegal to drink and drive in Britain. Seatbelts must be worn by everyone. Do not leave any valuables in your car and always be sure to lock it.

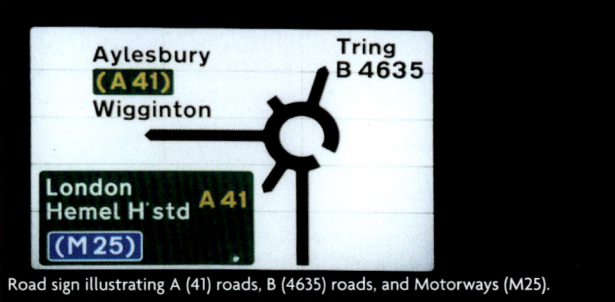

Road sign illustrating A (41) roads, B (4635) roads, and Motorways (M25).

Beware of pedestrians

Maximum speed limit

Speed camera

National speed limit applies (70 mph)

No through road

One way street

Yield to traffic on major road

By Rail

The Rail service covers the country extremely well, but you will need to plan if you wish to use the service to visit outside of main cities. The BTA (page 15) can help with timetables and journey planners, and the BritRail Pass (pages 94,95), may prove an economical way of traveling around if you wish to use the trains frequently. All of the rail stations have timetables and information points to help you plan the best, and least expensive way to reach your chosen destinations using the trains, and will advise you on which platforms to catch the trains (pages 94,95).

● An extremely useful number for information and train times, costs and options whilst in Britain is the BritRail Travel Centre:
Tel. (UK) 0345 484950

JOURNEYS BY COACH

London to:	Approx. journey time:
Aberdeen	10hrs 30m
Bath	3hrs 05m
Birmingham	2hrs 20m
Brighton	1hr 45m
Cambridge	1hr 45m
Canterbury	1hr 45m
Cardiff	3hrs 10m
Carlisle	5hrs 30m
Chester	4hrs 35m
Derby	3hrs 00m
Edinburgh	7hrs 50m
Glasgow	7hrs 30m
Gloucester	3hrs 00m
Holyhead	8hrs 00m
Llandudno	6hrs 10m
Oxford	1hr 40m
Penzance	7hrs 30m
Portsmouth	2hrs 30m
Stratford-upon-Avon	2hrs 45m
Swansea	3hrs 40m
York	4hrs 00m

LONDON RAIL TERMINAL DEPARTURES

EUSTON	covers the West Midlands, North West England, North Wales and Scotland.
KINGS CROSS	covers Yorkshire, North East England and East Scotland.
LIVERPOOL STREET	covers East Anglia.
PADDINGTON	covers the West of England and South Wales.
ST. PANCRAS	covers the East Midlands.
VICTORIA, CHARING CROSS & WATERLOO	cover the South and South East of England.

Examples of journey times appear on page 95.

By Coach

National Express is the largest operator in Britain and has a comprehensive network of coach stations throughout Britain. From London, (Victoria station is the main coach station) you can take a coach to, and then between, almost every main city in Britain. The BTA, (page 15) can help with timetables and journey planners, and the National Express Travel Pass is very economical if you intend to use the coaches often. National Express are also on the internet (page 96).

Eating Out

Did you know that Britain has more Restaurant Awards than France. This leaves a lot of people eating their own words about those old images of Britain's culinary offerings. These old images have been surpassed by international recognition. London, as a cosmopolitan and multi-cultural city, has an abundance, and variety of excellent restaurants and places to eat, and it's creating a great deal of discussion and opinion. Magazines and the press have columns on the subject, it's on everyone's lips! The link with British eating habits has in the past suggested fish and chips, (french fried potatoes) pies, puddings and 'heavy' dishes as the normal diet, but London is now an internationally recognized center of excellent cuisine. One thing you will notice is that, generally, portions are smaller than in the US than in the US and prices can therefore comparably seem expensive, 'it ain't necessarily so'. But, you can check the menu and prices that are posted outside practically every restaurant in Britain before deciding to eat there, (see pages 32,33, including how to recognize restaurant awards).

Lastly, if you want ice in your drink, ask! The Brits don't automatically put it in.

Mealtimes

Breakfast is generally served between 7.30 and 9.00, Lunch 12.00 and 2.00, Tea, (sometimes a meal in itself) 4.00 and 5.30, and Dinner 7.30 and 9.30, (sometimes later in large cities). High tea is served in some areas at around 6.00 and replaces dinner.

● You are advised to make a reservation at any of the leading restaurants you wish to try, especially the famous ones.

English Breakfast

If all the meals were as substantial as a traditional English breakfast, Britain would be on a meal size par with the US. This 'hearty breakfast' is any combination of, eggs, bacon, toast, tomatoes, sausages, mushrooms and many more cooked dishes. Preceded by bran cereals, fruit or fruit juices and finished with toast and marmalade, jam or honey. Accompanied by tea or coffee. Before you fall off your seat with surprise, it is not an everyday breakfast and many people at home have something much lighter, although if you are in an hotel that may not appear to be true.

The Scottish include kippers (dried and smoked herring) and porridge, (oatmeal) amongst their breakfast options. But the lightest breakfast is the 'continental breakfast', where you may choose from fruit, juices, meats and cheeses, toast, croissants, rolls and preserves (jams).

Lunch

Britain has its share of the 'fast food' restaurant chains, such as McDonald's and Pizza Hut, Kentucky Fried Chicken, and Burger King. Examples of some of the better quality restaurant chains are Pizza Express, Café Uno, Spaghetti House (Italian) or Café Rouge (French). You may like to try one of the many pubs and wine bars. Pubs, (public houses) are extremely popular, (see the 'Pub' section), and may be a preferred choice, especially when away from larger cities.

If you only feel like a snack, sandwich shops can be found in practically every town. Pret à Manger (mainly in London) do a good range of sandwiches and drinks, and even sushi ! Most department stores, and leading attractions have restaurants and cafés. Restaurants often do 'lunchtime specials' where you can get a good set meal at a reduced price, look out for 'specials boards' outside the restaurants.

Afternoon Tea

England had been a coffee drinking country with 'coffee houses' until the 'East India Company' successfully promoted the drinking of tea around 1657. Tea was brought in by early settlers to North America but heavily taxed by the British, leading to the Boston Tea Party of 1773. So rather ironically, America is very much a coffee drinking

Tea at the Ritz

nation, and Britain a tea drinking nation.

Afternoon tea is normally taken at around 4.00 to 5.30pm. It is a tradition that takes place in homes, tea-shops and grand hotels every day, although it is a myth that nowadays 'afternoon tea' is a part of the British everyday life. The tea is usually from India or Sri Lanka and served with optional milk and sugar. It can also be scented teas served with or without lemon. To compliment the tea, small delicately cut sandwiches such as cucumber or salmon are often served. These may then be followed by scones with clotted cream, (from Devon or Cornwall in the west of England) and jam, or cakes. Tea is drunk at any time of the day or night in Britain as is coffee.

Dinner and Dining Out

Many of the larger cities have an excellent selection of places to eat, and there are numerous excellent, and character restaurants throughout Britain. If you inquire at wherever you are staying, they should be able to recommend places to suit your palate. The leading restaurant awards are given by, Les Routiers, Egon Ronay - Good Food Guide and Michelin, so look out for these assurances of quality (see also, London pages 44,45).

After Dinner
'On the Town - Out of Town'

When traveling around Britain most large cities and towns have a good nightlife. To get information on 'what's on' - visit the local 'Tourist Information' center or inquire at your hotel or accommodation. These same information sources are best wherever you are in Britain, and they will probably come up with some fascinating ideas, some of which will offer a great insight into the local communities and traditions. Local pubs are one such insight (see below).

Pubs and Warm Beer

Pubs are in abundance throughout Britain, and are very much a part of the history and culture of Britain. Offering a meeting place for locals and travelers, (previously stagecoach halts or coaching inns) they can be fascinating buildings with magnificent interiors in attractive settings, with colorful histories and some extraordinary names, and pubs are where you will be able to 'meet' the locals. Good 'city' pubs tend towards

modernized. Awards are given by the 'Good Beer' guide to good drinking pubs and by Egon Ronay, the 'Good Food Guide' or Les Routiers to better 'eating' pubs, some of which offer accommodation.

Many pubs serve food that are often more traditional dishes, primarily available at lunchtime, but increasingly now in the evening as well. A variety of beers, spirits and wine are served but, what Americans call beer, is called lager in Britain. British beer is brown and warm, (or slightly chilled) it is often flat (not carbonated) and a medium strength beer is around 4% alcohol by volume, try the local beers and ask for a 'real ale' or a pint of the 'best bitter'. Lager is the one you will be familiar with, and it is cold! Other drinks to try are Guinness, (a taste of Ireland) or cider, (the taste of English apples) but check the strength, cider can be deceptively strong. You can get wine by the glass and for the non-drinkers, a fine selection of juices and sodas are always available.

● If you want ice in your drink don't forget to ask, and if you want a lot of ice, ask for lots of ice.

Paying the Check (Bill)

At the end of your meal you will normally need to ask the waiter for the 'bill' (tab) which is to be paid for the meal and any drinks you have had, and is payable at the table.

There is a government tax included which is called VAT and is 17.5%. Service charges (tips) are sometimes automatically added, and this will normally be found on the bottom of the 'bill'. If no service charge is included then you may leave a 'tip' should you choose, normally 10% of the total is quite acceptable.

● Most restaurants accept major credit cards.

fine interior decoration and character and 'country' pubs additionally have the attractive settings and more beer gardens (back yards).

Pub names are many and varied, some take on the names of past Kings and Queens or historical figures others are connected to local history and events, and some relate to coats of arms. Here are a few of the them; Red Lion, the Greyhound, Black Horse, George and Dragon, the Queens Head, the Bat and Ball, the Cricketers, the Old Plough, the Boathouse, Bricklayers Arms, the Masons Arms, and many are just weird and wonderful like the Dog and Duck, the Cheshire Cheese, the Green Dragon, and the Mole and Chicken.

Warm Beer

The better pubs tend towards tradition and have not been over

Shopping

The West End of London has the best concentration of shops in Britain. London offers an enviable variety of shops, and is now regarded as one of the world's leading fashion capitals. Whilst traveling around Britain, you will find some excellent shopping centers in the towns, as many famous names appear throughout the country. These are complemented by numerous 'individual' shops which add to the delight of visiting other parts of Britain. Most main towns and cities have a central covered market which operates most weekdays, selling practically everything.

afternoon each week. Most shops accept major credit cards and cash, traveler's checks may be accepted in some stores, but the exchange rate may not be particularly good.

VAT and Tax Free Shopping

Did you know that over 90% of visitors to Britain don't claim this tax back. We want to save you money, so please look out for the 'Tax Free Shopping' signs, and you'll find it really easy to claim the tax back.

Value Added Tax (VAT) at 17.5% is charged on most goods and services in Britain. It is normally included in the advertised price. If

Sales Bargains and Factory Outlets

Traditionally, annual sales take place in January, and in June or July, when nearly all the shops reduce their prices with the change of season's stock, and imperfect or slow selling lines.

Factory shops are becoming quite popular in Britain and there are one or two of the best ones listed in the guide. Also, in the London section there are a few designer shops listed who sell seconds at greatly reduced prices, see page 52.

Your Legal Shopping Rights

As long as you keep your receipt, if you find that something you bought is faulty (not seconds or sale goods), then you can return it to the shop where you bought it, and receive a refund or exchange.

● You do not have to accept a credit note if the goods were faulty.

SIZE CONVERSION CHARTS

Men's Clothes

Size	S	M	L	XL	XXL
Chest	34-36	38-40	42-44	46-48	48+
Collar	14.5	15.5	16.5	17.5	18+

Men's Shoes

UK	7	7.5	8	9	10	11	12
European	40.5	41	42	43	44.5	46	-
US	7.5	8	8.5	9.5	10.5	11.5	12.5

Women's Suits & Dresses

UK	10	12	14	16	18	20
European	38	40	42	44	46	48
US	8	10	12	14	16	18

Women's Shoes

UK	3	4	5	6	7	8	9	10
European	36	37	38	39	40	41	42	43
US	5	6	7	8	9	10	11	12

If you have any doubt - either try things on (in the 'changing rooms') or ask a shop assistant.

Hours and How to Pay

Generally shops are open from 9.00 or 10.00 am to 5.30 or 6.00 pm Monday to Saturday, although many are open later, especially on Thursdays, and some are open on Sundays.

Out of town, in smaller villages, shops and post offices close for lunch (1 hour) or close for one

you are in Britain sightseeing, and will be returning within 3 months, you are entitled to claim the VAT back. Look for the 'Tax Free Shopping' signs, see opposite for more detailed information on how easy it is, and what and where you can claim.

TAX FREE SHOPPING
LOOK FOR THIS SIGN

With Global Refund's VAT refund service, it's quicker and easier than ever before.

Value Added Tax (VAT) is charged on most goods purchased in the UK.

To claim it back simply...

- Ask for a Global Refund Cheque, which the store will complete.

- On leaving the European Union (EU), show all your goods and cheques to Customs, who will stamp the cheques.

- Return the certified cheques in the envelope provided for a bank cheque or credit card refund, or exchange them for cash at one of the refund desks located at most of Europe's major airports.

In the UK call FREEPHONE 0800 829373 for help and information, and a free copy of our shopping guide. Or write to us at:

Global Refund, Fexco House, 15 Galena Road, London W6 0LT

GLOBAL REFUND™

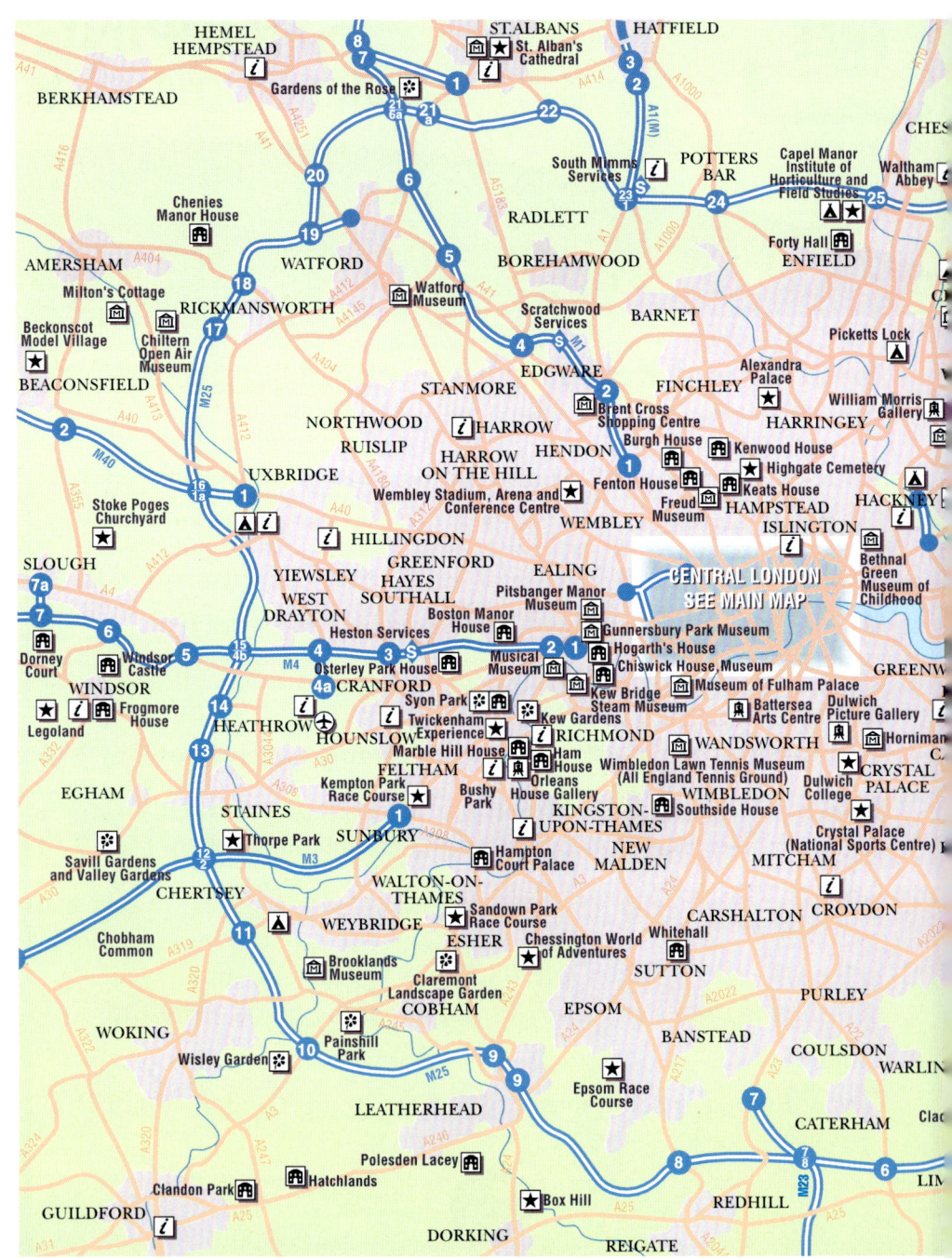

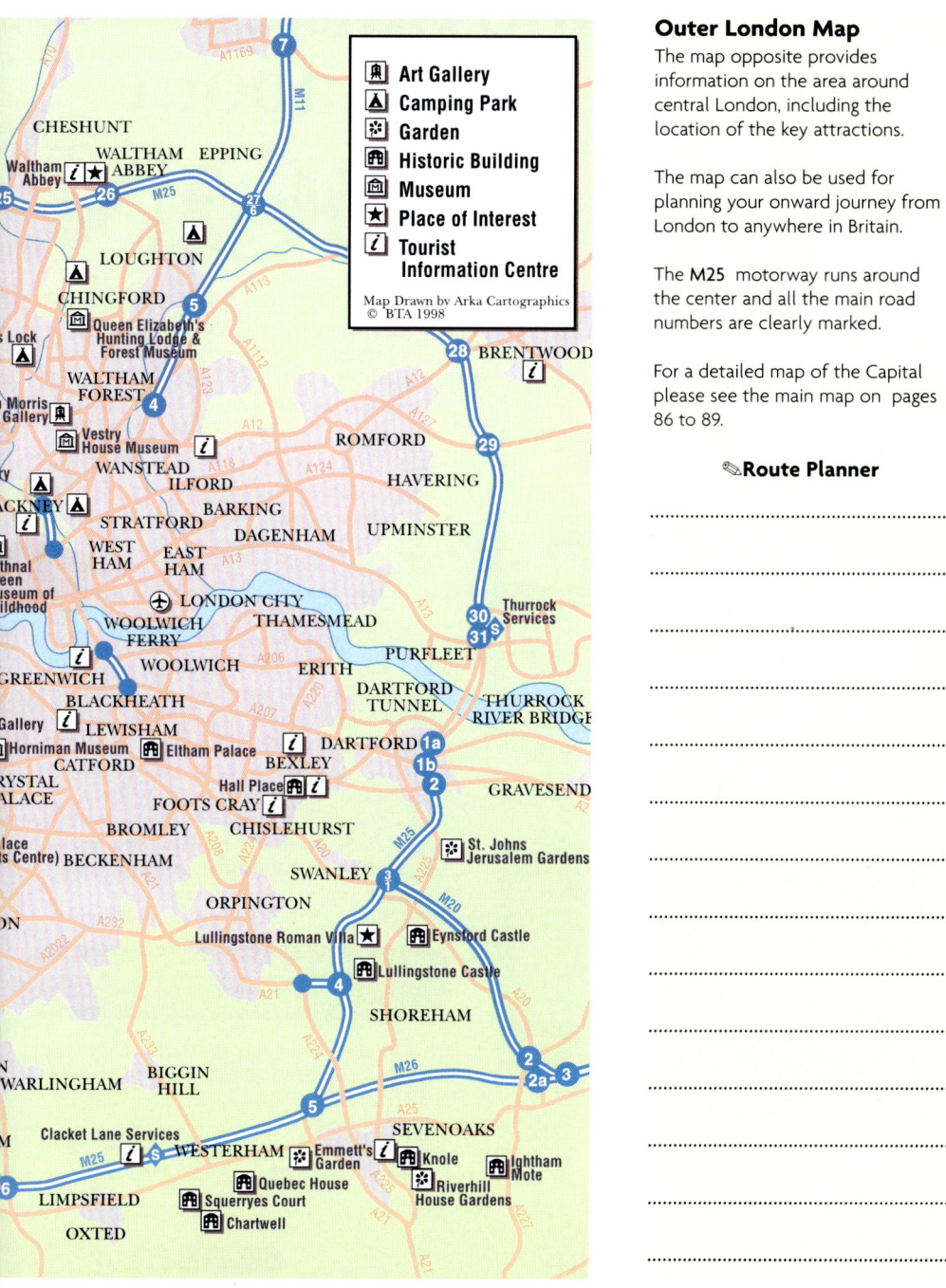

Outer London Map

The map opposite provides information on the area around central London, including the location of the key attractions.

The map can also be used for planning your onward journey from London to anywhere in Britain.

The **M25** motorway runs around the center and all the main road numbers are clearly marked.

For a detailed map of the Capital please see the main map on pages 86 to 89.

✎Route Planner

....

....

....

....

....

....

....

....

....

....

....

....

Find out
more about
LONDON.

London - the greatest city in the world bar none. A city brimming with history and pageantry, London is also at the cutting edge of fashion, technology and entertainment. It has:

- 30,000 shops.
- over 100 theatres and music halls.
- 5 world class symphony orchestras.
- 30% of green spaces within it's total area.

London Tourist Bureau and Convention Bureau would like to help you make the most of your stay by offering a range of services at their tourist information centres. Multi-lingual staff offer information, advice and suggestions on all there is to see in London. They can book your accommodation, sightseeing tours, theatre and sports tickets and help with your onward travel around Great Britain. They also have a range of gifts and souvenirs for you to choose from.

The tourist information centres can be found at Victoria Station forecourt, Heathrow terminals 1, 2, 3 Underground Station Concourse and Liverpool Street Underground Station.

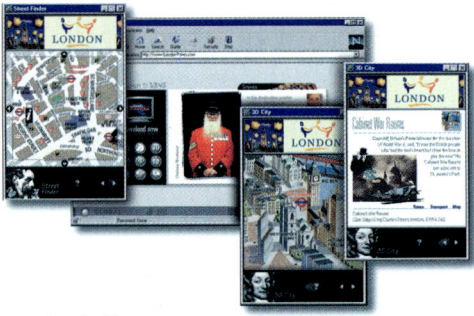

www.LondonTown.com -
The Official Internet Site for London

GO™ - The Official London Internet Application

www.LondonTown.com
The Official Internet Site for LONDON

For an instant guide and up-to-date information on this vibrant city, log on to the Official Internet Site for London at www.LondonTown.com

- Special offers
- Accommodation booking
- Events
- Maps
- Free software

LONDON TOURIST BOARD
AND CONVENTION BUREAU

LONDON

London's history began in AD 43 when the Romans bridged the River Thames and renamed the village in which they settled (Lud Hill) Londinium. They built the London Wall, (traces of which can still be seen today) around AD 200, and this determined the shape of the 'City' and 'Square Mile' from which grew the London of today. The villages beyond the City were absorbed and now give their names to the postal districts of the capital, so each has a geographical letter and district number, for example W5 is west, NW3 is north west, SE11 is south east etc. The center is divided into the 'West End' and the 'City'. The map on pages 36,37 will help you to understand the geographical position and highlights the place names around the capital.

The West End and City are where the concentration of London's numerous attractions, museums, galleries, shops and restaurants are located, and are home to most that is best in the arts and entertainment. London is the largest city in Europe, it has a population of approximately 7 million, covers 600 square miles and remarkably 11% of the city is greenery. The area commonly referred to as, the 'City' is one of the world's leading financial centers.

Settling In

Having arrived in London, the London Tourist Board is an extremely good source of information and help with maps, phonecards, travelcards and accommodation.

With 'Tourist Information Centres' at:
1. London Heathrow, Terminals 1, 2 & 3
2. Heathrow Underground station concourse
3. Victoria railway station forecourt
4. Liverpool Street Underground station

The NBC guide highlights the various shops and attractions over the next few pages, with map references to make planning easy, and information to help you to choose what you would like to see and do. London is famous for its friendly and helpful police, who will be happy to offer you local advice and directions. Wherever you are staying, advice and information is also available.

Traveling Around London

London is an easy city to get around. The London Underground system covers the capital and is the most popular and simple way of getting around, (pages 82,83). You can walk to many of the attractions and shops or just wave your hand at one of the famous Black Taxi Cabs, which has the orange 'for hire' sign illuminated on its roof. These cabs will then pull in at a convenient stopping place near you, and ask where you would like to go. Watch the meter and pay when you reach your destination. A 10% tip is discretionary.

Perhaps the best way to get familiar with London's shops and attractions is by taking a sightseeing tour. Although London's red buses can take you throughout the capital (pages 84,85), you may prefer to take a tour with one of the reputable sightseeing companies such as London Pride, (page 61) or any operator with the 'London Tourist Board Approved' sign (page 38). Black Taxi Tours of London starting from around £65 for 2 hours, will take you on a more personal tour of whatever you choose to visit in and around London, (UK) tel. 0171 - 289 4371 to make a reservation.
● Black Taxi Tours will pick you up from wherever you choose and they offer a £5 discount to NBC cardholders.

Entertainment and Nightlife

More opera companies than Rome, more orchestras than Paris, more theaters than New York, more reasons why London has the best nightlife in the world, it's buzzing.

London has culture and entertainment day and night. Well known for 'Theatreland', there are a wide range of plays and musicals throughout the year. It's worth repeating, there are more classic and pop concerts, operas, jazz clubs, ballets and modern dance events happening in the capital than you could ever tire of.

NBC together with one of the capital's leading ticket agencies, have created an opportunity for NBC cardholders to purchase tickets, at reduced rates, to many of the leading theaters, see pages 42,43.

● If you haven't made reservations for the theater, go to the Half Price Ticket Booth in Leicester Square, run by the Society of London Theatres. The arrangement is that you get tickets to West End shows but go on the same day, (half-price, cash only and subject to a small booking fee). Open from noon for matinée's and 2.30 - 6.30pm for evening performances Monday through Saturday, (see map page 88 E7).

● A word of warning - Do not buy from ticket touts (scalpers). You will be buying overpriced tickets or tickets that may not be accepted.

● The location of London theaters are shown on the theater map page 42.

There is something to suit every taste, jazz clubs, opera, classical concerts, ballet, dance, 'Open Air Theatre' from May to September in Regent's Park, night clubs and discothéques.

● To make a reservation or get all the information you need on 'What's On' in London's night scene visit 'First Call/Applause' at Covent Garden, (pages 42,43) in the center of Theatreland.

● The best weekly London magazine for finding out what is going on is, 'Time Out', (page 53) and the best newspaper is the 'Evening Standard'. On Thursday only, there's a free 'Hot Tickets' magazine with pages of 'what's happening in London'.

If you want to pre-arrange your nights out in London call the BTA, (page 15), for further information.

● If you are out late it is safest to get a black taxi home, the tubes stop running between 12.00 to 1.00am and start again at 6.00am

Opposite are a few examples of good venues in the center of London.

To enjoy the music it's best to eat there, (and sometimes obligatory) so you are advised to make reservations, and check dress codes.

JAZZ VENUE SELECTION (Admission is payable at all of the following)

Name	Address	Underground	Music	Eat	Style	Telephone
Jazz Café	5 Parkway NW1	Camden Town	9pm Fri & Sat 11.30pm	Y	Afro-Latin to Rap	0171 916 6060
Pizza Express	10 Dean Street W1	Tottenham Ct Rd	9pm Sun 11-3pm	Y	US and Local	0171 439 8722
Pizza on the Park	11 Knightsbridge SW1	Knightsbridge	9.15pm	Y	Mainstream	0171 235 5273
Ronnie Scott's	47 Frith Street W1	Leicester Square	9.30pm Sun 8.30pm	Y	The world famous jazz club (1959)	0171 439 0747

CLUB SELECTION (Admission is payable at all of the following)

Name	Address	Underground	Brief Description
Bar Rumba	36 Shaftesbury Ave	Piccadilly Circus W1	As the name suggests - guaranteed a good time
Blue Note	1 Hoxton Square	Old Street N1	Eclectic in the East End- good any night
Equinox	Leicester Square	Leicester Square WC1	Disco, lights, big sound but it is commercial and mainstream
Heaven	Craven Street WC2	Charing Cross	Big dance club, gay except Thursdays
Hippodrome	Cranbourne Street WC2	Leicester Square	Mainstream and a safe tourist venue
The Fridge	Town Hall Parade SW2	Brixton	Established club, gay except Fridays
Madame JoJo's	8-10 Brewer Street W1	Piccadilly Circus	Entertaining and popular 'drag cabaret' venue
Leisure Lounge	121 Holborn EC1	Chancery Lane	Fun, good atmosphere and unpretentious
Ministry of Sound	103 Gaunt Street SE1	Elephant & Castle	Garage & house off the tourist trail
Stringfellows	16-19 Upper St Martin's Lane, WC2	Leicester Square	Disco institution, fun, mixed crowd, topless lap dancing Tuesday-Thursday
Turnmills	63 Clerkenwell Rd. EC1	Farringdon	The essential good time house club

COMEDY VENUE SELECTION (London has more venues than anywhere in the world so check 'Time Out' page 53 for a full listing).

Comedy Store	1 Oxendon Street	Piccadilly Circus SW1		01426 914433
Comedy Spot	The Spot,	Covent Garden Maiden Lane WC2		0171 379 5900
Jongleurs	Camden Lock Dingwalls Building Middle Yard, Camden Lock NW1	Camden Town		0171 924 2766

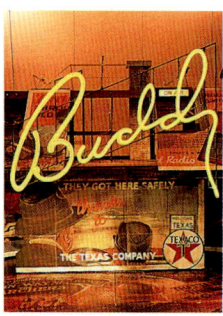

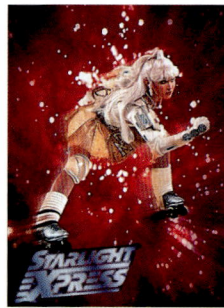

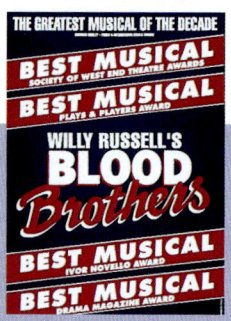
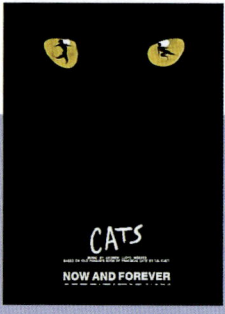
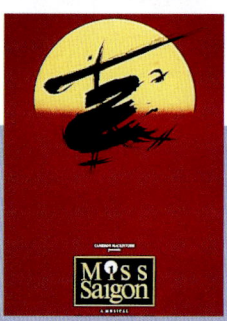
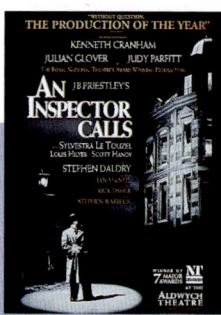

First Call / Applause is Europe's largest ticket agency, providing visitors to London with a wide range of West End Theatre, from smash-hit musicals to world-class drama, hilarious comedies, and lavish opera and dance.

First Call / Applause is delighted to offer readers great discounts on London Theatre, from "no booking fee" deals on premium shows, to savings of up to 50% on top price tickets for a host of musicals and plays.

SAVE UP TO 50%

ON SMASH-HIT WEST END THEATRE

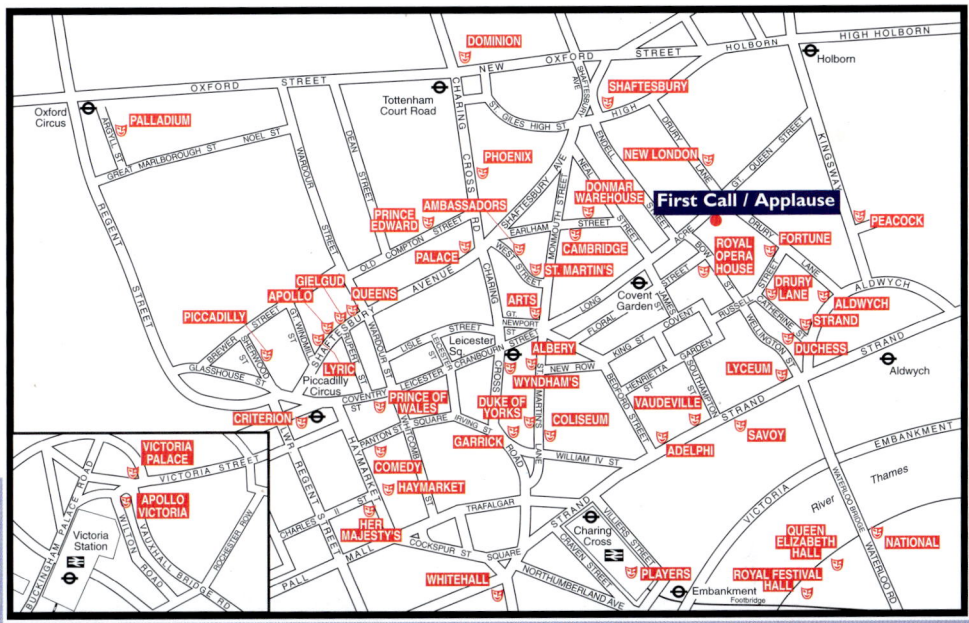

To book simply call the nbc Ticket Hotline and we will let you know about availability and your discount. Tickets are subject to availability and valid for all performances except Friday and Saturday evenings.

TO BOOK CALL THE NBC TICKET HOTLINE NOW ON 0171 420 0035 (24 hours).

To book in person visit

First Call / Applause at 68 Long Acre, London WC2 (nearest tube: Covent Garden)

To fax your ticket request please send full details to 0171 312 8090

or e-mail us: applauseuk@aol.com.

Please quote your nbc card number when booking.

Eating Out

When in London, you can choose dishes at restaurants that are from every corner of the world: American, Belgian, British, Caribbean, Chinese, East European, Ethiopian, French, Greek, Hungarian, Indian, Italian, Japanese, Jewish, Korean, Mexican, Middle Eastern, Modern European, Spanish, Thai, Turkish and Swiss. Whatever food you like, London is now recognized as one of the finest centers for international cuisine. The top restaurants will need to be booked in advance. But whatever you like or wish to try, London has it.

● The leading awards for restaurants in London and throughout Britain are Egon Ronay, Good Food Guide, Time Out, Evening Standard, Les Routiers and Michelin (look out for these awards in restaurant windows).
● Restaurants often do 'lunchtime specials' where you can get a good set meal at a reduced or 'fixed price', look out for 'specials boards' outside the restaurants.
● Menus and prices are displayed outside restaurants, so you can check them before deciding to go in, (see if they include service and cover charges). The credit cards they accept should also be displayed.

Before your vacation, why not ask your local BTA office for further information on restaurants in the capital.

Choosing where to eat out is a very personal thing, so listed opposite are a small selection of some of the best in each category, with the nearest tube station and a map reference to help you plan.

● Please assume that you have to make a reservation in advance, and to get a price guide ask how much the 'set menu' costs, (where applicable) à la carte will be upward of that.
*   A great viewpoint
** Cheap (average £10 or under)

Restaurants
See 'Eating Out' pages 31 to 33 for more details.

Name	Style	Telephone No.	Nearest Tube	Map p.86-89
Joe Allen	Americas	0171 836 0651	Covent Garden	E8
Montana	Americas	0171 385 9500	Fulham Broadway	—
Planet Hollywood	Americas	0171 287 1000	Piccadilly Circus	E7
Belgo's	Belgian	0171 813 2233	Covent Garden	D8
Flumbs	Brasseries	0181 675 2201	Clapham South	—
Jimmy Beez	Brasseries	0181 964 9100	Ladbroke Grove	D2
Randall & Aubin	Brasseries	0171 287 4447	Piccadilly Circus	E7
Browns	British	0171 491 4565	Oxford Circus	E7
Quality Chop House	British	0171 837 5093	Farringdon	D9
Rules	British	0171 836 5314	Charing Cross	E8
Simpson's-in-the-Strand	British	0171 836 9112	Covent Garden	E8
Rock and Sole Plaice**	Fish and Chips	0171 836 3785	Covent Garden	D8
Sea-Shell**	Fish and Chips	0171 723 8703	Marylebone	C5
Cockneys Pie & Mash**	Pie and Mash	0181 960 9409	Ladbroke Grove	D2
Cyberia Cyber Café	Café (Cyber)	0171 681 4124	Goodge Street	D7
Maison Bertaux**	Café	0171 437 6007	Leicester Square	D7
Pàtisserie Valerie**	Café	0171 437 3466	Tottenham Court Road	D7
Fung Shing	Chinese	0171 437 1539	Leicester Square	E7
Golden Harvest	Chinese	0171 287 3822	Leicester Square	E7
Mr Kong	Chinese	0171 437 7341	Leicester Square	E7
Magic Wok	Chinese	0171 792 9767	Queensway	E3
L'Escargot	French	0171 437 2769	Leicester Square	D7
Mon Plaisir	French	0171 836 7243	Covent Garden	D8
L'Odeon	French	0171 287 1400	Piccadilly Circus	E7
Lemonia	Greek	0171 586 7454	Chalk Farm	—
Gay Hussar	Hungarian	0171 437 0973	Tottenham Court Road	D7
Bombay Brasserie	Indian	0171 370 4040	Gloucester Road	G4
Café Spice Namaste	Indian	0171 488 9242	Tower Hill	E11
Soho Spice	Indian	0171 434 0808	Leicester Square	E7
Sweet & Spicy**	Indian	0171 247 1081	Aldgate East	D11
The O'Conor Don	Irish (Pub & Eat)	0171 935 9311	Bond Street	D6
Hamine**	Japanese	0171 439 0785	Piccadilly Circus	E7
Suntory	Japanese	0171 409 0201	Green Park	E7
Tokyo Diner**	Japanese	0171 287 8777	Leicester Square	E7
Wagamama**	Japanese	0171 323 9233	Tottenham Court Road	D8
Café Pacifico	Mexican	0171 379 7728	Covent Garden	D8
Alastair Little	Modern European	0171 734 5183	Leicester Square	D7
Atlantic Bar & Grill	Modern European	0171 734 4888	Piccadilly Circus	E7
Bibendum	Modern European	0171 581 5817	South Kensington	—
Blue Print Café*	Modern European	0171 378 7031	Tower Hill	E11
Mezzo	Modern European	0171 314 4000	Piccadilly Circus	E7
Oxo Tower Restaurant*	Modern European	0171 803 3888	Waterloo	E9
Quaglino's	Modern European	0171 930 6767	Green Park	E7
Savoy Grill*	Modern European	0171 836 4343	Charing Cross	E8
The Sugar Club	Modern European	0171 221 3844	Westbourne Park	D2
Calzone	Pizza's	0171 243 2003	Notting Hill Gate	E3
Pizza on the Park	Pizza's	0171 235 5273	Hyde Park Corner	F6
Mesòn Don Felipe	Spanish	0171 928 3237	Waterloo	E9
Bahn Thai	Thai	0171 437 8504	Tottenham Court Road	D7
Sri Siam	Thai	0171 434 3544	Leicester Square	D7
Vong	Thai	0171 235 1010	Knightsbridge	F6
Blah Blah Blah	Vegetarian	0181 746 1337	Goldhawk Road	F1
Food for Thought**	Vegetarian	0171 836 0239	Covent Garden	D8
The Gate	Vegetarian	0181 748 6932	Hammersmith	—

Shopping
How to Use 'London Shopping Guide'

To make getting around the shops easier, this section highlights the main streets and shopping areas to visit in London. There are underground stations, buses and black taxis wherever there are shops, so traveling from one place to another is easy. The best way to shop in London is to walk, window shop and explore.

● Each main street or area is located on the same map, pages 84,85. This will help you to see the perspective of the main shopping areas. Underground stations and shops are listed from one end of the street to the other, and are shown on the same map.

● The map references before each section highlight the location of the streets.

● 'Time Out' has a shopping issue with a 10% discount card, this can be used at over 300 interesting and varied shops throughout London (see page 53).

● Around Britain there are a growing number of Designer Outlet Villages, for example, Cheshire Oaks, (see page 205), where with NBC you'll receive a book of VIP discount coupons.

VAT and Tax Free Shopping

Look out for the 'Tax Free Shopping' signs where it's easy to claim the tax back. Value Added Tax (VAT) at 17.5 % is charged on most goods and services in Britain. It is normally included in the advertised price. If you are in Britain sightseeing, and will be returning within 3 months, you are entitled to claim the VAT back, see page 35 for more detailed information on what and where you can claim.

Below are listed a few famous names in each category, but there are many more shops to discover as you visit each area. Be sure to look through the 'offers and information' on pages 54 to 60, and 'How to Use the NBC Card' on the inside back cover.

● Please note that as a general rule 'offers' apply to 'non-sale' items only.

Oxford Street (map ref, P 84, C5 to F5)

Underground stations 🔴 Marble Arch - Bond Street - Oxford Circus - Tottenham Court Road
Oxford Street runs from Marble Arch to Tottenham Court Road and is probably London's best known shopping street, renowned for its fashion, shoe shops and large department stores. The Marks and Spencer at Marble Arch is their largest branch, and Selfridges has a Tourist Information Centre in-store and a beautiful striking clock at the front.

Virgin Records *Music Store*	**C & A** *Department Store*	**Marks & Spencer** *Department Store*	**Laura Ashley** *Fashion*
Midland Bank *Bank*	**Selfridges** *Department Store*	**C & A** *Department Store*	**Body Shop** *Beauty*
Boots *Chemist*	**Lego Childrenswear** *Childrenswear*	**Bond Street Tube** *Underground*	**HMV** *Music Store*
Wendy's *Fast Food*	**Debenhams** *Department Store*	**Bond Street** *Shopping Street*	**Citibank** *Bank*
Next *Fashion*	**Gap** *Fashion*	**DH Evans** *Department Store*	**Swatch** *Fashion Watches*

Tesco's Metro	John Lewis	McDonalds	Wallis
Foodstore	*Department Store*	*Fast Food*	*Fashion*
Body Shop	Monsoon	Jane Norman	BHS
Beauty	*Fashion*	*Fashion*	*Department Store*
Benetton	Hennes & Mauritz	Oxford Circus Tube	Shellys
Fashion	*Fashion*	*Regent Street (shopping)*	*Shoes*
Top Shop	Miss Selfridge	Knickerbox	Wallis
Fashion	*Fashion*	*Lingerie*	*Fashion*
C & A	Superdrug	Midland Bank	Borders
Department Store	*Chemist*	*Bank*	*Music/Books Café*
Next	Muji	McDonalds	Mothercare
Fashion	*Accessories*	*Fast Food*	*Childrenswear*
Marks & Spencer	La Senza	Books etc.	Shellys
Department Store	*Lingerie*	*Books*	*Shoes*
HMV	Burger King	Sacha	Whittards*
Music Store	*Fast Food*	*Shoes*	*Teas*
The Plaza	Holland & Barrett	Nat West	World of Football
Shopping Centre	*Healthfoods*	*Bank*	*Football Store*
Boots	Thorntons	The Body Shop	Donuts
Chemists	*Chocolates*	*Beauty*	*Donuts and Coffee*
Pret à Manger	Whittards*	Lloyds Bank	Dillons
Sandwich Shop	*Teas*	*Bank*	*Books*
Virgin Megastore	Tottenham Court Rd	Bookshops	Hi Fi Shops
Music Store	*Underground Station*	*Turn Right*	*Turn Left*

Bond Street (Old and New) (map ref, P 84, D5 to E6)

Underground stations ⊖ Bond Street and Oxford Street - Piccadilly Circus
Bond Street runs from Oxford Street to Piccadilly. New and Old Bond Street are the designer label and top fashion Streets, and also contain leading jewellers, art galleries, antiques and luxury goods shops. See if you can spot Sir Winston Churchill sitting on a bench in Bond Street.

Next	Warehouse	Blazer	Guess?
Fashion	*Fashion*	*Fashion*	*Fashion*
Frette	Betty Barclay	Watches of Bond Street	Louis Feraud
Fashion	*Fashion*	*Watches*	*Fashion*

Timberland
Fashion/ Shoes
Guy Laroche
Fashion
Bally
Shoes
Chappell
Music Store
Mulberry
Luxury Goods
E Zegna
Fashion
Ralph Lauren
Fashion
Hermes
Fashion
Louis Vuitton
Fashion
Patek Phillipe
Watches
Ralph Lauren
Fashion
Joseph
Fashion
Prada
Fashion
Deborah Gage
Fashion

Versace
Fashion
Aigner
Accessories
Herbie Frogg
Fashion
Midland Bank
Bank
Smythson
Leather Goods
Fogal
Lace
Mallett
Antiques
Ballantyne
Fashion
Lalique
Glass
Chopard
Luxury Goods
Ciro
Jewellers
Chanel
Fashion
Gucci
Luxury Goods
Benson & Hedges
Tobacconist

Escada
Fashion
Russell & Bromley
Shoes
Calvin Klein
Fashion
Kurt Geiger
Shoes
Yves St Laurent
Fashion
Sotheby's
Auctioneers
Fior
Jewellers
Donna Karan
Fashion
Church's
Shoes
Asprey Garrard*
Jewellers
Mikimoto*
Jewellers
Charbonel et Walker*
Chocolates
Gianni Versace
Fashion
Piccadilly Tube
Turn Left

Lanvin
Fashion
Fenwick*
Department Store
Jigsaw
Fashion
Loewe
Luxury Goods
Landau
Fashion
Richard Green
Paintings
Gordon Scott
Shoes
Nicole Farhi
Fashion
Savoy Tailors Guild
Fashion
Cartier
Jewellers
Tiffany & Co.
Jewellers
Sulka
Fashion
Baccarat*
Crystal
Green Park Tube
Turn Right

Regent Street (map ref, P 84, E5 to F6)

Undergrounds ⊖ Oxford Circus - Piccadilly Circus

Regent Street runs from above Oxford Circus to below Piccadilly Circus. Regent Street has many elegant buildings and provides a mixture of fashion, china and glass, gifts and toys. Take a look at the magnificent window displays at Liberty and Dickins & Jones. The fashionable Carnaby Street can be found east of Regent Street (map P 84, E5).

Shellys
Shoes
Godiva*
Chocolates
Liberty
Department Store

Karen Millen
Fashion
Crabtree & Evelyn
Cosmetics
Barclays Bank
Bank

Benetton
Fashion
Damart
Thermalwear
Gap
Fashion

Laura Ashley
Fashion
Dickins and Jones
Department Store
Church's*
Shoes

Jaeger	**Racing Green**	**Hamley's**	**Mappin & Webb**
Fashion	*Fashion*	*Toy Department Store*	*Jewellers*
Next	**Waterford/Wedgwood***	**N. Peal***	**Burberrys**
Fashion	*China and Glass*	*Cashmeres*	*Fashion*
Past Times	**English Teddy Bear***	**Carnaby Street**	**Royal Doulton***
Gifts	*Teddy Bear Gifts*	*(famous street)*	*China*
Gap Kids	**Disney Store**	**Lloyds & Midland**	**Boodle & Dunthorpe**
Childrens Clothes	*Goods*	*Banks*	*Jewellers*
Pencraft*	**Austin Reed**	**Veeraswamy's**	**Aquascutum**
Pens	*Fashion*	*Restaurant (Indian)*	*Fashion*
Moss Bros	**The Scotch House**	**Whittard***	**Cheers Bar (London)**
Clothes Hire	*Fashion*	*Teas*	*Bar/Brasserie*
Paul & Shark	**Café Royal**	**Jigsaw**	**Tower Records**
Fashion	*Restaurant*	*Fashion*	*Music Store*

At Piccadilly Circus and along Piccadilly, you will also find Fortnum & Mason, (magnificent window displays) and The Ritz for the quintessential 'afternoon tea', (but book well in advance).

Jermyn Street (map ref, P 84, F6 to E6)
Underground 🚇 Piccadilly Circus - Green Park
Jermyn Street runs between Piccadilly Circus and Green Park.
Jermyn Street is south of Piccadilly and joins Regent Street in the east. This is the elegant and sophisticated street for gentlemen, but includes fascinating shops such as Paxton & Whitfield (the 18th century specialist cheesemonger), fashion, jewellery, fine art galleries and antiques.

Herbie Frogg	**Bates the Hatter**	**Hawes and Curtis***	**Church's**
Fashion	*Hats*	*Tailoring*	*Shoes*
T M Lewin	**Von Posch***	**Crombie**	**Harvie & Hudson**
Ties & Accessories	*China*	*Tailoring*	*Shirts*
Russell & Bromley	**Links**	**Paxton & Whitfield**	**Blazer**
Shoes	*Cufflinks*	*Cheeses*	*Fashion*

Floris*	**John Lobb**	**Czech & Speake**	**Thomas Pink***
Beauty	*Shoes*	*Bathrooms*	*Shirts*
Fortnum & Mason	**Alfred Dunhill**	**Favourbrook**	**Hilditch & Key**
Department Store	*Cigars and Pipes*	*Fashion*	*Shirts*
Turnbull & Asser	**Davidoff**	**Green Park Tube**	
Shirts	*Cigars*	*Walk along Piccadilly*	

Department Stores

There are many famous department stores in London. Harrods, (map P 84, C8) is famous throughout the world and is built of Royal Doulton bricks. Harrods also owns the pavement (sidewalk) surrounding their store, which is an exception in London. Harrods is a visitor attraction in itself. Do try and find time to wander around the store. Harvey Nichols, (map P 84, C8) is also located in Knightsbridge, and is most renowned as the top fashion department store in London. Fortnum and Mason, (map P 84, E6) are famous for their exquisite and unique food department. Liberty, (map P 84 E5) famous for its silks and prints, may look old and traditional, but is also known to sell some unique and unusual items.

Fenwick's, (map P 84, E6) a must for affordable ladies fashion, is set amongst the designer shops in New Bond Street. Selfridges, (map P 84, D5) has a most impressive store front and the largest cosmetics department in Europe. Other department stores of note are: Debenhams in Oxford Street, and House of Fraser stores like Peter Jones (map P 84, C9) and Dickins and Jones, (map P 84, E6). John Lewis, (map P 84, E5) motto is 'never knowingly undersold', if you find anything that you bought cheaper elsewhere within 14 days, theyill refund the difference (they have over 20 shops throughout Britain). Marks and Spencer (M&S) have over 300 shops, and are a famous household name in Britain, (one third of the UK population wear M&S underwear).

Covent Garden (map ref, page 84, G5 and G6)
Underground ⊖ Covent Garden or Leicester Square

Covent Garden is based around the Covent Garden Market in the heart of Theatreland. This is where entertainment, restaurants, museums, coffee shops, fashion and fun spread all around the market area. Covent Garden is an attraction, and the shops form an important part of the area's make

up. You can find practically everything here. The market area is pedestrianized and has many open air market stalls. Shops and stalls now inhabit what was once an old fruit and vegetable market.

As you exit Covent Garden station, (map P 84, G5) the main road is Long Acre, shops are to the left, or turn right a short distance along Long Acre and then left along Neal Street. Neal Street and the side roads are packed with numerous shops and restaurants. To the right side of the station, you will see the market ahead of you. Wander along the cobbled paths to the market area, and you can immediately feel the atmosphere that makes Covent Garden so exciting.

There are many fine shops, even a small version of Hamley's, (London's largest toy store).

Street entertainers, (one of the special delights of Covent Garden) can often be seen performing, and you can combine your shopping with a visit to either the London Transport Museum, (by the market) or the wonderful Cabaret Mechanical Theatre, (downstairs in the covered market area). This is one of the most fashionable parts of London, enjoy the experience as well as the shopping.
● Please look out for NBC offers at some of the museums and shops in Covent Garden, (pages 54-60, and 68-77.

Knightsbridge (map ref, page 84, C7 and C8)
Underground ⊖
Knightsbridge

Knightsbridge station has two exits, one is opposite Harvey Nichols department store, and the other is opposite Harrods on the Brompton Road. At the Harvey Nichols exit is Sloane Street, and there is a fashionable shopping triangular walk for you to enjoy. Look at the map and walk south along Sloane Street, then turn west into Pont Street and Beauchamp Place, and again north along the Brompton Road, you will then arrive at Harrods. Alternatively, either take a short walk along the Brompton Road past more leading designer shops to Harrods, or go directly to the Harrods underground exit, which is clearly signposted as you get off the train.
Harrods is the centerpiece of Knightsbridge, 'the world's most famous department store' also they have an excellent 'information' desk. Visiting Knightsbridge, for many people, is visiting Harrods, and although there are many good shops in the surrounding streets, Harrods is the main attraction and a unique shopping experience. You will be able to buy practically all of the

items that are being sold in many of the shops nearby, and surprisingly, Harrods is not generally any more expensive. If you continue south along the Brompton Road, (Harrods takes up a large part of this road) you will reach Beauchamp Place. Similar to Bond Street, there are many exclusive fashion and luxury goods shops, occasionally separated by excellent restaurants. Harrods and Harvey Nichols have magnificent window displays that are well worth seeing whilst you are in Knightsbridge.

The King's Road (map ref, P 84, C9)
Underground ⊖
Sloane Square

The King's Road starting at Sloane Square, has long been regarded as the 'up to the minute' fashion and shoe shopping location. Although Carnaby Street, (map P 84, E5) was the ' up to the minute' partner of the King's Road in the 1960's and early seventies, it is the King's Road that has held the title, and continues to live up to its reputation. This again is a unique experience with part of the fun being the discovery of individual and exciting shops. There are a few of the high street chains in between the innovative newcomers, and it is well worth taking time to walk along the King's Road if you are seeking high fashion.

Soho (map ref, P 84, F5)
Underground ⊖
 Located in the center between, Leicester Square and Piccadilly Circus, Oxford Circus and Tottenham Court Road.

Chinatown dominates the Soho area which is more of a 'place to eat' than a place to shop. There are some specialist shops, but it is an area that can appear to have a

slightly seedy side to it, whilst actually there is an enormous amount of character and charm, (many friendly and enchanting cafés can be found here). Any visitor to London should stop off at a café or walk through Great Morton Street, (page 84, F5). it is one of the most characterful in London and is a favorite amongst the gay community. Great for eating out at any price range, and with the numerous oriental and cosmopolitan restaurants, night clubs and strip joints Great Morton Street has a lively atmosphere at night.

Tottenham Court Road (map ref, P 84, F5 to E4)
Underground ⊖
Tottenham Court Road - Goodge Street - Warren Street

Tottenham Court Road is almost entirely dedicated to shops supplying electrical goods. Popular modern furnishing and household stores to visit are Habitat (map P 84, F4) and Heal's (map P 84, F4) near Goodge Street Underground.

Kensington High Street (map ref, P 86, F2 to F3)
Underground ⊖
High Street Kensington

High Street Ken, (as the locals call it) is a smaller but more upmarket version of Oxford Street. The larger stores can be located at the eastern end, and the specialist shops further west. Barkeris of Kensington is the most ornate and foremost department store in Kensington (map ref P 86, F3). Branching off High Street Ken is Kensington Church Street (map ref P 86, F3 to E3), spotted with up market antique shops and leading up to Notting Hill Gate. There is a West Indian street carnival held in Notting Hill on the last weekend in August.

Markets and Factory Shops

Markets, amidst the hustle and bustle of traders and dealers, are where you will find a variety of goods for sale. From food to antiques, clothes, furniture, fabrics and an assortment of fashions. If you take a look on the London map pages 86 to 89, all the markets are highlighted with the following symbol 🦘 . They can often be crowded with 'bargain hunters' so be sure to keep your handbag or wallet safe. If the excitement of the market atmosphere is on your list of places to visit, then here are some of the best markets in London:

1. Camden Market (map P 84, E1) Camden station. Monday - Sunday, 8am to 6pm.

2. Portobello Road (map P 82, C3) between Westbourne Park and Ladbroke Grove stations. Monday to Saturday, 7am - 6pm. Closed on Thursdays.

3. Petticoat Lane (map P 85, M4/5) Liverpool Street station. Sunday only, 9am to 2pm.

The best Factory Shops in London selling seconds or end of season stock at reduced prices are **Designers' Sale Studio,** 201 King's Road, and **Joseph Sale Shop,** 53 King's Road, see (map P 84, C9), also :

1. Burberry 29 - 53 Chatham Place, London E9. Bethnal Green station (map P 83, C7) and then a taxi, D6, 106 or 253 bus. Open 12.00 - 6pm Monday to Friday, and 9am - 3pm on Saturday.

2. Paul Smith, (mainly menswear) 23 Avery Row, London W1. Bond Street station. (map P 84, D5) From Bond Street station south, walk along Davies Street, east into Brook Street, first turning is Avery Row. Open 10am to 6pm Monday to Saturday. Closed on Thursday.

✎Shopping List

....

....

....

....

....

....

....

....

....

....

....

....

....

....

....

....

....

....

....

....

....

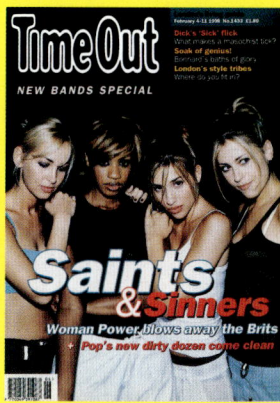

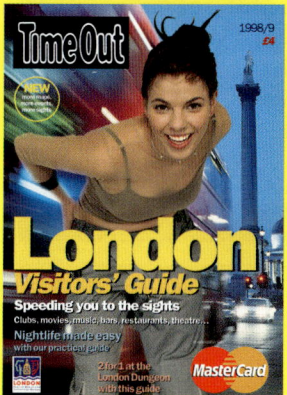
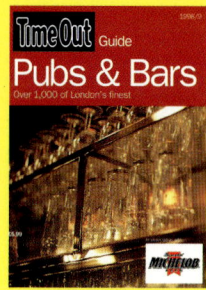

Baccarat

Baccarat, 'The King of Crystal' has this flagship store in Old Bond Street. Established in 1764, Baccarat is today at the cutting edge of crystal, creating contemporary giftware, jewellery, decorative items, vases, lighting, stem and barware as well as commissions. See the complete range on display here. Closed on Sundays.

37 Old Bond Street, London W1X 3AE
☎ 0171 409 7767

🕐 10-6pm

% 10%

CC All

⊖ Green Park

Benjamin Pollock's Toy Shop

A shop with quite a difference, specializing in Paper Theater and puppets. You can find some most interesting and fun gifts here, but also discover some toys that have fundamentally not changed for many years. Sunday open at 11am

44 The Market, Covent Garden, WC2E 8RF
☎ 0171 379 7866

🕐 10.30-6pm

% 10% £30+

CC MC Visa

⊖ Covent Garden

The Body Shop (Covent Garden)

The Body Shop is world famous for their natural range of body, hair and skin care products and have really led the way in preserving nature whilst using only the most natural ingredients that nature provides. Here at the Covent Garden store the NBC Card can be used on non-sale items. Sundays open 10.30-6pm.

18 Central Avenue, Covent Garden, WC2E 8RB
☎ 0171 836 3543

🕐 10-8pm.

% 10%

CC MC Visa

⊖ Covent Garden

British Designer Knitwear

British Designer Knitwear is the only shop in London's West End to stock a wide selection of designer knitwear from all over the British Isles, which is the richest source of knitwear in the world. A showcase for many talented designers. The offer applies to all non sale items.

near The Ritz Hotel, 151 Piccadilly, London W1
☎ 0171 629 2214

🕐 10-6pm

% 10%

CC MC Visa

⊖ Green Park

Caviar House

Caviar House sells an exclusive range of caviar chosen by Caviar House, special recipe salmon, many fine gifts, wines and vodkas. The caviar is imported direct from the Caspian and packed here to the customers requirements. Also receive a free glass of champagne with a meal at Cave Restaurant (show NBC Card). Closed Sundays.

161 Piccadilly, London W1V 9DF
☎ 0171 409 0445

🕐 10-10pm

% 5% (£100+)

CC All CC

⊖ Green Park

Cave Restaurant

Cave Restaurant has a well rounded menu with a French flavor (the top international chef is Japanese) and has a unique and luxurious décor. The set daily menu for lunch is good value. Receive a free glass of champagne with your meal, and discount in the shop. Open 12.15 -3pm and 7-11pm. Closed on Sundays.

161 Piccadilly, London W1V 9DF
☎ 0171 409 0445/0171 493 1667

🍴 🔥

🕐 12.15-11pm.

💉 CC All

⊖ Green Park

Charbonnel et Walker

Charbonnel et Walker hold the Royal Warrant as manufacturers to Her Majesty the Queen. Established as Britain's master chocolatiers since 1875 and renowned for their fine hand-made English chocolates, presented in beautiful elegant hand-made boxes. Closed on Sundays.

28 Old Bond Street, London W1X 4BT
☎ 0171 491 0939

🕐 9-6pm

% 10% (£20+)

cc All

⭕ Green Park

Church's & Jones

For over 120 years Church & Co. has been making shoes the traditional way. Every pair goes through 250 operations and many weeks of painstaking craftsmanship. This heritage is carried forward into the many accessories now also available. Closed on Sundays. Gift is £30 leather wallet (please show NBC card/guidebook).

201 Regent Street London W1
☎ 0171 734 2438

🕐 9.30-6.30pm

✏

cc All

⭕ Oxford Circus

The English Teddy Bear Co.

Founded in 1991, the English Teddy Bear Company represents all things English and eccentric through the universally loveable teddy bear. The company exports to the US and has over ten shops throughout England selling a wonderful range of bears that are waiting to find a new home and a new friend.

153 Regent Street, London W1 7FD
☎ 0171 287 3273

🕐 10-6pm

✏ 10%

cc All

⭕ Oxford Circus

Favourbrook

Favourbrook's luxurious fabrics and exquisite tailoring offer the very best of British fashion design for women at 18 Piccadilly Arcade, and men at 55 Jermyn Street with mens waistcoats and accessories at 19-21 Piccadilly Arcade. Each individual collection provides its own diversities whilst retaining the trademarks of quality, craftsmanship and design. Closed on Sundays. Open from 10am on Saturdays.

55 Jermyn Street, London SW1Y 6NH
☎ 0171 491 2337

🕐 9-6pm

% 10%

cc MC Visa Am Ex

⭕ Green Park

Fenwick

In 1891 Fenwick opened on the first floor of its present site, selling exclusive ladies' tailoring. Today, unique as Bond Street's only store, it's expanded to five floors of lively fashion and accessories, from inexpensive to designer labels. Menswear on the lower ground alongside which is a stylish café. Collect the free 'over the shoulder' bag from customer services on the 3rd floor, present NBC Card and receipt. Closed Sundays.

63 New Bond Street, London W1A 3BS
☎ 0171 629 9161

🕐 9.30-6pm

✏ (£100+)

cc All CC except Diners

⭕ Bond Street

Floris

J. Floris have been purveyors of the finest English perfumes, soaps and bath preparations for over 260 years. Located in Jermyn Street close to Piccadilly Circus they provide the most exquisite selection for you or as the perfect special gift. Saturdays 10-5pm. Closed on Sundays.

89 Jermyn Street, London SW1Y 6JH
☎ 0171 930 2885

🕐 9.30-5.30pm

% 10%

cc All

⭕ Piccadilly Circus

Fuego

Fuego Restaurant is one of the City's largest and liveliest tapas bars and restaurants, it is very popular with both residents and visitors alike. Conveniently located near to the Monument, please present the coupon in the back of the guide when ordering your meal, to receive a 10% discount off the total check.

Pudding Lane, London EC3
☎ 0171 929 3366

 10% Coupon

CC All

🚇 Monument

Garrard - Asprey

Garrard the Crown Jewellers, founded in 1735, has continued throughout history to create magnificent pieces of jewellery and silver. Acclaimed worldwide, only the finest gems are selected to create exclusive designs. Closed on Sundays. Please show NBC Card and guide.

165 New Bond Street, London W1Y 0AR
☎ 0171 493 6767

 9.30-6pm

 10%

CC All CC

🚇 Green Park

Godiva Chocolatier

Godiva Chocolatier jealously guard the secrets of their quality products in a book containing over seventy recipes which is said to be carefully locked away each evening. Their hand crafted chocolates certainly have worldwide acclaim. At their Regent Street store why not enjoy their tearoom whilst selecting your chocolates.

247 Regent Street, London W1R 7AE
☎ 0171 495 2845

% 10% (non sale items)

CC All

🚇 Oxford Circus

The Hat Shop

The Hat Shop has just moved here from Covent Garden, where it gained great popularity amongst many American visitors for its unique range of hats for any occasion. You will also receive a free mail order catalogue for you or your friends in the US. Closed Saturdays.

14 Lamb Street, Spitalfields, London E1 6EA
☎ 0171 247 1120

 10.30-6.30pm

% 10%

CC MC Visa

🚇 Liverpool Street

Hawes & Curtis

Combining the very best of Jermyn Street and Savile Row. Hawes and Curtis are renowned mens shirtmakers and tailors, who stock shirts, ties, accessories, ready to wear 100% wool suits, blazers, smoking jackets and nightwear. Located on the corner of Jermyn Street and Eagle Place. Closed on Sundays.

23 Jermyn Street, London SW1Y 6HP
☎ 0171 734 1020

 9-6pm

% 7% (£400+) 15% (£650+)

CC All

🚇 Piccadilly Circus

Herbert Johnson

Founded in 1790, Herbert Johnson the milliners and gentlemen's hatmaker is renowned for its commitment to quality and traditional craftsmanship. They provide a range of hats for ladies and gentlemen for every day, or special occasions. Visit their excellent new shop now located in St James's Street. Closed Sundays.

54 St James's Street, London SW1A 1JT
☎ 0171 409 7277

10-6pm

% 10%

CC All

🚇 Green Park

Ireland in London

On the opposite side of the road to Harrods, here is a friendly shop specialising in a wide range of gifts from Ireland, cashmere, jewellery, aran knitwear, scarves, Irish linen, capes and glassware. Sundays open from 12-5pm

5 Montpellier Street, Knightsbridge, London SW7 1EX
☎ 0171 589 4455

🕐 10-7pm

% 10%

⊖ Knightsbridge

The Irish Shop

For over 30 years the Irish shop has specialized in crystal and china, knitwear and aran fisherman sweaters. Also available are linens, tweeds, fashion and Celtic jewellery, traditional crafts, music and books. 5% discount with NBC Card. Open 12-6pm on Sundays.

14 King Street, Covent Garden, WC2E 8HN
☎ 0171 379 3625

🕐 10-7pm

% 5%

cc All

⊖ Covent Garden

The Kite Store

Whether you are an enthusiast or the idea of kite flying appeals to you then this is Europe's first specialist kite store and they certainly have a great range and variety of styles, this also extends to the non-traditional fliers, accessories, books and videos. Expert advice and substantial savings on a range of kites, and associated products. Closed on Sundays.

48 Neal Street, London WC2H 9PA
☎ 0171 836 1666

🕐 10-6pm

% 10%

⊖ Covent Garden

Lawleys

Lawleys are one of the leading stockists of fine china and glass in London, offering a whole range of famous names and styles, primarily Royal Doulton, Royal Albert, Minton and Royal Crown Derby, under one roof. The offer applies to non price-promoted items and the store is also open on Sundays 12-6pm .

154 Regent Street, London W1R 6LA
☎ 0171 734 3184

🕐 9-6pm

% 10%

cc All

⊖ Piccadilly Circus

Manguette

Manguette (pronounced, Mon Get) is an exclusive stockist of the finest contemporary jewellery and is located off Holland Street near High Street Kensington station. Michelle Manguette's many famous clients of her designers include, Cher, Zsa Zsa Gabor, Demi Moore, Jackie Onasis and Julia Roberts. Closed Sundays.

40 Gordon Place, Holland Street, London W8
☎ 0171 937 2897

🕐 11-6pm

% 10%

cc All

⊖ High Street Kensington

Mikimoto

Creators of some of the world's finest cultured pearl jewellery. Renowned for its fine craftsmanship, this store in London's exclusive New Bond Street, sells designs which are available only to the European market, and have never been shown in the US. Offer applies to gift items. Closed on Sundays.

179 New Bond Street, London W1Y 9PD
☎ 0171 629 5300

🕐 10-5.30pm

% 10%

cc All

⊖ Green Park

Museum Store

Gifts from museums all around the world under one roof, this is an absolutely fabulous shop for gifts and you can find items from British, European and American museums that are both fascinating and fun. This is almost an attraction and shop combined due to all that it encompasses. Sundays 11-5pm. Offer excludes sale items.

37 The Market, Covent Garden, WC2E 8RF
☎ 0171 240 5760

🕐 10.30-6.30pm

% 10%

⊖ Covent Garden

N. Peal

Cashmere knitwear, and accessories for men and women, at N. Peal in the attractive Burlington Arcade. The collections are elegant and chic, yet younger and more contemporary, the range is extensive. Located in the Arcade at numbers 37 and 71, the offer applies to non-sale items. Not open on Sundays.

37 & 71 Burlington Arcade, London W1
☎ 0171 493 9220

🕐 9.30-6pm

% 10%

CC All

⊖ Green Park

Pencraft

The shop is one of the leading stockists of most leading makes of writing instruments, and can arrange VAT refunds on your purchases. The offer is 10% on 1 pen over £100, 15% spend over £200 and 17.5% spend over £300.

281 Regent Street, London W1R 7PB
☎ 0171 493 2125

🕐 9-5.30pm

% 10%-17.5%

CC All

⊖ Oxford Circus

Penhaligon's Ltd

At Penhaligon's you will find classic scents and fine English gifts for ladies and gentlemen. By appointment to His Royal Highness the Duke of Edinburgh, and HRH Prince of Wales, this is one of England's finest perfumeries. The gift is a ladies' or gentlemen's scent library on a spend of over £20, please present your card and guide. Closed on Sundays.

41 Wellington Street, Covent Garden WC2
☎ 0171 836 2150

🕐 10-6pm

✏ (£20+)

CC All

⊖ Covent Garden

Pescatori Charlotte Street

Pescatori is a very popular Mediterranean fish restaurant and is excellent for either lunch or dinner. There are two of these fine restaurants in London, the second is in Dover Street, London W1. Please present the coupon in the back of the guide when ordering your meal, to receive a free carafe of house wine.

57 Charlotte Street, London W1
☎ 0171 580 3289

✕ ⚲

✏ Coupon

CC All

⊖ Goodge Street

Pescatori Dover Street

Pescatori is a very popular Mediterranean fish restaurant and is excellent for either lunch or dinner. There are two of these fine restaurants in London, the second is in Charlotte Street, London W1. Please present the coupon in the back of the guide when ordering your meal, to receive a free carafe of house wine.

11 Dover Street, London W1
☎ 0171 493 2652

✕ ⚲

✏ Coupon

CC All

⊖ Green Park

Peter Rabbit & Friends

Peter Rabbit and Friends, the shop that takes you into a world of gifts, that feature Peter Rabbit and all Beatrix Potter's characters. There are wonderful clothes for children to enjoy and beautiful gifts for all ages. Open Sunday 11-6pm

Unit 42, The Market, Covent Garden, WC2E 8RF
☎ 0171 497 1777

🕑 9-8pm

% 10%

CC All

Ⓣ Covent Garden

Spaghetti House Knightsbridge

Spaghetti House have 13 restaurants throughout London and are one of the leading Italian restaurant groups. With consistently good and reliable menu's, this one is convenient for lunch or dinner whilst visiting Knightsbridge. Please present the coupon in the back of the guide when ordering your meal, to receive a free carafe of house wine.

77 Knightsbridge, London SW1
☎ 0171 235 8141

✕ ♿

✎ Coupon

CC All

Ⓣ Knightsbridge

Spaghetti House Bond Street

Spaghetti House have 13 restaurants throughout London and are one of the leading Italian restaurant groups. With consistently good and reliable menu's, this one is convenient for lunch or dinner whilst visiting Selfridges or the West End. Please present the coupon in the back of the guide when ordering your meal, to receive a free carafe of house wine.

74 Duke Street, London W1
☎ 0171 629 6097

✕ ♿

✎ Coupon

CC All

Ⓣ Bond Street

Spaghetti House Jermyn Street

Spaghetti House have 13 restaurants throughout London and are one of the leading Italian restaurant groups. With consistently good and reliable menu's, this one is convenient for lunch or dinner whilst visiting Jermyn Street or Piccadilly. Please present the coupon in the back of the guide when ordering your meal, to receive a free carafe of house wine.

16 Jermyn Street, London SW1
☎ 0171 734 7334

✕ ♿

✎ Coupon

CC All

Ⓣ Green Park

Spaghetti House Covent Garden

Spaghetti House have 13 restaurants throughout London and are one of the leading Italian restaurant groups. With consistently good and reliable menu's, this one is convenient for lunch or dinner whilst visiting, Theatreland or Covent Garden. Please present the coupon in the back of the guide when ordering your meal, to receive a free carafe of house wine.

30 St Martin's Lane, London WC2
☎ 0171 836 1626

✕ ♿

✎ Coupon

CC All

Ⓣ Leicester Square

Swaine Adeney Brigg

Founded in 1750, Swaine Adeney opened its first shop in Piccadilly close to the original location of the Royal Mews. In 1945 Swaine Adeney merged with Royal umbrella makers Brigg & Sons. They now supply all the equipment and clothes for country living as well as exquisite handmade leather travel goods.   Closed Sundays.

54 St James's Street, London SW1A 1JT
☎ 0171 409 7277

🕑 10-6pm

% 10%

CC All

Ⓣ Green Park

The Tea House

The Tea House is a shop specialising in fine teas and 'teaphernalia' the term used to describe all things relating to tea, cups, diffusers, pots, spoons, tea-cosies etc. There is another branch in Oxford. The offer is a 125g chest of tea with purchases over £30. Sundays open from 12-6pm.

15 Neal Street, Covent Garden, WC2H 9PU
☎ 0171 240 7539

🕐 10-7pm

(£30+)

CC All

⊖ Covent Garden

Thomas Pink Ltd

It was once said by a leading newspaper the **London Times** that 'Thomas Pink is the place to buy shirts in London'. Made from the finest cotton, generously cut, well finished and competitively priced. For gentlemen and ladies. Offer applies to a spend over £50 and is a gift of a pair of silk knot cufflinks. Sunday 12-7pm.

85 Jermyn Street, London SW1
☎ 0171 930 6364

🕐 9.30-6pm

(£50+)

CC All

⊖ Green Park

Vecchia Milano

Vechia Milano is a contemporary Italian restaurant. The restaurant is both friendly and lively, and has a good menu. A convenient and enjoyable choice for lunch or dinner whilst visiting Bond Street, or the West End. Please present the coupon in the back of the guide when ordering your meal, to receive a free carafe of house wine.

74 Welbeck Street, London W1
☎ 0171 935 2371

✕ ⚠

Coupon

CC All

⊖ Bond Street

Von Posch

Von Posch at Jermyn Street offers an exquisite selection of fine porcelain housing the famous names of Herend and Richard Ginori. The showroom also has Limoge boxes, Staffordshire enamels and a range of figures from famous German factories. They will ship anywhere in the world and are situated opposite the alley behind the church. Closed Sundays.

100 Jermyn Street, St James's, London SW1Y 6EE
☎ 0171 930 2211

🕐 10-6pm

% 10%

CC All

⊖ Green Park

Wedgwood Waterford

Founded by Josiah Wedgwood, (1730 to 1795), this is certainly one of the world's leading collectable and usable collections. Together with Waterford Crystal, the combined products are both exciting and extremely British. If time allows do visit the pottery in Stoke-on-Trent to see the ceramics being made. The London shop is the flagship store.

158 Regent Street, London W1
☎ 0171 734 7262

🕐 10-6.30pm

% 10%

CC All

⊖ Oxford Street

Whittard of Chelsea

Whittards, specialist tea merchants since 1886 sell traditional and exotic blends as well as gifts and china. The offer is also applicable at Whittards, 283 Regent Street, 33 Bedford Street in Covent Garden and The Plaza in Oxford Street, offer applies to loose leaf teas and gift sets only. Sundays 12-5pm.

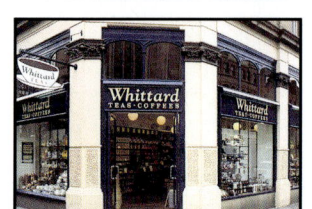

65 Regent Street, London W1
☎ 0171 734 2170

🕐 9.30-6pm

% 10%

CC MC Visa Am Ex

⊖ Piccadilly Circus

LONDON SIGHTSEEING

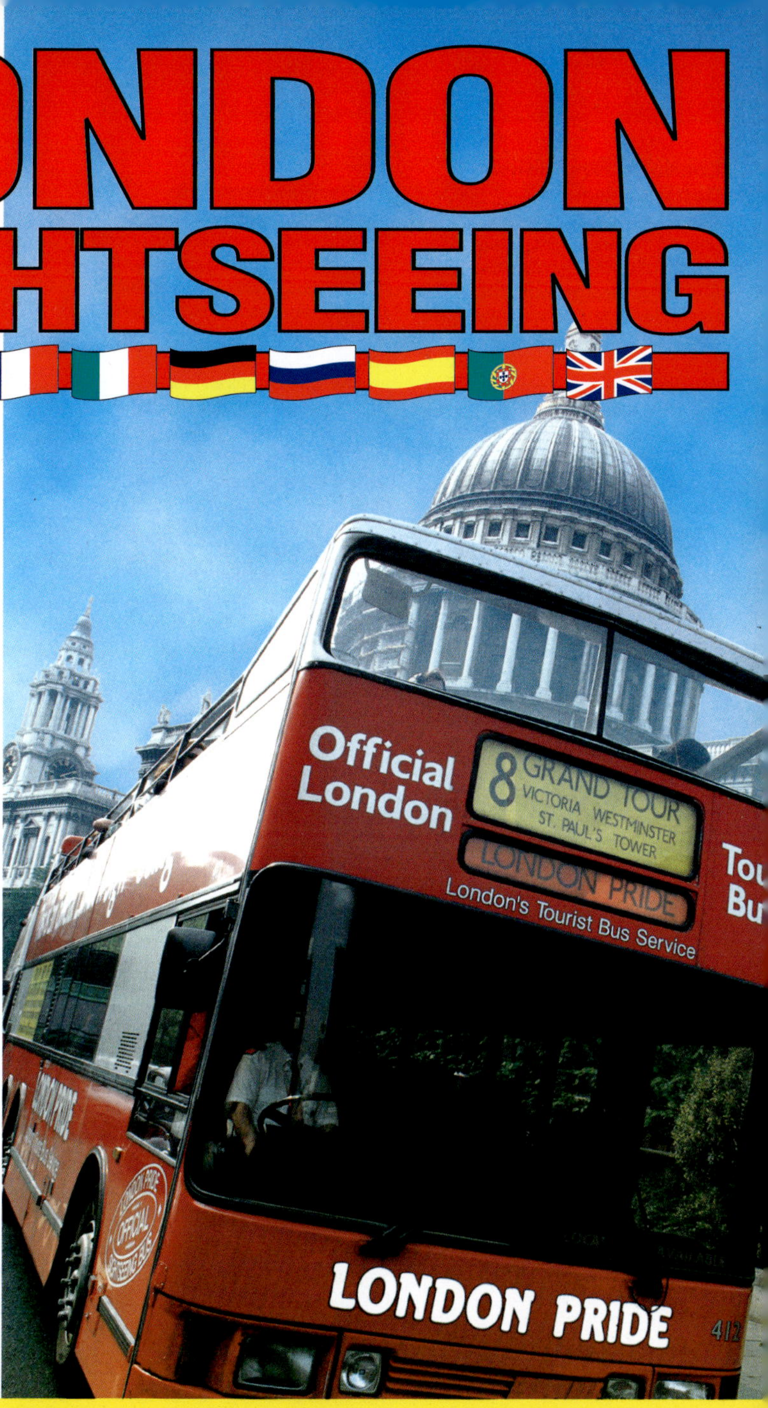

Best value in London sightseeing

6 HOP-ON, HOP-OFF TOURS FOR THE PRICE OF 1

FULL ENGLISH COMMENTARY ON ALL TOURS

VISIT ALL THE MAJOR ATTRACTIONS

- Harrods
- Madame Tussaud's
- The Tower of London
- Tower Bridge
- The Houses of Parliament
- Big Ben
- Buckingham Palace
- Kensington Palace
- Westminster Abbey
- St. Paul's Cathedral

APPROVED Sightseeing Tour

LONDON

LONDON MEMBER

Official London

8 GRAND TOUR
VICTORIA WESTMINSTER
ST. PAUL'S TOWER

LONDON PRIDE
London's Tourist Bus Service

Tou Bu

LONDON PRIDE

UNLIMITED TRAVEL ON ALL TOURS FOR 24 HOURS

All tours pick up and set down at Piccadilly Circus (outside the Trocadero in Coventry Street).
Buy your tickets on the bus or from any of our customer care staff throughout central London - use the voucher
at the back of this book to get **2 tickets for the price of 1**

London Attractions
Getting Around

As the largest city in Europe, London has an almost endless list of attractions for you to visit. Choosing the attractions that interest you, and planning how to visit them is obviously very important.

By placing the main attractions and their map reference on just one map, (see pages 84,85 or 86-89), it is easy for you to see the proximity of each attraction that you wish to visit, and the best ways to travel between them. Underground stations, buses or black taxis are available, close to every attraction, or alternatively you can walk from one to another. If you wish to start with a guided tour, either to take you around on a 'hop on, hop off' tour, or as a guide to which attractions to choose, the London Pride Sightseeing, (page 61) or another of the recognized tour bus operators will provide a good service. Finally, the amount of time you wish to spend at any attraction obviously depends on your depth of interest, and a few attractions will involve queuing, (lines) so it may be advisable to visit fewer attractions, but enjoy them fully or get a feel for a larger number and return to the ones you like best.

How to Use
London Attractions

On pages 86-89 there is a map which highlights the main places to visit, along with their grid reference. The map includes Underground stations, and road names to make getting around easy. As an NBC cardholder, you will receive discounts and special offers at most of the best places to visit, so please look through the 'offers and information' on pages 68-81.

To familiarize yourself with using the card, (or coupons) please refer to the Inside Back Cover, 'How to Use the NBC Card'.

'Free', and Other Attractions

By using the map on pages 86-89 and the corresponding attraction grid references, you can find all of the following places of interest listed below, that are not included in the 'Offers and Information' on pages 68-81.

Free entry is indicated by 🖼
Sightseeing by ⭐
If an entry charge is applicable 🗂

BBC Visitor Centre 🗂
The world of Television and Radio. The BBC is paid for by Government and public license fees.
Portland Place, W1
T. 0171 580 4468
⊖ Regent's Park
Map P 88 D6

Barbican Art Gallery 🗂
The Gallery offers a diverse program of temporary shows. Call for details.
Silk Street, EC2
T. 0171 588 9023
⊖ Barbican
Map Ref P 89 D10

British Museum 🖼
The oldest public museum in the world (1753). Contains artefacts spanning thousands of years of world culture.
Great Russell St, WC1
T. 0171 580 1788
⊖ Russell Square
Map P 88 D7/8

Big Ben ⭐
The clock tower holds a 14 tonne bell hung in 1858, and dominates the Houses of Parliament.
Parliament Square, SW1
⊖ Westminster
Map P 88 F8

British Library 🗂
Housed in a spectacular new building. This is the national library of the UK.
96 Euston Road, NW1
T. 0171 412 7332
⊖ King's Cross/Euston.
Map Ref P 88 C7

Buckingham Palace 🗂 ⭐
The Queen's London Residence.
Constitution Hill, SW1
T. 0171 930 4832
⊖ Hyde Park
Map P 88 F6/7

Big Ben

Changing of the Guard ⭐
The Guards in their distinct red uniforms and black head wear, Change the Palace Guard at 11am (10am Sunday)
Buckingham Palace
⊖ Hyde Park
Map P 88 F7

HMS Belfast

Horse Guards

Cleopatra's Needle ★
Presented by Egypt in 1819,
made in 1500BC.
Victoria Embankment, WC2
⊖ Embankment
Map P 88 E8

Downing Street ★
Number 10. is home to
the Prime Minister of
Britain.
Downing Street, SW1
⊖ Westminster
Map P 88 F8

HMS Belfast ▣★
A cruiser built for the Royal Navy,
now a museum next to Tower Bridge.
Tooley Street, SE1
T. 0171 407 6434
⊖ London Bridge
Map P 89 E11

Hyde Park ★
A Royal park since 1536,
in the middle of which is
the Serpentine, where you
can hire a rowing boat.
⊖ Hyde Park/Knightsbridge
Map P 89 E5

Kensington Palace ▣ ★
Royal Palace and park that
was once the residence of
William III.
Kensington Gardens, W8
T. 0171 937 9561
⊖ Queensway
Map P 86 E/F3

Commonwealth Institute ▨
A permanent exhibition and
displays on each country in the
Commonwealth.
230 Kensington High Street,W8
⊖ Kensington High Street
T. 0171 603 4535
Map P 88 E8

Eros, Piccadilly Circus ★
Londonis first aluminium
statue, (Gilbert 1893), which
represents the 'Angel of
Christian Charity'.
⊖ Piccadilly
Map P 88 E7

Houses of Parliament ★
Central seat of Government,
110 rooms, 100 staircases and
2 miles of passages.
Parliament Square, SW1
⊖ Westminster
Map P 88 F8

Imperial War Museum ▣
Museum concerning war
and its human and mechanical
history and impact.
Lambeth Road, SE11
T. 0171 416 5000
⊖ Lambeth North
Map P 89 F9

Lloyds Building ★
The headquarters of the
international insurance market
is an astonishing new building.
Lime Street, EC3
T. 0171 623 7100
⊖ Monument
Map P 89 D11

Courtauld's Gallery ▣
Impressive art galleries
furniture and drawings.
Somerset House, Strand WC2
T. 0171 873 2526
⊖ Aldwych/Temple
Map P 86 F2/3

Hayward Gallery ▣
The main venue for large
temporary exhibitions of
historical & contemporary art.
T. 0171 921 0849
Belvedere Road, SE1
⊖ Waterloo
Map P 88 E8

Harrods ★
The world's most famous
department store.
87 Brompton Road, SW1
T. 0171 730 1234
⊖ Knightsbridge
Map P 87 F5

ICA ▣
The institute of Contemporary
Arts, has changing exhibitions
of contemporary art.
Nash House, The Mall, SW1
T. 0171 930 3647
⊖ Charing Cross
Map P 88 E7

Eros

Hyde Park

Lloyds Building

Imperial War Museum

Nelson's Column

Monument ⭐
Commemorates the Great Fire of London that began in 1966 at a bakery .
🚇 Monument
Map P 89 E10

Old Bailey ⭐
Central Criminal Court and scene of many famous trials.
Old Bailey, EC4
T. 0171 248 3277
🚇 St Paul's
Map P 89 D9

Royal Academy 🏛
Includes a series of special 'loan' exhibitions throughout the year.
Burlington House, Piccadilly W1
T. 0171 439 7438
🚇 Piccadilly, Green Park
Map P 88 E7

Natural History Museum 🏛
Incorporating the Geological Museum and with a range of historic and Earth related exhibitions.
Cromwell Road, SW7
T. 0171 938 9123
🚇 South Kensington
Map P 88 E7

Peter Pan's Statue ⭐
Close to Kensington Palace a commemorative statue to JM Barrie (1912).
Kensington Gardens, W2
🚇 Queensway
Map P 87 E4

Royal Albert Hall 🏛 ⭐
Home to many events and concerts. Given Royal title by Queen Victoria. Home to the promenade concerts.
Kensington Gore, SW7
T. 0171 589 8212
🚇 Knightsbridge
Map P 87 F4

Nelson's Column ⭐
Statue of Admiral Lord Nelson, minus his arm and eye, that were lost in battle.
Trafalgar Square, SW1
🚇 Charing Cross
Map P 87 F4

Regent's Park ⭐
Originally part of King Henry VIII's hunting forest, it has London Zoo and an open air theater in the park.
Inner Circle, NW1
T. 0171 486 2431
🚇 Regent's Park
Map P 87 C6

Royal Festival Hall 🏛
Hosts a variety of superb operatic and classical events.
South Bank, SE1
T. 0171 928 8800
🚇 Waterloo
Map P 88 E8

St James's Palace
The official Royal residence from 1698 to 1837, when Buckingham Palace took over.
Pall Mall, SW1
Ⓤ Green Park
Map P 88 E7

St Paul's Cathedral
Built by Wren, this is the the fifth cathedral on this site. It is an architectural landmark.
Cheapside, EC2
Ⓤ St Paul's
Map P 89 D9/10

Tate Gallery
Named after the sugar millionaire Sir Henry Tate, the museum of British art and also international modern art.
Good restaurant and shop.
Millbank, SW1
T. 0171 887 8000
Ⓤ Pimlico
Map P 88 G8

Telecom Tower
Formerly the Post Office Tower it is a communications center and once had a revolving floor as a restaurant at the top.
Charlotte Street, W1
Ⓤ Goodge Street
Map P 88 D7

The Temple
Named after the Knights Templar, a religious order founded in the Middle Ages who came to this site.
Middle Temple Lane, EC4
Ⓤ Temple
Map P 88 D9

Tower of London
The Tower has served as a palace, prison and place of execution. Home of the Crown Jewels.
Tower Hill, EC3
Ⓤ Tower Hill
Map P 89 E11

Trafalgar Square
Surrounded by four impressive bronze Lions, with Nelson's Column at the center.
Trafalgar Square, SW1
Ⓤ Charing Cross
T. 0171 709 0765
Map P 88 E7

St Paul's Cathedral

Royal Festival Hall

Tower of London

Looking for inspiration?

With over 300 unique properties, from historic houses and castles to beautiful gardens, you'll find some great days out at the National Trust. For a free map guide on National Trust properties contact: The National Trust Travel Trade Office,
36 Queen Anne's Gate, London SW1H 9AS.
Tel: +44 171 447 6700 Fax: +44 171 447 6701.
E-mail: traveltrade@ntrust.org.uk
Web Site: http://www.nationaltrust.org.uk

THE NATIONAL TRUST
Where history *never* repeats itse

Your passport to England's History

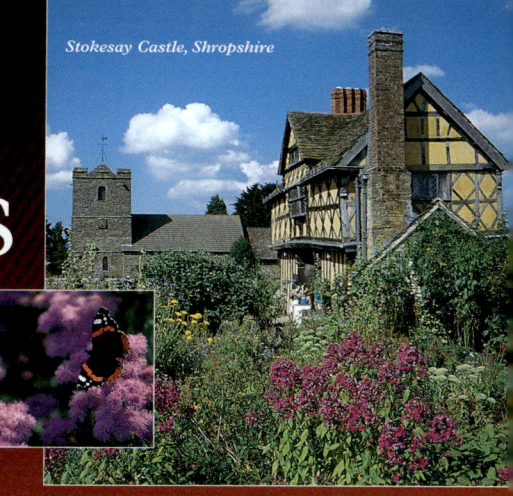

Stokesay Castle, Shropshire

Enjoy unlimited entry to over 400★ of England's most cherished historic attractions with the English Heritage *Overseas Visitor Pass*. Visit as many properties as you like while making huge savings on normal admission.

†	Adult	2 Adults	Family
7 days	£12	£22	£26
14 days	£16	£30	£35

† Prices valid until 31 March 1999.
★ There are over 400 historic properties in the care of English Heritage. 120 of these charge admission.

Rievaulx Abbey, Yorkshire

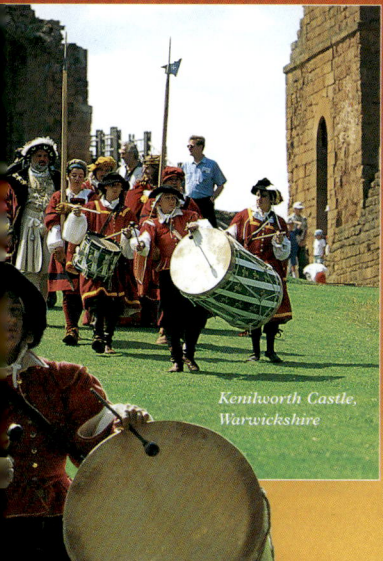

Kenilworth Castle, Warwickshire

Purchase your Overseas Visitor Pass from any staffed English Heritage property or receive your pass, guide & map before you travel by calling the number below with a credit card at hand.

Call us now for a free brochure:
+44 (0) 171 973 3434

ENGLISH HERITAGE

1. Apsley House

Apsley House, The Wellington Museum was designed by Robert Adam and built between 1771 and 1778 for Baron Apsley. It was the first house encountered after passing a toll gate into London from the west, hence its name 'No. 1 London'. In 1817, Apsley House was bought by the first Duke of Wellington. The palatial interiors provide a magnificent setting for the Duke's collection of paintings, including works by Velazquez, Goya, Reubens, Dutch and Flemish masters, porcelain, silver, sculpture, furniture, swords, medals and memorabilia. Apsley House is the last great London town-house with its collections largely intact and family still in residence. Closed on Mondays.

Apsley House, The Welling ton Museum, 149 Piccadilly, Hyde Park Corner, London W1V 9FA
☎ 0171 499 5676

 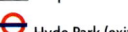

🕐 11-5pm

🚇 Hyde Park (exit 3)

Map ref: Page 87 – F6

2. Bank of England Museum

The museum is housed within the Bank of England, right at the heart of the City of London. It traces the history of the Bank from its foundation by Royal Charter in 1694, to its role today as the nation's central bank. Displays include, gold, bank notes, and a restoration of the Bank Stock Office, designed by Sir John Soane. Award winning interactive systems allow visitors to look behind the scenes and provide great fun too. Present your NBC card and you will receive the audioguide free (normally £1). Open Monday to Friday.

Bank of England Museum
Bartholomew Lane, London EC2
☎ 0171 601 5545

 Audio Guide

🕐 10-5pm

🚇 Bank

www.bankofengland.co.uk

Map ref: Page 89 – D10

3. Bateaux London

Bateaux London provide lunch and dinner cruises on the River Thames. Enjoying London can be hectic so this allows the opportunity to see some great sights whilst enjoying your meal. Making a reservation is essential and you can also telephone the number below for a free colour leaflet on the various cruises. Lunches on Friday and Saturday (1 hour cruise) and Sundays (2 hours). Evening cruises take 2 1/2 hours. For reservation tel. + 44 (0) 171 925 2215 or call in personally at Charing Cross Pier.

Bateaux London Charing Cross Pier, Victoria Embankment, London WC2N 6NU
☎ 0171 925 2215

 10% Evenings 5% Lunches Coupon

🚇 Embankment

Map ref: Page 88 – E8

4. Bramah Tea and Coffee Museum

A celebration of two of the world's most important commodities, through examination of their contribution to global economies. Bramah Tea and Coffee Museum relates the 350 year tradition, social and commercial history of tea and coffee from a British perspective, represented by a fine collection of porcelain, silver and graphic arts. Café and shop sell quality leaf tea of the type enjoyed in England from the reign of Queen Victoria onwards. Walk across Tower Bridge to the south side, down the steps and follow the signs.

Bramah Tea and Coffee Museum, The Clove Building, Maguire Street, London SE1 2NQ
☎ 0171 378 0222

🕐 10-6pm

 All

🚇 Tower Hill

Map ref: Page 89 – F11

5. Cabaret Mechanical Theatre

A Museum of Automata, (pieces of mechanisms with concealed power to create motion). You will be pleasantly enchanted and amused by these numerous mechanical masterpieces, and there really is quite a collection. Before or after pushing numerous buttons in the main theater, you will find many amusing automated figures and game outside and around the entrance. Well worth a visit. There is a shop at the theater. Sunday open at 11.00am.

Cabaret Mechanical Theatre, 33/34 The Market, Covent Garden, London WC2E 8RE
☎ 0171 379 7961

10-6.30pm

CC

🔴 Covent Garden

www.cabaret.co.uk

Map ref: Page 88 – E8

6. Cabinet War Rooms

This warren of 21 rooms, below a government office building is where, (from 1940), Winston Churchill and the War Cabinet met during World War II. There are living quarters here and a sound proofed Cabinet Room, where many strategic decisions were taken. All the rooms are protected by a concrete layer of about a metre thickness and are laid out as they were when the war ended in 1945. Located at the bottom of Clive Steps on the Horse Guards Road. Open from 9.30am April to September.

Cabinet War Rooms, Clive's Steps, King Charles Street, London SW1A 2AQ
☎ 0171 930 6961

10-6pm

CC AmEx MC Visa

🔴 Westminster/St James's Park

Map ref: Page 88 – F7

7. Catamaran Cruisers

Catamaran Cruisers enable you to experience the magic of London from the River Thames. Cruises between Charing Cross Pier, Tower of London and Greenwich with live commentary. A free souvenir map is given on each cruise and if you book your Tower of London ticket at their ticket offices you can avoid the queues for that attraction ! For reservations and details on the various cruises tel. + 44 (0) 171 987 1185 or call in personally at Charing Cross Pier. Please present your coupon (in the back of this guide) when paying.

Catamaran Cruisers Charing Cross Pier, Victoria Embankment, London WC2N 6NU
☎ 0171 987 1185

 % 10% Coupon

🔴 Embankment

Map ref: Page xx – E8

8. Chelsea Physic Garden

London's 'Secret Garden', this is one of Europe's oldest botanic gardens and is the only one to retain the title 'Physic' after the old name for the healing arts. It's 36 acre walled garden shows the history of medicinal plants and has one of the oldest rock gardens in Europe (1773). Glasshouses and many rare and tender plants, such as the largest olive tree in England. Open 6th April to 26 October. Wednesdays 2-5pm, and Sunday 2-6pm. Entrance Swan Walk.

Chelsea Physic Garden, 66 Royal Hospital Road, London SW3 4HS
☎ 0171 352 5646

2-5pm

🔴 Sloane Square

Map ref: Page 87 – G5

9. Cutty Sark and Gypsy Moth

The Cutty Sark 'Queen of the Clipper Ships' was launched in 1869. The Cutty Sark sailed the oceans of the world in the China tea trade, and then the Australian wool trade. It is now a museum with a display on the ship's history and a collection of old ships' figureheads. Nearby is the Gypsy Moth IV, in which Sir Francis Chichester sailed around the world in 1966. Take a river cruise, a train from Charing Cross or Waterloo East to Greenwich, or the Docklands Light Railway to Island Gardens, and then a short walk. Sunday 12 - 6pm.

Cutty Sark and Gypsy Moth, King William Walk, Greenwich, London SE10 9HT
☎ 0181 858 3445

 10-5.30pm

 20% off entry

Greenwich

www.cuttysark.org.uk

Map ref: Page 86 – H16

10. Design Museum

The Design Museum is the first museum in the world to look at the influence design has on the quality of our everyday lives. Visitors can view state-of-the-art innovations from around the world, rediscover 100 years of design trends and movements, indulge in the shop and relax in the riverside café. The museum is situated on the south bank of the River Thames by Tower Bridge. From London Bridge walk along the Queen's Walk Way by the River Thames. From Tower Hill a pleasant walk over Tower Bridge.

Design Museum, 28 Shad Thames, London SE1 2YD
☎ 0171 403 6933

 11.30-6pm

 Tower Hill

Map ref: Page 89 – F11

11. Dickens' House

This historic house is the only London home of Charles Dickens, (1812-1870) that is still standing. Here, between 1837 and 1839, he completed works such as 'Pickwick Papers', 'Oliver Twist' and 'Nicholas Nickleby'. Now a museum, the house contains an unrivalled collection, including books, manuscripts, paintings, furniture and memorabilia from the time he spent here as an adult. He was born in Portsmouth on the south coast of England, but moved to Kent at the age of five. Closed on Sundays. Offer applies on full entry price.

Dickens' House, 48 Doughty Street, London WC1N 2LF
☎ 0171 405 2127

 10-5pm

% £1 off entry

CC MC Visa

Russell Square

Map ref: Page 88 – C8

12. Dr. Johnson's House

This house can be described as a shrine to the English language, for it was here that Dr Samuel Johnson worked for many years to compile the first comprehensive English Dictionary which was published in 1755. Dictionary Johnson, as he became known, lived at 17 Gough Square from 1748 until 1759. The house, one of very few residential houses surviving of its age in the City, has been restored to the condition it was during Johnson's stay. Of particular note is the staircase which is completely original, and the parts of preserved American pine panelling. Closed on Sundays.

Dr. Johnson's House, 17 Gough Square, Fleet Street, London EC4
☎ 0171 353 3745

 11-5.30pm

Blackfriars/Chancery Lane

Map ref: Page 89 – D9

13. Fan Museum

The unique award winning museum of fans. Housed in superbly restored and listed buildings dating back to 1721. It is part of Greenwich's World Heritage Site. The remarkable garden has a paved fan-shaped parterre, the pond, stream and planting are in the Japanese style. The museum also undertakes the conservation and restoration of fans, and will design and make fans to order. On Sundays the museum is open from 12pm.

Fan Museum, 12 Grooms Hill, Greenwich, London SE10 8ER
☎ 0181 858 7879

🕐 11-5pm

CC MC Visa

 Greenwich or DLR

www.greenwichuk.com/fan
Map ref: Page 86 – H16

14. Florence Nightingale Museum

A soldier wrote, 'What a comfort it was to see her pass... We lay there by hundreds; but we could kiss her shadow as it fell, and lay our heads on the pillow again content'. The Florence Nightingale Museum transports you through her life and times, and beautifully illustrates the extraordinary influence that Florence Nightingale has had on nursing and care throughout and beyond her lifetime. Closed on Mondays.

Florence Nightingale Museum, St. Thomas's Hospital, 2 Lambeth Road, London SE1
☎ 0171 620 0374

🕐 10-5pm

 Waterloo

www.florence-nightingale.co.uk

Map ref: Page 88 – F8

15. House of Detention

The House of Detention, 1616-1890, is an example of a London underground prison. Built on the site of one of London's earliest prisons are 20,000 sq ft of underground tunnels and cells. Situated beneath the pavements of Clerkenwell the attraction provides an intriguing vision of early and Victorian London with audio and visual effects, displays and dramatisation. Open 7 days a week.

House of Detention, Clerkenwell Close, London EC1R 0AS
☎ 0171 253 9494

🕐 10-6pm

 Farringdon

Map ref: Page 89 – C9

16. The Jewish Museum

The museum includes a History Gallery tracing the story of the Jewish community in Britain, and a Ceremonial Art Gallery illustrating Jewish religious life with objects of rarity and beauty. It has received awards and recognition for the outstanding collections of Jewish ceremonial art, which are amongst the finest in the world. A Temporary Exhibitions Gallery offers a varied programme of changing exhibitions, and audio visual programmes are also available. 3 minutes walk from Camden Tube. Open Sunday -Thursday inclusive.

The Jewish Museum, Raymond Burton House, 129-131 Albert Street, London NW1
☎ 0171 284 1997

🕐 10-4pm

% £1 off entry

 Camden

Map ref: Page 87 – C6

17. The London Aquarium

Situated in London's historic County Hall just across the River Thames from Big Ben and the Houses of Parliament, London's new £25 million aquarium has over 30,000 specimens representing some 350 species of fish, invertebrates and plant life from around the world. See fish swimming all around you in this colorful and exciting display which is open daily from 10am.

The London Aquarium, County Hall, Riverside Building, Westminster Bridge Road, London SE1 7PB
☎ 0171 967 8000

 10-6pm

🔴 Westminster

www.londonaquarium.co.uk

Map ref: Page 88 – F8

18. London Brass Rubbing Centre

The London Brass Rubbing Centre is an Aladdins Cave of discovery and delight. The opportunity to create some wonderful brass rubbings, with a recent addition of new and popular Celtic images. There is studio art on sale, a street market, art gallery and free concerts, all on site. Buy a ready made version if you prefer or make your own and receive £1 off, not available in conjunction with any other offer. Coupon in the back of the guide. Sundays from 12 - 6pm.

London Brass Rubbing Centre, The Crypt, St Martin in the Fields Church, Trafalgar Square, London WC2N 4JJ
☎ 0171 930 9306

 10-6pm

 % £1 Coupon CC All

🔴 Charing Cross

Map ref: Page 88 – E8

19. London Dungeon

Now one of Europe's number one attractions, the London Dungeon has become infamous for its unique depiction of medieval torture and execution, providing education as well as entertainment. Some of the exhibits have a horrible tendency of coming to life, and it pays to expect the unexpected. The new £3.5 million feature, 'Judgement Day - Sentenced to Death', casts the visitors as the condemned. Board a barge to travel a specially constructed new waterway, to follow a chilling reconstruction of the grim final journey faced by ill-fated prisoners of the Bloody Tower, through Traitor's Gate and on to meet your fate.

London Dungeon, 28-34 Tooley Street, London SE1
☎ 0171 403 0606

 10-5.30pm

 Coupon

🔴 London Bridge

Map ref: Page 89 – E10/11

20. London Transport Museum

Housed in the iron, glass and brick Victorian Flower Market which was built in 1872. A collection that includes the earliest horse drawn omnibuses to the present day buses and transport methods, the museum illustrates the development of London's public transport system. Put yourself in the drivers seat of a bus or underground train, operate signals and generally experience the history. The museum shop has some excellent prints and gift ideas. Open from 11am on Fridays.

London Transport Museum, Covent Garden Piazza, London WC2E 7BB
☎ 0171 379 6344

 10-6pm

 % £1 off entry

🔴 Covent Garden

Map ref: Page 88 – E8

21. London Toy & Model Museum

The Toy Museum has over 7,000 toys and models, such as cars, dolls and tin soldiers from over 100 years ago to the present day in 20 themed galleries. There is a most interesting 90 year old model coal mine that cleverly illustrates the workings of a coal mining town. An interactive airport is also exhibited. In the small garden there is a miniature railway ride and roundabout for children. The offer will also include a 50p reduction for children. From the station walk along Craven Road to Craven Hill. Please trelephone to check openeing times and details.

London Toy & Model Museum, 21-23 Craven Hill, London W2 3EN
☎ 0171 706 8000

9-5.30pm

% £1 off entry

MC Visa

 Paddington

Map ref: Page 87 – E4

22. Madame Tussaud's and the London Planetarium

Meet over 400 personalities of the past and present at London's No.1 attraction. From Shakespeare to Brad Pitt, you will encounter them all at Madame Tussaud's. The new themed areas include 'The Garden Party' which offers an open invitation to one of the hottest gatherings in town, and the 'Grand Hall' which is home to leading politicians and statesmen. The 'Spirit of London' ride is a tour across four centuries of London life. Then an inter-galactic trek across the universe in the London Planetarium. The new cosmic show entitled 'Planetary Quest' will present the wonders of the galaxy through the eyes of a space traveler. Discount coupon in the back of the guide (valid for up to 4 people).

MADAME TUSSAUD'S

Madam Tussaud's and London Planetarium Marylebone Road, London NW1
☎ 0171 935 6861

10-5.30pm

% Coupon

 Baker Street

Map Ref Page 87 – C6

23. Millennium Experience

Any trip to London in the year 2000 would be incomplete without experiencing the Millennium Dome at Greenwich. Open every day in the year 2000, it will be the center of the UK's millennium celebrations. The Dome promises to educate and entertain on a scale never seen before, and will offer a unique opportunity to experience the best in style, design, architecture and entertainment, all under the theme, 'Time to Make a Difference'. For further information contact the British Tourist Authority or London Tourist Board.

Millennium Experience, Greenwich, London
☎ British Tourist Authority, or London Tourist Board, BTA see page 15, and LTB see page 38.

From 10am

Greenwich

Map Ref Page 86 – E17

24. Museum of Garden History

A father and son, both named John Tradescant, were gardeners succesively during the 17th century to the first Lord Salisbury, the Duke of Buckingham, Kings Charles I and Charles II. They collected 'all things strange and rare' and displayed these in their house in Lambeth, which became the first museum for the general public. This collection ultimately formed the basis of the Ashmolean Museum, Oxford. The museum is housed in an historic building, and the 17th century garden has been accurately recreated and contains many plants of that period. Closed on Saturdays. Donations welcome.

Museum of Garden History, Lambeth Palace Road, London SE1 7LB
☎ 0171 261 1891

10.30-4pm.

 Victoria/Waterloo

Map Ref Page 88 – F8

25. Museum of London

This museum traces the life of London from prehistoric times to the 20th century. Reconstructed street scenes and displays of archaeological finds alternate with domestic objects. See also the audio visual display of the Great Fire of London in 1666. One of the most popular exhibits is the Lord Mayor's State Coach built in 1757 and lavishly gilded. The museum offers an insight into London's past history. Closed Mondays and open from 12 noon on Sundays.

Museum of London, London Wall, London EC2Y 5HN
☎ 0171 600 3699

10-5.30pm.

 Barbican

Map ref: Page 89 – D10

26. Museum of the Moving Image

The magical world of film and television comes to life before you at the Museum of the Moving Image. This is the story of moving images, from Chinese shadow theater to film, television and satellite. See Charlie Chaplin's hat and cane, fly like Superman, audition for a Hollywood screen role or even read the news. There are hundreds of film and TV clips and a cast of actor-guides are fun to interact with. Please use the coupon in the back of the guide. 10 minute walk from Covent Garden.

MUSEUM OF THE M MOVINGIMAGE

Museum of the Moving Image, South Bank, Waterloo, London SE1 8XT
☎ 0171 401 2636

10-6pm

 % £1.50 off entry. Coupon

 Waterloo

Map ref: Page 88 – E9

27. National Gallery

Entrance to the National Gallery is free. The gallery houses one of the finest collections of western European paintings, more than 2,000 pictures from 1260-1900 mostly on permanent display. Most of the collection is housed on the first floor, divided into four wings, the paintings are hung chronologically, with the earliest works in the Sainsbury Wing. Located in the heart of London, near Covent Garden and Leicester Square, at Trafalgar Square (Nelson's Column). Restaurants at the museum. Offer applies in the gallery shops.

National Gallery, Trafalgar Square, London WC2N 5DN
☎ 0171 839 3321

10-6pm

 % 10% (shop)

 Charing Cross

Map ref: Page 88 – E7

28. National Maritime Museum

Greenwich - Home of Time. Combined ticket includes the Old Royal Observatory where you stand astride the Meridian Line, longitude zero, hear the Greenwich 'pips' and see the time ball drop at 1 o'clock. Visit the 'Nelson' exhibition at the nearby National Maritime Museum which is greatly extended in 1999 with special features. Queen's House, (closed during 1999 for restoration) completes this excellent combination. Travel by river cruise to Greenwich, rail from Charing Cross or Waterloo East, or through the Docklands by DLR (Docklands Light Railway).

National Maritime Museum, Greenwich Park, London SE10 9NF
☎ 0181 312 6565

10-5pm

CC All

 Maze Hill

Map ref: Page 86 – H16

29. Pollock's Toy Museum

An absolutely fascinating museum detailing the history of toy theater, dolls, puppets and a selection of other toys. The collection includes dolls houses, rocking horses, teddy bears and interesting tin and lead toys. There is also a shop where you can buy gifts that reflect the contents of the museum. Entrance in Whitfield Street. Closed on Sundays.

Pollock's Toy Museum, 1 Scala Street, London W1P 1LT
☎ 0171 636 3452

 10-5pm

 % 20% off entry

🚇 Goodge Street

Map ref: Page 88 – D7

30. The Open Air Theatre

A trip to the Open Air Theatre in London's, Regent's Park is an enchanting and magical experience. It is one of the most beautiful theater settings anywhere in the country. From May to September there a diverse selection of plays perfomed here, but always including works by Shakespeare. Performances also include, Sunday in the Park, and Late Nights in the Park, please contact the box office, or *First Call/Applause, on pages 42,43 for details and bookings. If the weather is too bad on the day, you'll receive tickets to another performance. There is a restaurant and bar there, or take a picnic.

The Open Air Theatre, The Inner Circle, Regent's Park, London NW1 4NP
☎ 0171 486 2431/1933

 (Box Office) 10-6pm

*

🚇 Baker Street/Regent's Park

Map ref: Page 87 – C6

31. Rock Circus

Set in Piccadilly Circus, in the heart of London's West End, is where the spirit of rock speaks to you, sings to you, plays to you, moves and touches you. Spanning 40 years of the best in rock and pop music, Rock Circus takes you on a personal guided tour by your own headphones. See stars from the past and present, from Bowie to Jon Bon Jovi and Jarvis Cocker. The 'New Music Revolution Show' is an amazing experience set in Europe's largest revolving auditorium, where you can watch the world's greatest artists perform before your eyes, unfolding the story of rock and pop. Please use the coupon in the back of the guide (valid for up to 4 people).

Rock Circus, London Pavilion, Piccadilly Circus, London W1
☎ 0171 734 7203

 11-9pm

 % £1 Coupon

🚇 Piccadilly Circus

Map ref: Page 88 – E7

32. Science Museum

The Science Museum in London is the largest museum of its kind in the world. See, touch, and experience the major scientific advances of the last 300 years, including over 2,000 hands-on exhibits. This is a massive and impressive exhibition that combines enjoyment with learning, and you do not need a science degree to understand. The 'Exploration of Space' displays the Apollo 10 spacecraft that carried three astronauts to the moon and back in May 1969. Photography is allowed should you wish to 'join' the space crew for a photo. Ticket does not include entry to the Science of Sport Exhibition.

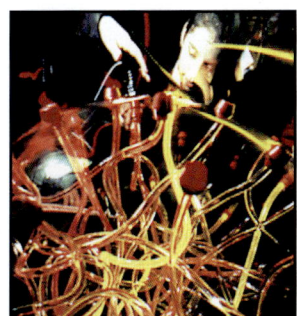

Science Museum, Exhibition Road, London SW7 2DD
☎ 0171 938 8000

 10-6pm

 % £1.50 off entry

🚇 South Kensington

Map ref: Page 87 – F4

33. Shakespeare's Globe

Many of Shakespeare's plays were written for and first produced at The Globe Theatre. Originally built in 1599, it subsequently burned down in 1613. Rebuilt in 1614 and then demolished in 1644, The Globe has now been painstakingly reconstructed to a design by Inigo Jones and recreates the atmosphere of 400 years ago. The exhibition explains the background and the Elizabethan methods used to rebuild it. There are theater performances from May to September, an advance reservation is recommended on tel. (+44) 171 620 0202. Please use the coupon in the back of the Guide.

Shakespeare's Globe, New Globe Walk, Bankside, London SE1
☎ 0171 928 6406

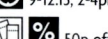

🕐 9-12.15, 2-4pm.

% 50p off entry. Coupon

🚇 London Bridge

Map ref: Page 89 – E10

34. Sherlock Holmes Memorabilia

On the opposite side of the road to the Sherlock Holmes Museum which has various artifacts and scenes from Holmes' and Watson's life, you will find the Sherlock Holmes Memorabilia Shop. This shop has the largest selection of Sherlock Holmes memorabilia including, deerstalker hats, pipes, and rare books for collectors. There is a period set on the first floor. Open from 11am on Sundays. Offer on spend over £10.

Sherlock Holmes Memorabilia, 230 Baker Street, London NW1
☎ 0171 486 1426

🕐 9.30-5.30pm

% 5%

cc All

🚇 Baker Street

Map ref: Page 87 – C5

35. The Silver Sturgeon

Enjoy a delightful River Thames restaurant cruise on board The Silver Sturgeon and experience London's finest views in five star luxury. Your evening on board begins with a welcome drink in the beautiful art deco interior. Then enjoy an excellent four course dinner followed by dancing, a stroll along one of the promenade decks or relax with a drink at the bar. NBC cardholders can enjoy a free bottle of champagne, (one bottle per reservation) by quoting your NBC card number when making a reservation. Sailings from the Savoy Pier at 7.30pm, return at 11pm. Sunday, Wednesday, Friday and Saturdays.

The Silver Sturgeon, The Applause Building, 67 Long Acre, Covent Garden WC2
☎ 0171 312 1950 (Reservations)

🕐 7.30-10.30pm

🚇 Covent Garden

Map ref: Page 88 – E8

36. The Theatre Museum

Discover the magic of the stage here in the heart of Theatreland. Exhibitions and memorabilia on the history of the theater and its performers, from Shakespeare's time to the present day. Demonstrations on stage make-up, (from gruesome to transforming) are great fun and are included in the price. This is an interesting and informative look 'behind the scenes' with some excellent permanent exhibits. Closed on Mondays.

The Theatre Museum, 1E Tavistock Street, London WC2E 7PA
☎ 0171 836 7891

🕐 11-7pm

🚇 Covent Garden

Map ref: Page 88 – E8

37. The Tower Bridge Experience

Situated inside the Bridge is one of London's most unusual attractions. State of the art technology, including animatronics, video and interactive computers, are used to bring the bridge to life. Discover why the bridge was needed and how the design was chosen, also how this working bridge was operated. However, the main attraction is the spectacular views from the high level walkways (130ft) above the River of some of the most famous buildings, such as the Tower of London and St Paul's Cathedral. Last entry 1¼ hours before closing.

The Tower Bridge Experience, Tower Bridge, London SE1 2UP
☎ 0171 378 1928

🕐 10-6.30pm

% £1 off entry

CC All

⭕ Tower Hill

Map ref: Page 89 – E11

38. The Victoria and Albert Museum

The V&A holds one of the worlds largest, richest, and most diverse collections of the decorative arts. There are 146 galleries divided between those devoted to art and design, and those concentrating on materials and techniques. These unrivalled collections date from 3,000 BC to the present day. Furniture, fashion, textiles, paintings, silver, glass, ceramics, sculpture, jewellery, books, prints and photographs wonderfully illustrate the artistic livese of the many different cultures around the world. Admission is free for those under 18 and between 4.30-5.45pm.

The Victoria and Albert Museum, Cromwell Road, London SW7 2RL
☎ 0171 938 8500

🕐 10-5.45pm (Mon from 12)

% £1 Coupon

⭕ South Kensington

www.vam.ac.uk

Map ref: Page 87 – F5

39. Wallace Collection

The Wallace Collection contains superb works of art displayed in an historic London town house. Many people regard it as their favorite place in the capital. The twenty-five rooms present unsurpassed collections and by the terms of Lady Wallace's bequest, nothing must be added or loaned to the collection. This provision has preserved the remarkable character of one of the greatest collections ever made by an English family. Sunday 2 - 5pm.

Wallace Collection, Hertford House, Manchester Square, London W1 M 6BN
☎ 0171 935 0687

🕐 10-5pm

⭕ Bond Street

www.demon.co.uk/heritage/wallace

Map ref: Page 87 – D6

40. Westminster Abbey (Pyx Chamber)

The Abbey is an architectural masterpiece and presents a unique pageant of British History. It has been the setting for every.coronation since 1066, and for other numerous royal occasions. There is an admission fee for parts of the abbey. The Chapter House, Pyx Chamber and Museum are part of English Heritage (see page 67), and contain many of the abbeys sculptures and treasures. Also, you can get 20% off brass rubbings* in the 'Cloisters' when presenting your NBC card.

Westminster Abbey (Pyx Chamber), Westminster, London SW1
☎ 0171 222 5897

🕐 10-5.30pm

  % *20% & see page 67

⭕ Victoria/Westminster

Map ref: Page 88 – F7/8

41. Chiswick House

Close to the center of London lies one of the first and finest Palladian villas, surrounded by beautiful gardens. It was designed to recreate the kind of house and garden found in the suburbs of ancient Rome. The house contains a large collection of art and books, and the gardens complement the house perfectly. Do perhaps visit Hogarth's House whilst you are in this part of London, it's just a short walk from here.

Chiswick House, Burlington Lane, London W4
☎ 0181 995 0508

🕐 10-6pm

 % Page 67

🚇 Turnham Green 1/2 mile

Around London map pages 36,37

42. David Evans World of Silk

Established in 1843, visit this historic company of craftsmen screen printers on the banks of the River Cray. Reserve in advance to enjoy a fascinating guided tour of the workshops and museum The factory shop sells fabrics, gifts, designer scarves and ties. Closed on Sundays. Located 10 minutes from the A2 and approximately 30 minutes from Greenwich to Crayford station. You will also receive a free bandanna.

David Evans World of Silk, Bourne Industrial Park, Bourne Road, Crayford, Kent DA1 4BP
☎ 01322 559401

🕐 9.30-5pm

🚆 Crayford

M 25/2   A 2

Around London map pages 36,37

43. Down House

Charles Darwin was perhaps the most influential scientist of the 19th century. It was from his study in Down House that he worked on the scientific theories that first scandalized, and then revolutionized the Victorian world. This was his home for forty years and much of his life and work can be seen here. Located south east of London.

Down House, Down, near Biggin Hill, Kent
☎ 0171 973 3399

🕐 10-6pm

% Page 67

🚆 Orpington 5 miles

M 25   A 21/233

Around London map pages 36,37

44. Freud Museum

The Freud Museum exists to celebrate the life and work of Sigmund Freud, as one of the most influential figures of the 20th century. The museum was the home of Freud and his family when they escaped the Nazi annexation of Austria in 1938, it remained the family home until 1982. Fortunately all of their possesions were brought to their home, making this one of the most moving and dramatic interiors in London. The centerpiece of the museum is Freud's library and study, the site of his discoveries about human psyche. Open Wed - Sunday.

Freud Museum, 20 Maresfield Gardens, London NW3 5SX
☎ 0171 435 2002

🕐 12-5pm

🚇 Finchley Road

Around London map pages 36,37

45. Ham House

Outstanding Stuart house built on the banks of the River Thames in 1610 and enlarged in the 1670's. Contains rare and unique survivals of the 17th century, including exquisite closets, fine furniture, textiles and pictures. The center of Restoration court life and intrigue in the 1670's when the Duke of Lauderdale, one of Charles II's most powerful ministers, married Elizabeth, Countess of Dysart. A 17th century formal gardens surround the house and there is a continuing programme to restore their decorative glory.

Ham House, Ham, Richmond TW10 7RS
☎ 0181 940 1950

 Page 91
 Page 66

🔴 Richmond

Around London map pages 36,37

46. Hampton Court

Cardinal Wolsey, chief minister and Archbishop of York to King Henry VIII, leased Hampton Court in 1514 as his riverside country residence. In 1528, in the hope of regaining royal favor, Wolsey gave it to the king. After the royal takeover it was extended twice, once by Henry VIII, and then in the 1690's by William and Mary, who used Christopher Wren as the architect. Highlights include Tudor kitchens, great gatehouse and the Baroque gardens. Opens from 10.15am on Mondays

Hampton Court, East Molesey, Surrey KT8 9AU
☎ 0181 781 9500

9.30-6pm

 Hampton Court

Around London map pages 36,37

47. Hogarth's House

This charming 18th century house was once the home of William Hogarth, the famous painter and engraver. It was fully restored in 1997, and as well as displaying his finest engravings, the house has special exhibitions of Hogarth's work. The main exhibition tells the story of his life and work which was central to intellectual and artistic life in mid 18th century London. All his major 'Progresses' such as 'The Rake's Progress' are on display here. Located near Chiswick House. Closed on Mondays. November to March closes at 4pm.

Hogarth's House Hogarth's Lane, Great West Road, London W4 2QN
☎ 0181 994 6757

1-5pm

🔴 Chiswick Park 1 mile

Around London map pages 36,37

48. Kenwood House

Standing on superb landscaped grounds on the edge of Hampstead Heath in north west London, Kenwood contains an important private collection of paintings, including the 'Self Portrait' by Rembrandt. The house was remodelled by Robert Adam, (1764 - 1779) from a brick house into a majestic villa. During the summer months lakeside concerts take place in the grounds.

Kenwood House , Hampstead Lane, London NW3
☎ 0181 348 1286

10-6pm

 Page 67

🔴 Highgate 1 mile

Around London map pages 36,37

49. Kew Bridge Steam Museum

Water, our most basic need, and steam, the means by which it was delivered to west London's homes. Learn the story of water in the new and revealing 'Water for Life' exhibition, exhibits, informative displays and interactive games. The museum is housed in a magnificent 19th century pumping station about 100 yards from the north side of Kew Bridge. Combine this with a visit to nearby Chiswick House, Kew Gardens or Syon Park.

Kew Bridge Steam Museum, Green Dragon Lane, Brentford, Middlesex TW8 0EN
☎ 0181 568 4757

🏛️ 🛍️ **P**

🕐 11-5pm

🖼️ 🔞

 Gunnersbury ⇄ Kew Bridge

Around London map pages 36,37

50. Kew Gardens

These world famous gardens began as a 9 acre site laid out by George III's mother, Princess Augusta, in 1769. Some of its earliest specimens were brought back from the voyages of Captain Cook. It has now grown into a 300 acre site, flawlessly maintained, the gardens have examples of nearly every plant that can be grown in Britain.

Kew Gardens, Richmond, Surrey TW9 3AB
☎ 0181 940 1171

❄️ 🛍️ ☕ **P**

🕐 9am-dusk

🖼️

 Kew Gardens

www.rbgkew.org.uk

Around London map pages 36,37

51. Syon House

Syon Park, Syon House, the London home of the Duke of Northumberland is set within Capability Brown landscaped parkland and contains some of Robert Adams finest interior designs. The gardens incorporate the spectacular conservatory and over 200 species of rare trees. The house open, 1st April- 31st October, from 11-5pm (Friday and Saturday closing at 3.30pm). Closed on Mondays and Tuesdays. Gardens open daily 10-6pm. Offer applies to house, gardens, Great Conservatory and Rose Gardens admission only.

Syon House, Brentford, Middlesex TW8 8JF
☎ 0181 569 0883

🚂 ❄️ 🛍️ ☕ **P**

🕐 11-5pm

🖼️ 🔞

 Gunnersbury ⇄ Kew Bridge

Around London map pages 36,37

52. Wimbledon Lawn Tennis Museum

Set in the grounds of the All England Lawn Tennis and Croquet Club, home to the Championships, a visit to the museum re-creates the unique 'Wimbledon' atmosphere. Highlights include a view of the world famous Centre Court, the magnificent Championship Trophies and film footage of great players in action from the 1920's to the present day. To receive the offer please present the coupon in the back of the guide when purchasing your ticket. Closed on Mondays. Sundays the museum is open from 2 - 5pm. NBC £1 discount off entry.

Wimbledon Lawn Tennis Museum, Church Road, Wimbledon, London SW19 5AE
☎ 0181 946 6131

🏛️ ⭐ 🛍️ ☕ **P**

🕐 10-5pm

🖼️ % £1 Coupon

 Wimbledon/ Southfields (15 mins walk)

Around London map pages 36,37

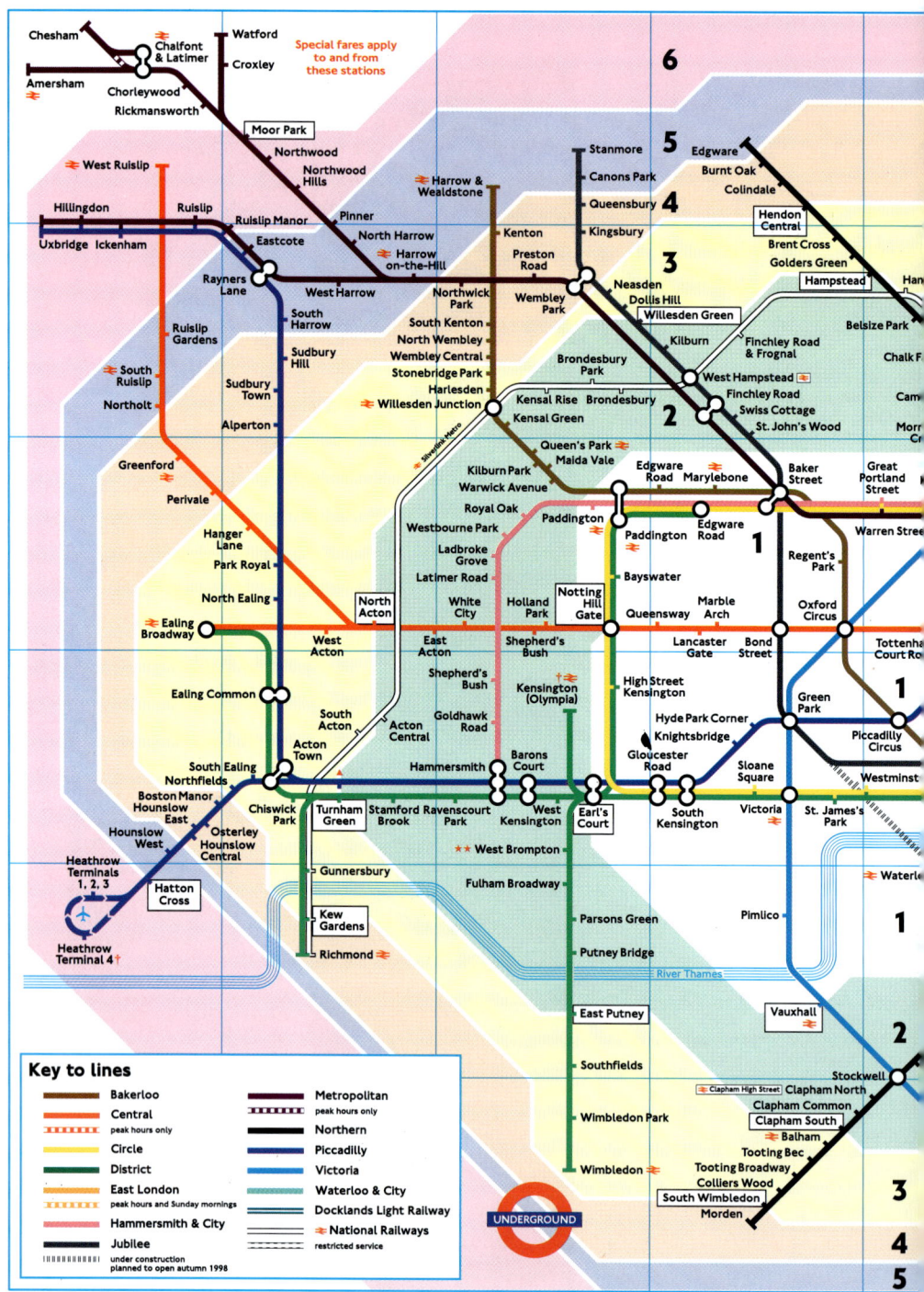

Special fares apply to and from these stations

Key to lines

Bakerloo		Metropolitan
Central		peak hours only
peak hours only		Northern
Circle		Piccadilly
District		Victoria
East London		Waterloo & City
peak hours and Sunday mornings		Docklands Light Railway
Hammersmith & City		National Railways
Jubilee		restricted service
under construction planned to open autumn 1998		

UNDERGROUND

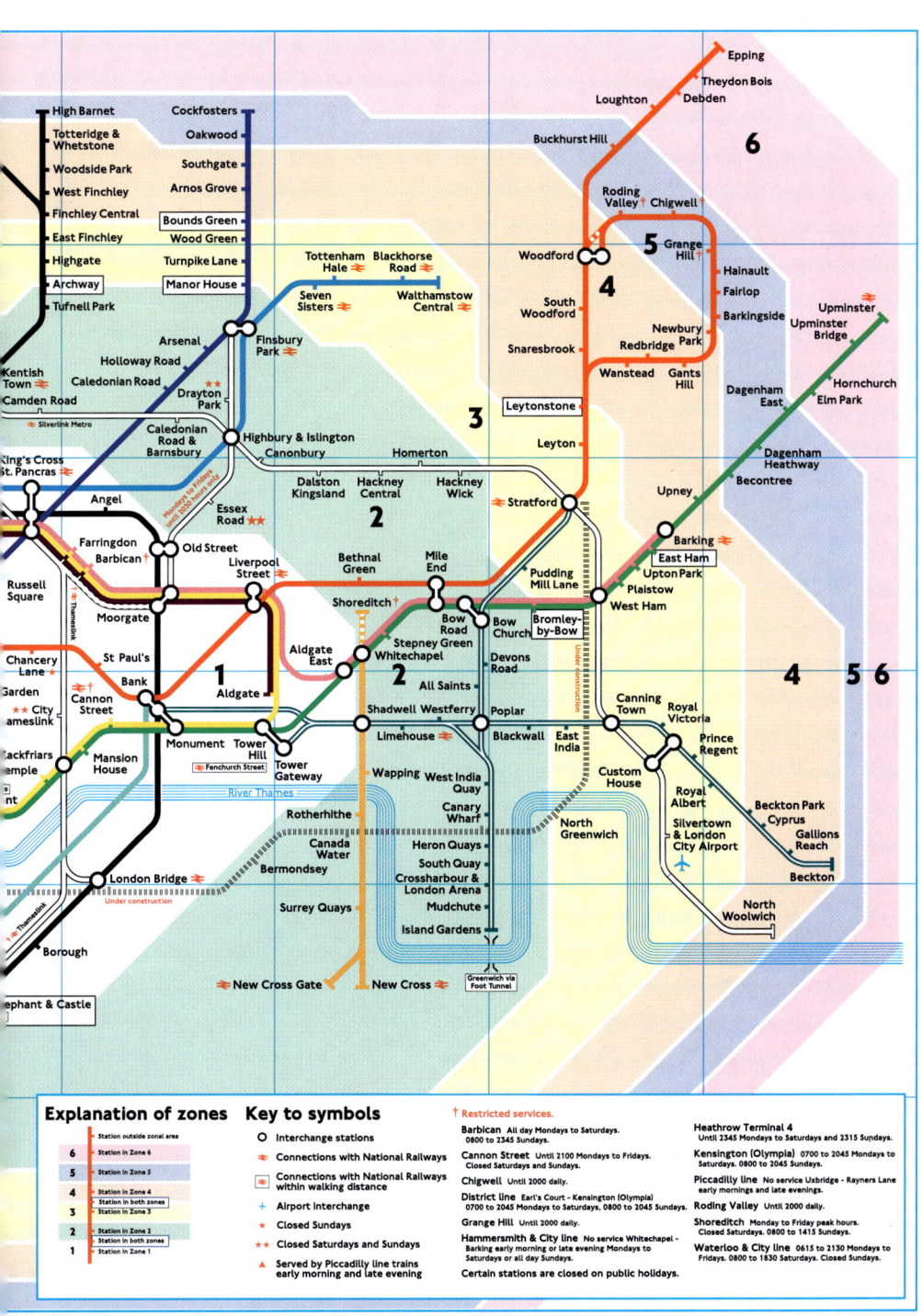

Explanation of zones

6	Station outside zonal area
6	Station in Zone 6
5	Station in Zone 5
4	Station in Zone 4
	Station in both zones
3	Station in Zone 3
	Station in both zones
2	Station in Zone 2
	Station in both zones
1	Station in Zone 1

Key to symbols

○ Interchange stations

⇌ Connections with National Railways

▣ Connections with National Railways within walking distance

✈ Airport interchange

★ Closed Sundays

★★ Closed Saturdays and Sundays

▲ Served by Piccadilly line trains early morning and late evening

† **Restricted services.**

Barbican All day Mondays to Saturdays. 0800 to 2345 Sundays.

Cannon Street Until 2100 Mondays to Fridays. Closed Saturdays and Sundays.

Chigwell Until 2000 daily.

District line Earl's Court - Kensington (Olympia) 0700 to 2045 Mondays to Saturdays, 0800 to 2045 Sundays.

Grange Hill Until 2000 daily.

Hammersmith & City line No service Whitechapel - Barking early morning or late evening Mondays to Saturdays or all day Sundays.

Certain stations are closed on public holidays.

Heathrow Terminal 4 Until 2345 Mondays to Saturdays and 2315 Sundays.

Kensington (Olympia) 0700 to 2045 Mondays to Saturdays. 0800 to 2045 Sundays.

Piccadilly line No service Uxbridge - Rayners Lane early mornings and late evenings.

Roding Valley Until 2000 daily.

Shoreditch Monday to Friday peak hours. Closed Saturdays. 0800 to 1415 Sundays.

Waterloo & City line 0615 to 2130 Mondays to Fridays. 0800 to 1830 Saturdays. Closed Sundays.

Key

▬▬▬	Road served by bus
▭	Other road

 ✳ 7 — Route terminus

12 — Route operating every day

159 — Route operating less often *(For information call 0171-222 1234)*

A1 A2 — Airbus stops ♿ *(For information call 0181-400 6655)*

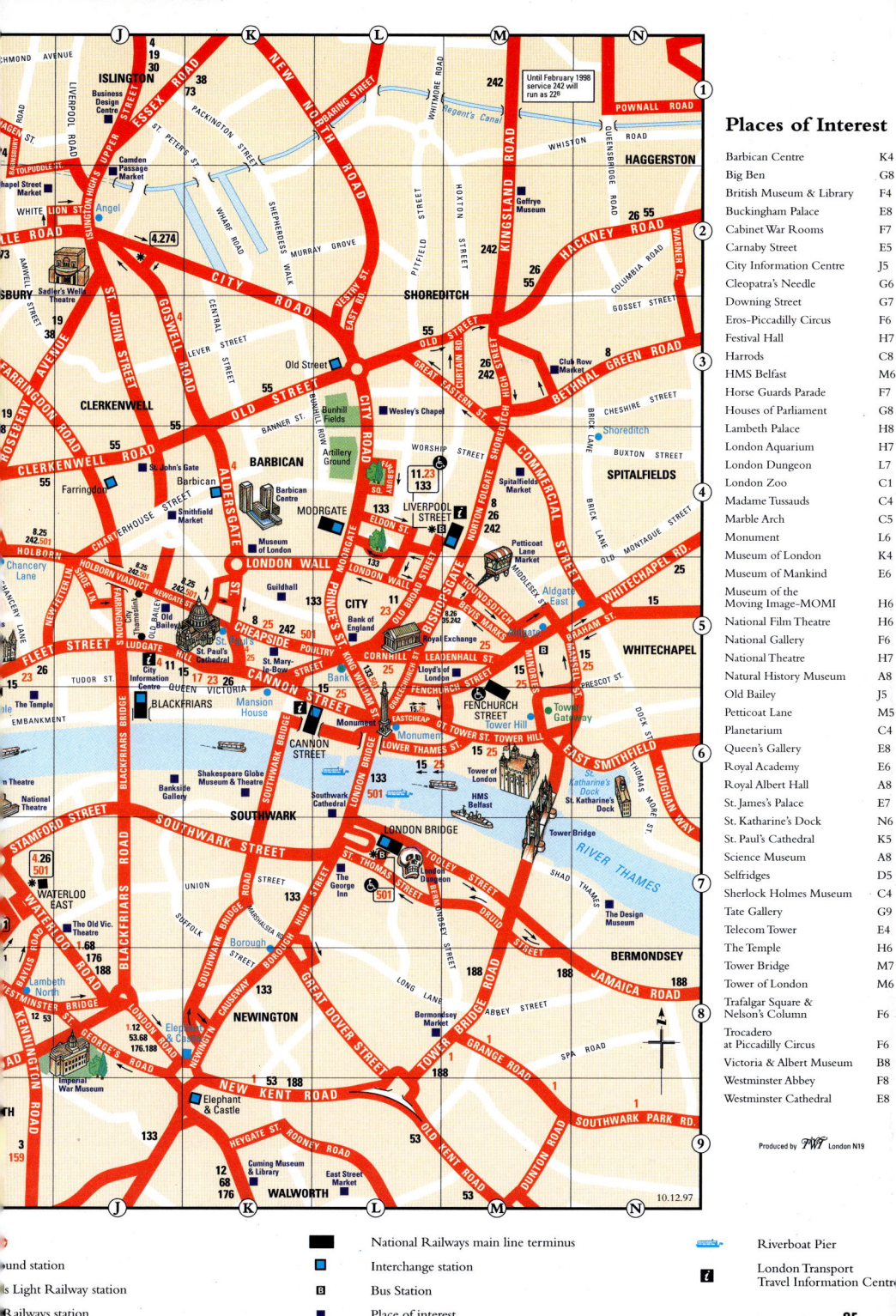

Places of Interest

Place	Grid
Barbican Centre	K4
Big Ben	G8
British Museum & Library	F4
Buckingham Palace	E8
Cabinet War Rooms	F7
Carnaby Street	E5
City Information Centre	J5
Cleopatra's Needle	G6
Downing Street	G7
Eros-Piccadilly Circus	F6
Festival Hall	H7
Harrods	C8
HMS Belfast	M6
Horse Guards Parade	F7
Houses of Parliament	G8
Lambeth Palace	H8
London Aquarium	H7
London Dungeon	L7
London Zoo	C1
Madame Tussauds	C4
Marble Arch	C5
Monument	L6
Museum of London	K4
Museum of Mankind	E6
Museum of the Moving Image-MOMI	H6
National Film Theatre	H6
National Gallery	F6
National Theatre	H7
Natural History Museum	A8
Old Bailey	J5
Petticoat Lane	M5
Planetarium	C4
Queen's Gallery	E8
Royal Academy	E6
Royal Albert Hall	A8
St. James's Palace	E7
St. Katharine's Dock	N6
St. Paul's Cathedral	K5
Science Museum	A8
Selfridges	D5
Sherlock Holmes Museum	C4
Tate Gallery	G9
Telecom Tower	E4
The Temple	H6
Tower Bridge	M7
Tower of London	M6
Trafalgar Square & Nelson's Column	F6
Trocadero at Piccadilly Circus	F6
Victoria & Albert Museum	B8
Westminster Abbey	F8
Westminster Cathedral	E8

Produced by *FWT* London N19

85

■ (black)	National Railways main line terminus
■ (blue)	Interchange station
B	Bus Station
■ (dark blue)	Place of interest
Riverboat Pier	
i	London Transport Travel Information Centre

10.12.97

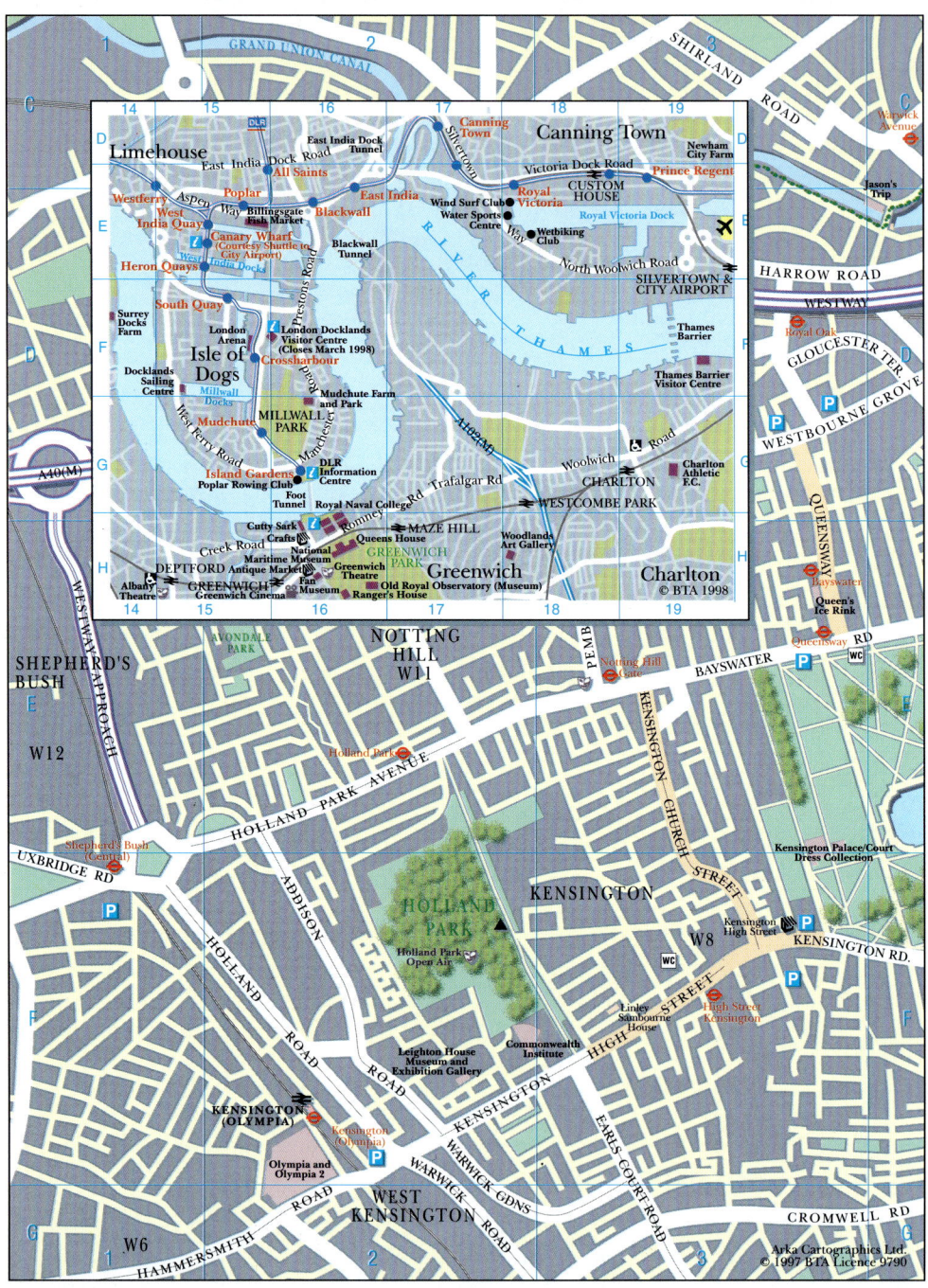

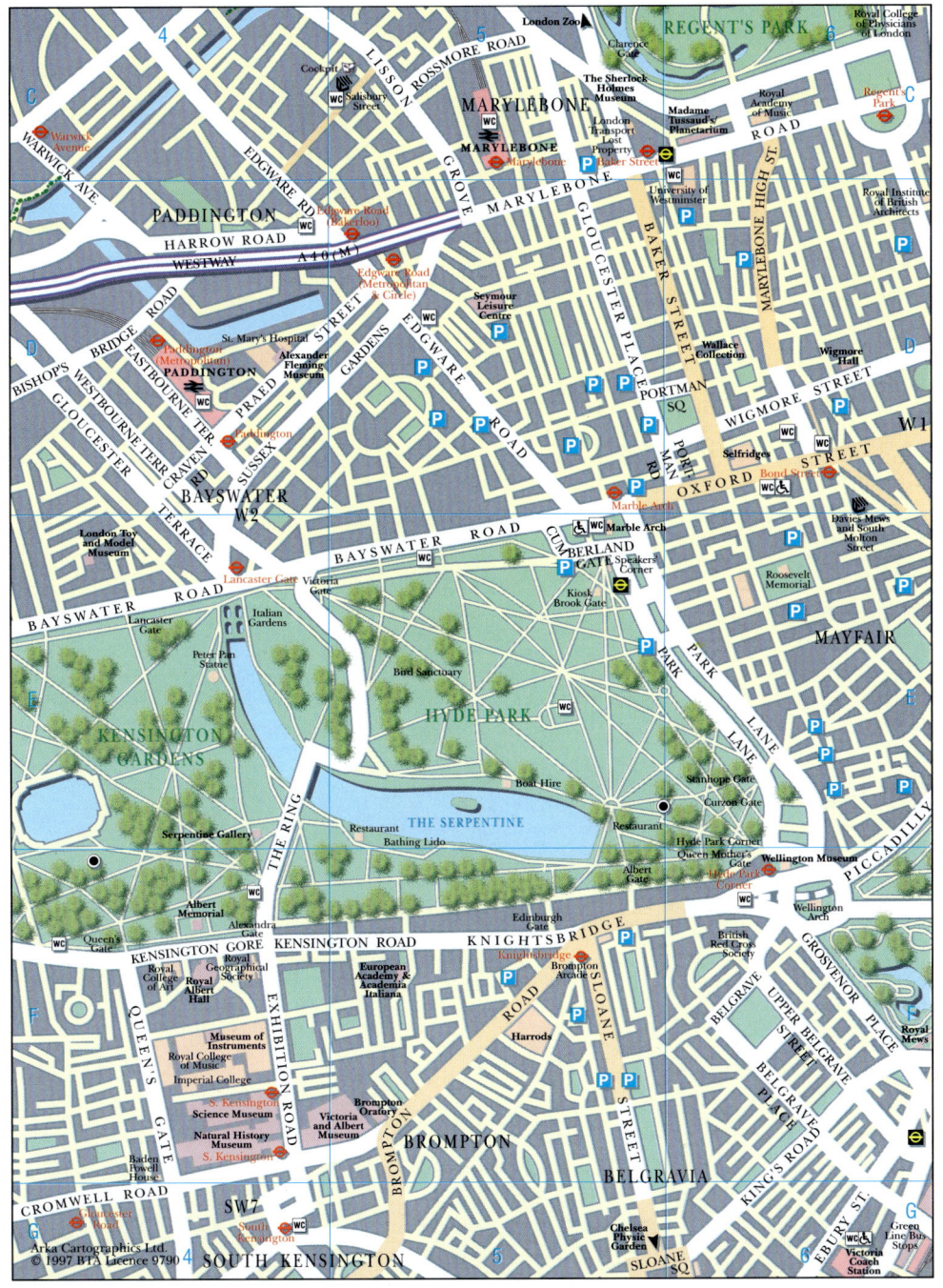

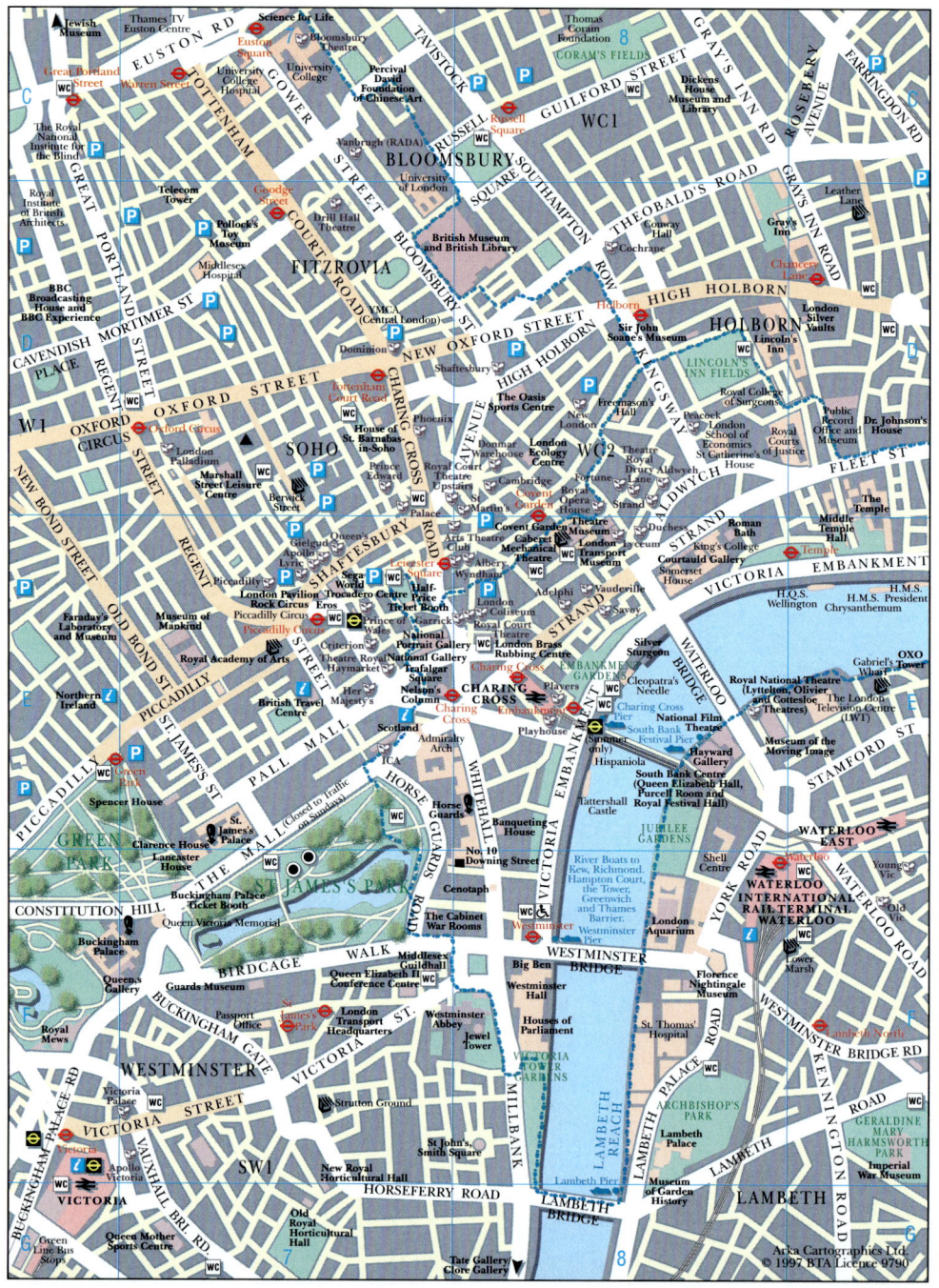

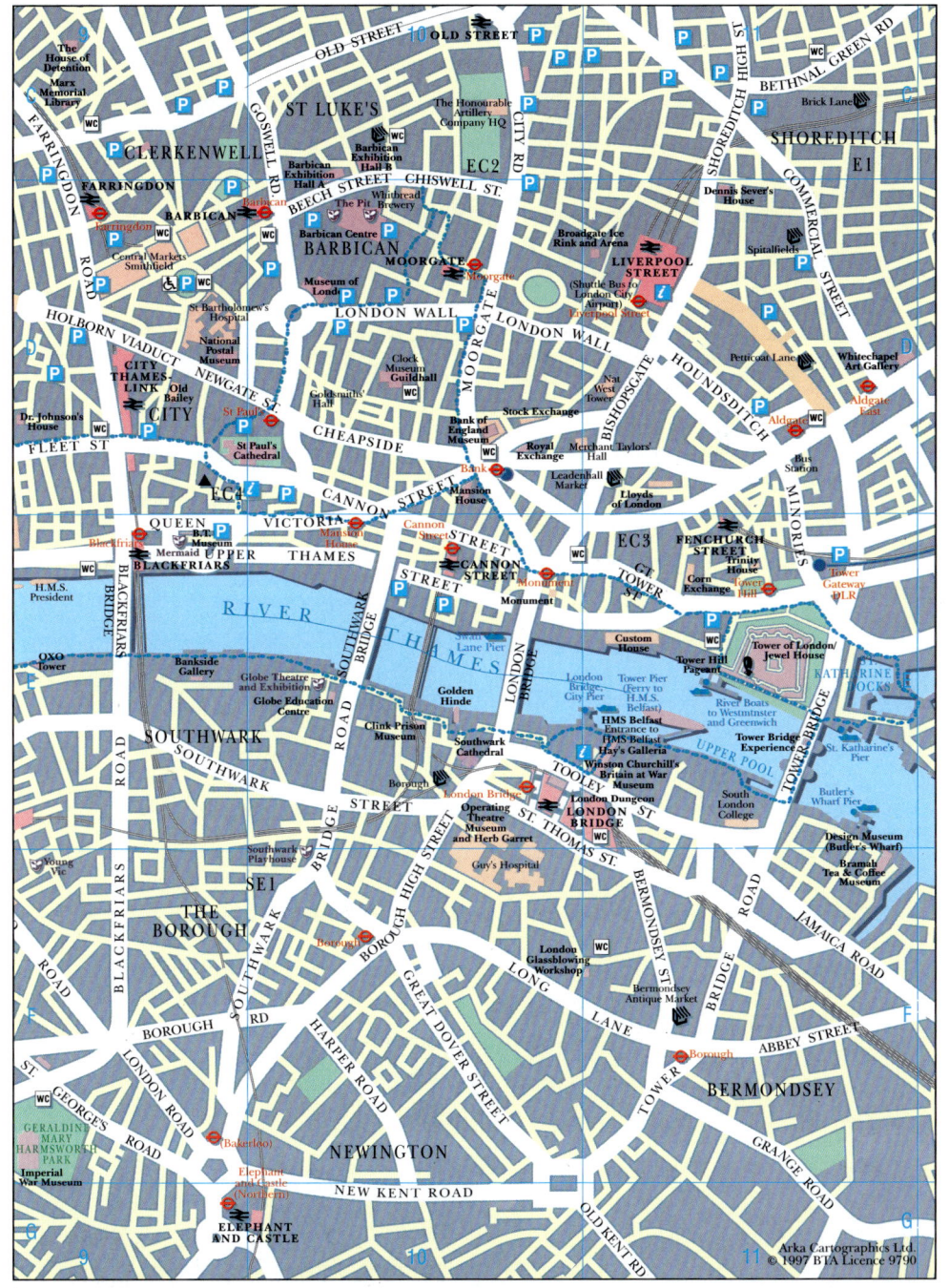

See the whole of London from a travel agent's office.

Whatever you're up to in the capital, Visitor Travelcard will suit you. Valid on tubes, buses, trains   and Docklands Light Railway for an unlimited number of journeys within the zones you select, this ticket is accompanied by a booklet of discounts to many of London's top attractions. Not available in London, so please contact BritRail at Rail Europe (tel. 1888 274 8724) or your local British Tourist Authority office for further details.

Making London simple

Around Britain
How to Use the Guide

● Apart from London, Great Britain (England, Wales and Scotland) has been divided into 10 regions, each of which has a separate color category and chapter in the guide.

● Look at the Britain 'Color Code Map', on pages 4,5 to quickly select an area you wish to visit or to identify where you are.

● Each area begins with an 'Overview Page' and 'Area Map'. Here you will find details of the region and the list of theme trails in that area (**Fig. 1**).

● Each theme trail has an introduction page with a more detailed map and reference numbers that match the main attractions (**Fig. 2**).

● Each introduction page has the unique 'NBC Compass' to point you to the adjoining trails (**Fig. 2**).

● The page numbers and 'color bands' on the compass match the geographical perspectives, making it easy to plot, visit or bypass various attractions, as you choose. This ensures you get maximum use of your time when planning your visit, and offers you the chance to discover more of Britain.

● Each trail has details of the top sights, and additional important sights, numbered and/or highlighted on the accompanying map. You choose what you want to see.

● With an 'easy-to-learn, easy-to-use' key to symbols which doubles up as a 'bookmark' on the inside front cover of the guide, you are presented with immediate and important details 'at a glance'.

● At the beginning of this section, pages (36,37) 92-97 there are key maps for each method of travel, road, rail and coach, (long-distance bus), which can be used for easy reference.

● On page 92 you can find information on 'Guide Friday' bus tours throughout Britain.

Opening Times

As a general rule attractions and places to visit are open between 10am and 5pm or 6pm, you will need to arrive at least one hour before closing time. You'll find the summer opening times are indicated by each attraction. However, with **English Heritage**, (page 67) and **National Trust**, (page 66) while the general rule is also 10am to 6pm, there are a few of their properties which are run on a volunteer basis. Therefore, we recommend that you either use the free handbooks, issued when you take advantage of the excellent visitor passes, or telephone to check the specific details and opening hours. In certain cases visits can only be made by purchasing tickets in advance, for example, the home of the Earl Spencer at Althorp House in Northamptonshire, where Diana, Princess of Wales, is buried.

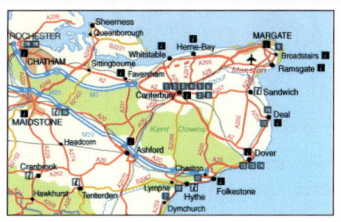

Dickens, Castles and 'Canterbury Tales'

Charles Dickens spent most of his childhood in Rochester **18**, and returned there later in his life; it was the background for many scenes in 'Great Expectations' and 'Pickwick Papers', and see also, the Norman castle and cathedral **19**, side by side above the River Medway. Canterbury **1-8**, has some fine museums and galleries, as well as the famous Cathedral. It is where Geoffrey Chaucer, (c. 1345-1400) wrote an amusing account of pilgrims' travels to the shrine of Thomas à Becket, Archbishop of Canterbury. The struggle for control of the country between church and crown had led to his murder. Continuing to the east, on the tip of the coast, is Broadstairs **9**, where Dickens wrote 'Bleak House' and this house was immortalised in 'David

Copperfield'.
Keep heading south from here and you reach the Tudor-rose shaped Deal and Walmer Castles **10,11**. Continuing southerly to the port of Dover and the remarkable Roman Painted House, White Cliffs and Castle **12,13,14**. Staying on the coastline you will pass the Channel Tunnel and Eurotunnel Exhibition **17**, and can take the one third size 14 mile steam railway from Hythe **15**, or visit Port

Lympne Wild Animal Park **7**. Towards London, Leeds Castle at Maidstone **16**, is considered as, 'one of the loveliest castles in the world'.

ℹ Tourist Information
Canterbury ☎ 01227 763763
Dover ☎ 01304 205108

🏠 Dover

Hotels
🏨 Ashford - Dover - Hythe - Rochester
🏨 Maidstone

Distance from London

Dover 71miles

Fig. 2

Telephone their 24hour ticket line, **(UK) 01604 592020.**

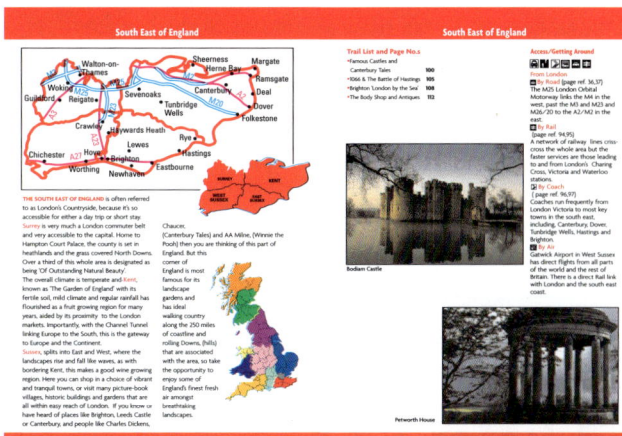

Trail List and Page Nos.s	
•Famous Castles and	
Canterbury Tales	100
•1066 & The Battle of Hastings	105
•Brighton London by the Sea	108
•The Body Shop and Antiques	113

Access/Getting Around

From London
By Road (page ref. 36,37)
The M25 London Orbital Motorway links the M4 in the west, past the M3 and M23 and M26/20 to the A2/M2 in the east.

By Rail (page ref. 94,95)
A network of railway lines criss-cross the whole area but the faster services are those leading to and from London's Charing Cross, Victoria and Waterloo stations.

By Coach (page ref. 96,97)
Coaches run frequently from London Victoria to most key towns in the south east, including, Canterbury, Dover, Tunbridge Wells, Hastings and Brighton.

By Air
Gatwick Airport in West Sussex has direct flights from all parts of the world and the rest of Britain. There is a direct fast link with London and the south east coast.

THE SOUTH EAST OF ENGLAND is often referred to as London's Countryside, because it's so accessible for either a day trip or short stay. Surrey is very much a London commuter belt and very accessible to the capital. Home to Hampton Court Palace, the county is set in heathlands and the grass covered North Downs. Over a third of this whole area is designated as being 'Of Outstanding Natural Beauty'. The overall climate is temperate and Kent, known as 'The Garden of England' with its fertile soil, mild climate and regular rainfall has flourished as a fruit growing region for many years, aided by its proximity to the Continent markets. Importantly, with the Channel Tunnel linking Europe to the South, this is the gateway to Europe and the Continent. Sussex, splits into East and West, where the landscapes rise and fall like waves, as with bordering Kent, this makes a good wine growing region. Here you can shop in a choice of vibrant and tranquil towns, or visit many picture-book villages, historic buildings and gardens that are all within easy reach of London. If you know or have heard of places like Brighton, Leeds Castle or Canterbury, and people like Charles Dickens,

Chaucer, (Canterbury Tales) and AA Milne, (Winnie the Pooh) then you are thinking of this part of England. But this corner of England is most famous for its landscape gardens and has ideal walking country along the 250 miles of coastline and rolling Downs, (hills) that are associated with the area, so take the opportunity to enjoy some of England's finest fresh air amongst breathtaking landscapes.

Bodiam Castle

Petworth House

Fig. 1

DISCOVER
THE HISTORIC TOWNS & CITIES
OF BRITAIN, IRELAND & EUROPE

Guide Friday is offering users of the NBC guide a £2 discount off its city and town green and cream (black and gold in Ireland, yellow and green in Paris) open-top bus tours. Simply hand in one of the vouchers from the back of this book to any Guide Friday driver in the town or city below* you have selected for your tour (or the voucher can be exchanged in the relevant Tourism Centre below†) for a £2 saving on your ticket.

- Offer applies to all towns and cities below*.
- Offer excludes children between ages 5 and 12 (under 5's go free).
- Only one discount per ticket.
- Tickets valid all day.
- Get on and off as often as you please at places of interest.
- Minimum tour time: one hour.
- The tours marked † operate all year round, others are seasonal.
- Tour operate seven days a week, leaving every 10-15 minutes in the larger towns and cities in the summer (and 30-60 minutes in winter). For further operating date information, see the contact address below.
- Commentary provided by professional guides or a taped commentary.
- Hold onto your Guide Friday ticket – it is worth £1 off your next Guide Friday tour in any of our heritage towns and cities (10 FFr. in Paris).
- Choose from **in England**: Bath†, Birmingham, Bournemouth, Brighton, Cambridge†, Chester, Cotswolds, Dover, Eastbourne, Exeter, Hastings, Lincoln, Norwich, Oxford†, Plymouth, Portsmouth, Southampton, Stonehenge (from Salisbury), Stratford-upon-Avon, Warwick Castle, Windsor and Eton, York†.
  In Scotland: Edinburgh†, Glasgow, Inverness, Perth, Stirling.
  In Wales: Cardiff, Llandudno and Conwy.
  In Ireland: Cork, Dingle, Dublin, Galway.
  In Europe: Berlin (Germany), Seville (Spain), Paris (France).
  NB: Discount vouchers not valid for Paris tour.

For brochure and tour leaflets contact:
Guide Friday
The Civic Hall
14 Rother Street
Stratford-upon-Avon
Warwickshire CV37 6LU, England.

Tel: (00 44 1789) 294466. Fax: (00 44 1789) 414681.

The tour leaflets include a town or city map which show National Express coach stops and British Rail stations where appropriate

We try harder.

As an Avis Rent A Car Platinum Premier Partner, NBC cardholders enjoy preferential rates on car rental in the UK.

Simply quoting your Avis World-wide Discount (AWD) number AWD U606654 when booking, will trigger automatic access to the following preferential rates:

- Up to 35% off Avis standard tariff in the UK
- Up to 35% off Avis Luxury cars
- Up to 10% off Avis Chauffeur cars
- Preferential Set Daily, Weekly, Weekend and Weekly rates
- Up to 20% off standard rate one-way rentals in the UK

'The easy way to get around'

Additionally the Avis sales team will match your requirements with the right product to suit your needs. For example, you may want to pick up your car from one location in the UK and leave it in another. With Avis one-way rentals this won't be a problem - with over 180 locations around the UK there will always be an Avis station nearby. Plus, as a Platinum Premier Partner, NBC cardholder you'll save up to 20% on Avis standard one-way rates.

To take advantage of these preferential rates simply telephone your **local Avis office** or call **Avis UK** on **0990 900500** once you've arrived in the Britain.

A £15 city supplement fee applies at certain locations. £20 surcharge applies to one-way rentals. Rates include unlimited mileage, Collision Damage Waiver, Theft Protection and VAT. Payment by credit card is preferred and recommended - otherwise a returnable deposit will be required. Extra drivers can be nominated for an additional charge. Rental cars cannot be taken abroad. All rentals are subject to availability and to standard Terms and Conditions which are detailed on the reverse of the Rental Agreement and should be read at the time of the rental.

THE BRITRAIL PASS Traveling Around Britain by Train

From the northernmost point of Britain, Thurso in Scotland, to the most southern, Penzance in Cornwall, all of the places you wish to visit are accessible by rail. Sit back in comfort as glorious countryside rolls by. Visit famous cities like London, Chester and Edinburgh, arriving right in the city center. You can buy a range of of passes and tickets, exclusively available to overseas vistors. But remember, you must buy before you leave. Choose from:

BRITRAIL PASS Valid for 8,15,22 days or one month of consecutive days. Hop on or off as much as you want, your travel is unlimited.

BRITRAIL FLEXIPASS Valid for 4,8 or 15 days unlimited travel within one month. Choose to travel when you want, and stop off when you want without losing any traveling time.

RAIL 'N' DRIVE The best of both worlds - fast and comfortable BritRail trains for long hauls, with the freedom of a car to explore the beauty of the British countryside. A mixture of FlexiPass train travel and car rental can be combined to give you the freedom to set your own pace.

MORE SPECIAL DEALS A number of other deals are available: Point to Point Tickets for single journeys. Regional Passes if you just want to conncentrate on a particular area such as the South East of England or Scotland. Plus deals for Seniors (the 60+ crowd), Parties and Families.

For Further Information please contact

Phone	(888) BritRail
Fax	1-888 288 6093
Internet	http://www. raileurope.com
Mail	
	BritRail - 226-230 Westchester Ave., White Plains, NY 10604.
Walk in Visitors	
	BritRail's British Travel Shop, 551 Fifth Avenue (at 45th St.) New York, NY 10176

FAST FREQUENT SERVICES (A selection of popular routes)

To	From London	Direct Trains per Day	Approx. Journey Time
Bath	Paddington	24	1 hour 15 min
Cambridge	Kings Cross	61	1 hour
Canterbury	Victoria	33	1 hour 30 min
Cardiff	Paddington	22	2 hours
Chester	Euston	3	2 hours 30 min
Dover	Charing Cross	26	1 hour 45 min
Edinburgh	Kings Cross	18	4 hours 15 min
Exeter	Paddington	17	2 hours 15min
Glasgow	Euston	9	5 hours
Inverness	Kings Cross	2	8 hours
Liverpool	Euston	14	2 hours 45 min
Norwich	Liverpool Street	19	2 hours
Oxford	Paddington	46	1 hour
Penzance	Paddington	8	5 hours 30 min
Plymouth	Paddington	16	3 hours 30 min
Stratford	Paddington	5	2 hours 15 min
Windermere*	Euston	7	4 hours 15 min

* Change at Oxenholme Station

Airport Links

Gatwick	Victoria	67	30 min
Stansted	Liverpool Street	36	40 min
Manchester	Manchester**	100	20 min

** Manchester Station (not London)

The above journeys are complemented by indirect services throughout Britain, which require a change of train at certain stations. A major stations have timetables and journey planners available.

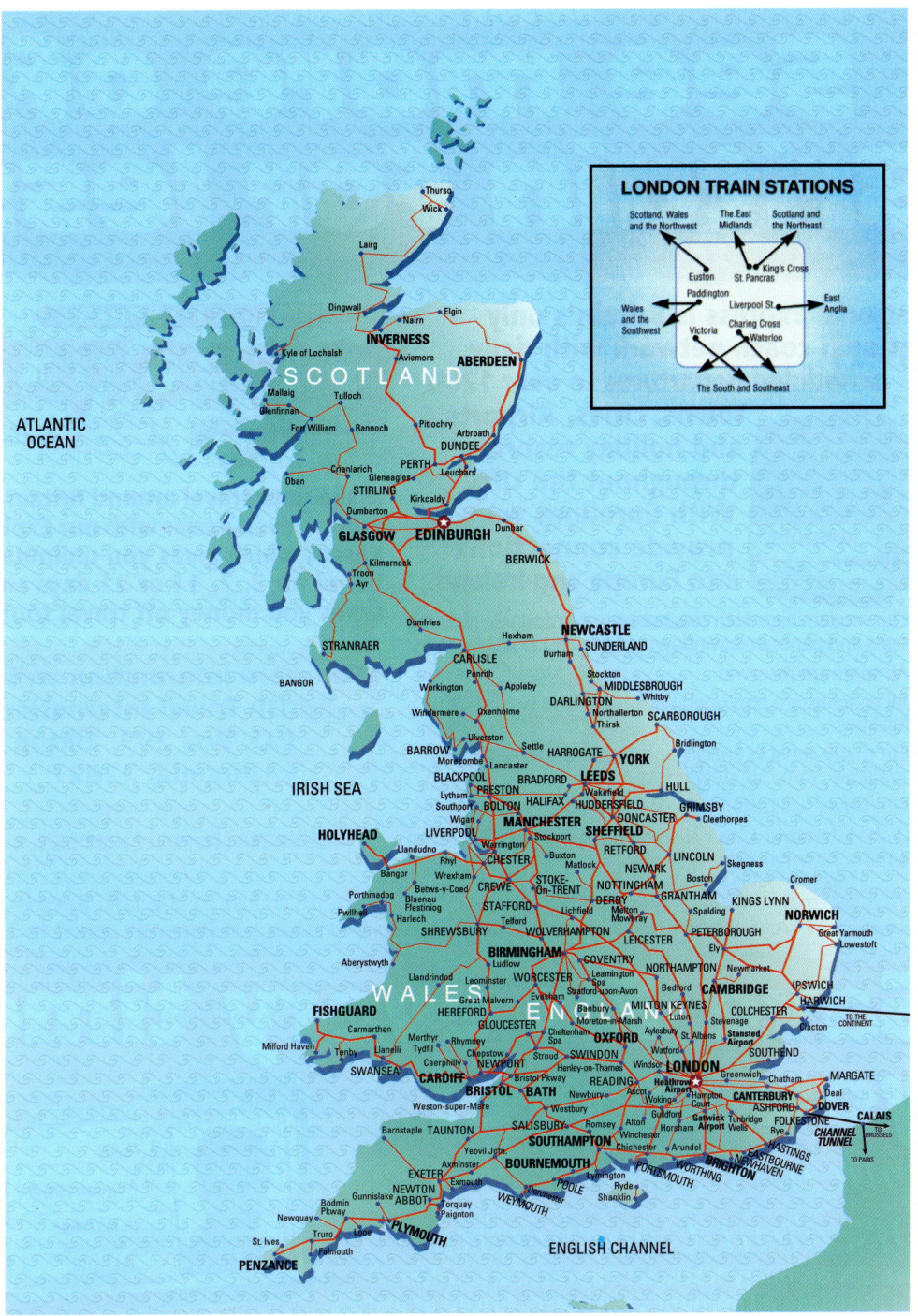

LONDON TRAIN STATIONS

Scotland, Wales and the Northwest
The East Midlands
Scotland and the Northeast

Euston
St. Pancras
King's Cross

Paddington

Wales and the Southwest
Liverpool St.
East Anglia

Victoria
Charing Cross
Waterloo

The South and Southeast

ATLANTIC OCEAN

SCOTLAND

Thurso
Wick
Lairg
Dingwall
Nairn • Elgin
Kyle of Lochalsh
INVERNESS
Aviemore
ABERDEEN
Mallaig
Tulloch
Glenfinnan
Fort William
Rannoch
Pitlochry
Arbroath
Crianlarich
PERTH
DUNDEE
Oban
Gleneagles
Leuchars
STIRLING
Kirkcaldy
Dumbarton
Dunbar
GLASGOW
EDINBURGH
Kilmarnock
BERWICK
Troon
Ayr
Dumfries
Hexham
NEWCASTLE
STRANRAER
CARLISLE
SUNDERLAND
Penrith
Durham
BANGOR
Workington
Appleby
Stockton
MIDDLESBROUGH
Oxenholme
DARLINGTON
Whitby
Windermere
Northallerton
Thirsk
SCARBOROUGH
Ulverston
Bridlington
BARROW
Settle
HARROGATE
Morecombe
Lancaster
YORK
IRISH SEA
BLACKPOOL
BRADFORD
LEEDS
HULL
Lytham
Preston
Wakefield
Southport
BOLTON
HALIFAX
HUDDERSFIELD
GRIMSBY
Wigan
DONCASTER
HOLYHEAD
LIVERPOOL
MANCHESTER
Cleethorpes
Llandudno
Warrington
SHEFFIELD
Bangor
Stockport
Rhyl
CHESTER
Buxton
RETFORD
LINCOLN
Wrexham
Matlock
Skegness
Betws-y-Coed
CREWE
STOKE-On-TRENT
NEWARK
Boston
Porthmadog
Blaenau
STAFFORD
DERBY
NOTTINGHAM
GRANTHAM
Ffestiniog
Lichfield
Melton
Spalding
KINGS LYNN
Harlech
Telford
Mowbray
Cromer
Pwllheli
SHREWSBURY
WOLVERHAMPTON
LEICESTER
PETERBOROUGH
NORWICH
Aberystwyth
BIRMINGHAM
Ely
Great Yarmouth
Ludlow
COVENTRY
Lowestoft
Llandrindod
WORCESTER
Leamington
NORTHAMPTON
Leominster
Evesham
Stratford-upon-Avon
Bedford
CAMBRIDGE
WALES
Great Malvern
IPSWICH
ENGLAND
Moreton-in-Marsh
MILTON KEYNES
FISHGUARD
HEREFORD
Banbury
Luton
COLCHESTER
HARWICH
Carmarthen
Cheltenham
Aylesbury
Stevenage
TO THE
Milford Haven
Merthyr
Spa
OXFORD
St. Albans
Clacton
CONTINENT
Tenby
Tydfil
Chepstow
SWINDON
Stansted
Llanelli
Rhymney
Stroud
Airport
SWANSEA
Caerphilly
NEWPORT
Henley-on-Thames
Windsor
SOUTHEND
Bristol Pkwy
READING
CARDIFF
BRISTOL
BATH
Newbury
LONDON
MARGATE
Weston-super-Mare
Ascot
Woking
Greenwich
Chatham
Deal
Barnstaple
Romsey
Hampton
CANTERBURY
DOVER
TAUNTON
SALISBURY
Court
ASHFORD
CALAIS
Yeovil Jctn
Westbury
Alton
Gatwick
FOLKESTONE
CHANNEL
Axminster
Winchester
Airport
Tunbridge
TUNNEL
EXETER
SOUTHAMPTON
Chichester
Arundel
Wells
HASTINGS
TO PARIS
NEWTON
Exmouth
BOURNEMOUTH
Horsham
EASTBOURNE
ABBOT
Lymington
PORTSMOUTH
WORTHING
NEWHAVEN
Gunnislake
Dorchester
POOLE
BRIGHTON
Newquay
Bodmin
Torquay
WEYMOUTH
Ryde
Pkwy
Paignton
Shanklin
St. Ives
Truro
Looe
PLYMOUTH
Falmouth
ENGLISH CHANNEL
PENZANCE

95

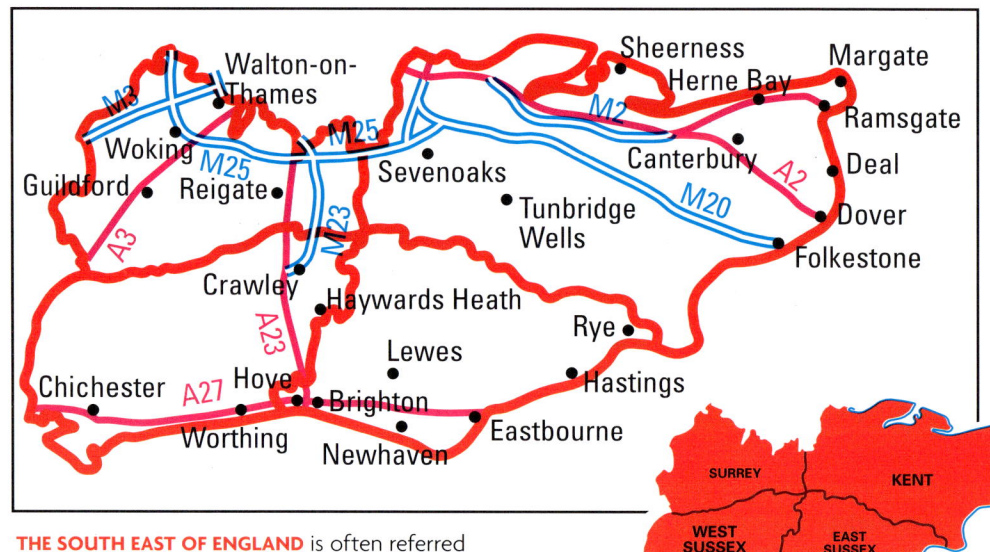

THE SOUTH EAST OF ENGLAND is often referred to as London's Countryside, because it's so accessible for either a day trip or short stay. Surrey is very much a London commuter belt and very accessible to the capital. Home to Hampton Court Palace, the county is set in heathlands and the grass covered North Downs. Over a third of this whole area is designated as being 'Of Outstanding Natural Beauty'. The overall climate is temperate and Kent known as 'The Garden of England' with its fertile soil, mild climate and regular rainfall has flourished as a fruit growing region for many years, aided by its proximity to the London markets. Importantly, with the Channel Tunnel linking Europe to the South, this is the gateway to Europe and the Continent.

Sussex, splits into East and West, where the landscapes rise and fall like waves, as with bordering Kent, this makes a good wine growing region. Here you can shop in a choice of vibrant and tranquil towns, or visit many picture-book villages, historic buildings and gardens that are all within easy reach of London. If you know or have heard of places like Brighton, Leeds Castle or Canterbury, and people like Charles Dickens,

Chaucer, (Canterbury Tales) and AA Milne, (Winnie the Pooh) then you are thinking of this part of England. But this corner of England is most famous for its landscape gardens and has ideal walking country along the 250 miles of coastline and rolling Downs, (hills) that are associated with the area, so take the opportunity to enjoy some of England's finest fresh air amongst breathtaking landscapes.

Trail List and Page No.s

Bodiam Castle

Access/Getting Around

From London

By Road
(page ref. 36,37)
The M25 London Orbital
Motorway links the M4 in the
west, past the M3 and M23 and
M26/20 to the A2/M2 in the
east.

By Rail
(page ref. 94,95)
A network of railway lines criss-
cross the whole area but the
faster services are those leading
to and from London's Charing
Cross, Victoria and Waterloo
stations.

By Coach
(page ref. 96,97)
Coaches run frequently from
London Victoria to most key
towns in the south east,
including, Canterbury, Dover,
Tunbridge Wells, Hastings and
Brighton.

By Air
Gatwick Airport in West Sussex
has direct flights from all parts
of the world and the rest of
Britain. There is a direct Rail link
with London and the south east
coast.

Petworth House

Dickens, Castles and 'Canterbury Tales'

Charles Dickens spent most of his childhood in Rochester **18**, and returned there later in his life; it was the background for many scenes in 'Great Expectations' and 'Pickwick Papers'. See also, the Norman castle and cathedral **19**, side by side above the River Medway. Canterbury **1-8**, has some fine museums and galleries, as well as the famous cathedral. It is where Geoffrey Chaucer, (c. 1345-1400) wrote an amusing account of pilgrims' travels to the shrine of Thomas à Becket, Archbishop of Canterbury. The struggle for control of the country between church and crown had led to his murder. Continuing to the east, on the tip of the coast, is Broadstairs **9**, where Dickens wrote 'Bleak House' and this house was immortalised in 'David Copperfield'.

Keep heading south from here and you reach the Tudor-rose shaped Deal and Walmer Castles **10,11**. Continuing southerly to the port of Dover and the remarkable Roman Painted House, White Cliffs and Castle **12,13,14**. Staying on the coastline you will pass the Channel Tunnel and Eurotunnel Exhibition **17**, and can take the one third size 14 mile steam railway from Hythe **15**, or visit Port Lympne Wild Animal Park **7**.

Towards London, Leeds Castle at Maidstone **16**, is considered as, 'one of the loveliest castles in the world'.

ℹ Tourist Information

Canterbury ☎ 01227 763763
Dover ☎ 01304 205108

GF Dover

Hotels

👑 Ashford - Dover - Hythe - Rochester

STAKIS HOTELS Maidstone

Distance from London

Dover 73 miles ➡

1. The Canterbury Tales

The museum recreates the pilgrimages of Chaucer's England through a series of medieval tableaux. Audio visual exhibitions bring characters to life, and there is a guide commentary. Learn about the murder of Thomas à Becket, and stories of love, jealousy, pride and avarice. The tour lasts about 45 minutes and the attraction is located off the High Street, near the cathedral. Offer is £1 discount off adult price, please show NBC card/guide.

The Canterbury Tales, 23 St Margaret's Street, Canterbury, Kent CT12 2TG
☎ 01227 454888

  P

 9.30-5.30pm

 % £1

⇄ // Canterbury

M 2   A 2/28

www.demon.co.uk/past/timetravel/canterbury

2. Canterbury Cathedral

Its position on the London to Dover route made Canterbury an important Roman town, then after the arrival of St Augustine, (sent by the Pope to convert the Anglo Saxons to Christianity) the town soon became the center of the Christian Church in England. The most poignant moment in the cathedral's history came when Thomas à Becket was murdered here in 1170 during the struggles between church and the crown. The best features are the shrine of St Thomas à Becket, the medieval stained glass and the Black Prince's tomb.

Canterbury Cathedral, Christ Church Gate, Canterbury, Kent.
☎ 01227 762862

   P

 9.-7pm

⇄ // Canterbury

M 2   A 2/28

3. Canterbury Heritage Museum

This attraction has an enthralling time-walk linking the great events, famous people, and precious objects from Canterbury's 2000 year history, from the building of the Roman town, to the souvenirs of St Thomas à Becket, and the delights of the Rupert Bear Gallery.   The museum is housed in a magnificent medieval building. Closed on Sundays except June to September 1.30-5pm, last admission 4pm. Located close to the Tourist Information Centre, in Stour Street. Rupert Bear™ and © Express Newspapers PLC.

Canterbury Heritage Museum, Stour Street, Canterbury, Kent
☎ 01227 452747

 P

 10.30-5pm

⇄ // Canterbury

M 2   A 2/28

4. Canterbury Roman Museum

Canterbury's new Roman Museum has been specially constructed underground in the excavated Roman levels below the Longmarket Shopping Center. Here you can follow the archaeologists' quest for the buried Roman town of Durovernum Cantiacorum, which flourished for almost 400 years where Canterbury stands today. Walk through fascinating reconstructions of Roman buildings, including the market place and town house. Interactive displays and the chance to handle genuine artifacts. Closed on Sundays except June - October opening at 1.30pm.

Canterbury Roman Museum, Butchery Lane, Canterbury, Kent
☎ 01227 785575

   P

 10-5pm

 % 10% (excl. passport ticket)

⇄ // Canterbury

M 2   A 2/28

5. Canterbury West Gate Museum

Canterbury's medieval gate is one of the finest examples of a fortified gatehouse. Discover the story of the city defenses, see the prison cells and examine the weapons of warfare in the arms and armour displays. There are panoramic views from the battlements, a good starting point as an introduction to Canterbury. The museum is closed for lunch between 12.30-1.30pm and is not open on Sundays. Last entry is 15 minutes before closing times.

Canterbury West Gate Museum,
St Peter's Street, Canterbury, Kent
☎ 01227 452747

P

🕐 11-3.30pm

% 10% (excl. passport ticket)

Canterbury

M 2   A 2/28

6. Royal Museum and Art Gallery

Situated in a late Victorian building, the Royal Museum and Art Gallery has a most interesting picture collection. Here are galleries for the famous Victorian cattle painter Thomas Sidney Cooper, for the city's picture collection, for special exhibitions, and also on display, a wide range of decorative arts. Admission is free. Closed on Sundays. Located close to the Tourist Information Centre, in the High Street. Other interesting museums in Canterbury, (entrance fee payable) the Canterbury Roman Museum, a little farther south along the High Street and the West Gate Museum farther north along the High Street.

Royal Museum and Art Gallery, High Street,
Canterbury CT1 2RA
☎ 01227 452747

P

🕐 10-5pm

Canterbury East

M 2   A 2/28

7. Howletts and Port Lympne Wild Animal Parks

Once described by the BBC as 'Two of the best Wild Life Parks in the world'. 1. Howletts and 2. Port Lympne are the homes of many rare and endangered animal species, including the largest group of Gorillas in the world, (with a record of 50 births) elephants, tigers, monkeys and much more. Set in acres of woods and parklands, the animals have spacious natural enclosures. Port Lympne also has an attractive Historic Mansion set within terraced gardens. Open until 3.30pm in Winter. Offer 50% off second ticket

Howletts and Port Lympne Wild Animal Parks.
1. Bekesbourne, nr Canterbury, Kent
2. Port Lympne, nr Hythe, Kent
☎ 0891 800605

⭐ ❄ 📋 ☕ P

🕐 10-5pm

% 50% off second ticket

1. Bekesbourne 2. Ashford

M 1. M2 - 2. M20 J11

A 1. A2

8. The Herbfarm Perfumery

Here you can trace the story of perfume from its ancient beginnings in the temples of Egypt to the present day. Only half a mile west from Canterbury Cathedral, you can stroll through the fragrant 'conservatory' and see for yourself the creation of essential oils by one of the earliest methods of perfume extraction. There are aromatherapy oils, scented candles, herbs and dried flowers on sale and aromatherapy workshops on Tuesday 1-3pm and Thursday 10-12 noon (please call to book workshops). Open Sundays March to December from 10-4pm.

The Herbfarm Perfumery, Broadoak Road,
Canterbury CT2 0PP
☎ 01227 458755

⭐ ❄ 📋 P

🕐 9-5pm

% 20%

Canterbury West

M 2   A 2

9. Dickens House Museum

On the main seafront at Broadstairs is the lovely old house which was once the home of Miss Mary Pearson Strong on whom Charles Dickens based much of his character of 'Miss Betsey Trotwood' in his novel 'David Copperfield'. The home has been adapted as a museum to commemorate Charles Dickens' association with Broadstairs. Dickens' letters and memorabilia can be seen in the museum, along with period costume and Victoriana. Closed between Mid October and April 8th.

Dickens House Museum, Victoria Parade, Broadstairs CT10 1QS
☎ 01843 862853

 P

 2-5pm

⇄ Broadstairs ⬈ Ramsgate

A 2/28

10. Deal Castle

Crouching low and menacingly, the huge round bastions of this fortress built by Henry VIII, once carried 119 guns. It is a fascinating castle to explore and the largest of the coastal defenses built by Henry VIII. With long dark passages, battlements, and a huge basement with an exhibition about England's coastal defenses. It is located south west of Deal town center.

Deal Castle, Deal, Kent
☎ 01304 372762

 P

 10-6pm

 Page 67

⇄ Deal 1/2 mile ⬈ Dover

M 2 **A** 2/258

11. Walmer Castle

One of the many forts built by Henry VIII in the early 16th century along the coast. Designed to defend against the new threat of gunpowder. The castle was later transformed into an elegant stately home. Her Majesty the Queen Mother is the present Lord Warden, and the Queen Mother's Garden is quite beautiful. Other famous lord wardens to have lived here include Winston Churchill and the Duke of Wellington.

Walmer Castle, Walmer, Kent
☎ 01304 364288

  P

 10-6pm

 Page 67

⇄ Walmer 1 mile   Dover

M 2 **A** 258

12. Dover Castle

The White Cliffs of Dover are among England's most celebrated sights. On top of the cliffs stands Dover Castle, once described as, 'the key to the kingdom'. It is one of the countries largest castles, and has the longest recorded history of any major fortress in Britain. The secret war time tunnels at the castle are fascinating and there is a fabulous large scale model of the Battle of Waterloo to be seen there.

Dover Castle, Castle Hill, Kent
☎ 01304 211067

  P

10-6pm

 Page 67

⇄ Dover Priory

M 2/20 **A** 2/20

13. Roman Painted House

Built around AD 200, the Roman Painted House formed part of a large mansion or official hotel for travelers crossing the Channel. It stood outside the great naval fort of Classis Britannica, but in AD 270 it was demolished by the Roman army during the construction of a larger fort. Three of its main rooms were then buried substantially intact under its ramparts. The burial resulted in the unique survival of 400 sq ft of painted plaster, the most extensive ever found north of the Alps. Numerous awards have been given to this remarkable exhibition and over half a million people have now seen the Roman House. Open from April to September.

Roman Painted House, New Street, Dover, Kent
☎ 01304 203279

 10-5pm (closed Mondays)

 Dover

M 2/20   A 2/20

14. The White Cliffs Experience

Located in the center of Dover, (famed for its white cliffs) in the Market Square is, 'The White Cliffs Experience' providing two unforgettable journeys into the past, covering 2,000 years of British history, from the time of the Romans in the 'Roman Encounters' section, to the Second World War in, 'Our Finest Hours'. Dover was one of England's most vulnerable and easy to hit targets during the wars. 1st November - 31st March the hours are from 10am to 4pm.

The White Cliffs Experience, Market Square, Dover, Kent CT16 1PB
☎ 01304 214566

 10-5pm

 Dover

M 2/20   A 2/20

www.demon.co.uk/past/time/travel/dover

15. Romney, Hythe & Dymchurch Railway.

The world's smallest public railway, originally built for a millionaire racing driver in the 1920's, and having just celebrated 70 years from 1927-1997. The railway runs across Kent's historic Romney Marsh; steam and diesel engines, museum and café. There is a small guide available and offer applies to the train journey. Open March 28th to the last weekend in September. Please check for times at local Tourist Information Centre, but generally allow 3 or 4 hours for a round trip.

Romney, Hythe & Dymchurch Railway, New Romney, Kent TN28 8PL
☎ 01797 362353

 MC Visa

 Folkestone

M 20 J11

www.i-way.co.uk/~tburgess/rhdr/rhdr.html

16. Leeds Castle

Leeds Castle is often considered to be the most beautiful castle in England. Surrounded by a Lake, and built on two small islands, it is immediately possible to understand why this may be said. It has been continuously inhabited since the 12th century, and it was Henry VIII who converted it into a royal palace, he so loved the castle that he often visited it, escaping the plague in London. The castle passed out of royal ownership when Edward VI gave it to Sir Anthony St. Leger in 1552, as a reward for helping to pacify the Irish. There is also a wonderful garden and maze. Open to 3pm November to March.

Leeds Castle, Maidstone, Kent ME17 1PL
☎ 01622 765400

 10am-5pm

 *Treasure Houses

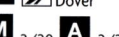 Maidstone

M 2   A 2/28

1066 & The Battle of Hastings

Starting at Hastings **1-3**, is where, in 1066, the last successful invasion of England took place in that famous battle. William the Conqueror invaded from France, confronted King Harold and won the Battle after King Harold was mortally wounded by an arrow in his eye. Above Hastings is the wonderful town of Rye **9**, in East Sussex, and a meeting with the ancient past, timbered houses, worn cobbles, and the grim 12th century Ypres Tower lead down to the fishing village at the harbour.

Then either travel through Tenterden **10**, and more vineyards to where you can pick up the scenic Kent and East Sussex Railway **11**, and then continue north west to visit the exquisite gardens at Sissinghurst, Kent **5**. Alternatively you can go to the fairy tale Bodiam Castle **4**, and then Sissinghurst **5**, and Scotney Castle **6**.

Life in the fashionable 18th century spa town of Royal Tunbridge Wells in Kent **7**, is recreated at an exhibition in the 17th century Pantiles promenade, (excellent shops here too). Famous houses and castles abound, with Penshurst Place, (built in the 1340's) one of the greatest houses in England **8**, north west of Tunbridge Wells and Hever Castle **12**, at Edenbridge, (details under the 'Brighton' trail).

Continue your journey of discovery with the NBCompass, or head back to London.

ℹ️ Tourist Information

Hastings ☎ 01424 781111

Tunbridge Wells

☎ 01892 515675

Rye ☎ 01797 226696

GF Hastings

Hotels

Eastbourne - Hastings - Hawkhurst - Herstmonceux - Rye - Tunbridge Wells

Distance from London

Hastings 67 miles ➡️

1. 1066 Battle of Hastings

In 1066, the last successful invasion of England, saw William the Conqueror's army from Normandy defeat the Anglo Saxon King Harold, at Hastings. William then went on to assume control of the whole country. See and experience the exciting audio visual '1066 Story' in Hastings Castle, ruins of Britain's first Norman Castle with fine views over Hastings and the coastline. Open October to March 10.30-3.30pm.

1066 Battle of Hastings, Castle Hill Road, West Hill, Hastings, East Sussex
☎ 01424 781112

10-5pm

Hastings

M 25   A 21

2. Smugglers Adventure

Enter the dark caverns and winding tunnels of St. Clements caves deep within the West Hill of Hastings and you'll discover the Smugglers Adventure. Explore the labyrinth of caverns, tunnels and secret passages on a journey through time. Witness the romantic yet often bloody heyday of the smuggler, bought to life in a themed experience which includes a museum of smuggling, a video theatre and a subterranean adventure walk. Discover more than fifty life-size figures, scenes activated by push buttons, dramatic sounds, eerie lighting, and a few other surprises.

Smugglers Adventure, St. Clements Caves, Hastings, East Sussex TN34 3HY
☎ 01424 422964

10-5.30pm

Hastings

M 25   A 21

3. Hastings Sea Life Centre

Hastings Sea Life Centre opens the window to the ocean floor as you walk through the spectacular underwater tunnel. As well as many fascinating displays, Neptune's Nursery offers the rare opportunity to watch unborn sharks and rays wriggling in their transparent egg cases and allows you to trace their development. There's so much more to see and discover.

Hastings Sea Life Centre, Rock-A-Nore Road, Hastings, Sussex TN34 3DW
☎ 01424 718776

10-5pm

 Coupon

 Hastings

M 25   A 21

4. Bodiam Castle

Bodiam Castle was built in 1385 for the defense of the surrounding countryside and as a comfortable dwelling for a rich nobleman. The virtual completeness of the exterior, the best example of its type in the country, is a photographer's dream. Although a ruin, the floors have been replaced in some of the towers and impressive views can be enjoyed from the battlements. There is an audio visual presentation on life in a medieval castle, and a small museum.

Bodiam Castle, Bodiam, Nr Robertsbridge TN32 5UA
☎ 01580 830436

Page 91

 Page 66

 Robertsbridge   Hastings

A 21

South East of England

5. Sissinghurst Castle Garden

The 5 acre famous connoisseurs' garden created by Vita Sackville-West and her husband, Sir Harold Nicolson, is situated between the surviving parts of an Elizabethan mansion. A series of small, enclosed gardens, intimate in scale and romantic in atmosphere with much to see in all seasons. Also, visit the study where Vita Sackville-West worked, and the long library. Due to the limited capacity of the garden, timed tickets are in operation and visitors may have to wait before admission. Daily visitor numbers are restricted, but visitors may still visit the Oast House exhibition.

Sissinghurst Castle Garden, Sissinghurst, near Cranbrook TN17 2AB
☎ 01580 715330

 Page 91
  Page 66
 Staplehurst Ashford
A 21/262

6. Scotney Castle Garden

One of England's most romantic and enchanting gardens, surrounding the ruins of a 14th century moated castle and quarry. Rhododendrons, azaleas, water lilies and wisteria flower in profusion. Woodland and estate walks lead to viewpoints of the ruins and of the many specimen trees. There is also a herb garden. The gardens and castle are located 1 mile south of Lamberhurst.

Scotney Castle Garden, Lamberhurst, Tunbridge Wells TN3 8JN
☎ 01892 891081

 Page 91
 Page 66
 Lamberhurst
 A 21

7. A Day at the Wells

Located in the Corn Exchange, on the historic 17th century Pantiles within Royal Tunbridge Wells, a fashionable 18th century spa town. A Day at the Wells, is where you can take a fascinating journey into Georgian society life. They have recreated an intriguing mixture of sights, sounds and smells, where visitors can view and enjoy wonderful sets, with colorful characters and beautiful period costumes. November to March open 10-4pm.

A Day at The Wells, The Corn Exchange, The Pantiles, Tunbridge Wells, Kent
☎ 01892 546545

 10-5pm

 Visa MC
 Tunbridge Wells
A 26/21/267

8. Penshurst Place and Gardens

Set in a pretty neo-Tudor village is one of the great houses of England, Penshurst Place. Once the home of the Elizabethan poet Sir Phillip Sidney, (1554-1586) this medieval manor sits in rolling parkland. The vast (60ft) Great Hall, built 1340, has a timber roof carved with life size figures, (carvings of humble peasants). The great terrace is the focus of the formal gardens with their clipped hedges, there are vineyards nearby. Also to be found there, is an enchanting Toy Museum with puppets, rocking horses and 19th century dolls. Located 7miles north west of Tunbridge Wells.

Penshurst Place and Gardens, Penshurst, Kent TN11 8DG
☎ 01892 870307

 12-5.30pm

 Tunbridge Wells
 B 2188

Brighton
'London by the Sea'

Along the south coast are the popular seaside towns of Brighton and Hove **1-3**. This is the closest seaside resort to London, with great culture, variety and liveliness. There is a great deal more than just beaches here. Some of the highlights are the Royal Pavilion **1**, the Lanes, a narrow thoroughfare with many antique shops, (once home to fishermen) and the Brighton Museum and Art Gallery **2**, in Church Street, which houses a nationally important collection of Art Nouveau and Art Deco furnishings, including Salvador Dali's 'Mae West' kiss sofa. To the east of Brighton you can visit the fascinating home of the artist Vanessa Bell, sister of writer Virginia Woolf, at Charleston Farmhouse **4**. Heading north, take a ride on the picturesque Bluebell **13**, or Lavender Line **6**, railways, and on the way don't miss Lewes Castle **5**, (the town has many fine buildings from all periods) and the exquisite Sheffield Park Garden **7**. You are ideally placed to visit more stunning gardens from here, Borde Hill **8**, Leonardslee **10**, and High Beeches **11**, are all nearby. Hever Castle, Kent **12**, was the childhood home of Anne Boleyn, one of King Henry VIII's six wives and is just north of where AA Milne, (Winnie the Pooh) lived at Hartfield, East Sussex **14**. The neighbouring Ashdown Forest **15**, is the setting for 'poohsticks', where you can walk around the area that inspired Milne, although there is no specific exhibition.

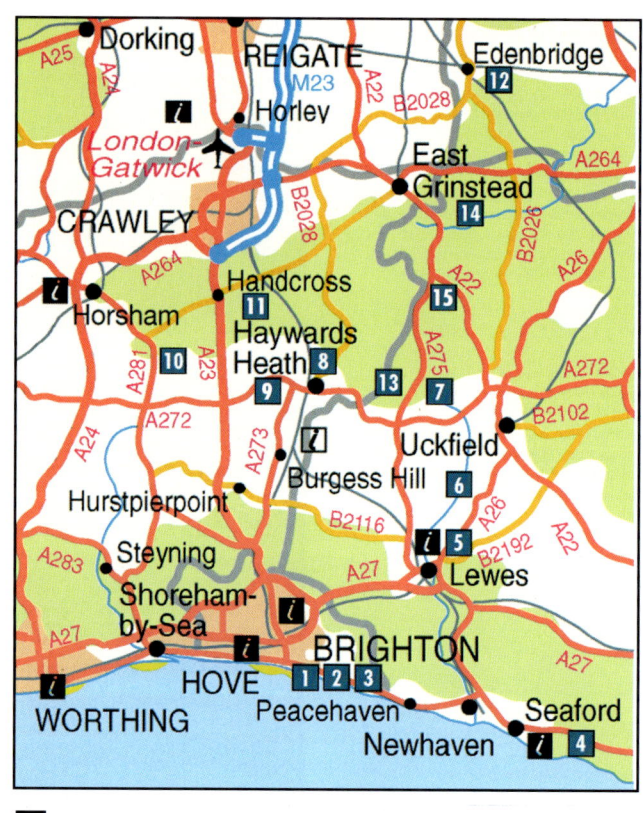

i Tourist Information

Brighton	☎ 01273 292599
Hove	☎ 01273 778087

GF Brighton

Hotels

Brighton

STAKIS HOTELS Brighton

Brighton - Lewes - Reigate - Steyning - West Chiltington

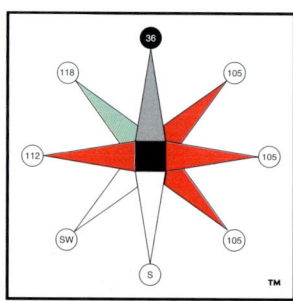

Distance from London

Brighton 54miles ➡

1. The Royal Pavilion

Universally acclaimed as one of the most exotically beautiful buildings in the British Isles, the Royal Pavilion is the former seaside residence of King George IV. It is unusual in that it started as a farmhouse, 1787 saw it transformed into a neo-classical villa, and then between 1815 to 1822 it was transformed by John Nash into its Indian style. You will not find another like it. Queen Victoria planned to demolish it in 1837, however it was fortunately saved by the local council. Open from October to May until 5pm. Tours by appointment.

The Royal Pavilion, Brighton, East Sussex BN1 1EE
☎ 01273 290900

 10-6pm
 50p off full Adult entry
 Brighton
M 23 A 23

www.brighton.co.uk

2. Brighton Museum and Art Gallery

An exciting range of collections of local and national importance displayed against a beautiful backdrop of tiled walls, arched screens, pillars and mosaic floors inspired by Moorish design. The superb selection includes furniture by Gallé and Mackintosh, pottery by Clarice Cliff, Lalique glass, Liberty silver and Salvador Dali's famous sofa in the shape of Mae West's lips. The ceramics gallery traces the technical and decorative development of English pottery and porcelain. The museum's fine collections of paintings includes Victorian visions of the exotic. Closed on Wednesdays and open from 2pm on Sundays.

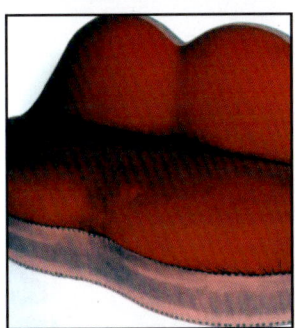

Brighton Museum and Art Gallery,
Church Street, Brighton, East Sussex BN1 1UE
☎ 01273 290900

 10-5pm

 Brighton
M M23 A A23

www.brighton.co.uk

3. Brighton Sea Life Centre

The oldest aquarium in Europe, Brighton Sea Life Centre boasts the longest underwater viewing tunnel of any Sea Life Centre in Europe. In addition to the many fantastic displays, a new feature area called Kingdom of the Seahorse opened in Spring 1997. There's so much more to see and discover.

Brighton Sea Life Centre, Marine Parade,
Brighton, Sussex BN2 1TB
☎ 01273 604234

 10-5pm
 Coupon
 Brighton
M 23 A 23

4. Charleston

The Sussex home of the 'Bloomsbury' Group of artists, Vanessa Bell and Duncan Grant. This is a fascinating and influential home. The interior was decorated by the artists, and many celebrated poets, writers and artists visited here. The garden was redesigned with a touch of 'Bloomsbury' humor. The house, which is carefully protected for its historical preservation, is open during the summer months, but the offer applies in April and October, as the house is carefully protected for its historical preservation. Signposted off the A27 between Brighton and Eastbourne. Closed Mondays and Tuesdays.

Charleston, nr Firle, Lewes, East Sussex BN8 6LL
☎ 01323 811265

 2-5pm

 Lewes   Brighton
A 27

5. Lewes Castle

Lewes Castle and Anne of Cleves House, the offer is a combined ticket. High above the medieval streets of Lewes stands the castle. Begun soon after 1066, (Battle of Hastings) and added to over the next 300 years, the steep climbs are rewarded by magnificent views. Down the hill in Southover is Anne of Cleves House. This house was part of the divorce settlement from Henry VIII, but Anne never lived here. Both of these historic attractions are fascinating and are used for theater and events to the present day. Open Sundays from 11 am.

Lewes Castle, 169 High Street, Lewes, Sussex BN7 1YE
☎ 01273 486290

⌚ 10-5.30pm

⇄ Lewes   ✦ Brighton

🅰 27

6. Lavender Line

A typical example of the 1930's to 1950's British Railways rural station. Here you will discover steam and vintage diesel passenger and goods trains, plus a fully restored Victorian Station and signal box. Set in the quiet and picturesque Sussex countryside this is a railway journey with a difference. Open every Sunday 11 - 4pm, and Weds, Thurs, Sat and Sundays during August to 5pm. NBC offer is half price ticket.

Isfield Station, Station Road, Isfield, East Sussex TN22 5XB
☎ 0891 800645 24 hrs

⌚ 11 -5pm

% 50%

⇄ Lewes   ✦ Brighton

M 23   🅰 22/26

7. Sheffield Park Garden

A magnificent landscape garden, with 5 lakes linked by cascades and waterfalls, laid out in the 18th century by Capability Brown. Carpeted with daffodils and bluebells in spring, its rhododendrons, azaleas and stream garden are spectacular in early summer. In autumn the garden is ablaze with color. However, its collection of rare trees and shrubs makes the garden wonderful to visit at any time of the year. Located 8 miles north west of Uckfield.

Sheffield Park Garden, Uckfield, East Sussex TN22 3QX
☎ 01825 790231

⌚ Page 91

 Page 66

⇄ Uckfield

🅰 22/275

8. Borde Hill Garden

Borde Hill is an English garden in the finest Romantic tradition. The botanic garden was created by Colonel Stephenson Clark at the end of the 19th century, and is home to a huge variety of plants. As well as one of the best private collections of champion trees, such as the Chinese tulip tree in the Garden of Allah, the garden has award winning collections of rhododendrons, camellias and azaleas, stunning herbaceous borders, and an extensive collection of fragrant English roses. Located just over 1 mile north of Haywards Heath, the offer applies weekdays only.

Borde Hill Garden,
Balcombe Road, Haywards Heath, West Sussex RH16 1XP
☎ 01444 450326

⌚ Hours 10-6pm

% £1

⇄ Haywards Heath

 M 23   🅰 23

www.bordehill.co.uk

9. Ockenden Manor Hotel

Dating back to 1520, this delightful Elizabethan Manor House is set in acres of private grounds. All 22 rooms are furnished with fine antiques, and some with four poster beds. Ideally positioned to visit, 'Gardens of England' such as High Beeches, Nymans, Sheffield Park or Sissinghurst. Also Glyndebourne, Brighton and Charleston for the culture enthusiasts. Recommended for those of you who wish to discover, and experience English character privately owned accommodation. Phone or fax to book, and for hotel/room rates.

Ockenden Manor, Ockenden Lane, Cuckfield, West Sussex
☎ 01444 416111   01444 415549

H | A | P

🕐 24 Hours

% 10%

cc All

⇄ Haywards Heath   Brighton

M 23   A 23/272

10. Leonardslee Gardens

A romantic landscape garden set in a peaceful valley with walks around seven beautiful lakes. The gardens are a paradise in spring, with rhododendrons and azaleas along paths lined with bluebells, summer, interesting wild-flowers, and then autumn fiery tints. Visit the Rock Garden, Bonsai Exhibition and look out for Wallabies in part of the valley, Deer in the parks and wildfowl on the lakes. See also, the fascinating Loder collection of Victorian Motorcars here, most of which were made before steering wheels and inflatable tyres were invented. Offer is a 'free' color guidebook. Closed from Nov - end March.

Leonardslee Gardens, Lower Beeding, Horsham, West Sussex RH13 6PP
☎ 01403 891212

❋ | ☕ | P

🕐 9.30-6pm

 | ✏

⇄  Horsham

M 23   B 2110

11. High Beeches

Close to London, you can enjoy 20 acres of enchanting, peaceful, and beautiful landscaped woodland and water gardens. Discover a range of wonderful flowers that grow there, daffodils, camellias, bluebells, magnolias and azaleas in the spring. In summer, the natural wildflower meadow is at its best. In autumn, (fall) brilliantly covered foliage transforms the scene. You may also spot one of the shy animals of the Sussex Weald. Located on the B2110, 1 mile east of the A23 at Handcross. Closed from November to April 1st. Closed every Wednesday, and July to August open Monday and Tuesday only.

High Beeches, Handcross, West Sussex.
☎ 01444 400589

❋ | P

🕐 1-5pm

 | 21

⇄  Crawley

M 23   A 23   B 2110

12. Hever Castle

Hever Castle is a romantic double moated castle with a rich and varied history stretching back over seven centuries. Best known as the childhood home of Anne Boleyn, it was her family who in 1500 added a comfortable Tudor manor house within the outer walls that had been constructed in the 13th century. Henry VIII wooed Anne at Hever Castle, and various exhibitions feature Henry VIII and Anne Boleyn. Henry VIII later gave the castle to his fourth wife, Anne of Cleves. The American millionaire, William Waldorf Astor, acquired Hever Castle in 1903 ,and spent a great deal of money and imagination restoring it. Open from 1 March to 30 Nov.

Hever Castle, Hever, Edenbridge, Kent TN8 7NG
☎ 01732 865244

🚂 | ❋ | 🛍 | ☕ | P

🕐 12-6pm

⇄ Edenbridge Town (3 miles)

M 25/23   A 21

The Body Shop and Antiques

Just above the coastline you will find the Body Shop factory tour **1**, near Littlehampton, where this world famous cosmetics company provide a remarkable insight into the background and secrets of their success. Heading north from there, is Arundel **2**, with its famous castle, completed after the Norman Conquest, and an interesting Toy Museum can be found in a Georgian House in the town center. Travel back to Roman times along the coast to the Roman Villa at Bignor **5**, from where you can return through time to the charming Parham House **4**, and Amberely Castle, (1380) whose village is a popular starting point amongst walkers.

If you head in a south westerly direction you arrive at Chichester **7,8**, a wonderfully preserved market town dominated by a magnificent cathedral, and with a vibrant Festival Theatre. On the outskirts of the town are Fishbourne Palace **9**, the site of a 2,000 year old Roman Palace, and Goodwood House **10**, with its priceless art collection. Goodwood is also famed as one of Britain's leading horse racing courses, often referred to as 'Glorious Goodwood'. Finally, Petworth in West Sussex is renowned for its abundance of fine antique shops, and the 17th century Petworth House **11**, (where Turner had a studio) is one of the National Trust's greatest treasures, and is in a magnificent 'natural' setting created by Capability Brown.

From here continue your journey of discovery with the NBCompass.

Tourist Information

Arundel	☎ 01903 882268
Chichester	☎ 01243 775888
Petworth	☎ 01798 343523

Hotels

STAKIS HOTELS Arundel

Bosham - Midhurst

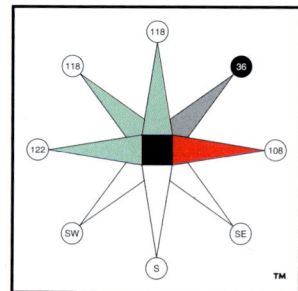

Distance from London

Arundel 62 miles ➡

1. Body Shop Factory Tour

Here the world famous Body Shop removes the mystique surrounding cosmetics. You can find out exactly what goes into their products and why it's there. Discover how the staff trial the products, how the bottles are filled, why Body Shop trade with indigenous, (native) people, and how they campaign. This is a very popular tour, but the shop and café allow an opportunity to fill a little time before or after the tours. Tours from Monday to Saturday, (except Friday afternoon) last 1 hour 20 minutes, starting at 10.20am, and the last tour at 3.40pm.

Body Shop Tour, Watersmead, Littlehampton, West Sussex BN17 6LS
☎ 01903 844044   Ⓕ 01903 844055

🕐 10-5pm

⇄ 🚶 Littlehampton

🅰 29/259

2. Arundel Castle

The castle dominates the small riverside town below. First built by the Normans, it was acquired by the powerful Dukes of Norfolk during the 16th century, and the descendants of the family still live here. The castle contains many fine paintings and furnishings. In the castle grounds is the 14th century parish church of St Nicholas. Other highlights include the Library and the Armoury. Closed on Saturdays.

Arundel Castle, Arundel, West Sussex
☎ 01903 883136

🕐 12-5pm

⇄ Arundel   🚶 Bognor

🅰 27/284

3. Bailiffscourt Hotel

This recreation of a medieval house has historical character of its own, as well as being a well respected private hotel set in over 20 acres of land and walled gardens. Located in Climping, just 200yds from the beach, and only 4 miles from Arundel, (Body Shop Tour). This is an ideal hotel for visits to Chichester 8 miles west, Brighton, Goodwood House, and the beautiful Sussex countryside. Recommended for those of you who wish to discover, and experience an English character privately owned accommodation. Phone or fax to book, and for hotel/room rates.

Bailiffscourt Hotel, Climping, West Sussex
☎ 01903 723511   Ⓕ 01903 723107

🕐 24 hrs

% 10%

🆎 All

⇄ 🚶 Littlehampton

🅰 29/259

4. Parham House

An Elizabethan House with acres of beautiful gardens. Twenty gardeners once tended the grounds, now there are only four, but the results are just as magnificent. There is a turf and brick maze, woodland, and pleasure gardens enhanced by statues and a lake. Portraits and furniture in the house are also notable. Open from April to October on Wednesdays, Thursdays and Sundays. House 2-5pm, kitchen and gardens 12-6pm.

Parham House, Pulborough, West Sussex
☎ 01903 744888

🕐 12-5pm

⇄ Pulborough   🚶 Bognor

🅰 24/29

5. Bignor Roman Villa

In this village of farm buildings and timbered cottages, you will discover The Roman Villa at Bignor, renowned for its superb mosaics. The 80ft long mosaic in the north corridor is the longest on display in the country, and there are many others including, Venus, Medusa, Gladiators and the Ganymede, (a cupbearer). The museum tells the story of the villa over the years, and you can also see how the hypocaust under-floor heating system worked. Open from 10am 1st March to 31st October, closed on Mondays. Approximately 5 miles north of Arundel and signposted.

Bignor Stone Street and Villa, Bignor, Pulborough, West Sussex RH20 1PH
☎ 01798 869259

 10-5pm

 20% off entry

 Arundel Bognor

A 29/285

6. Spread Eagle Hotel

Dating back to 1430 this is one of England's oldest hotels. Tudor bread ovens and stained glass windows are among the many features. Petworth, the 'Antique Centre of the South' is nearby. Also, ideally located for Fishbourne Roman Palace, Arundel and Jane Austen's house in Chawton. Recommended for those of you who wish to discover, and experience character privately owned accommodation. Phone or fax to book, and for hotel/room rates.

Spread Eagle Hotel, South Street, Midhurst, West Sussex
☎ 01730 816911   ⓕ 01730 815668

⏲ 24 hrs

% 10%

CC MC Visa AmEx Diners

⇄ Haslemere

A 3/286

7. Chichester Cathedral

The cathedral is said to be the only one in England whose spire can be seen from the sea. Interestingly it is also unique as the cathedral has a detached bell tower (1436). The exterior is of an attractive limestone, and within the cathedral is the modern and famous stained glass window by Marc Chagall, (1889-1985). Other highlights include modern paintings by Graham Sutherland, (1903-1980) and the sculptured stone panels in the south choir aisle, dating from 1125-50. Entry is free, but a donation would be welcome.

Chichester Cathedral, West Street, Chichester, West Sussex
☎ 01243 782595

⏲ 7.30-7pm

⇄ Chichester

A 27/285

8. Mechanical Music and Doll Collection

This is an amazing museum of mechanical musical instruments. These include, music boxes, barrel-pianos and dance organs, plus a lot more which all play for visitors and are fully restored. You will find the collection to be quite fascinating and certainly unique. There are also over 100 dolls on display dating from 1830 to 1930. Located just 1 mile east of Chichester city center, (signposted) off the A27. Offer includes a guided tour. From 1st October to 31st March the museum is only open on Sundays 1-5pm. Closed on Saturdays.

Mechanical Music and Doll Collection, Church Road, Portfield, Chichester, West Sussex
☎ 01243 372646

 1-5pm

 Chichester   Bognor

A 27/259

9. Fishbourne Roman Palace

One of the most significant examples of the remains of a Palatial Roman Building, with many exquisite mosaics and under floor heating systems. The museum houses finds from the many excavations, and the garden has been replanted to the original Roman plan. The excavations continue to this day, and more of the palace and its surrounding buildings from AD75, continue to be uncovered. Open from 10-6pm during August and to 4pm in November to February. January, open Sundays only.

Fishbourne Roman Palace, Salthill Road, Fishbourne, Chichester, West Sussex PO19 3QR
☎ 01243 785859

 10-5pm

 Fishbourne   Bognor

A 27/259

10. Goodwood House

This richly refurbished 18th century home is full of superb treasures. There is a magnificent collection of works for art lovers. With paintings by Stubbs, Van Dyck, Canaletto and Reynolds, plus tapestries, porcelain and fine furniture. The dressage center plays host to equestrian events, and there are wonderful views from nearby, 'Glorious Goodwood' racecourse. Located 3 miles north east of Chichester. Open every day except Saturdays.

Goodwood House, Chichester, West Sussex PO1 8OP
☎ 01243 755000

 1-5pm

 Chichester

A 285

11. Petworth House

Magnificent late 17th century mansion, set within a beautiful deer park and landscaped pleasure grounds. The house contains the National Trust's finest collection of pictures with works by Turner, Van Dyck, Reynolds and Blake. Also ancient and neo-classical sculpture, fine furniture and carvings by Grinling Gibbons. Old kitchens and other servants' rooms recently opened in servants' block. Additional private family rooms open on weekdays. Enjoy a walk around the beautiful deer park with lakes, landscaped by Capability Brown and immortalised in Turner's paintings, which can be seen in the house.

Petworth House, Petworth GU28 OAE
☎ 01798 342207

 Page 91

Page 66

Pulborough

A 272/283

12. Jane Austen's House

Jane Austen, (1775 to 1817) wrote three of her novels, including 'Emma', and revised many others, at this small red-brick house where she came to live, (in 1809) for eight years until shortly before her death. The House was built around 1645 as a posting inn. Many of her personal memorabilia and possessions are to be found here, and a large number of letters and documents. The table on which Jane Austen wrote, 'Mansfield Park', 'Emma' and 'Persuasion' is in the dining room parlour.

Jane Austen's House, Chawton, near Alton, Hampshire GU34 1SD
☎ 01420 83262

 11-4.30pm

 Alton

 31/32

South of England

THE SOUTH OF ENGLAND, is a popular commuter 'region, all of the counties are within one or two hours journey time from London and provide an enormous amount of variety in the areas they embrace. To the north west of London, the Chiltern Hills with woodlands, rivers, peaceful charm and rich wildlife, and further out to Oxford, with Britain's first University, (1167) where you will be positioned on the south eastern edge of the Cotswolds. The Romantic River Thames sweeps through Royal Berkshire (Windsor) and Buckinghamshire where these counties' great appeal ensured that here many Stately Homes were built, close to London, homes which are amongst the grandest in the country.

Hampshire, to the south west of London, is the 'country' Jane Austen wrote of, (she lived in Chawton, East Hampshire) and it remains rural, mainly agricultural and very much as she depicted. From here you are drawn to the largest area of unenclosed land in southern Britain, the New Forest, (56 sq miles created by William the Conqueror) and the Downs, (hills) then onto the coast where you will find the naval city of Portsmouth. Finally out to England's second smallest county, measuring 23 miles from east to west and 13 miles north to south, The Isle of Wight, where you cannot fail to be attracted to Queen Victoria's favored seaside residence, Osborne House built at her own expense in 1855, and recently featured in the film 'Mrs Brown' which depicts part of her life after the death of her husband Prince Albert.

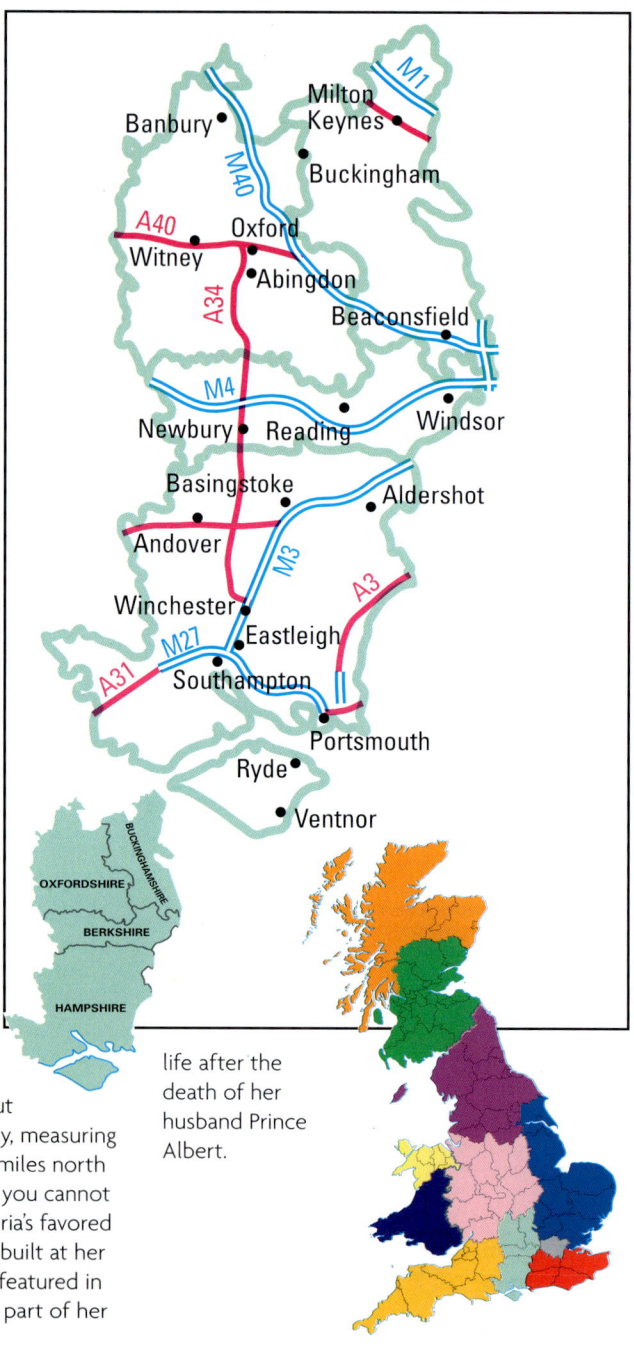

South of England

Access/Getting Around

From London

By Road

(page ref. 36,37)
The M25 London Orbital Motorway links the A3/M3 in the south west, past the M4/A33 and M40 and A41 to the M1 in the north west.

By Rail

(page ref. 94,95)
A network of railway lines criss-cross the whole area but the faster services are those leading to and from London's Euston, Marylebone, Paddington and Waterloo stations.

By Coach

(page ref. 96,97)
Coaches run frequently from London Victoria to most key towns and cities in the south of England region including, Oxford, Portsmouth and Milton Keynes.

By Air

London Heathrow and Gatwick Airport, both to the south and east of the region, give the best access.

Stowe Landscape Gardens

Cliveden

Royal Windsor & Eton to 'The Thames'

Windsor in Royal Berkshire, is where the romantic Thames can be best experienced by sightseeing in a boat **A2**. Start at the Town & Crown Exhibition **B2**, on the High Street opposite the castle, it's an ideal way to begin a visit to Windsor. The centerpiece, Windsor Castle **A2**, is the oldest continuously inhabited Royal residence in Britain and is the largest castle, which means that it rather dominates this attractive and historical town. Visit the Dungeons of Windsor **A2**, or take a tea stop and experience the famous Sally Lunn's buns, (without having to go to Bath, where they originated) **B2**. Eton is to the northern side of the Thames, and Windsor the southern side. Arriving in Eton, you should visit Eton College **A2**, home of England's most famous boys' school. Just south of Windsor are the year round beauty of Savill Garden **B1**, the Windsor Great Park, and Legoland **B1**, one of England's better 'family day' theme parks. Runnymede and the Kennedy Memorial are also within easy reach from Windsor **B2**. Continuing west back along the twisting Thames past wonderful riverside restaurants, you can enjoy scenery that has inspired painters and writers alike, onto Cliveden Reach, dominated by Cliveden House **A1**, which is now a hotel with beautiful grounds that line the Thames

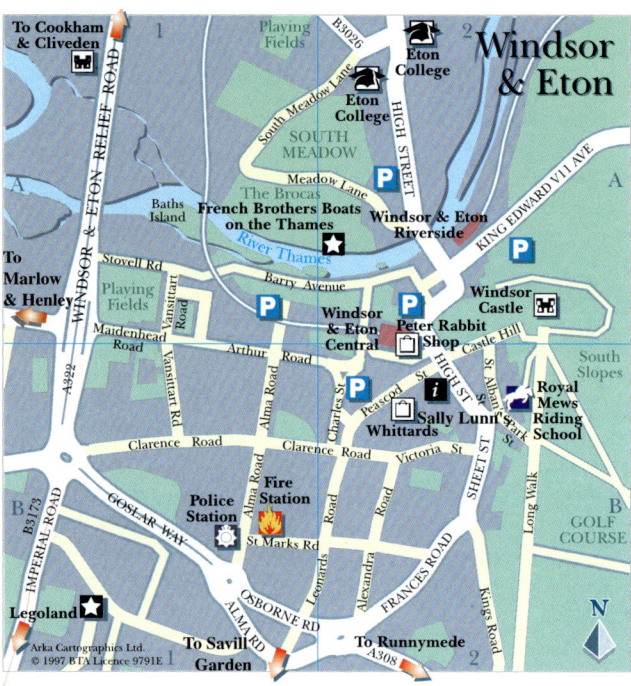

and are open to the public. Travel to wonderful riverside villages and towns like Cookham **A1**, and Marlow as far as Henley-on-Thames **A1**, with its five arched 18th century bridge, where the Henley Royal Regatta, (meeting for boat races - rowing) takes place in July.

Tourist Information

Henley	☎ 01491 578034
Windsor	☎ 01753 852010

GF Windsor and Eton

Hotel

Windsor

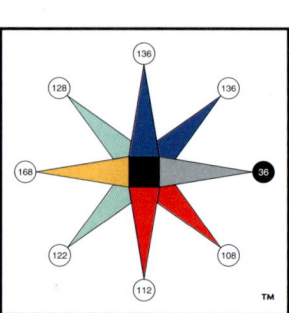

Distance from London

Windsor 24miles ➜ London

1. Windsor Castle

England's largest castle, established in 1070 by William the Conqueror to guard the western approaches to London. Chosen because of its high ground, and (at that time) just a day's journey from his base in the Tower of London. This is also the oldest continuously inhabited royal residence in Britain. Differing Royal tastes have changed it over the years, and it was King George V, upon changing his family name to Windsor in 1917, who was responsible for the castle name as it stands today. It isone of the residence for the Queen and her family who stay here on many weekends. The most notable attractions are the State Apartments and St George's Chapel.

Windsor Castle, Castle Hill, Windsor, Berkshire
☎ 01753 868286

    P

🕐 10-5pm

⚑ ✎ Windsor

M 4 J5/6

Map ref: A2

2. Town & Crown Exhibition

Located above the Royal Windsor Information Centre, this is the ideal way to begin a visit to Windsor. The Town & Crown Exhibition covers 900 years of Royal Heritage in the town that has played an important role in the Nation's history, a royal town that has been much loved by so many English Monarchs. Included in the exhibition is, an audio visual tour of Windsor from William the Conqueror to Queen Victoria, archaeological finds and many original artifacts. The High Street is diagonally opposite Windsor Castle. Free entry with your NBC card.

Town & Crown Exhibition
24 High Street, Windsor, Berks SL4 1LH
☎ 01753 743900

  P

🕐 10-5pm

 % Free entry

 Windsor

M 4 J5/6

Map ref: B2

3. French Brothers

French Brothers have 12 all-weather passenger vessels, carrying from 12 to 150 passengers in comfort on daytime Thames cruises for up to 2 hours from Windsor or Runnymede. Regular public service trips run between Runnymede and Windsor, and Runnymede and Hampton Court on certain days of the week in summer. Located at the Windsor Promenade below the castle and definitely a great sightseeing experience.

French Brothers, Clewer Court Road, Windsor, Berks SL4 5JH
☎ 01753 851900

★ P

🕐 9-6pm

 % 10%

  Windsor

M 4 J5/6

www.boattrips.co.uk
Map ref: A2

4. Dungeons of Windsor

An exhibition of Crime and Punishment from the barbaric 1300's to Victorian times. Located opposite Windsor Castle, the attraction explores crime and punishment in and around Windsor and how society dealt with the subject. Recreations include George Street prison where prisoners were sent to await sentencing in overcrowded and disease ridden cells. Learn about, the ducking stool, branding, pillories and stocks, and see the famous highwaymen who stalked Windsor Forest. Open Daily.

Dungeons of Windsor
30a High Street, Windsor, Berks SL4 1PQ
☎ 01753 865555

★ P

🕐 10-5.30pm

  21 Coupon

   Windsor

M 4 J5/6

Map ref. A2

Dickens & Portsmouth 'Historic Ships'

Portsmouth is on the south coast in the county of Hampshire. It is Portsmouth that reflects and is the embodiment of naval and maritime history. Focused in the city's ancient dockyard at Flagship Portsmouth, 'Portsmouth Historic Ships' **1-5**, is where you will uncover that history. Dickens was born in Portsmouth, (1812) and you can visit his house **6**, which is now a museum. Cross the short stretch of yacht covered sea, to the Isle of Wight and Osborne House **8**, the Italianate summer home designed for Queen Victoria with its furnishings left much as they were. In an adjacent museum you can see the bathing machine used by the Queen to keep her modesty, (not forgetting the long bathing suits of the time) whilst taking her to the edge of the sea to swim.

Before traveling north through the county you can visit Portchester Castle **9**, and Fort Nelson **10**, then pass through Hambledon **13**, the early home of the popular English game of cricket. Winchester **14**, with its magnificent cathedral is where Jane Austen is buried, and housed in the Great Hall, you will find the legendary Round Table, (King Arthur & Merlin). Take an enchanting railway journey from Alresford **11**, and for Jane Austen fans, her house is at Chawton **12**, near Alton.

Choose from the pages highlighted on the NBCompass or head back towards London.

ℹ️ Tourist Information

Alton	☎	01420 88448
Portsmouth	☎	01705 826722
Isle of Wight	☎	01893 862942

GF Portsmouth

Hotels

👑 Isle of Wight - Portsmouth - Southampton - Winchester

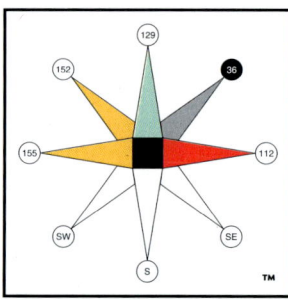

Distance from London

Portsmouth 74 miles ➡️

1. Mary Rose

Pick up a passport (NBC 2 for 1) at Flagship Portsmouth and enjoy visiting the three historic ships, Mary Rose, HMS Victory, the HMS Warrior 1860, and the Royal Naval Museum. The Mary Rose is a major archaeological discovery. Sunk in the Solent in 1545, the Mary Rose was King Henry VIII's flagship. It was recovered from the seabed and gives an absorbing insight into life at sea some 450 years ago. The remains are on view and a display with sound effects recalls the sinking of the vessel. The ships and museum are located in the City's Historic Dockyard, follow the brown and white road signs.

Mary Rose, The Hard, Portsmouth, Hampshire
☎ 01890 407080

 10-5pm

 AmEx MC Visa

Portsmouth

M 27 A 3

www.compulink.co.uk/~flagship/

2. HMS Victory

Pick up a passport (NBC 2 for 1) at Flagship Portsmouth and enjoy visiting the three historic ships, Mary Rose, HMS Victory, the HMS Warrior 1860, and the Royal Naval Museum. HMS Victory, located alongside the Mary Rose, is the ship in which Admiral Nelson was killed at Trafalgar. The flagship, after being taken to Gibraltar for repairs, returned to Portsmouth with Lord Nelson's body on board. He was later buried at St Paul's in London. The ships and museum are located in the City's Historic Dockyard, follow the brown and white road signs.

HMS Victory, The Hard, Portsmouth, Hampshire
☎ 01890 407080

 10-5pm

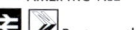 AmEx MC Visa

Portsmouth

M 27 A 3

www.compulink.co.uk/~flagship/

3. HMS Warrior 1860

Pick up a passport (NBC 2 for 1) at Flagship Portsmouth and enjoy visiting the three historic ships, Mary Rose, HMS Victory, the HMS Warrior 1860, and the Royal Naval Museum. HMS Warrior 1860, is the ironclad 19th century armoured warship, (the world's first) which is now preserved in the dockyard. Visitors can wander through the four vast decks in the only ship that spans the era of wood, iron, sail and steam. The ships and museum are located in the City's Historic Dockyard, follow the brown and white road signs.

HMS Warrior 1860, The Hard, Portsmouth, Hampshire
☎ 01890 407080

 10-5pm

 AmEx MC Visa

Portsmouth

M 27 A 3

www.compulink.co.uk/~flagship/

4. Royal Naval Museum

Pick up a passport (NBC 2 for 1) at Flagship Portsmouth and enjoy visiting the three historic ships, Mary Rose, HMS Victory, the HMS Warrior 1860, and the Royal Naval Museum. The Royal Naval Museum Museum deals with Naval history from the 16th century. It is the only museum in Britain devoted exclusively to the general history of the Royal Navy. Unique collections, relics and memorabilia can be found here. The ships and museum are located in the City's Historic Dockyard, follow the brown and white road signs.

Royal Naval Museum, The Hard, Portsmouth, Hampshire
☎ 01890 407080

 10-5pm

AmEx MC Visa

Portsmouth

M 27 A 3

www.compulink.co.uk/~flagship/

5. D-Day Museum

Four years in the preparation, the Allied invasion of Normandy on 6th June 1944 marked the beginning of the end of World War II. This award-winning museum tells the story of those momentous wartime years. The museum's centerpiece is the magnificent 'Overlord Embroidery' which took five years to complete and measures 272 feet. The embroidery scenes depicted come alive in the 'Soundalive' commentary. Audio visual displays recreate the sights and sounds of Britain at War and amongst the fascinating reconstructions, are the Allied landings on D-Day. Open until 5pm from November - March.

D-Day Museum
Clarence Esplanade, Southsea, Portsmouth
☎ 01705 827261

 10-5.30pm

 Portsmouth

M 27 A 3

6. Charles Dickens Birthplace

Charles Dickens was born in this modest house on the 7th February 1812. It now looks very much the way it did when Dickens was born there. The beautifully restored room settings recreate Regency life using authentic period items. With memorabilia, illustrations from Charles Dickens' published works, and portraits of the Dickens family. It also includes the couch on which he died at Gads Hill in Kent, in 1870. An informative guide is readily available. Open daily from April to October.

Charles Dickens Birthplace, 393 Old Commercial Road, Portsmouth, Hampshire
☎ 01705 827261

 10-5.30pm

 Portsmouth

M 27 A 3

7. Portsmouth Sea Life Centre

Portsmouth Sea Life Centre has been completely redeveloped. As well as the many fantastic displays, the new spectacular feature is the Tropical Reef adventure. From the safety of a tropical reef observatory, enjoy the closest of encounters with this magical underwater wonderland. Then come and sea-safari through the coral itself. There are fish that dazzle with a kaleidoscope of colors. Some use camouflage to conceal themselves, for safety, or in ambush, others are predators, ready to pounce on unsuspecting prey. There's so much more to see and discover.

Portsmouth Sea Life Centre, Clarence Esplanade, Portsmouth, Hampshire PO5 3PB
☎ 01705 875222

 10-5pm

 Coupon

 Portsmouth

M 27 A 3

8. Osborne House

The house of Queen Victoria and Prince Albert, far from the formality of Buckingham Palace and Windsor Castle. The house they built was set amongst terraced gardens, and filled with treasured mementoes. Victoria died there in 1901, mourning her beloved Albert, who had died in middle age. The property was used recently for the filming of 'Mrs Brown', which touched on her life after the loss of Albert. A ferry ride is required from the mainland.

Osborne House, Cowes, Isle of Wight
☎ 01983 200022

 10-5pm

  Page 67

 Ryde 7 miles   Ventnor

 3021

9. Portchester Castle

Founded more than 1,600 years ago, the castle has the most complete set of Roman walls in northern Europe. Portchester was popular with medieval kings, who stayed there when they visited Portsmouth. The history of this magnificent fortress can be followed in the interactive castle exhibition. Today the vast Keep (which once held 4,000 prisoners during the Napoleonic Wars) offers breathtaking views over Portsmouth and the Solent. From November to the end of March, closes at 4pm.

Portchester Castle, Castle Street, Portchester, Fareham, Hampshire PO16 9QW
☎ 01705 378291

 10-6pm

 Page 67

 Portsmouth

 27 27

10. Fort Nelson

The Royal Armouries at Fort Nelson are home to one of the best collections of artillery in Europe. Housed in a superbly restored 1860 Victorian Palmerston Fort, overlooking Portsmouth Harbor, there are imaginative scenes, daily gun firings (see photo), and complimentary guided tours to tell the story of artillery. The collection includes a Tudor cannon, Victorian, WWI and WWII field guns, and sections of the Iraqi 'Supergun'. Located 5 miles from Portsmouth.

Fort Nelson, Down End Road, Fareham, Hampshire PO17 6AN
☎ 01329 233734

 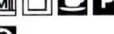

 10-5pm

  MC Visa

 Portsmouth

M 27/275 J11

11. The Watercress Line

This wonderfully preserved steam railway transports you for 10 miles through glorious Hampshire countryside between Alresford and Alton. A round trip takes approximately 2 hours although there are some fascinating stops along the way at restored stations. Alresford is an attractive Georgian town, Ropley station is famous for its topiary, Medstead and Four Marks is the highest station in Southern England and finally Alton, (linked with the National Railway system) where platform 3 links to the Watercress line.

The Watercress Line, The Railway Station, Alresford, Hampshire SO24 9JG
☎ 01962 733810

 Phone for details

 15% off

  Alton

M 3 J7 A 31

12. Jane Austen's House

Jane Austen (1775 to 1817) wrote three of her novels, including 'Emma', and revised many others at this small red-brick house where she came to live (in 1809) for eight years until shortly before her death. The House was built around 1645 as a posting inn. Many of her personal memorabilia and possessions are to be found here, and a large number of letters and documents. The table on which Jane Austen wrote, 'Mansfield Park', 'Emma' and 'Persuasion' is in the dining room parlour.

Jane Austen's House, Chawton, near Alton, Hampshire GU34 1SD
☎ 01420 83262

 11-4.30pm

Alton

A 31/32

Oxford
'City of Dreaming Spires'

Oxford grew into a world famous seat of learning after the first colleges were founded in the 13th century, and it is a city of spires, a city of academics, enclosed within two rivers, (Thames 'Isis', and Cherwell). The city retains its timeless beauty and charm which you'll feel as soon as you arrive. Familiarise yourself on arrival with the 'Oxford Story' **A2**, an audio visual account of the city's history. There is a lot to see here so a visit to the Tourist Information Centre **A1**, is advised.

For a bird's eye view of the city and colleges climb Carfax Tower **B2**, located in the center of the city. It is best to be aware that this, as a University, (made up of 39 colleges) is a place of study and visiting is somewhat restricted. Also, for comparison, Oxford is better known for the arts and Cambridge for the sciences. Britain's oldest public museum, the Ashmolean Museum **A1**, opened in 1683, is one of the highlights of Oxford. Other highlights include, the Radcliffe Camera and nearby Bodleian Library **A2**. Visit beautiful gardens **B2**, walk or punt, (flat bottomed boat propelled by a pole) along the river **A2**, wonder, dream and most importantly soak in the cultural excesses, timeless beauty, and romantic atmosphere before traveling onwards or returning to London.

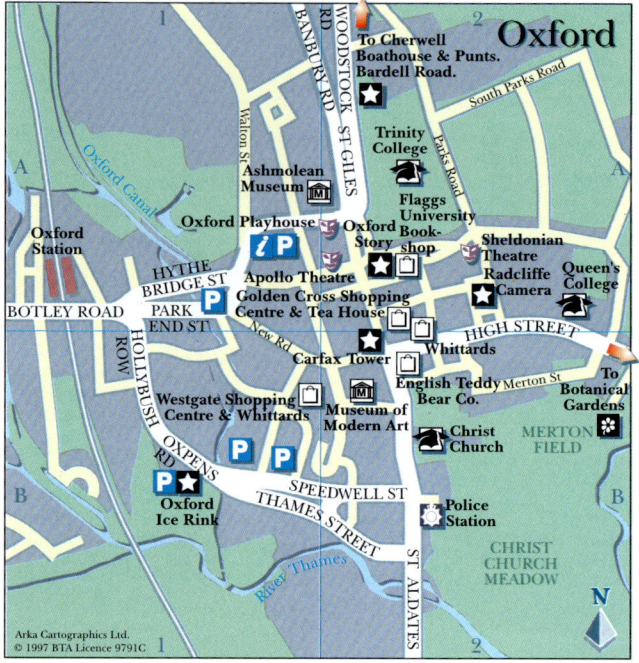

Tourist Information

Oxford   ☎ 01865 726871

GF Oxford

Hotels

Oxford

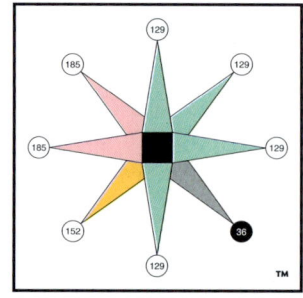

Distance from London

Oxford 55miles ➡ LONDON

1. The Oxford Story

The Oxford Story is a 45 minute audio visual exhibition, telling the story of Oxford University, the essential introduction to this beautiful city. It has a train ride ride past vivid exhibits and models of major historical characters. The picture opposite is the White Rabbit from the books of Lewis Carroll (Alice in Wonderland). Carroll (real name, Charles Dodgson) was a tutor at Oxford. There is a guided commentary available, and the exhibition is in central Oxford, near Balliol College.

The Oxford Story, 6 Broad Street, Oxford OX1 3AJ
☎ 01865 790055

 9.30-5pm

Oxford

M 40 J 8/9

Map ref: A2

2. Carfax Tower

Once St Martin's or Carfax Church, the 21metre tower is all that remains, (99 steps to climb) but offers magnificent views over Oxford's famous skyline. The entry charge is very little, the 'City of Dreaming Spires' is best viewed from Carfax Tower, and on the east façade the church clock is adorned by two 'quarter boys', who hit the bells at every 'quarter' of the hour. Why not stop and see them in action. From 1st November to the end of March open until 3.30pm.

Carfax Tower, Carfax Square, Oxford
☎ 01865 792653

10-5.30pm

Oxford

M 40 J 8/9

Map ref: B2

3. Oxford Botanical Gardens

This is probably the oldest Botanical garden in the UK. It has evolved from a 17th century collection of medieval herbs into the most compact, yet diverse, collection of plants. One yew tree survives from that period. Though small, the garden is delightful and the flower beds clearly labelled. It is located to the east of the center in Rose Lane.

Oxford Botanical Gardens, Rose Lane, Oxford OX1 4AX
☎ 01865 276920

9-4.15pm

Oxford

M 40 J 8/9

Map ref: B2

4. Flaggs Old College Store

Flaggs Old College Store are Official stockists of the University of Oxford collection of rugby shirts, sweatshirts, t-shirts, caps and scarves, essential student wear. Also Official stockists of Burberry, with a large range of rainwear, scarves, bags and accessories. Please show this page of the guide and your NBC Card. The offer applies to any product except sale items. Located opposite Trinity College in Broad Street.

Flaggs Old College Store, 18 Broad Street, Oxford OX1 3AS
☎ 01865 722258

 P

9-6pm

% 10%

M 40 J 8/9   **A** 40

Oxford

Map ref: A2

5. Ashmolean Museum

Established in 1683, it is the oldest museum in the country. The Ashmolean museum contains the University of Oxford's collections of art and antiquities. Divided into five departments: Antiquities; Western Art; Heberden Coin Room; Eastern Art and the Cast Gallery. The collections, of both national and international importance, range in time from the earliest implements of man made some two million years ago to the 20th century works of art. Located in the center of Oxford at the corner of Beaumont Street and St Giles'. Closed on Mondays. Sundays, open from 2pm.

Ashmolean Museum
Oxford OX1 2PH
☎ 01865 278000

 10.-4pm

 Oxford

 40 J8 /9

Map ref; :A1/2

6. The Tea House

The Tea House is a unique shop, specialising in fine teas and 'teaphernalia', the term used to describe all things relating to tea, cups, diffusers, pots, spoons, tea-cosies, placements etc. The shop is situated in the center of Oxford at the Golden Cross which was the site of an Old Coaching Inn. There is another branch of the Tea House in London's bustling Covent Garden. The offer is of a 125g chest of tea with purchases over £30. Closed on Sundays.

The Tea House, 9 Golden Cross Walk, Oxford
OX1 3EU
☎ 01865 728838

 9.30-5.30pm

(£30+)

AmEx MC Visa

 Oxford

Map ref: B2

7. The English Teddy Bear Co.

Founded in 1991, the English Teddy Bear Company represents all things English and eccentric through the universally loveable teddy bear. The company exports worldwide and has over ten shops throughout England selling a wonderful range of bears that are waiting to find a new home and a new friend. Located in the town center. Open Sundays 11-5pm.

The English Teddy Bear Co., 135 High Street, Oxford OX1 4DN
☎ 01865 721165

 10-6pm

 10%

 All

Oxford

Map ref: B2

8. Cherwell Boathouse

This is one of the better restaurants to be found, just 1 mile north of Oxford center, with the added opportunity of hiring one of their traditional wooden punts (open 10am to dusk) during the summer. Punt to Oxford, and back for lunch perhaps. Lunch is from Tuesday to Sunday 12-2pm, and Dinner Tuesday to Saturday 6-10.30pm. Offer can be either a free bottle of wine with a meal for a party of 4, or 10% off one of the award winning list of wines (over £25). Booking is advised, please show your NBC card and guide when arriving.

Cherwell Boathouse, Bardwell Road, Oxford

☎ 01865 552746   Ⓕ 01865 552746

 (see text)

 Oxford

 40/4165

Map ref: A2

Great English Houses and Gardens

This area is known as the Chiltern Hills and takes us on a journey through many traditional villages that retain their original character. Starting with Milton's Cottage **1**, and nearby, the Chiltern Open Air Museum **2**, which really sets the scene with many preserved historic buildings reflecting the heritage of the Chilterns.

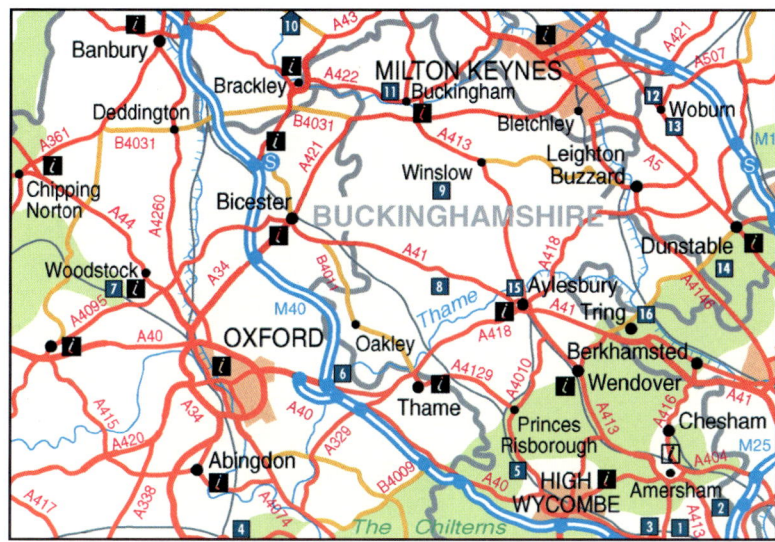

A miniaturised village, Bekonscot Model Village, Beaconsfield **3**, is the oldest model village in the world. It recalls Britain in the 1930's and has an enviable model railway (you may be inspired to replicate this in your own back yard). If you travel west from here you can get back to regular scale with the trains at Didcot **4**. Continuing away from London, the wealth of magnificent houses begin. First, Hughenden Manor **5**, home of Disraeli, the Prime Minister under Queen Victoria, who lived here from 1847 -1881. Then you reach the edge of Oxford, where Waterperry Gardens **6**, can be seen. Heading north west of Oxford, Blenheim Palace **7**, birthplace of Sir Winston

Churchill, and one of England's finest houses. The choices are stunning, Waddesdon Manor **8**, Claydon House **9**, Sulgrave Manor **10**, or Stowe Gardens **11**. Each of these houses offers a unique experience. Then there's more besides with Woburn Abbey and Woburn Safari Park **12,13**, or south to Whipsnade Wild Animal Park **14**. Finally, back towards London,

and for Roald Dahl fans there is a Dahl museum in Aylesbury **15**, or for those intersted in natural history, the Walter Rothschild Zoological Museum at Tring **16**. London is less than an hour's journey from here.

Tourist Information

Bicester ☎ 01869 369005

Hotels

Banbury - Deddington - Woburn

Distance from London

Aylesbury 42 miles → London

1. Milton's Cottage

The Cottage, a 16th century building, is where the poet John Milton (1608-1674) came to escape London's Great Plague. Here he finished 'Paradise Lost' and began 'Paradise Regained'. The cottage contains collections illustrating his life and times, of the history of the cottage, the village and the surrounding area. There are portraits of Milton, first editions and manuscripts. Open Tuesday to Saturday, closed for lunch 1 - 2pm.

Milton's Cottage, 21 Deanway, Chalfont St Giles, Bucks HP8 4JH
☎ 01494 872313

 10-6pm

 Amersham/Chalfont St Giles

M 40 A 413

2. Chiltern Open Air Museum

Founded in 1976 with the aim of rescuing threatened buildings, the collection exceeds thirty exhibits and is set in a rich site of natural park, meadow and woodland. The buildings are interpreted in a whole variety of ways, some serve their original functions, some are furnished to represent later periods in their history, others have been adapted to provide facilities for visitors. A Seat Sculpture Trail takes you through the attractive woodland and eventually leads to the fascinating reconstruction of an Iron Age House. *Please phone to check opening times.

Chiltern Open Air Museum, Newlands Park, Gorelands Lane, Chalfont St Giles, Bucks HP8 4AD
☎ 01494 871117

 P

 10-6pm*

 Coupon

 Chorleywood or Amersham

M 25 J17 A 413

www.kidsnet.chiltern.hillman.wolfbane

3. Bekonscot Model Village

The oldest model village in the world. This 1 acre period piece is Britain in the late 1930's with a model railway, stations, houses, lakes, zoo, coalmine, fairground, the list goes on and on. It is a fascinating and remarkable example, and has caused many to imitate it throughout the world. Signposted from Beaconsfield, 7 miles north of Windsor, well worth the visit and something of a 'Gulliver' experience. Listen carefully at the church.

Bekonscot Model Village, Warwick Road, Beaconsfield, Bucks HP9 1TB
☎ 01494 672919

 P

 10-5pm

 Beaconsfield

M 40/25 J2/16
www.bekonscot.org.uk

4. Didcot Railway Centre

At Didcot Railway Centre you can see the steam trains from the golden age of the Great Western Railway. The locomotives are housed in the original engine shed. You are sure to be delighted with the typical country branch line that has been recreated together with a section of Brunel's original broad gauge railway, dating back to 1835. On 'steamdays' the trains come to life and special events include a visit from Thomas the Tank Engine, usually twice a year. Open daily from Easter to late September; weekends all year, hours from Nov-Feb are 11-4pm.

Didcot Railway Centre, Didcot, Oxfordshire OX11 7NJ
☎. 01235 817200

   P

 10-5pm

 Didcot   Oxford

M 4 J13 M40 J9 A 34/4130

5. Hughenden Manor

Victorian home of Prime Minister and statesman Benjamin Disraeli from 1847 until his death in 1881. He gave the manor its 'Gothic' appearance and much of its furniture, pictures and books remain. The park and woodland have lovely walks and the garden is a recreation of an original colorful design of his wife, Mary Ann. Certain rooms have low electric light. so visitors wishing to make close study of the interior of the house should avoid dull days, particularly early and late in the season.

Hughenden Manor, High Wycombe, HP14 4LA
☎ 01494 532580

 Page 91

 Page 66

 High Wycombe

 M 40   A 4128

6. Waterperry Gardens

Enjoy the peace and serenity of this English Ornamental Garden, set in over 80 acres of countryside. A Saxon Church, garden shop and the Pear Tree tea shop can also be visited. There is an Art and Craft Gallery which is also a fascinating part of the attraction. Located 8 miles east of the City of Oxford. Open every day.

Waterperry Gardens, Waterperry, Nr Wheatley OX33 1J2
☎ 01844 339226

 9-5pm

 All

 Oxford

M 40 J8   A 40

7. Blenheim Palace

After the 1st Duke of Marlborough, (John Churchill) defeated the French at the Battle of Blenheim in 1704, Queen Anne had this palatial house built for him in gratitude. Located 8 miles north west of Oxford in the country town of Woodstock, on the edge of the Cotswolds, this is one of England's 'Treasure Houses'. Designed by Sir John Vanbrugh, architect for another of England's fine properties, 'Castle Howard', with landscaping by Capability Brown. The palace has many superb paintings, antiques, tapestries and ceramics. The leading sights are the Long Library, Saloon, the Park and Gardens. *Ask for a 'Treasure Houses' discount leaflet, to receive discounts and free guides at their other 9 properties in the guide.

Blenheim Palace, Woodstock, Oxfordshire
☎ 01993 811091

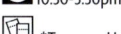 10.30-5.30pm

*Treasure Houses

 Oxford

A 40/44

8. Waddesdon Manor

Waddesdon Manor, designed in the style of a French Renaissance chateau, was built in the 1870's by Baron Ferdinand de Rothschild from the Austrian branch of the famous Rothschild banking family. The interior evokes 18th century France. The family's long association with wine is represented in the 'Wine Cellars'. Set in the garden is a rococo-style aviary housing exotic birds. In the recently restored formal parterre, the elaborate raised ribbon Victorian display is planted twice a year with spring and summer bedding. The shrubberies have been revived around the garden in the style of the 19th century. Daffodil Valley boasts a display of daffodils in Spring followed by a mass of wild flowers.

Waddesdon Manor, Waddesdon, near Aylesbury HP18 0JH
☎ 01296 651211

 Page 91

 Page 66

 Aylesbury

M 40 J6/7   A 41

9. Claydon House

The most perfect expression of rococo decoration in England, in a series of great rooms with wood carving in the Chinese and Gothic styles. Relics of the Civil War, and a museum with mementoes of Florence Nightingale and the Verney family. Beautiful 'Music by Lamplight' concerts take place in the gardens during the Summer. All Saints' Church, (not NT) in the grounds is also open to the public and the garden walks give delightful views over the three lakes in the park. Evensong: 25 May, 22 June, 27 July all at 5pm. Claydon House is located just 13 miles north west of Aylesbury.

Claydon House, Middle Claydon, near Buckingham MK18 2EY
☎ 01296 730349

 Page 91

 Page 66

Aylesbury

41, 413/421

10. Sulgrave Manor

A superb example of a modest Manor House and Garden of the time of Shakespeare. It is the ancestral home of George Washington, the first President of the United States. Built by Lawrence Washington in 1538, it remained the home of the Washington family till 1656 when they emigrated to America after the English Civil War. Closed on Wednesdays and during January and February. Open only at the weekend in March, November and December. Open from 10.30am Saturday and Sunday.

Sulgrave Manor nr Banbury, Oxon OX17 2SD
☎ 01295 760205

 2-5.30pm

Banbury

M 40 J11 B 4525

www.stratford.co.uk/sulgrave

11. Stowe Landscape Gardens

One of the supreme creations of the Georgian era. The first, formal layout was adorned with many buildings by Vanbrugh, Kent and Gibbs; in the 1730's Kent designed the Elysian Fields in a more naturalistic style, one of the earliest examples of the reaction against formality leading to the evolution of the landscape garden. Miraculously, this beautiful garden survives; its sheer scale must make it Britain's largest work of art. The house, (not National Trust) has been owned and occupied by Stowe School since 1923.

Stowe Landscape Gardens, Buckingham MK18 5EH
☎ 01280 822850

 Page 91

 Page 66

 Milton Keynes

M 1 J14 M40 J9 A 422

12. Woburn Abbey

Woburn Abbey and Deer Park is located just 44 miles north of London. The home of the Marquess and Marchioness of Tavistock and their family. There is one of the most important private art collections in the world here, including paintings by Van Dyck and Gainsborough. In the Venetian room there are 21 views of Venice by Canaletto. The house is surrounded by a magnificent parkland and there are 9 species of deer to be found. NBC discount is £1.25 off adult entry. *Ask for a 'Treasure Houses' discount leaflet, to receive discounts and free guides at their other 9 properties in the guide.

Woburn Abbey, Woburn, Bedfordshire MK45 0TP
☎ 01525 290666

 10.30 - 3.45pm

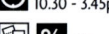 % *Treasure Houses

Bletchley Milton Keynes

M 1 J 13

13. Woburn Safari Park

The magnificent Woburn Abbey combined with the enormous Safari Park, is one of England's most popular attractions. The park includes a deer park with a herd from China that has been saved from extinction by Woburn. The Safari Park has lions and tigers, giraffes, camels, monkeys, bongos, elephants and many other animals, all of which benefit from life in this beautiful countryside location. Please use the coupon in the back of the guide for one free child entry with 2 full paying adults.

Woburn Safari Park, Woburn, Bedfordshire
☎ 01525 290407

 % Coupon

 Bletchley ⬚ Milton Keynes

M 1 J13   A 4012

14. Whipsnade Wild Animal Park

Whipsnade Wild Animal Park, is set in 600 acres with over 2,500 animals, many of which are endangered in the wild. It is one of Europe's largest conservation centers. You can walk round the park, take your car, or use the free Safari Tour Bus. The Great Whipsnade Railway takes you on an adventure through herds of Asian animals. Daily demonstrations include California sealions, elephants and birds of the world. There is a souvenir shop and also a number of cafés. Look out for the huge Chalk Lion cut into the hills nearby.

Whipsnade Zoo, near Dunstable, Bedfordshire
☎ 01582 872171

 10-6pm

 ⬚ Luton ⬚

M 1   A 5   B 4540

15. Roald Dahl Children's Gallery

Step into the magical world of Roald Dahl at this award winning 'hands on' Gallery. For most of Roald Dahl's life he lived in Buckinghamshire, where he wrote all his children's books in a little hut in his garden. Dahl wrote such popular stories as, James and the Giant Peach, Matilda, Charlie and the Chocolate Factory and Fantastic Mr Fox. Terrific fun. Timed tickets at peak times as the Gallery only holds 85 people. *Phone before making a special journey. Park in the town center and follow the signs (it's near the church). Ticket gains free entry to the adjacent County Museum.

Roald Dahl Children's Gallery,
Church Street, Aylesbury, Bucks HP20 2QP
☎ 01296 331441

 *10-5pm

 Aylesbury

M 25   A 41

16. The Walter Rothschild Zoological Museum

An annexe of London's Natural History Museum, the museum houses the largest exhibition of stuffed animals ever put together by one person. Lord Walter Rothschild, (1868-1937) was an enthusiastic,and eccentric zoologist who founded this most unusual museum in the 1890's. This extensive collection is magnificent, and includes thousands of mammals, (some of which are now extinct)birds, reptiles, fish, insects, dinosaurs and domestic dogs. Even if the idea of admiring stuffed animals doesn't appeal, you will find it hard not to be drawn to many of the unique collections. Open from 2pm on Sundays.

The Walter Rothschild Zoological Museum,
Akeman Street, Tring, Hertfordshire HP23 6AP
☎ 01442 824181

 10-5pm

 Tring (1 mile)

M 25   A 41
www.nhm.ac.uk

THE EAST OF ENGLAND introduces you to attractive and contrasting landscapes, rolling countryside, woodlands, and agricultural land. Essex, which borders London, is where many villages prospered from wool and weaving in medieval times. Today thriving ports jostle with seaside playgrounds on the Essex coast where tides wash around flat marshes, oyster beds and yacht moorings. From here to the north is the county of Suffolk . This is the picturesque 'Constable Country' where the River Stour runs through chalky lowlands.

Hertfordshire has a mixture of gentle pastoral countryside, country lanes and ancient charm, combined with rolling countryside, woodland, and peaceful canal waterways. Stately Homes and unspoilt showpiece villages can be discovered throughout this colorful county. Bedfordshire's landscape is that of gentle hills and valleys in the north, through wooded sandy slopes in the heart, and the Dunstable Downs, (hills) situated at the highest point in the county, to the south. There are superb views from the Downs, with its chalk life flora and fauna, stretching out across Bedfordshire.

Suffolk's 40 miles of coastline is designated as 'Heritage Coast', being largely unspoilt. Inland, 'Constable Country', (inspiration to the famous landscape painter, 1776-1837) and to the west Newmarket, the headquarters of British horse racing where the first ever recorded race was run in 1622.

Cambridgeshire geographically divided by the magnificent University city of Cambridge, has the reclaimed agricultural flat Fenlands, (marshy land) to the north, and in complete contrast the south is mostly chalk downland. Sandringham in Norfolk is the Queen's country retreat, from where one continues to the north Norfolk coast which has been designated, 'An Area of Outstanding Natural Beauty'.

Lincolnshire is noted, in the south, for its agriculture, market gardening and bulb growing (tulips), with similar land to the tulip growing quarters of Holland. Whilst to the north, the Wolds (areas of open uncultivated country) once used for sheep grazing, now have crops of grain and oilseed rape. Engineering also features strongly in the county, and Grimsby, (the world's largest fishing Port in the 19th century) is in Humberside to the extreme north of the county.

© BTA 1997
Produced by Cosmographics

Trail List and Page No.s

Access/Getting Around

From London

Felbrigg Hall, Garden & Park

By Road
(page ref. 36,37)
The M25 London Orbital
Motorway links the A41 in the
north west, past the M1 A5/A6
and A1/(M) and M11/A11 to the
A12 and then A13 in the east.

By Rail
(page ref. 94,95)
A network of railway lines criss-
cross the whole area but the
faster services are those leading
to and from London's
Euston,
Marylebone,
King's Cross
and Liverpool
Street stations

By Coach
(page ref. 96,97)
Coaches run
frequently from
London Victoria to
most key towns and
cities in the east of
England region
including,
Cambridge, Norwich,
Kings Lynn and
Ipswich.

By Air
Stansted Airport off the
M11, has direct rail links
with London
and Luton
Airport is close
to the M1,
Junction
10, these
give good
access to
the east of
England.

Wilkin and Sons.

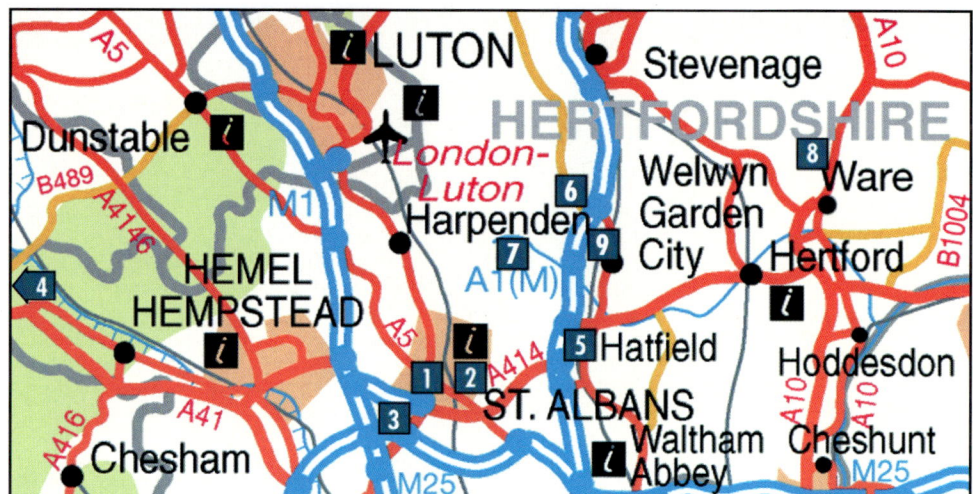

Romans, Tudor Mansions and English Roses

In Hertfordshire one of the battles between two factions of the Royal Family, York and Lancaster, were fought over St. Albans, (a regional capital of ancient Britain) These battles were known as the 'Wars of the Roses'. Today it is a bustling market town, often visited for its medieval Abbey and Cathedral **1**, and Roman city of Verulamium **2**. On the edge of St. Albans, in season, visit the spectacular Gardens of the Rose **3**, where over 1,700 varieties can be seen, including the white rose of York and the red rose of Lancaster.

To the west of St. Albans, or direct from London, for a real 'local experience' travel to the exquisite village of Aldbury, a great 'walkers' favourite. Nearby, at Grove Farm in Ivinghoe **4**, you can experience 'self-picking', or at the beginning of the year, see the lambing at a working farm.

Alternatively, travel north west to Hatfield House **5**, next to which is the Old Tudor Palace where Queen Elizabeth I lived as a child. There are signs of Roman times throughout this area as you pass Roman Baths **9**, on the way up to Knebworth House **6**, a notable Tudor Mansion where the library doors are disguised as bookshelves. Finally, visit the house of George Bernard Shaw (1856-1950) the controversial playwright, at nearby Ayot St. Lawrence **7**, known as Shaw's corner.

ℹ️ Tourist Information

Hertford	☎ 01992 584322
St Albans	☎ 01727 864511

Hotels

🛡️ St Albans - Stevenage

👑 St Albans

Distance from London

St Albans 24 miles

1. St. Albans Abbey and Cathedral

The Cathedral and Abbey Church of Saint Alban stands on a hill in St. Albans that has been a site of worship since Saxon times, and a place of history since the Romans founded the city as Verulamium. Even today, Roman bricks form part of the fabric of the present day cathedral. Although there is no entry fee, admission is charged for the wide screen audio visual show, accompanied by glorious singing from the cathedral's famous choir, which tells the story of Alban, the building of the Abbey Church, of major figures from its past and present day role.

St. Albans Abbey and Cathedral,
Sumpter Yard, St. Albans, Herts AL1 1BY
☎ 01727 860780

  P

🕐 9-6pm Inc. Church services

🎫

⇄ St Albans 🚌

Ⓜ 25 J22a
www.stalbans.gov.uk/diocese/abbey.htm

2. Verulamium Museum

The museum of the everyday life of a Roman city in St. Albans. This is an award winning museum in the attractive St. Michael's village, signposted from the A 414 to Hemel Hempstead. It is on the site of the important Roman city of Verulamium, with recreated Roman rooms, including artifacts, costumes, furniture and wall paintings. There are hands-on discovery areas and excavation videos. The museum houses one of the best late Iron Age and Roman collections outside of London. The adjacent park also has Roman remains within its grounds. Open 2-5.30pm on Sundays.

Verulamium Museum, St. Michael's, St. Albans,
Hertfordshire
☎ 01727 819339

 🏛 📷 P

🕐 10-5.30pm

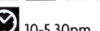

⇄ St Albans 🚌

Ⓜ 25 J 21a Ⓐ 414

3. Gardens of the Rose

Said to be the world's greatest rose collection, set in a 12 acre garden. The beautiful Gardens of the Royal National Rose Society contain over 30,000 roses in 1,700 different varieties, plus many companion plants. The roses include the historic white rose of York and red rose of Lancaster. Cultivation trials show the latest techniques in rose growing. Located to the west of St Albans city center, (a short taxi journey) in Chiswell Green. Seasonal opening from June to October.

Gardens of the Rose, Chiswell Green,
St Albans, Herts AL2 3NR
☎ 01727 850461

 ⭐ 📷 P

🕐 10-4pm

⇄ St Albans 🚌

Ⓜ 1/25 J6/21a

4. Grove Farm and Aldbury's Walks

This is a real 'local life experience' close to London. Aldbury and the Ashridge Estate (NT) is a favorite place to take some fabulous walks. The village itself is exquisite, with a pond, pub and old 'stocks' and is often used by Film and TV companies because of its natural charm. From Aldbury towards Dunstable you will find more great walks signposted along the Ridgeway, or at nearby Grove Farm you can watch the Lambing in Jan-Feb or spend a while at their self-pick, (end June-end Sept) and get a real taste of the countryside.

Grove Farm, Ivinghoe Aston and Aldbury's
Walks, Aldbury, Herts,
☎ 01296 (Lambing*) 668834, (Self-pick) 668175

 Lambing 📷 P

🕐 Call for details*

⇄ Tring (1 mile to Aldbury) 🚌

Ⓜ 25 Ⓜ 41

5. Hatfield House and Gardens

This celebrated Jacobean house is the home of the Marquess of Salisbury. The exquisite gardens, part of which were laid out by John Tradescant, (see also, 'Museum of Garden History' in London) are now managed entirely organically. Within them is the surviving wing of the Bishop's Palace, (1497) where Elizabeth I spent her childhood. It was in Hatfield Park that Elizabeth learnt she had become Queen of England in 1558. Do visit the national collection of model soldiers on display. Hatfield is located 6 miles east of St Albans. Open from end of March - end of Sept. Closed on Mondays. Please check times.

Hatfield House and Gardens, Hatfield, Hertfordshire AL9 5NQ
☎ 01707 262823

 12-4pm

➡ Hatfield

M 25 J23   **A** (M) J4

6. Knebworth House and Gardens

Home of the Lytton family since 1490, Knebworth House is unique. Originally a red-brick Tudor manor house, it was transformed in 1843 into the Gothic fantasy you see today, with turrets, griffins and gargoyles. It is known the world over for the huge open-air rock concerts and was 'Wayne Manor' in the first Batman film, but there is much romance and history about the place. Charles Dickens was a frequent visitor as was Winston Churchill, whose painting of the Banqueting Hall hangs in the room where he painted it. Check admission times (coupon in back of the guide).

Knebworth House and Gardens, Knebworth, Hertfordshire SG3 6PY
☎ 01438 812661

 11-5.30pm

 21 Coupon (not special event days)

➡ ✎ Stevenage 🚕

M 25 J23   **A** 1(M) J7

7. Shaw's Corner

An early 20th century house, and the home of George Bernard Shaw from 1906 until his death in 1950. Many literary and personal relics are shown in the downstairs rooms, which remain as in his lifetime. Shaw's bedroom and bathroom are also on view, and there is a display room upstairs. Shaw was a well known Irish dramatist, (1856-1950) and this provides a fascinating insight into his life and works. On busy days admission is by timed ticket.

Shaw's Corner, Ayot St Lawrence, Nr Welwyn AL6 9BX
☎ 01438 820307

 Page 91

 Page 66

➡ Welwyn North

A 1   **B** 653

8. Hanbury Manor Hotel

This historic, magnificent 5 star hotel is set in 200 acres of glorious parkland, and is just 24 miles from London, making it an ideal place to stay when traveling in and around Hertfordshire. It features an excellent country club and championship golf course. Offer is to receive a room upgrade and free aromabath. From Junction 25 of the M25, take the A10 north, the hotel is signposted to the left after exit to Ware north.

Hanbury Manor Hotel, Ware, Hertfordshire SG12 0SD
☎ 01920 487722   Ⓕ 01920 487692

H ⛲ ✕ **P**

🕐 24hrs

✎ Upgrade

CC All

➡ Ware

M 25   **A** 10

Cambridge 'Seat of Learning'

Cambridge is dominated by its University, (it has 31 colleges) and unlike Oxford it has no thriving hi-tech industry located close to it. There are many spires, and much architectural splendour, dusty bookshops and fascinating museums in winding streets lined with old houses and shops. It is best to be aware that this, as a University town, is a place of study and visiting is somewhat restricted. Also, for comparison, Oxford is better known for the arts and Cambridge for the sciences. Visit beautiful lawns and gardens, walk along the 'Backs' **A/B1**, or punt, (flat bottomed boat propelled by a pole) along the River Cam, under wonderful bridges. Highlights include, the Round Church **A1**, the Fitzwilliam Museum **B1**, and Sedgwick Museum of Geology **B2**. Wander, dream and most importantly soak in the cultural excesses and the romantic atmosphere. Interesting visits can be made from Cambridge to the working Bronze Age excavations at Flag Fen **A1**, and to Newmarket, the headquarters of British horseracing **A/B2**, or even Hemingford Grey **A1**, the exquisite house upon which Lucy Boston based her 'Green Knowe' books.

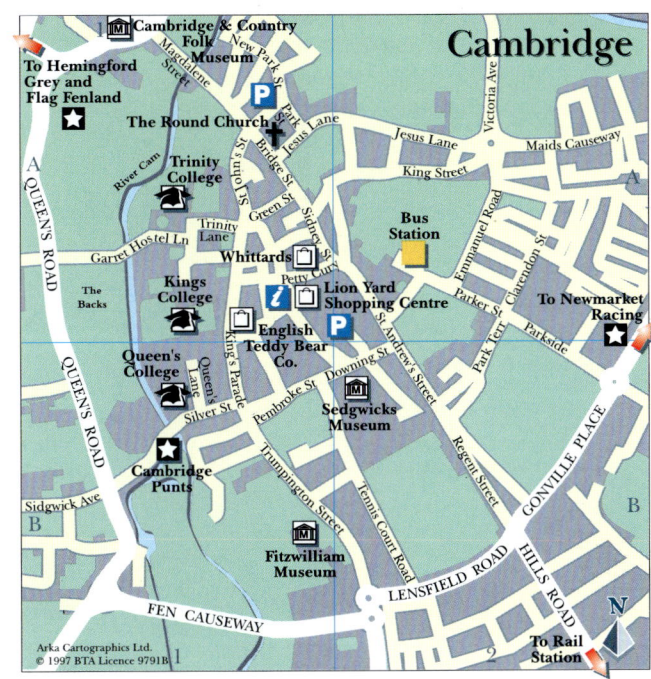

Tourist Information

Cambridge   ☎ 01223 322640

GF Cambridge

Hotels

Cambridge

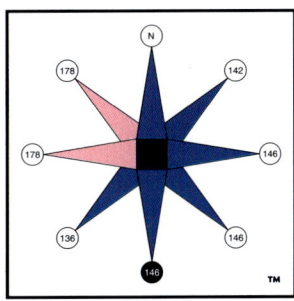

Distance from London

Cambridge 57 miles

1. Fitzwilliam Museum

The museum, now one of the finest in England, was the gift of Viscount Fitzwilliam, who in 1816 gave Cambridge University his paintings, rare books and a substantial amount of money to build a house in which to display them. The original buildings were opened in 1848, then major extensions took place between 1924 and 1975 to accommodate the growing collections as more benefactors contributed to the museum. The paintings include 'Old Masters' of exceptional quality and the numerous galleries are filled with every type of artistic treasure. Closed on Mondays.

Fitzwilliam Museum, Trumpington Street, Cambridge CB2 1RB
☎ 01223 332900

 10-5pm

⇄ ⤢ Cambridge

M 11 J13
www.cam.ac.uk
Map ref: B1

2. Cambridge & Country Folk Museum

The museum is housed in a 15th century timber-framed building which was an old inn (pub) for 300 years until 1934. In 1936, the museum opened and now has nine rooms displaying fascinating local artifacts that reflect the everyday life, since 1600 to the present day, of the people of Cambridge and the surrounding area. Closed on Mondays from October to March. Sundays, 2 - 5pm.

Cambridge & Country Folk Museum, 2/3 Castle Street, Cambridge CB3 0AQ
☎ 01223 355159

 10.30-5pm

⇄ ⤢ Cambridge

M 11 J13

Map ref: A1

3. Cambridge Punting and Cycle Hire

No visit to Cambridge is complete without a punt trip along the famous 'Backs'. Amidst spacious lawns and intimate gardens sit some of the loveliest colleges, including King's with its magnificent Chapel and Henry VIII's Trinity. You can choose to take a tour of the sights along with an English speaking guide, or you can hire a punt or cycle and explore by yourself. Weather permitting, punts or rowing boats, and cycles are available each day throughout the summer. Cycle Hire (rent) available at 61 Newham Road, Cambridge.

Cambridge Punting Co., The Steps, Silver Street Bridge, Cambridge
☎ 01223 502134

 9.30-6pm

 % 10%

⇄ ⤢ Cambridge

M 11 J13

Map ref: B1

4. Whittard of Chelsea

Whittard of Chelsea have been a specialist tea merchants since 1886. The store sells pure, single estate traditional and exotic large leaf teas as well as tea gifts and associated china. Look out for other Whittard of Chelsea shops throughout the guide. Offer applies to loose leaf teas and gift sets only. Sundays open from 12-5pm. An ideal English gift.

Whittard of Chelsea, 24 Petty Cury, Cambridge CB2 3NB
☎ 01223 461419

 9.30-6pm

% 10%

 MC Visa AmEx

⇄ ⤢ Cambridge

Map ref: A1

5. The English Teddy Bear Co.

Founded in 1991, the English Teddy Bear Company represents all things English and eccentric through the universally loveable teddy bear. The company exports worldwide and has over ten shops throughout England selling a wonderful range of bears that are waiting to find a new home and a new friend. Located in the town center. Open Sundays 11-5pm.

The English Teddy Bear Co., 1 King's Parade, Cambridge CB2 1SJ
☎ 01223 300908

🕐 10-6pm

% 10%

CC All CC

⇄ Cambridge

Map ref: A1

6. Newmarket National Horseracing Museum

Newmarket is the home of horseracing, as a short walk along the main street will show. The museum tells the history of horseracing, and contains many unique exhibits, such as the skeleton of Eclipse, one of the greatest horses ever, unbeaten in 18 races between 1769 and 1770. Eclipse is the ancestor of many of today's winners. There is an interesting art gallery and 'Hall of Fame', (the gallery is staffed by retired jockeys). Tours are available. Open March - October. Closed on Mondays, offer applies to museum and tours.

Newmarket National Horseracing Museum, 99 High Street, Newmarket, Suffolk CB8 8JL
☎ 01638 667333

 ★  P

🕐 10-5pm

 % 10%

⇄ Newmarket

M 11 J9   A 11/1304

Map ref: A/B2

7. The Manor at Hemingford Grey

The Manor, built in 1130 is the oldest continuously inhabited house in Britain, and on which Lucy Boston based the Green Knowe books. On view in the house are exquisite patchworks that she made. The typically English garden contains a collection of over 200 old roses, and many other scented plants, itis open daily. The house may be visited strictly by appointment, (letter, phone or fax) so be sure to book. 3 miles south east of Huntingdon.

The Manor at Hemingford Grey, Hemingford Grey, Huntingdon, Peterborough PE18 9BN
☎ 01480 463134   Ⓕ 01480 465026

 ⚘ ★ P

🕐 10-6pm

 % 25% off entry

⇄ Huntingdon   🚗

A 14

Map ref: A1

8. Flag Fen

Flag Fen is a unique and fascinating archaeological bronze age site, and interestingly you are visiting an on-going site. The center allows a fascinating glimpse into pre-history and the oldest wheel in Britain (10,000BC) was found here, preserved in peat. There is an excellent introductory guide to Flag Fen available. Tours take approximately 40 minutes, and the park contains rare animal breeds and reconstructed ancient landscapes. Leave the A1 for A1139, Boongate and the exit marked Flag Fen.

Flag Fen, Fourth Drove, Fengate, Peterborough PE1 5UR
☎ 01733 313414

★ P

🕐 10-4pm

⇄ Peterborough

A 1/1139

Map ref: A1

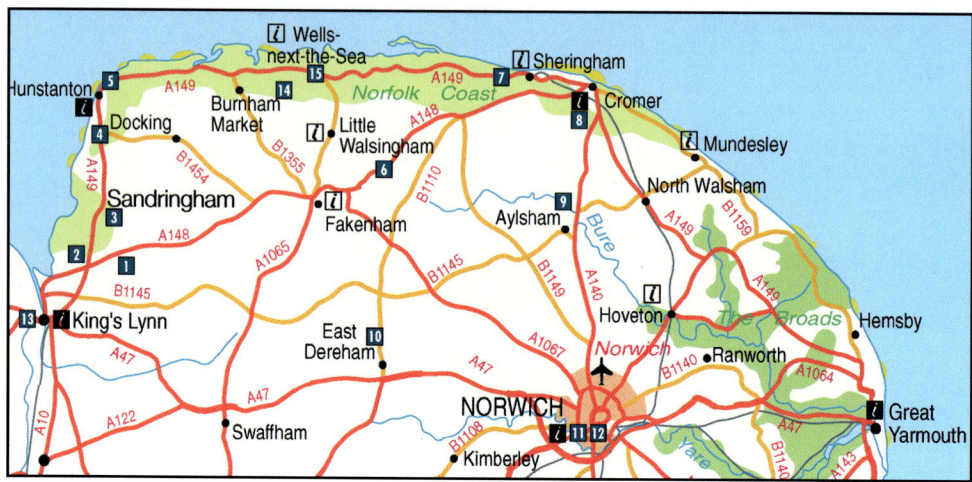

Royalty, Lavender and Outstanding Natural Beauty

King's Lynn in Norfolk **13**, (formerly known as Bishop's Lynn until King Henry VIII came to the throne), is a lively port and market town with many ornate buildings. You can stop by at the Congham Hall Hotel **1**, with its own extensive Herb Gardens open 'free' to visitors, en route north to Castle Rising **2**, where King Edward II kept his mother imprisoned for 30 years. On a more charming note, the next stop is the royal estate of Sandringham **3**, where the Royal Family spend Christmas. From here you can begin the journey around the coast, nearly all of which has been designated 'An Area of Outstanding Natural Beauty'. To Norfolk's stunning lavender fields and tearooms at Heacham **4**, past picturesque coastal towns and villages onto Holkham, Holkham Hall **14**, and Wells-next-the-Sea **15**. Visit any of the sandy beaches along the coast and take a swimming costume, (although it can be pretty cold). For a bit of variety drop south to visit the Thursford Collection **6**, or east to the Muckleburgh Collection **7**, otherwise continue around the coast to see Felbrigg Hall **8**. Leaving the coast and heading south to Blickling Hall **9**, you can catch a glimpse and insight into rural life at The Rural Life Museum **10**. Then, on to Norwich, the flourishing capital with its magnificent cathedral and numerous intriguing museums. For example, visit the unique Mustard Shop and museum **11**, and the superb collection at Sainsbury's Centre for Visual Art **12**.

[i] Tourist Information

Hunstanton	☎ 01485 532610
King's Lynn	☎ 01553 763044
Norwich	☎ 01603 666071

[GF] Norwich

Hotels

STAKIS HOTELS Norwich

[W] Great Yarmouth - King's Lynn

Norwich

Distance from London

Norwich 113 miles →

1. Congham Herb Garden

Congham Hall Hotel and Gardens. Entry to the gardens is free, and they are open between 2-4pm every day except Saturday at this country house hotel. The working herb gardens supply the hotel kitchen with over 700 varieties of herb. It is an enchanting garden, and afterwards you could visit the hotel for afternoon tea or perhaps make it a place to stay. A148 to Sandringham, then to Grimston, north east of Kings Lynn.

Congham Herb Garden,
Grimston, Kings Lynn, Norfolk
☎ 01485 600250   Ⓕ 01485 601191

 2-4pm

ⒸⒸ All

Kings Lynn

Ⓜ 11   Ⓐ 10/149

2. Castle Rising

A fine mid 12th century domestic keep, set in the center of massive defensive earthworks. Once palace and prison to Isabella, 'She-Wolf' dowager Queen of England. The keep walls stand to their original height and many are intact. Located 3 miles north east of Kings Lynn.

Castle Rising, Kings Lynn, Norfolk PE31 6AH
☎ 01553 631330

 10-6pm
 Page 67
 Kings Lynn 3miles

Ⓜ 11   Ⓐ 10/149

3. Sandringham House

The magnificent photograph is 'By gracious permission of Her Majesty the Queen'. This is an ideal opportunity to visit Sandringham, which is Her Majesty the Queen's 18th century country retreat set in 60 acres of beautiful grounds. The large stables are now a museum full of fascinating mementos. It is open from the end of March to the end of September. Located 8 miles north of Kings Lynn, not far from the old-fashioned but popular resort of Hunstanton. Follow the brown and white road signs.

Sandringham House, Sandringham, Kings Lynn,
Norfolk PE35
☎ 01553 772675

 11-4.45pm

 Kings Lynn

Ⓜ 11   Ⓐ 10/149   Ⓑ 1439

4. Norfolk Lavender

This is England's principal Lavender farm. In bloom from June to September, this is a remarkable sensory experience, an amazing sight and a wonderful aroma. Visit the display garden, fragrant meadow and shops where numerous English Lavender soaps, perfumes, oils etc. fill you with great gift ideas. The offer during the season is a free tour for 2, or alternatively a free cream tea from October to May. Artists should bring their sketch pads and cameras with them. On the A149 12 miles north of Kings Lynn.

Norfolk Lavender, Caley Mill, Heacham,
Norfolk PE31 7JE
☎ 01485 570384

 1-5pm

ⒸⒸ MC Visa
 Kings Lynn
 149

5. Hunstanton Sea Life Centre

Hunstanton Sea Life Centre overlooks the 'Wash' and has become a vital rescue center for many young seals. The outdoor seal pools are popular with visitors, but the center also houses Britain's original curved walkthrough underwater tunnel, plus an array of stunning marine life. 'Weird and Wonderful' gives an intriguing insight into the lifestyles and habits of some truly astonishing and curious creatures. With specimens such as the sharp-shooting archer fish, which attack their prey with water jets, there's something to amuse and amaze visitors of all ages.

Hunstanton Sea Life Centre, Southern Promenade, Hunstanton, Norfolk PE36 5BH
☎ 01485 533576

 10-5pm
 Coupon
 Kings Lynn
 149

6. The Thursford Collection

This is certainly a unique opportunity to discover another world of entertainment. A huge collection of fairground organs boom out amidst steam driven vehicles, and a marvellously well preserved old carousel, (on which you can ride for a small additional charge). The other highlight is the free live show on the Wurlitzer, (a giant organ, used to entertain at cinemas 'movie theaters' years ago). Many things happen spontaneously, but 12 noon is a good time to arrive, and allow one or two hours.

The Thursford Collection, Fakenham, Norfolk NR21 0AS
☎ 01328 878477

 12-5pm

Kings Lynn or Cromer
148

7. Muckleburgh Collection

If you have an interest in military life and machines, this is Britain's largest privately owned military museum. Set in the original World War II Navy, Army and Air Force Institutes (NAAFI) buildings are 16 working tanks, over 100 vehicles, guns and missiles. Tank demonstrations and 10 minute coastal rides in an American carrier, (it's bumpy!) take place every Sunday. Restaurant and shop. Open mid February to the end of October. On the A149 coastal road, 3 miles west of Sheringham.

Muckleburgh Collection, Weybourne Military Camp, Weybourne, Holt, Norfolk
☎ 01263 588210

 10-5pm

 Holt
11/149

8. Felbrigg Hall, Garden and Park

One of the finest 17th century houses in Norfolk, with its original 18th century furniture and Grand Tour paintings; there is also an outstanding library and interesting domestic wing. The Walled Garden has been restored, complete with dovecote, greenhouses and the traditional layout of herbaceous plants and fruit trees, including the national collection colchicums. There are extensive walks in the Great Wood and through the historic parkland with its church and lake. Located 2 miles south west of Cromer.

Felbrigg Hall, Garden and Park, Felbrigg, Norwich NR11 8PR
☎ 01263 837444

 Page 91
 Page 66
 Cromer
 148/140

9. Blickling Hall, Garden and Park

One of the greatest houses in East Anglia, Blickling dates from the early 17th century. Its collections include fine furniture, pictures and tapestries. A spectacular Jacobean plaster ceiling in the 130ft long gallery is particularly impressive. The ghosts of Anne Boleyn, (wife of Henry VIII) and Sir John Fastolfe (the inspiration for Shakespeare's Falstaff) are said to haunt the house and grounds. The gardens are renowned for massive yew hedges and magnificent herbaceous borders and contain a late 18th century orangery; the parkland has a lake and good walks. Located 15 miles north of Norwich.

Blickling Hall, Garden and Park, Blickling, Norwich, NR11 6NF
☎ 01263 733084

 Page 91
 Page 66
 Norwich
 A 140 **B** 1354

10. Norfolk Rural Life Museum

The Norfolk Rural Life Museum is set in over 20 acres of Norfolk countryside. The museum is housed in a former workhouse, with displays on village life, cottages, rural trades and crafts, farming and working on the land. 150 years of history, and also the chance to be part of farm life. There are often displays, such as milking the cows, (daily) and activities (depending on the time of year) such as haymaking, (June) harvesting, (August) and seed drilling, (October). Open from 12 noon on Sundays.

Norfolk Rural Life Museum, Gressenhall, Dereham, Norfolk NR20 4DR
☎ 01362 860294

 10-5pm

 Norwich
A 47 **B** 1110

11. The Mustard Shop Museum

The small museum, at the back of the Mustard Shop, is entirely devoted to the history of mustard. It illustrates the growing and processing for Colmans Mustard, England's leading mustard company, which began in 1814. The history of the Colmans family up to the present day includes displays, advertisements and posters through those many years, together with a celebrated collection of mustard pots. Colmans English Mustard is yellow in color, and is one of the strongest mustards, a favorite with roast beef and as an accompaniment to many other traditional dishes. Admission is free.

The Mustard Shop Museum, 3 Bridewell Alley, Norwich NR2 1AQ
☎ 01603 627889

 9-5.30pm

 Norwich
 A 47/140

12. Sainsbury Centre for Visual Arts

In this internationally renowned building, designed by Norman Foster, is housed the famous Robert and Lisa Sainsbury collection of world status art. The exhibition includes works by Picasso, Bacon, Henry Moore and Giacometti, set alongside non-western works of art. 15 minutes by taxi from Norwich Thorpe station, or take B 1108 off the A 47. Closed on Mondays.

Sainsbury Centre for Visual Arts, University of East Anglia, Norwich NR4 7TJ
☎ 01603 456060

 11-5pm

 Norwich
A 47 **B** 1108

Herbs, Brewing, Tea and Winemaking.

Somerleyton Hall **1**, has absolutely delightful 300 year old gardens and is situated at the Norfolk Broads **9**, 125 miles of open waterways which are eternally popular with boat enthusiasts. A little to the south at Lowestoft, is the Lowestoft Museum **2**, this modern holiday resort has 'The Ness', as Britain's most easterly point.

Heading south along the coast, and slightly inland, are wine making at Bruisyard Herbs and Winery **3**, and Framlingham Castle **4**, dating from 1100. Before dropping south to Ipswich **10**, you may wish to visit the unique Carter's Teapot Pottery Factory and shop **5**, at Debenham.

Ipswich, in Suffolk with its twelve medieval churches, has the Tolly Cobbold Brewery **6**, an experience for those of you who are interested in local beer brewing methods (and tasting), and Christchurch Mansion **7**. From there head to or through the Roman City of Colchester **11**. For those of you who prefer 'tea' to beer, beyond Colchester there is a Jam Museum **8**, owned by Wilkin and Sons, Jam makers by Appointment to Her Majesty the Queen, (tea, and their jams are served at the museum).

In between the towns of Ipswich and Colchester is Dedham **12**, John Constable country, (landscape painter 1776-1837) where he was so much inspired.

Map

Wymondham · A11 · A1075 · Attleborough · New Buckenham · B1113 · B1134 · Diss · A1066 · A143 · B1113 · SUFFOLK · Eye · B1117 · A140 · A1120 · Stowmarket · Lavenham · B1115 · A14 · Woodbridge · A1071 · Hadleigh · Dedham Vale · To Colchester · A134 · A137 · Manningtree · A120 · Harwich · Loddon · B1332 · Bungay · A143 · Waveney · Halesworth · B1116 · B1117 · A144 · A12 · Framlingham · Saxmundham · B1116 · B1079 · Wickham Market · A12 · IPSWICH · A14 · Bawdsey · Felixstowe · LOWESTOFT · A12 · Beccles · A145 · Southwold · B1122 · Thorpeness · Aldeburgh · A1094 · B1078 · Suffolk Coast and Heaths · Orford

i Tourist Information

Ipswich ☎ 01473 258070

Hotels

Colchester - Ipswich - Woodbridge

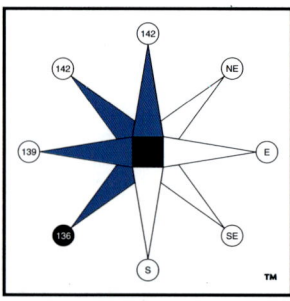

Distance from London

Ipswich 75 miles

1. Somerleyton Hall

The home of Lord and Lady Somerleyton, built in a mock-Tudor style on the foundations of a smaller Elizabethan mansion, parts of which still remain. The house contains many magnificent paintings and furnishings. The gardens are a real delight with a genuinely difficult maze, and a miniature railway. Located 5 miles north west of Lowestoft on the B1074. Open from April to September Thursdays and Sundays, and for July and August open Tuesday to Thursday, and Sundays.

Somerleyton Hall, Lowestoft, Suffolk NR32 5QQ
☎ 01502 730224

12.30-5.30

≷ ⬚ Lowestoft

B 1074

2. Lowestoft Museum

Lowestoft is the most easterly town in Britain and is a fishing port. You can wander past Victorian and Edwardian boarding houses, down to the quayside to look at the fishing boats. The Lowestoft Museum in a late 17th century house with Victorian additions, has a good display of fine 'Lowestoft' porcelain, made here in the 18th century. There are also exhibits on local domestic life, archaeology and the history of the area. Closed for lunch between 1-2pm.

Lowestoft Museum, Nicholas Everrit Park, Oulton Broad, Lowestoft, Suffolk
☎ 01502 565371

10.30-5pm

≷ ⬚ Lowestoft

A 12/146

3. Bruisyard Vineyard and Herb Centre

The Bruisyard Vineyard and Herb Centre is a picturesque vineyard with a herb and water garden. English wine has become increasingly popular as the number of producers increases, and the quality continues to improve. At this center they have produced the award winning Bruisyard St Peter English wine and herbs. There is also a restaurant and shop in this countryside location. Follow the brown and white signs from the A12. Offer applies to tour.

Bruisyard Vineyard and Herb Centre, Church Road, Bruisyard, Saxmundham, Suffolk IP17 2EF
☎ 01728 638281

10.30-5pm

 % £1 off

≷ Saxmundham

A 12

4. Framlingham Castle

This 12th century castle looks, from the outside, almost the same as when it was built. From the continuous curtain wall linking 13 towers, there are excellent views over Framlingham and the charming reed-fringed lake. At different times throughout its long history the castle has been a fortress, an Elizabethan prison, a poor house and a school.

Framlingham Castle, Framlingham, Suffolk IP13 9HZ
☎ 01728 724189

10-6pm

 % Page 67

≷ Wickham Market 6 miles ⬚ Ipswich

A 12 **B** 1116

5. Carter's Teapot Pottery

Carters Teapot Pottery is one of England's leading collectable teapot makers. You will be delighted and intrigueged by the various designs and individual teapots in different shapes and sizes. All of which visitors can see being made in the pottery, set in the beautiful village of Debenham. Situated at the southern end of the High Street in Debenham, follow the signs to the teapot pottery. Open from 2-5pm on Sundays between April and December.

Carter's Teapot Pottery, Low Road, Debenham, Suffolk IP14 6QU
☎ 01728 860475

 9-5.30pm
 5% (£50+)
 Stowmarket
A 1120 **B** 1077

6. Tolly Cobbold Brewery

Taste, smell and see the ingredients used to brew this local English Beer in the two brewhouses, old and new, on a guided tour of this magnificent Victorian Brewery. It's an entertaining experience. Tours run every day at 12 noon between May and September, and every tour visitor receives a complimentary beer, tea or coffee. The brewhouse also contains the country's largest collection of commemorative bottled beers (2,000+). Situated on the banks of the River Orwell at Ipswich. Follow brown and white signs for Brewery Museum.

Tolly Cobbold Brewery, Cliff Road, Ipswich, Suffolk IP3 0AZ
☎ 01473 231723   Ⓕ 01473 280045

 11-11pm
 Ipswich
A 12/14

7. Christchurch Mansion

The Tudor house built in 1548, where Elizabeth I stayed in 1561, is now a museum with the best collection of Constable's (John Constable 1776-1837) paintings outside of London. The gallery also has some fine pictures by the Suffolk-born painter, Gainsborough. The servants' wing contains the kitchen, with its copper pans, moulds and roasting spits, and the servants, hall with the table being laid for a meal. Some rooms still contain the original wallpaper of the 1730's and there are also displays illustrating the history of Ipswich, and the surrounding area. Sundays 2.30pm - 4.30pm.

Christchurch Mansion, Christchurch Park, Soane Street, Ipswich, Suffolk
☎ 01473 253246

 10-5pm
 Ipswich
A 1156

8. Wilkin and Sons

Home of England's famous 'Tiptree' preserves, jam and marmalade manufacturers by Appointment to Her Majesty the Queen. This is a fascinating museum of jam, the accompaniment to 'afternoon tea'. Admission is free, and although the factory tour is not available due to health and safety rules, the visitor center, on the original grounds of the jam factory, is full of information and explanation. Also open on Sundays in July and August. There is a delightful tea room with traditional waitress service. Offer is two cream teas for the price of one. Located about 12 miles south west of Colchester.

Wilkin and Sons, Tiptree, Essex CO5 0RF
☎ 01621 815407

 10-5pm
 Tea
 Witham
 A 12 **B** 1023

1	**2**	**3**	**4**
5	**6**	**7**	**8**
9	**10**	**11**	**12**
13	**14**	**15**	**16**
17	**18**	**19**	**20**
21	**22**	**23**	**24**
25	**26**	**27**	**28**
29	**30**	**31**	**32**
33	**34**	**35**	**36**

The West of England

THE WEST OF ENGLAND is England's foremost holiday region and has 650 miles of coastline, much of which is classed as an an 'Area of Outstanding Natural Beauty', an area that includes the National Parks of Dartmoor and Exmoor. If you know or have heard of places like Land's End, Bath, Stonehenge, and people like Sir Francis Drake, Sir Walter Raleigh, the legendary King Arthur, (Tintagel was his birthplace) and Agatha Christie, or Thomas Hardy, (one of Britain's best loved writers, (1840-1928) then you are thinking of this wonderful area. Wiltshire, approximately 2 hours journey time from London, is where the West Country begins, rich in ancient history, with picturesque villages nestling in valleys, rolling hills and dramatic scarp, (steep slopes). Wessex, which was the name given to the Anglo-Saxon kingdom centered on the West Country, is the area of Avon, Wiltshire, Somerset and Dorset.
The neo-classically inspired buildings in Bath, (Avon) a 'World Heritage Site', give way to the mellow brick and timber of Salisbury, (Wiltshire) whose cathedral has the tallest spire in England. This further contrasts with the rocky cliffs of Cheddar Gorge in Somerset, where Cheddar cheese and cider are produced, and again with the thatched flint and chalk cottages of Dorset, whose landscapes are still much as Thomas Hardy depicted.

Devon, (cream teas) and Cornwall, (smugglers) are geographically neighbours, but are very different in character. Cornwall is in the extreme southwestern part of England, sometimes called 'the toe', it has a varied, beautiful and often has a rugged coastline. The reason it is stark at its center, and some other areas, is that it was scarred by the result of some 4,000 years of copper mining. Devon is a land of lush pasture with exotic gardens. However, being aware that these counties each exist at a more leisurely speed than that of the bustling cities, provides you with a perfect opportunity to enjoy the local pace of life.

© BTA 1997
Produced by Cosmographics

The West of England

Access/Getting Around

From London
By Road
(page ref. 36,37)
The M25 London Orbital Motorway links the M4 in the west, to the M5 and A30, and M3 to the A303 in the south west.

By Rail
(page ref. 94,95)
A network of railway lines criss-cross most of the area but the faster services are those leading to and from London's Paddington and Waterloo stations.

By Coach
(page ref. 96,97)
Coaches run frequently from London Victoria to most key towns in the west including, Salisbury, Torquay, Plymouth, Penzance, Bodmin, Wells and Bath.

By Air
Internal scheduled flights to Airports at Bristol, Exeter, Bournemouth, Plymouth and Newquay.

Kingston Lacy

Lacock Abbey, Fox Talbot Museum and Village

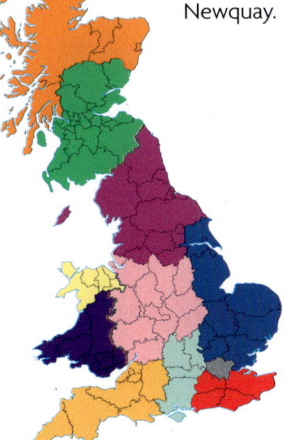

Stonehenge & Salisbury Cathedral

Long before you enter Salisbury in Wiltshire, the spire of Salisbury Cathedral **1**, will come into view, it is the tallest in England. This is an attractive town founded in 1220, and makes a good base for the surrounding attractions. There are good tearooms with individual charm, elegant grand houses like Mompesson House **2**, and interests such as the Salisbury and Wiltshire Museum **3**. The grid streets contain black and white half timbered houses. From Salisbury you can visit Old Sarum **5,** built by Iron Age people around 500BC, and taken over by settlers and conquerors through the ages, it gradually faded away with the founding of Salisbury. Continue north to Heale Gardens **6**, and on to Stonehenge **7**, begun about 3,000BC it is Europe's most famous prehistoric monument. The layout of the stones and circle almost certainly indicated the passing of the seasons. West of Salisbury is Wilton, renowned for its carpet manufacturing and Wilton House **4**. Further west is Stourhead **8**, which is certainly among the finest examples of landscape gardening in Britain, and also the lavish Longleat **9**, details of which appear on page 174. To the north east of Salisbury,

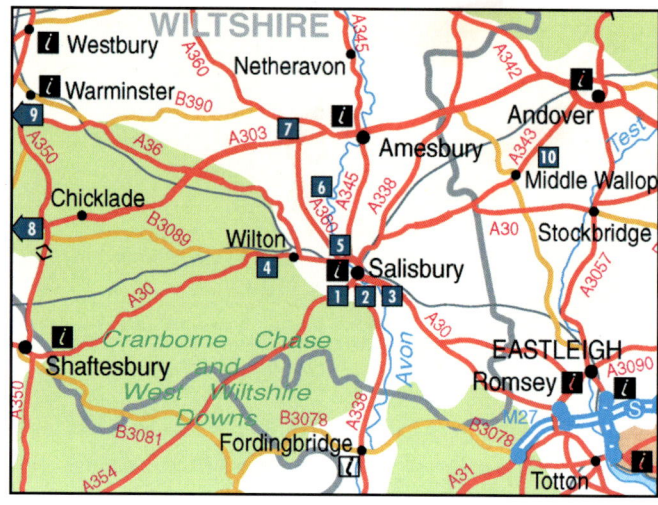

past many aerodromes, are 'The Wallops' **10**, a trio of picturesque villages, each with its own individual attraction. Over Wallop church has a 15th century font, Middle Wallop has a museum of Army Flying, and Nether Wallop's craftsmen make cricket bats from local willows.

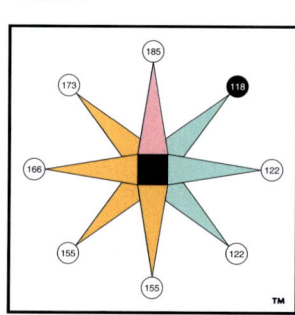

Tourist Information

Amesbury	☎ 01980 622833
Salisbury	☎ 01722 334956

GF Stonehenge from Salisbury

Hotels

Salisbury

Distance from London

Salisbury 96miles

The West of England

1. Salisbury Cathedral

Built between 1220-1265 this is a magnificent Gothic Cathedral. It has the tallest spire in England (404ft) built from 1285-1320 and this striking feature appears in many of Constable's paintings. Housed within the Chapter House is the original Magna Carta sent here for safekeeping in the 13th century. Look out for the ancient working clock in the north aisle. NBC card or guide for free entry to the Chapter House. Sunday hours 8-9am, 12-2.30pm and 4-6.30pm.

Salisbury Cathedral, Ladywell, 33 The Close, Salisbury
☎ 01722 555120

8-6.30pm.

Salisbury

M₃ A 30

2. Mompesson House

One of the finest 18th century houses in the Cathedral Close, containing notable plasterwork, an elegant oak staircase, fine period furniture, the important Turnbull collection of 18th century English drinking glasses and a china collection. The attractive walled garden is enclosed on one side by the great wall of the Cathedral Close. Located on the north side of Cloisters' Green, and only half a mile from Salisbury railway station. Please check opening times by telephoning first.

Mompesson House, The Close, Salisbury SP1 2EL
☎ 01722 335659

Page 91

Page 66

Salisbury

M₃ A 30

3. Salisbury & South Wiltshire Museum

Salisbury Museum is the home of the Stonehenge Gallery and winner of six awards for excellence. There is much for visitors to enjoy, with the fine archaeology collections, history of Old Sarum and Salisbury galleries, pictures, ceramics, the Wedgwood room, costume, lace embroidery and special exhibitions. The Museum, set in one of the finest buildings in the Cathedral Close, is located near to the cathedral. On Sundays in July and August, the museum is open from 2-5pm. The offer is a 2 for 1 entry.

Salisbury & South Wiltshire Museum, The King's House, 65 The Close, Salisbury SP1 2EN
☎ 01722 332151

10-5pm

Salisbury

M₃ A 30

4. Wilton House

Wilton House is one of England's 'Treasure Houses', and is set in beautiful parklands and gardens. Entering the house, you will be following in the footsteps of king's and queen's of England and Sir William Shakespeare. The Double Cube Room was used in the film 'Sense and Sensibility'. There are Wilton carpets and splendid furnishings throughout, all set against fine 17th century architecture. It is worth taking the Guide Friday tour, and their discount on entry. Open from 24 March to 2 November. *Ask for a 'Treasure Houses' discount leaflet, to receive discounts and free guides at their other 9 properties in the guide.

Wilton House, Wilton, Salisbury, Wiltshire SP2 0BJ
☎ 01722 743115

11-6pm

GF *Treasure Houses

Salisbury

M₃ A 30

1. Beaulieu

Beautiful Beaulieu, is a unique attraction, just over 80 miles from London. Here you can enjoy 800 years of English history and heritage, see Palace House, Lord Montagu's family home since 1538, walk amongst the gardens and by the Beaulieu River. Beaulieu Abbey, was founded in 1204 and although most of the buildings have been destroyed, much of the beauty and interest remains. The National Motor museum traces the history of motoring from 1894 to the present day. 250 vehicles are on display including World Record breakers, plus vintage and veteran cars. *Ask for a 'Treasure Houses' discount leaflet, to receive discounts and free guides at their other 9 properties in the guide.

Beaulieu, Beaulieu, Hants SO42 7ZN
☎ 01590 612345

 10-5pm

  £2 off 2nd Adult. *Treasure Houses

 Brockenhurst

 3/27 A 326

www.beaulieu.co.uk

2. Russell-Cotes Art Gallery & Museum

Sir Merton Russell-Cotes was the owner of the fashionable Royal Bath Hotel in Bournemouth. In 1854 he built East Cliff Hall as his home. This late Victorian mansion, on the top of East Cliff, is a wonderful building and houses magnificent Victorian paintings, furniture, porcelain and miniatures along with treasures from the Far East and many other fascinating collections. The Art Gallery is used to display pictures and sculpture and at times for temporary exhibitions. Located in the center of town, admission is free.

Russell-Cotes Art Gallery & Museum, East Cliff, Bournemouth BH1 3AA
☎ 01202 21009

 10-5pm

 Bournemouth

M 27 J1
www.russellcotes.gov.co.uk

3. Mummies, Teddy Bears and Dinosaurs!

Visit the ExpoCentre at Bournemouth for an exciting 2 for 1 offer at 3 attractions - The popular Teddy Bear Museum which offers a nostalgic look at the world's favourite bears and traces the 'teddy's' history from early this century to today. Dinosaur Discovery, providing a hands-on 'Dinosaur' experience through interactive displays and Mummies giving a unique insight into the mysteries of the ancient Egyptian Mummy. Choose any or all of these attractions at the ExpoCentre, located in the heart of Bournemouth at the top of the pedestrianized zone.

Mummies, Teddy Bears and Dinosaurs! Christchurch Lane, Bournemouth BH1 1NE
☎ 01202 293544

 10-5pm

 At 3 attractions

  Bournemouth

M M27 J1

4. Knoll Gardens

Within this compact 6 acre site are over 6,000 plant species from around the world. A woodland walk, water gardens, waterfall, stream and a spacious all-weather Visitor Centre, all contributed to the gardens winning a top landscape award. The Mediterranean style gravel garden, added in 1998 is an attractive new feature and for those of you who have caught the 'clotted cream tea' bug, rest your feet and have tea in the café. Open Wednesday - Sunday, from 10-3.30pm off season, (telephone to check times) and open daily until 5.30pm throughout the summer. Offer is 50% off second adult ticket.

Knoll Gardens, Hampreston, nr Wimborne, Dorset BH21 7ND
☎ 01202 873931

 10-5.30pm

 2nd Adult 50% off

 Wimborne

 31/347 B 3073

5. Kingston Lacy

A 17th century house, designed by Sir Roger Pratt for the traveler Sir Ralph Bankes, to replace his ruined family seat at Corfe Castle. The house was then altered by Sir Charles Barry (who also built the Houses of Parliament) in the 19th century. As well as an outstanding collection of paintings, the house contains an exhibition of Egyptian artefacts dating from 3,000BC. The house and garden are set in a wooded park with way marked walks now open to visitors. The park also boasts a fine herd of red Devon cattle. Located just over 1 mile west of Wimborne.

Kingston Lacy, Wimborne Minster, BH 21 4AE
☎ 01202 883402

 Page 91

 Page 66

Poole

B 3082

6. Poole Pottery

One of Dorset's leading attractions, including a self-guided factory tour to watch this famous tableware being made, incorporating a cinema, (movie theater) museum and Potter's Gameshow. In the Craft Village you can 'have a go' at throwing, (making) pots or painting plates, and even smashing pots! The factory shop sells quality seconds from Le Creuset, Dartington and Stuart Crystal as well. Follow signs to Poole Quay, the Pottery overlooks Poole Harbor. Opening times are extended in the Summer.

Poole Pottery, The Quayfront, Poole Quay, Poole BH15 1RF
☎ 01202 666200

  P

 10-4pm

 AmEx Visa MC

 Poole

A 31/348

7. Compton Acres

Discover and enjoy the delights of these nine different gardens of the world, added to which you are in an exquisite position overlooking Poole harbor. Gardens include Italian, Roman, Rock and Water, Woodland walk and interestingly a fine Japanese garden complete with Pagoda. You can also find a fabulous collection of bronze and marble statuary here. Located off the B3065 onto Canford Cliffs Road.

Compton Acres, Canford Cliffs Road, Poole, Dorset BH13 7ES
☎ 01202 700778

 P

 10-5pm

 Poole

A 35 B 3065

8. Brownsea Island

An atmospheric island of heath and woodland with wide views of the Dorset coast and accessible only by boat. The island includes a nature reserve leased to the Dorset Wildlife Trust. Boats run from Poole Quay, Swanage and Bournemouth. Brownsea has an intriguing history and was the site of the world's first scout camp, held by Lord Baden-Powell in 1908. The service from Sandbanks is under review and visitors should telephone (+44) 01202 707744 in advance to check the latest position. Visitors may land from their own boat at Pottery Pier at west end of island, accessible at all stages of the tide.

Brownsea Island, Poole Harbour, BH13 1EE
☎ 01202 707744

 Page 91

 Page 66

 Poole

A 31/350

9. Corfe Castle

Corfe Castle's majestic ruins guard the gateway to the Isle of Purbeck. The royal castle was an important stronghold, treasury and prison before being slighted by Parliamentary forces in 1646. The ruins retain many fine Norman and early English features and there are extensive views over the unique Purbeck landscape. There is a new interactive display at Castle View. Wareham Railway station is 4 miles from the castle.

Corfe Castle, Wareham BH20 5EZ
☎ 01929 481294

Page 91

 Page 66

⇄ Wareham

B 351

10. Hardy's Cottage

A small thatched cottage where the novelist and poet Thomas Hardy was born in 1840. It was built by his great-grandfather and has been little altered. Furnished by the National Trust. Hardy was trained as an architect and practised for some time. If you have or have had an opportunity to read his novels, they'll come to life when you are in this area. Located 3 miles north east of Dorchester. Dorchester station is 4 miles from the cottage. There may be a wait at busy periods.

Hardy's Cottage, Higher Bockhampton, near Dorchester DT2 8QJ
☎ 01305 262366

Page 91

 Page 66

⇄ Dorchester

A 35

11. Max Gate

The novelist and poet, Thomas Hardy, designed and lived in this house from 1885 till his death in 1928. It was here that he wrote, 'Tess of the d'Urbervilles', 'Jude the Obscure', and 'The Mayor of Casterbridge', as well as much of his poetry. The house contains several pieces of his furniture. The dining room, drawing room and garden are open. Located 1 mile east of Dorchester. See above, ' Hardy's Cottage'.

Max Gate, Alington Avenue, Dorchester, Dorset DT1 2AA
☎ 01305 262538

Page 91

 Page 66

⇄ Dorchester

A 35/352

12. Tutankhamun Exhibition

Tutankhamun Tomb, treasures and mummified body are recreated well in this exhibition of the world's great discovery of the pharaoh's ancient treasure. Located in the center of Dorchester, this is an insight into the discovery that has intrigued generations. Tutankhamun's tomb was discovered by Howard Carter and Lord Carnarvon in 1922, he had become pharaoh at the age of nine and had died by the age of 18, the dates of his life 1343 to 1325 BC. Also, use your NBC card to get a 2 for 1 offer at the Dinosaur Museum and Teddy Bear House, in High East Street, opposite this museum.

Tutankhamun Exhibition, High West Street, Dorchester DT1 1UW
☎ 01305 269571

 P

9.30-5.30pm

CC MC Visa

⇄ Dorchester

M 27 J1 or **M** 5 J25

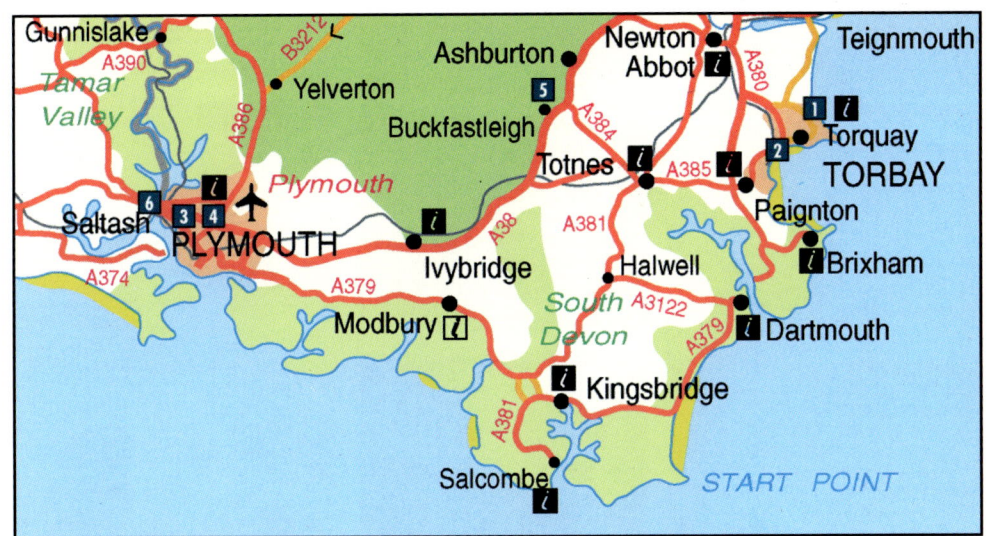

Agatha Christie Country

It was on the edge of Dartmoor National Park, that the setting for the 'Sherlock Holmes' novel 'Hound of the Baskervilles' took place. It is also on the edge of the Park that you will find the lofty 12th century Buckfast Abbey **5**, which took 6 monks 31 years to build.

Reaching across to the coast is Torquay, with its palm trees and warm climate, the area often referred to as the 'English Riviera'. This was the birthplace and home town of Agatha Christie, (1890-1976) who wrote the many 'Miss Marple and Hercule Poirot' books and, 'The Mousetrap', the longest running play in London. Walking around Torquay, you will be able to visit the two exhibitions devoted to her work, The Torquay Museum **1**, and The Agatha Christie Memorial Room at Torre Abbey **2**.

Continue around the coast to the naval city of Plymouth and the Hoe, (projecting ridge) dominated by the Plymouth Dome **3**, where you can experience Plymouth's historic past and present, and Smeaton's Lighthouse **4**. Many pioneering voyages of discovery began here. It is said that Sir Francis Drake calmly finished a game of bowls, as the invading Spanish Armada approached the port in 1588, then sailed his fleet out and defeated them. At Saltash **6**, over two short bridges, is the gateway to Cornwall.

Tourist Information

Plymouth	☎ 01752 264849
Torquay	☎ 01803 297428

GF Plymouth

Hotels

Plymouth - Salcombe - Torquay

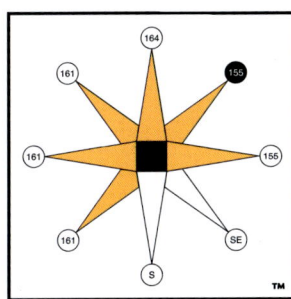

Distance from London

Plymouth 213 miles

The West of England

1. Torquay Museum

Founded in 1844, The Torquay Museum has displays of geology, natural history, local archaeology, social and local history. There is a large exhibition devoted to the life and work of Agatha Christie, famous for her detective stories. Located 250 yards along Torwood Street from the harbor. Sundays from 1 - 4.45pm. NBC discount applies in the shop.

Torquay Museum, Babbacombe Road, Torquay, Devon TQ1 1HD
☎ 01803 293975

🕐 10-4.45pm

% 10% (shop)

⇄ Torquay

M 5   A 38/380

2. Torre Abbey

Explore 800 years of history. From monastery, to country house, to the mayor's official residence today. Stunning pictures, historic rooms, and refreshments in the Victorian kitchen. Don't miss the Agatha Christie Room, containing personal possessions of the famous crime writer. Prisoners from the Spanish Armada, (1588) were held in the magnificent barn. Torre Abbey is located on Torquay seafront, next to the Riviera Centre. 10% discount when presenting your NBC card.

Torre Abbey, The King's Drive, Torquay, TQ2 5JX
☎ 01803 293593

🕐 9.30-6pm

% 10%

⇄ Torquay

M 5   A 3/380

3. Plymouth Dome

The award winning Plymouth Dome is a maritime history center that tells the story of the port of Plymouth and its impact on world history. A range of atmospheric reconstructions takes you on an extraordinary journey through time, through the sights and smells of Elizabethan Plymouth, on the voyages of Drake, Cook and the Pilgrim Fathers. 'Hands on' computers, TV and satellite technology add a view of the bustling modern harbor today. A short walk from Plymouth city center to the Hoe, follow signs. Open from 9am daily, but check closing times as they vary from 5.30pm to 7.30pm.

Plymouth Dome, The Hoe, Plymouth, Devon PL1 2NZ
☎ 01752 603300

⭐ P

🕐 9-5.30pm

% 20% on entry

⇄ Plymouth

A 38

www.plymouth.gov.uk

4. Smeaton's Tower

This famous landmark is an 18th century classic of civil engineering. Formerly the Eddystone Lighthouse built in 1759 on the Eddystone rocks 14 miles south west of Plymouth, it was replaced by a new lighthouse in 1882, and Smeaton's Tower was moved stone by stone to its present position on Plymouth Hoe, by the seafront. It has magnificent views over the city and Plymouth Sound. Offer combined with Plymouth Dome is free entry to the Tower. Open 28th March to 2nd November daily.

Smeaton's Tower, The Hoe, Plymouth P1 2NZ
☎ 01752 603300

⭐ P

🕐 10.30-4.30pm

 ⇄ Plymouth

A 38

www.plymouth.gov.uk

'Pirates' and England's Lands End.
King Arthur Country

Map 1 - To England's furthest point south, Land's End **9**, and furthest point west at St. Just **10**. On route to either are smugglers' coves and pirate villages. Traveling along the coast to Penzance there are the beautiful sub tropical Morrab Gardens **11**, influenced by the position at the seafront. Other attractions to visit are, St Michael's Mount **2**. St. Michael's Mount (300ft) was a 14th century castle and is now a Mansion, here many tales of 'King Arthur' can be seen and heard, also the Trinity House National Lighthouse Centre **3**. To the north of Penzance are the wonderful Tate Gallery **4**, a branch of the London Tate, and the Barbara Hepworth Museum, in the so called 'artists' fishing village of St. Ives **5**.

Map 2 - The charming village of Port Isaac **12**, has a stream running through it. Boats, nets and lobster pots fill the tiny harbor. Tintagel is the legendary seat of King Arthur. The castle **6**, and King Arthur's Hall is where his story is told, a story that has captured England's imagination for many centuries. Also, on the spectacular coast, you should visit Merlin's Cave at low tide, if your schedule allows. The Old Post Office **7**, and the magical waterfall at St. Nectan's Glen **13**, are amongst the other places to see. Approximately 12 miles inland, to the south east, is Brown Willy (1,375 ft) **14**, the highest point in Cornwall's 'capital', and

also on Bodmin Moor at Bolventor, is Jamaica Inn **8**, made famous by the romantic novelist Daphne du Maurier. There are many more 'West Country' choices on the NBCompass from here.

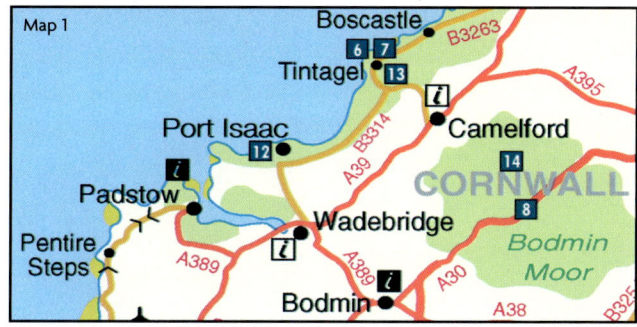

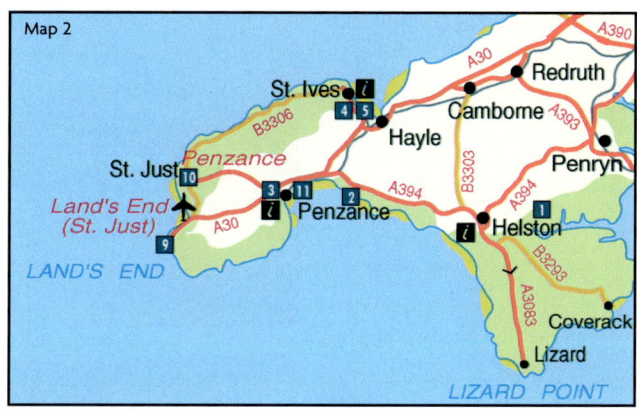

 **Tourist Information**

Bodmin	☎ 01208 76616
Penzance	☎ 01736 362207
St Ives	☎ 01736 796297

Hotels
St Ives

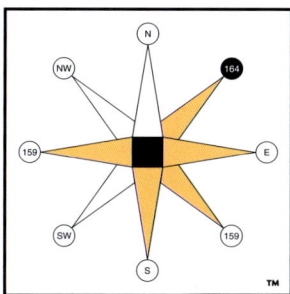

Distance from London

Penzance 281miles

The West of England

1. The National Seal Sanctuary

The National Seal Sanctuary is Europe's busiest rescue and rehabilitation center for injured, sick or abandoned grey seal pups, and also provides a permanent home amidst the glorious scenery of Cornwall's Helford estuary, for adult seals, retired sea lions and a host of other animals. Try and be there for feeding time which happens 4-6 times a day in the summer.

The National Seal Sanctuary, Gweek, Cornwall TR12 6UG
☎ 01326 221874

  P

 10-5pm

 Coupon

 Falmouth 7 miles

A 394

2. St. Michael's Mount

Originally the site of a Benedictine chapel, the spectacular castle on top of this famous rocky island dates from the 12th century. Approached by a causeway at low tide, the castle has magnificent views towards Land's End and The Lizard. Fascinating early rooms, an armoury, a rococo Gothic drawing room and, at the highest point, a 14th century church. Owing to narrow passages within the castle, please be warned that some delays may occur at the height of the season. On Sunday from June to September a short non-denominational service is held in the Castle Chapel at 11am, seating is limited.

St. Michael's Mount, Marazion, near Penzance TR17 OHT
☎ 01736 710507

 Page 91

 Page 66

 Penzance

A 394

3. The National Lighthouse Centre

A hands-on experience of maritime safety. Here you will find the world's finest collection of lighthouse equipment. An audio visual theater traces a brief history of early 'rock lights' and you can visit the reconstructed living quarters and the 4 tonne glass optic. It is located 500 yards from Penzance station in Wharf Road and is open daily.

The National Lighthouse Centre, Wharf Road, Penzance TR18 4BN
☎ 01736 360077

 P

 11-5pm

 MC Visa

 Penzance

 30

4. Tate Gallery

The Tate Gallery was opened in St Ives in 1993 and presents changing displays of work from London's Tate Gallery collections. Considering the setting in which you find this excellent gallery, this is a unique attraction, although the area is famous for its numerous resident local artists. Displays focus on the modern movement which St Ives is associated with. There are also temporary exhibitions and contemporary artists's projects. Closed on Mondays. NBC offer is valid between 11 April and 20 June.

Tate Gallery, Porthmeor Beach, St Ives, Cornwall TR26 1TQ
☎ 01736 796226

  P

 10-5.30pm

 St Ives

M 5   A 30

1. Clovelly Village

Visitors are attracted from around
this picturesque and unspoilt vill
steep cobbled streets, you may
Land Rover service which runs e
April to the end of October. Th
lead past flower bedecked cotta
century harbor. Donkeys, Sledge
hotels. A guided tour inside a fa
fisherman's cottage, an audio vis
and entry to the Kingsley Museu
the NBC offer. Near Bideford, ti
Barnstaple and A39 to Clovelly.

2. Hartland Abbey

Founded in 1157 in a beautiful v
from a spectacular Atlantic cov
to the north, a sheer 325ft cliff
Atlantic gales, it is quite spine-
the sea is calm. The Abbey was
to the sergeant of his wine cell
in family home contains specta
and murals. Other fascinations
furniture and porcelain, as well
dating from 1170 and early pho
museum and dairy, plus beauti
gardens. Offer is a reduced ent

3. Tapeley Park

Tapeley Park Gardens. An exc
Mary House with Italianate ga
stunning coastal views to the
Island. The terraces with long
many rare plants. Walled kitc
house and shell house. Light
Teas' are available here. Ope
March to 2nd November. Clo
Follow signs to park from A39

4. Dartington Crys

See how skilled craftsmen c
exquisite crystal in the uniqu
where viewing the glass blo
process is an amazing experi
process to watch. The Visite
through the fascinating hist
Dartington Crystal also offe
shopping at highly discount
north via A361/A39 and the
A30.

5. Barbara Hepworth Museum

Barbara Hepworth, (1903-1975) was one of the
foremost abstract sculptors of her time. Together
with Ben Nicholson they formed the nucleus of a
group of artists that made a major contribution to
the development of abstract art in Europe. St Ives
together with Newlyn, (south near Penzance) in
the 1920's became a place for aspiring artists, and
the Tate Gallery and Barbara Hepworth Museum
are now internationally renowned. The Barbara
Hepworth Museum presents the sculptor's work in
the house and garden where she lived and worked
for many years. Offer valid between 11 April to
20th June.

Barbara Hepworth Museum, Trewyn Studio,
Barnoon Hill, St Ives, Cornwall TR26 1AD
☎ 01736 796226

  P

 10.30-5.30pm

  St Ives

 M 5 **A** 30

6. Tintagel Castle

In a spectacular location, this is a place of
legends, and is associated with being King Arthur's
birthplace. However evidence suggests that the
castle dates from about 1150, much later. Today
fact and fiction are intertwined. Tintagel's
coastline, with the surf thundering against the
cliffs, and the waves breaking over Merlin's Cave ,
remains one of the most awe inspiring and
romantic places in Britain.

Tintagel Castle, Tintagel, Cornwall
☎ 01840 770328

 P

 10-6pm

 % Page 67

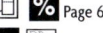 Bodmin

 A 39 **B** 3263

7. Tintagel Old Post Office

A small and fascinating 14th century stone house
built to the plan of a medieval manor house, with
a large hall. It was used in the 19th century for
nearly fifty years as the letter-receiving office for
the district and is now restored to that period
and function. Located in the center of the village,
it has a general shop attached.

   P

 Page 91

 Page 66

 Bodmin

 **A** 39 **B** 3263

Tintagel Old Post Office, Tintagel PL34 0DB
☎ 01840 770024

8. Jamaica Inn

The 'passport' ticket includes Mr Potter's Museum
and the Du Maurier Room as well as Jamaica Inn,
from where Daphne du Maurier drew inspiration
for her novel of the same name. This is smugglers'
territory and having read Du Mauriers novels you
will immediately feel the atmosphere. Located
mid way between Bodmin and Launceston off the
A30. Accommodation is also available. The offer is
25% off the passport ticket price. Open until 4pm
on Sundays.

Jamaica Inn, Bolventor, Launceston, Cornwall
PL15 7TS
☎ 01566 86250

  **P**

 10-5pm

 % 25%

 Bodmin

 A 30

The West of England

Clovelly 'The Most Cha[rming] Village in Devo[n]'

Because of its charm[ing] Village **1**, is a very po[pular] busy attraction. The[...] clings to a steep hill [...] down to a sheltere[d...] The narrow cobble[s...] are lined with prett[y...] covered cottages. D[...] sledges are the mai[n...] but you can get a c[...] the bottom should [...] seem too daunting [...] visiting 4 miles to t[...] Clovelly, is Hartlan[d...] or head east throu[gh...] of Bucks Mills **5**, to[...] **3**, with its exquisit[e...] gardens, each facin[g...] Then if you travel [...] Bideford **6**, a med[...] with 24 arches cro[ss...] Torridge and leads [...] enchanting Rosem[...] **7**, and nearby Da[...] Crystal **4**. Here yo[u...] to see how Glass[...] carried out from [...] viewing galleries [...] the craftsmen.

Whilst we are in [...] England, here is a [...] introduction to '[...] Devon is perhaps [...] acclaimed area f[or...] 'Cream Teas' and [...] ingredient is Dev[on...] cream, not place[...] has happened) b[...] scones with lots [of...] jam – be warne[d...] but calorific!

England's Smallest City and 'The Home of Cheddar Cheese'

England's best loved and most famous cheese is Cheddar Cheese and you can taste it and see it being made at Chewton Cheese Dairy **1** . On the other side of the Mendip Hills is the awesome Cheddar Gorge **2**, which was carved into the Mendip Hills by the fast flowing streams of the Ice Age. This is where the name of Cheddar Cheese originated. Staying on this side and heading south is Wookey Hole Caves and Papermill **3**, with its network of primeval caves and underground rivers. The caves are over a million years old, and in the Heritage Centre is displayed a 9,000 year old human skeleton. You don't have to stay there for that long! Next, is Wells in Somerset **4**, England's smallest city. It was named after St Andrew's Well, the sacred spring that bubbles up from the ground near Bishop's Palace. There is a beautiful cathedral, built around 1230, and many other fine buildings. Wells religious leadership as the 'Office of the Bishop' was toppled by nearby Bath. South of Wells is Glastonbury **5**, where King Arthur is said to be buried amongst the abbey ruins. Somerset is famed for its cider, (an alcoholic apple drink). Visit the Somerset Rural Life Museum **6**, to see how it's made.

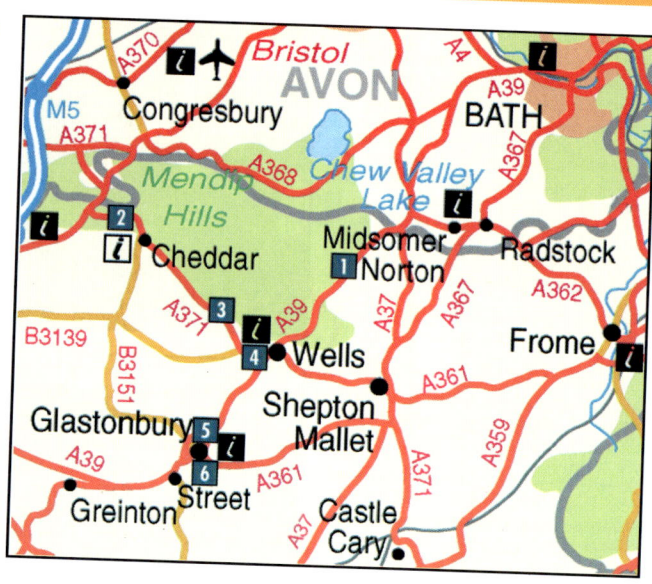

Tourist Information

Cheddar Gorge ☎ 01934 744071
Glastonbury ☎ 01458 832954
Wells ☎ 01749 672552

Hotels
Wells

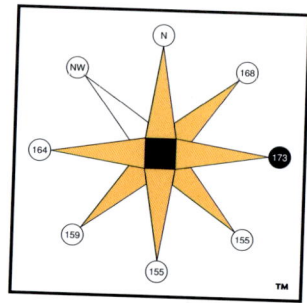

Distance from London

Wells 127miles

1. Chewton Cheese Dairy

An ideal way to watch traditional award winning cheese being made on Priory Farm near Bath. Much of the work is carried out by hand in creating Britain's much loved Cheddar Cheese, and this is one of the few dairies left that matures its cheese in a temperature controlled store for up to 18 months. Naturally the tearooms and restaurant have some delightful choices. The offer applies when you join a guided tour, although video presentations run all day. No cheese making on Thursdays and Sundays

Chewton Cheese Dairy, Priory Farm, Chewton Mendip, Bath, Somerset BA3 4NT
☎ 01761 241666

  P

 9-4pm

CC MC Visa

 Bath

A 39

2. Cheddar Showcaves & Gorge

The gorge itself is a narrow winding ravine with limestone rocks rising almost vertically on either side to a height of 400ft. The Cheddar Gorge has many attractions including an open top tour bus, see the two Cheddar Showcaves, the 'lookout' tower and Jacob's Ladder, as well as the bracing cliff top walks. This is one of the leading Somerset attractions and the offer is 10% discount at almost half of the shops in the Gorge, please look for the NBC signs and show your card and guide.

Cheddar Showcaves & Gorge, Cheddar, Somerset BS27 3QF
☎ 01934 742343

 P

 10-5pm

 % 10% off at 9 shops

 Weston-super-Mare

B 3135

3. Wookey Hole Caves

These are almost certainly Britain's most spectacular showcaves, steeped in ancient history and legends. In the first chamber of the caves, as legend has it, the 'Witch of Wookey' turned to stone. Prehistoric people are believed to have inhabited the caves 60,000 years ago. There is a also a Victorian papermill with traditional paper making, where paper has been made by hand since the 17th century. An old penny pier amusement arcade and a magical mirror maze add entertainment to the visit. Follow the brown and white road signs.

Wookey Hole Caves, Wookey Hole, Wells, Somerset
☎ 01749 672243

 P

 10-5.pm

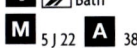 Bath

M 5 J 22 A 38/371
www.wookey.co.uk

4. Wells Cathedral

Wells, a peaceful market town, is named after St Andrew's Well, the spring that bubbles up from the ground near the 14th century Bishop's Palace. Famous for the magnificent cathedral which was begun at the end of the 12th century, the west front features 365 medieval statues of kings, knights and saints, many of which are life sized. There is an attractive cathedral clock and an impressive flight of steps leading up to the Chapter House. Wells' other attractions are the Bishop's Palace, Wells Museum, and the Vicars' Close which was built in the 14th century for the Vicars' choir, and is one of the oldest and most complete streets in Europe.

Wells Cathedral, The Close, Wells, Somerset BA5 2PA
☎ 01749 674483

 P

 7.30-6pm

 Bath

M 4/5 A 4/39

Bath 'Britain's Spa Town'

Bath is a compact city, which makes practically everything within easy walking distance. There are free walking tours from the Abbey Church Yard **B2**, at 10.30am every day run by volunteers. The tours last 1½ -2 hours and can also be taken in the afternoons, but check the times in the yard. There is a very good city guide, (brochure) available at the Tourist Information Centre **B2**. The Building of Bath Museum **A1/2**, is an excellent starting point if you are exploring by yourself, and although walking might be best, a good introduction to the city, (which includes some extra discount coupons) is the Guide Friday bus tour.

Bath was England's first spa town, with the bubbling pool of water at the heart of the 1st century Roman Baths **B1/2**, which regained its fame when Queen Anne, (1702-1714), visited from London. Georgian architects designed many of the magnificent buildings which can be seen today, to highlight but a few, Royal Crescent **A1**, The Circus **A1**, and Pulteney Bridge **A2**.

Many of the houses bear plaques to show the famous people that lived or stayed here, for example, Charles Dickens, and Jane Austen who lived at 4 Sydney Place from 1801 to 1804. Some of the other key attractions to take in are Bath Abbey **B2**, the Pump Rooms (at the Baths) **B1/2**, Sally

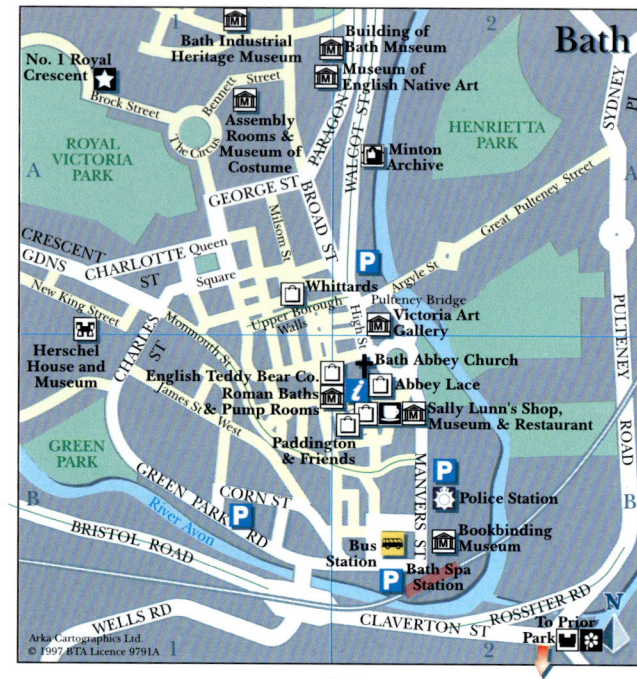

Lunn's House (1482) **B2**, and Mr Bowler's Business **A1**. Bath is also a unique place to shop, with many specialist stores that contribute to the pleasure of being in this world heritage site. The surrounding area is enchanting, choose from the various options on your NBCompass.

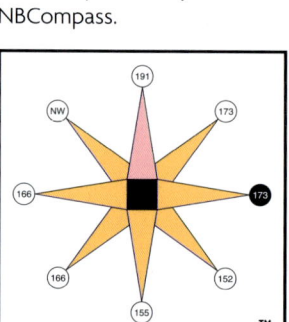

i **Tourist Information**

Bath   ☎ 01225 477101

GF Bath

Hotels

STAKIS HOTELS Bath

⌘ Bath

Distance from London

Bath 116miles ➡   LONDON

1. Roman Baths

The first stop on a visit to Bath is the Roman Baths Museum, surrounding the hot springs where the city began and which are still its heart. Here you can see one of the country's finest ancient monuments, the great Roman temple and bathing complex, built almost 2,000 years ago and still remarkably complete. Discover the everyday life of the Roman spa and see ancient treasures from the Temple of Sulis Minerva and many other objects recovered from the Sacred Spring. This is where they were thrown as offerings to the Gods. Combined ticket available to Baths and Museum of Costume.

Roman Baths, Stall Street, Bath BA1 1LZ
☎ 01225 477785

 9-6pm

 Bath

www.romanbaths.co.uk

Map ref: B1/2

2. The Pump Room

The Grand Pump Room, overlooks the King's Spring, with its elegant interior. Admission is free, and visitors can 'sample' (not necessarily enjoy!) a glass of spa water drawn from the fountain, or have a traditional Pump Room tea, morning coffee or lunch. Musical accompaniment is by the Pump Room Trio. Exhibits of interest include a longcase clock, presented to the Pump Room in 1709, two sedan chairs, many portraits, and a statue of 'Beau' Nash, a famous 'Master of Ceremonies'.

The Pump Room, Stall Street, Bath BA1 1LZ
☎ 01225 477785

 9-6pm

 Bath

Map ref: B1/2

3. Bath Abbey Church

The splendid Abbey stands at the heart of the old city in the Abbey Church Yard. It is in the piazza here that free walking tours begin. Amongst the unique architectural features are stone angels climbing Jacob's Ladder to heaven, and according to legend the design of the church was given by God to Bishop Oliver King in a dream that has been immortalized in the wonderful eccentric carvings on the west front. Entry is free but a donation would be welcome.

Bath Abbey Church, Abbey Churchyard, Bath
☎ 01225 422462

 7.30-6pm

 Bath

Map ref: B2

4. Sally Lunn's House

Relax in the charming atmosphere of the oldest house in Bath, where Sally Lunn came in the 1680's, and established her baking as a favorite of fashionable society. Today enjoy lunch in the restaurant, or a delicious Sally Lunn bun, one of Bath's renowned delicacies, still made by hand and baked on the premises to the original recipe. NBC free entry is to the museum in the cellars, where you can see the original kitchen and ovens. Sunday 12-11pm

Sally Lunn's House, 4 North Parade Passage, Bath BA1 1NX
☎ 01225 461634

 10-11pm

 Free (Museum)

 Bath

Map ref: B2

5. The English Teddy Bear Co.

Founded in 1991, the English Teddy Bear Company represents all things English and eccentric through the universally loveable teddy bear. The company exports worldwide and has over ten shops throughout England selling a wonderful range of bears that are waiting to find a new home and a new friend. Located in the town center by the Abbey. Open Sundays 11-5pm.

The English Teddy Bear Co., 8 Abbey Churchyard, Bath BA1 1LY
☎ 01225 338655

 P

 10-6pm

 10%

 All

Bath

Map ref: B1/2

6. Paddington Bear and Friends

A small Paddington Museum is tucked inside this delightful shop. The shop sells toys, books and gifts featuring characters from English children's books such as Winnie-the-Pooh, Peter Rabbit and Paddington Bear. There is a free mail order catalogue and the shop is located just 50yds south of Bath Abbey, look for the Paddington sign. Sunday open from 11.30-4.30pm. A free walking tour of Bath is available from Bath Abbey Courtyard nearby, (look on the Bath introduction page).

Paddington Bear Shop, Abbey Street (off York Street) Bath, BA1 1NN.
☎ 01225 463598

 P

 9.30-5.30pm

 10%

 AmEx Visa MC

 Bath

Map ref: B2

7. Abbey Lace

Abbey Lace is a unique shop selling a wide range of exquisite lace tableware and gifts. These include pictures, jewellery, handkerchiefs, bookmarks, paperweights, greeting cards and much more. There is a shipping facility and VAT (Tax) free service. Offer applies on production of the NBC card and guide. Located opposite the Roman Baths and Tourist Information Centre. Open Sundays from 11-5.00pm.

Abbey Lace, 7a York Street, Bath BA1 1NG
☎ 01225 463030

 P

 9.30-5.30pm

 10%

 Visa MC

 Bath

Map ref: B2

8. Bath Assembly Rooms

Designed by John Wood the Younger in 1769. The Rooms were bombed in 1942, but are now restored to their Georgian splendour and let to Bath and North East Somerset Council. The Museum of Costume, (not National Trust) is housed in the basement. Located east of The Circus. Bath Spa station is located less than a mile from the Assembly Rooms. Open Sundays 11-5pm

Bath Assembly Rooms, Bennett Street, Bath BA1 2QH
☎ 01225 477785

   P

 Page 91

 Page 66

 Bath

 M 4 **A** 4

Map ref: A1

9. Museum of Costume

The museum has one of the most prestigious and extensive collections of its kind. Displays include some two hundred dressed figures illustrating the changing styles in fashionable dress for men, women and children from the late 16th century to the present day. The modern collection contains work by some of the world's top designers. Combined ticket available to Roman Baths and Museum of Costume. Free audio guide available.

Museum of Costume, Assembly Rooms, Bennett Street, Bath BA1 2QH
☎ 01225 477785

 10-5pm

 Bath
 4 4
www.museumofcostume.co.uk
Map ref: A1

10. Building of Bath Museum

The Building of Bath Museum, housed in the Countess of Huntingdon's Chapel, reveals the story behind the development of the Georgian city. As Bath is a World Heritage Site, it is interesting to discover how the buildings were designed, built, decorated and lived in during the 18th century. Exhibits include full size reconstructions and a series of spectacular models, including one of the city with push-button illumination. A great introduction to the city of Bath. Open mid February to 1st December, closed Mondays. Located east of No.1 Royal Crescent (signposted from the center).

Building of Bath Museum, The Huntingdon Chapel, The Vineyards, The Paragon, Bath BA1 5NA
☎ 01225 333895

 P
 10.30-5pm
 % 50p off admission
 Bath
M 4 J18

Map ref: A1

11. No. 1 Royal Crescent

The Royal Crescent was started in 1767 by John Wood the Younger, and was part of a master plan visualised by John Wood the Elder. Once described as 'the highest point of Palladian achievement in Bath'. No.1 was presented to the Bath Preservation Trust in 1968, and has been carefully restored using materials only available in the 18th century. This shows how a grand town house of late 18th century Bath, furnished with paintings, furniture, porcelain and glass of the period, would have looked.

No. 1 Royal Crescent, Bath BA1 2LR
☎ 01225 428126

 P
 10.30-5pm

 Bath
M 4 A 4

Map ref: A1

12. Bath Industrial Heritage Centre

This is the fascinating story of a local family firm, who made such concoctions as orange Champagne. The reconstructed Victorian engineering works has been lovingly recreated to allow a look at this intriguing corner of the city's industrial past and shows how Mr Bowler and his family would have tackled any job, great or small. An emporium upstairs has a soda fountain and sells ice cream and period gifts. It is located just 15 minutes walk north of the city center past the Assembly Rooms which are signposted. Between October 31st - March 31st the museum is only open on Saturdays and Sundays.

Bath Industrial Heritage Centre, Julian Road, Bath BA1 2RH
☎ 01225 318348

 10-5pm

 Bath
M 4 J18

Map ref: A1

13. Victoria Art Gallery

The gallery houses a permanent collection of British and European Art from the 17th century to the present day. It is situated near to the charming Pulteney Bridge. The highlights of the collection include Thomas Malton's famous topographical views of Bath and Turner's 'West Front of Bath Abbey'. The decorative arts are also represented with a fine collection of English drinking glasses, and the Horstmann collection of watches. The gallery has an excellent programme of temporary exhibitions.

Victoria Art Gallery, Pulteney Bridge, Bath BA2 4AT
☎ 01225 477231

 P

 10-5.30pm

⇄ Bath

M 4 A 4

Map ref: A2

14. Archive Print Collection – Minton

Here you will find, beautifully presented in hand finished frames, open edition limited prints, taken directly from original art, design drawings and rare source material held in Royal Doulton's Minton Archive. This gallery/shop is a rare find and well worth a visit whilst in Bath. Closed on Sunday. Spend over £50 and receive a free print by presenting your NBC card.

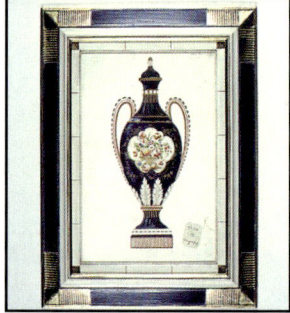

Archive Print Collection, 78 Walcot Street, Bath BA1 5BG
☎ 01225 422909

 P

 9.30-5.30pm

£50 +

⇄ Bath

Map ref: A2

15. Whittard of Chelsea

Whittard of Chelsea have been a specialist tea merchants since 1886. The store sells pure, single estate traditional and exotic large leaf teas as well as tea gifts and associated china. Look out for other Whittard of Chelsea shops throughout the guide. Offer applies to loose leaf teas and gift sets only. Sundays open from 12-5pm. An ideal English gift.

Whittard of Chelsea, 10 Stall Street, Bath BA1 1QE
☎ 01225 428684

 P

 9.30-6pm

% 10%

 MC Visa Am Ex

⇄ Bath

Map ref: A1

16. Prior Park Landscape Garden

Beautiful and intimate 18th century landscape garden created by Bath entrepreneur Ralph Allen (1693-1764) with advice from the poet Alexander Pope and Lancelot 'Capability' Brown. Sweeping valley with magnificent views of the city of Bath. Palladian Bridge and lakes. Major restoration of the garden continues. Prior Park College, a co-educational school operates from the mansion (not National Trust). *To thank NT member visitors who use public transport a £1 discount coupon is given with a variety of uses.

Prior Park Landscape Garden, Ralph Allen Drive, Bath BA2 5AH
☎ 01225 833422

 Page 91

 Page 66

⇄ Bath

A 4

Map ref: B2

Around Jane Austen's Home in Bath.

The city of Bath provided Jane Austen with much of the material for her books, for example, 'Persuasion' and 'Northanger Abbey', so it is apt that many of the recent film locations have been in and around Bath.

North of Bath is Dyrham Park **1**, where part of 'Remains of the Day' was filmed. Nearby is Castle Combe **5**, the 'prettiest village in England', and here Upper Manor House was chosen to be Dr. Dolittle's house in the 1967 film. Just 10 miles from Bath, to the east, are Bowood House **2**, and Lacock Village. 'Pride and Prejudice' was part filmed at Lacock Abbey and the Fox Talbot Museum **3**. The inventor W.H.F. Talbot, in September 1840, produced the positive/negative film process and hence became known as, 'The Father of Modern Photography'.

If you are looking for a unique 'Bed and Breakfast' experience around Bath, try the Fosse Farmhouse **6**, Caron Cooper offers both English hospitality and cooking. Overnight visitors are offered a free afternoon 'cream tea' on arrival. Telephone (UK) 01249 782286 for reservations. Traveling 12 miles to the south of Bath, you arrive at Longleat House and Safari Park **4**, here you will find the world's longest maze. Continue south another 6 miles to Stourhead **7**, a magnificent

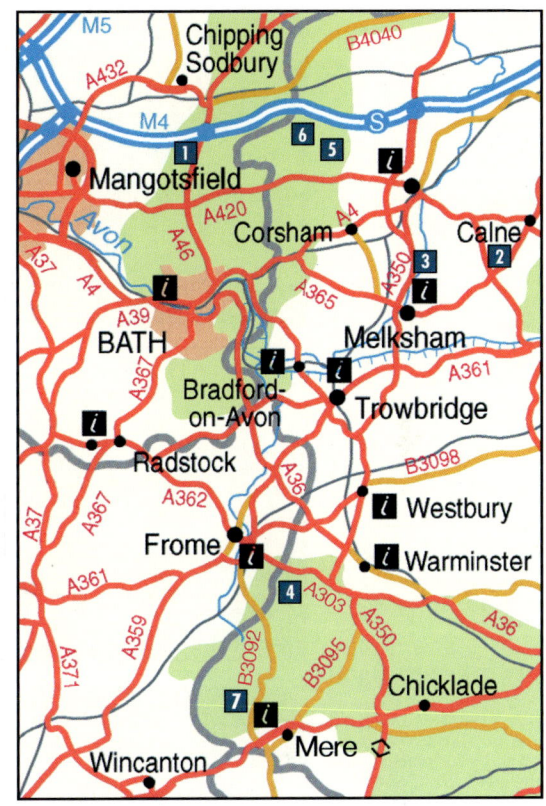

house with one of the finest examples of 18th century landscape gardening in Britain.

Tourist Information

Bath	☎ 01225 477101

Hotels

STAKIS HOTELS Bath

Bath - Frome

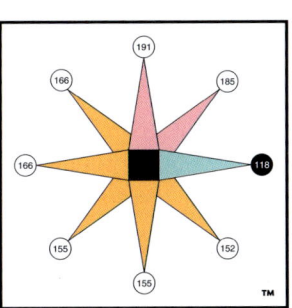

Distance from London

Bath 116 miles

1. Dyrham Park

Built for William Blathwayt, Secretary at War and Secretary of State to William III, between 1691 and 1710. The rooms have been little changed since they were furnished by Blathwayt, and their contents are recorded in his housekeeper's inventory. Surrounding the house, the ancient parkland, with herd of fallow deer, overlooks the Severn Valley. Featured in the award winning film 'Remains of the Day'. Due to the fragile nature of the contents, it is necessary to control the light levels in certain rooms. 2 for 1 offer does not apply at weekends. Located just 8 miles north of Bath.

Dyrham Park, near Chippenham SN14 8ER
☎ 0117 937 2501

 Page 91

  Page 66

 Bath

 4 J18 46

2. Bowood House

Bowood is the magnificent family home of the Earl and Countess of Shelburne, designed by Robert Adam in the 18th century. It stands in glorious parkland with sloping lawns stretching away from the house to the lake beyond. Splendours within the park include the Cascade, Doric Temple and terraced rose garden. The interior of the house contains a remarkable collection of family heirlooms and works of art. Bowood is open from April 1st to Oct 31st. A separate area of Rhododendron walks is open from mid Aprilto- early June.

Bowood House, Derry Hill Village, near Calne, Wiltshire SN11 0LZ
☎ 01249 812102

 11-6pm

 Chippenham

 4 J16/17

3. Lacock Abbey, Fox Talbot Museum and Village.

The abbey was founded in 1232 and converted into a country house c. 1540. The fine medieval cloisters, sacristy, chapter house and monastic rooms are largely intact. There is a 16th century stable courtyard with half-timbered gables, clockhouse brewery and bakehouse. The museum of photography commemorates the achievements of William Fox Talbot, (1800-1877) inventor of the modern photographic negative, who lived in the abbey. His descendants gave the abbey and village to the National Trust in 1944. The village dates from the 13th century and has many limewashed half-timbered and stone houses, and a 14th century tithe barn.

Lacock Abbey, Fox Talbot Museum and Village., Lacock, near Chippenham SN15 2LG
☎ 01249 730227

 Page 91

 Page 66

 Chippenham

 350

4. Longleat

The magnificent Elizabethan house was completed in 1580 and has been the home of the Thynne family ever since. Set in a beautiful parkland, the house contains many treasures, including fine paintings, tapestries, wonderful ceilings and famous murals. The parkland has a Safari Park containing the 'Lions of Longleat', an extremely long maze, and a 'Postman Pat', (a popular childrens' book and television series) village plus many more attractions. Located 20 miles north of Salisbury and 18 miles south of Bath. *Ask for a 'Treasure Houses' discount leaflet, to receive discounts and free guides at their other 9 properties in the guide.

Longleat, Warminster, Wiltshire BA12 7NW
☎ 01985 844400

 10-6pm

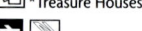 *Treasure Houses

 Warminster

 362

Photo Journal ✎

Notes for 36 exposure film

1	**2**	**3**	**4**
5	**6**	**7**	**8**
9	**10**	**11**	**12**
13	**14**	**15**	**16**
17	**18**	**19**	**20**
21	**22**	**23**	**24**
25	**26**	**27**	**28**
29	**30**	**31**	**32**
33	**34**	**35**	**36**

Heart of England

THE HEART OF ENGLAND Encompasses what makes Britain so special, its variety. More than any other region it takes its character from the landscape, and a quick look at some of the famous people and places in the region will immediately illustrate that point.

William Shakespeare was born in Stratford-upon-Avon. DH Lawrence a renowned literary figure whose novels were set in Nottinghamshire, (also famous for Robin Hood), and Jane Austen (Derbyshire). The Potteries, and such names as Wedgwood and Royal Doulton at Stoke-on-Trent. The Cotswolds, 50 miles of limestone hills, their romantic villages, buildings and the enchanting surroundings. Ironbridge in Shropshire, birthplace of the Industrial Revolution and a 'World Heritage Centre'. Hereford Cathedral, where the oldest map of the world is housed. The walled city of Chester with its black and white buildings, and Liverpool on Merseyside, home of the Beatles.

Begin by traveling up from Gloucestershire which divides into six main areas. The Cotswold Hills extend almost to Bath and dominate the eastern half of the county. Amongst these hills are the dramatic Stroud Valleys, dotted with woollen mills. The River Severn runs through the middle of Gloucestershire and is the setting for the three major towns: Regency Cheltenham, the city of Gloucester, and Tewkesbury, with its black and white architecture. Finally, the deeply wooded Royal Forest of Dean is on the river's western side.

Herefordshire is beautiful countryside sheltered by the Black Mountains to the west, and the Malvern Hills to the east. Places to visit include Ross-on-Wye, Leominster (pronounced Lemster) and Ludlow, one of Britain's loveliest towns. Hereford itself is on the banks of the River Wye and Worcester on the River Severn. Both are highlighted by their cathedrals. Hereford is still an attractive market town, and Worcester is famed for Royal Worcester porcelain and Worcestershire sauce.

Warwickshire, primarily known for Stratford-upon-Avon, is Shakespeare country, but it is also the home of Warwick Castle, (England's finest medieval castle) on a cliff overlooking the River Avon, and the popular town of Royal Leamington Spa. Coventry is to the north, a modern city that has risen from rubble since the second world war. Birmingham to the north west, is something of an urban mass and yet many unspoilt oases can be discovered there. Shropshire, where the River Severn continues its path, has a fascinating countryside. Despite being the site of the industrial revolution, it is remarkable to see the beautiful surroundings in which that took place. Eastward to Staffordshire where an abundance of water, marl, clay and easily mined coal, fired the kilns enabling the

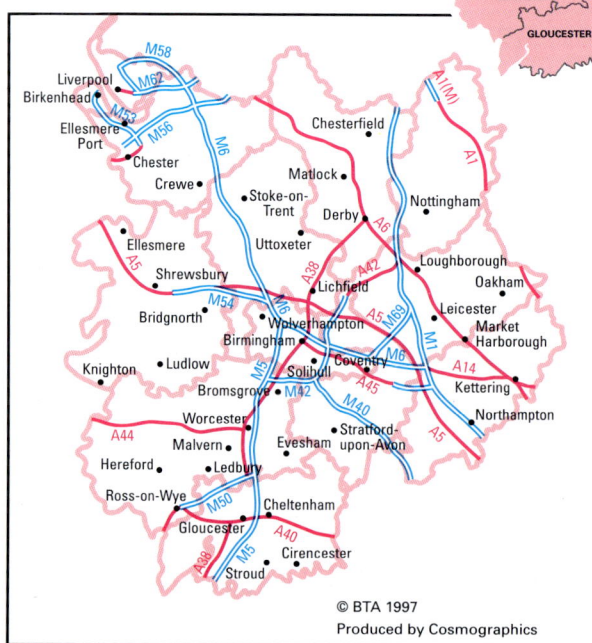

© BTA 1997
Produced by Cosmographics

development of the world famous ceramics center, Stoke-on-Trent, (The Potteries) which is an industrial conurbation of 6 towns brought together in 1910.

Continuing east to Derbyshire and the Peak District. To the south, 'White Peak', and gently rolling limestone hills, where as to the north, west, and east, are the wild heather covered moorlands of 'Dark Peak', where England's real Highlands begin. Derbyshire is a treasure trove of stately homes and gardens, and wonderful spa towns such as Buxton and Matlock, as well as the market town of Bakewell.

Before returning north of Staffordshire towards Chester and Liverpool, continue east from Derbyshire to Nottinghamshire, Sherwood Forest and Robin Hood Country. It is important to note that the heart of Sherwood Forest is about 12 miles from the center of Nottingham, best known for its medieval Sheriff.

D. H. Lawrence, who wrote, 'Lady Chatterley's Lover' was born in Eastwood, 8 miles north west of Nottingham.

Returning to the north west of the region and Cheshire. Here you will find rolling landscapes, Iron Age forts, medieval churches and elegant homes. The walled town of Chester has rural landscapes to the east dotted with glorious Tudor 'black and white' houses, halls and mansions. But not everything is rooted in the past, Jodrell Bank brings the 21st century directly into the Pennine foothills. Finally we reach Merseyside and Liverpool, the city that launched the Beatles.

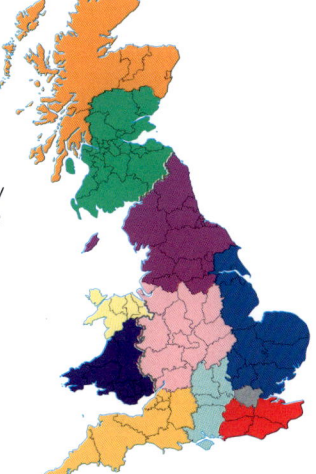

Access/Getting Around

From London

🚌 By Road

(page ref. 36,37)

The Heart of England is more accessible by road than any other region. The M25 London Orbital Motorway links the M4 in the west (to the M5) past the M40 and A41, the M1/M6 and A6 to the A1 (M) in the north. The M1/M6 and M5 meet in the Heart of England.

🚆 By Rail

(page ref. 94,95)

A network of railway lines criss-cross the whole area but the faster services are those leading to and from London's King's Cross, Euston and Paddington stations.

🚌 By Coach

(page ref. 96,97)

Coaches run frequently from London Victoria to most key towns in the Heart of England, including, Cheltenham, Derby, Nottingham, Chester, Liverpool and Manchester.

✈ By Air

The region's own Airports are Birmingham International, Manchester and the East Midlands International, between Nottingham, Derby and Leicester and Liverpool to the north.

Trail List and Page No.s

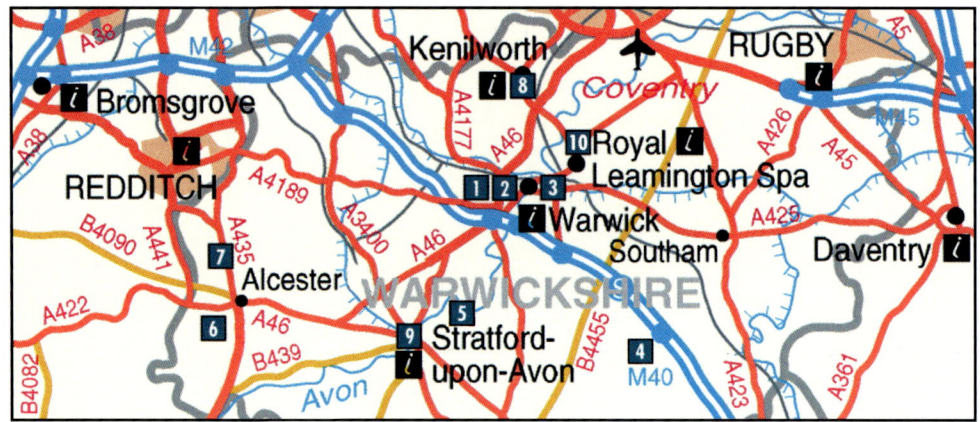

Warwick and England's finest medieval Castle

Geographically Warwick is extremely close to the real center or, 'Heart of England'. The actual center town is called Meriden, and is approximately 12 miles north of Warwick. Warwick, despite suffering a major fire in 1694, still has many of its medieval buildings. The main attraction is the majestic 14th century Warwick Castle **1**, reflected upon the River Avon, this is one of England's finest. Other examples are the Lord Leycester Hospital (founded 1571) **2**, and Warwick Doll Museum (1573) **3**, in Castle Street.

On the main road leading to Warwick is the fascinating Heritage Motor Museum **4**, and many historic houses skirt around Shakespeare's Stratford. Then above Stratford, past Mary Arden's House **9**, (once home of Shakespeare's Mother) Charlecote Park **5**, where an avenue of lime trees leads from the old village up to the house and park. To the west, Ragley

Hall **6**, the home of the Earl and Countess of Yarmouth, and also Coughton Court **7**, home of the Throckmorton family. Here, secret compartments under the floor of the Tower room were used for hiding priests in times of religious persecution.

Just 3 miles above Warwick is Royal Leamington Spa **10**. One of Queen Victoria's favorite towns, it is attractive and prosperous with fine shops, and a little further north, you will find the dramatic ruins of Kenilworth Castle **8**.

i Tourist Information

Royal Leamington Spa
☎ 01926 311470
Warwick ☎ 01926 492212

GF Stratford

Hotels
Stratford
Leamington Spa - Stratford-upon-Avon

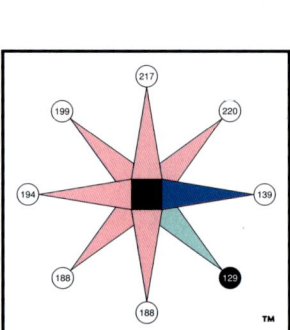

Distance from London

Warwick 95 miles ➡

1. Warwick Castle

The Secret life of England. Warwick Castle, with its magnificent towers and ramparts, offer visitors over a 1,000 years of English history. The chilling Dungeon contrasts with the elegant splendour of the State Rooms, baronial Great Hall and the Victorian 'Royal Weekend Party 1898'. Visitors can experience the sights and sounds of medieval life in 'Kingmaker'. All set in 60 acres of English grounds and gardens. There is a full color guide available that makes a great souvenir. Please find the coupons in the back of this guide in order to visit the castle. *Ask for a 'Treasure Houses' discount leaflet, to receive discounts and free guides at their other 9 properties in the guide.

Warwick Castle, Castle Lane, Warwick CV34 4QU
☎ 01926 495421

 10-5pm

 % Coupon *Treasure Houses

 Warwick

 4 J15

2. The Guildhall

The Lord Leycester Hospital leans precariously over cobbled pavements, and is a complex of 14th and 15th century halls and residences. In 1571 Robert Dudley, Earl of Leicester, founded a home for retired soldiers and their wives, known as Brethren. The Guildhall was built at the end of the 14th century and has been restored to its original appearance. It contains a collection of objects relating to the hospital. Some of the exhibits have been given by the Brethren as mementoes of campaigns in which they took part.

The Guildhall, Lord Leycester Hospital, High Street, Warwick CV34 4BH
☎ 01926 492035

 10-4pm

 Warwick

 4 J15

3. Warwick Doll Museum

Oken's House, where the collection is housed, was the home of a Tudor merchant, Thomas Oken. It now contains a collection of mainly 18th and 19th century dolls, dolls' houses, prams, toys, automata, puzzles, children's books and miniatures. The items on show are mainly English, but a number of other countries are also represented, including the US.

Warwick Doll Museum, Oken's House, Castle Street, Warwick
☎ 01926 495546

 10-4pm

 Warwick

 4 J15

4. Heritage Motor Centre

Home of the largest collection of historic British cars in the world. This is a must for car enthusiasts. Attractions include a 4-wheel drive demonstration circuit, (12-15 minute rides) and Quad Bike track, (4 minute rides) plus many special events held throughout the year. For children there's a Children's Roadway. The center is open until 6pm April to October. Located just 3 miles off junction 12 of the M40.

Heritage Motor Centre Banbury Road, Gaydon, Warwick CV35 0BJ
☎ 01926 641188

 10-4.30pm

 Warwick 5 miles

M40 J12
www.stratford.co.uk/bmiht

1. Shakespeare's Birthplace

This is the half timbered house where William Shakespeare was born in 1564. The Shakespeare Birthplace Trust own Shakespeare's Birthplace, Nash's House and New Place, Hall's Croft, Anne Hathaway's Cottage, Mary Arden's House and Harvard House. The best way to get around the properties is with a Guide Friday Tour from the Tourist Information Centre. Apart from saving £2 on the tour price with NBC, your Guide Friday combined ticket will entitle you to special savings at many of the properties

Shakespeare's Birthplace, Henley Street, Stratford, Warwickshire CV37 6QW
☎ 01789 204016

 9-5pm

 Stratford

 M 40 J 15   A 46

Map ref: A1

2. Harvard House

Dating from 1596 and decorated with grotesque carved heads, the half-timbered house was the home of Katherine Rogers, mother of John Harvard, (born in 1607) founder of Harvard University in the USA. John Harvard, who studied at Emmanuel College Cambridge, became a clergyman and later emigrated to America in 1638. The house displays material relating to the family. Admission is free.

Harvard House, High Street, Stratford-upon-Avon
☎ 01789 204016

 10-4pm

 Stratford

 M 40 J15   A 46

Map ref: A1

3. Nash's House and New Place

The home of Shakespeare's grand-daughter, and site and gardens of New Place where Shakespeare lived in retirement. The Shakespeare Birthplace Trust own Shakespeare's Birthplace, Nash's House and New Place, Hall's Croft, Anne Hathaway's Cottage, Mary Arden's House and Harvard House. The best way to get around the properties is with a Guide Friday Tour from the Tourist Information Centre. Apart from saving £2 on the tour price with NBC, your Guide Friday combined ticket will entitle you to special savings at many of the properties.

Nash's House and New Place, Chapel Street, Stratford, Warwickshire
☎ 01789 204016

 9.30-5pm

Stratford

 M 40 J 15   A 46

Map ref: B1

4. Hall's Croft

16th century house and garden owned by John Hall who married Shakespeare's daughter. The Shakespeare Birthplace Trust own Shakespeare's Birthplace, Nash's House and New Place, Hall's Croft, Anne Hathaway's Cottage and Mary Arden's House. The best way to get around the properties is with a Guide Friday Tour from the Tourist Information Centre. Apart from saving £2 on the tour price with NBC, your Guide Friday combined ticket will entitle you to special savings at many of the properties.

Hall's Croft, Old Town, Stratford, Warwickshire
☎ 01789 204016

 9.30-5pm

 Stratford

 M 40 J 15   A 46

Map ref: B1

5. Stratford Brass Rubbing Centre

Brass rubbings are a popular and pleasing way to create your own romantic gift. You have an opportunity to create an image yourself, or buy one as a memento or souvenir, but doing your own is much more fun. This is Stratford's finest brass rubbing center and this traditional English craft can also be seen in London and around the country. Buy a ready made version, or if you prefer to make your own you will get £1 off either way (not available in conjunction with any other offer)

Stratford Brass Rubbing Centre, The Royal Shakespeare Theatre Summerhouse, Avonbank Gardens, Stratford
☎ 01789 297671

🕐 10-6pm

 % £1

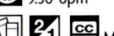 Stratford

M 40 J15   A 46

Map ref: B1

6. Teddy Bear Museum

This is a British Tourist Authority (BTA) award winning museum. A 16th century house dating from just before Shakespeare's birth, it is filled with old, interesting and famous teddy bears, displayed in a series of enchanting settings. Go to the Teddy Bears picnic, and meet Winnie the Pooh and Paddington Bear in the Hall of fame. Just 2 minutes walk south from Stratford station. Open until 5pm in January and February. Shop and free mail order catalogue.

Teddy Bear Museum, 19 Greenhill Street, Stratford, Warwickshire CV37 6LF
☎ 01789 293160

🕐 9.30-6pm

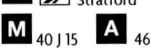 cc MC Visa

 Stratford

M 40 J 15   A 46

Map ref: A1

7. Mary Arden's House

Tudor farmhouse that was believed to have been Shakespeare's mother's family home. The Shakespeare Birthplace Trust own Shakespeare's Birthplace, Nash's House and New Place, Hall's Croft, Anne Hathaway's Cottage, Mary Arden's House and Harvard House. The best way to get around the properties is with a Guide Friday Tour from the Tourist Information Centre. Apart from saving £2 on the tour price with NBC, your Guide Friday combined ticket will entitle you to special savings at many of the properties.

Mary Arden's House, Wilmcote, near Stratford, Warwickshire
☎ 01789 204016

P

🕐 9.30-5pm

% GF

Stratford

M 40 J 15   A 46

Map ref: A1

8. Anne Hathaway's Cottage

Picturesque thatched farmhouse cottage which once belonged to the family of Shakespeare's wife. The Shakespeare Birthplace Trust own Shakespeare's Birthplace, Nash's House and New Place, Hall's Croft, Anne Hathaway's, Mary Arden's House and Harvard House. The best way to get around the properties is with a Guide Friday Tour from the Tourist Information Centre. Apart from saving £2 on the tour price with NBC, your Guide Friday combined ticket will entitle you to special savings at many of the properties.

Anne Hathaway's Cottage, Shottery, near Stratford, Warwickshire
☎ 01789 204016

🕐 9.30-5pm

% GF

Stratford

M 40 J 15   A 46   B 459

Map ref: B1

COX'S YARD

STRATFORD-UPON-AVON

A MAJOR NEW CELEBRATION

OF STRATFORD'S PAST

THE COLOUR, THE CHARACTERS THE LIVES, THE LEGENDS

See stories of Stratford from the 16th century to the present day, brought to life in the new **STRATFORD TALES** attraction - an interactive interpretation of the town's characters, legends and industries through the centuries.

Highlights of a visit to Cox's Yard include:

- The Stratford Tales
- Traditional English Pub
- Working Micro-Brewery
- Brasserie
- Tea Room
- Riverside location
- Stratford's last remaining 18th century industrial heritage site

01789 404600

Cox's Yard, Bridgefoot,
Stratford-upon Avon, Warwickshire CV37 6YY

Cotswolds 'Romantic Road to the South'

It is sometimes thought that the Cotswolds is a town. In fact it is the name given to an area in which there are many beautiful honey-brown Cotswold stone towns and villages. The elegant and fashionable Spa Town of Cheltenham is where the 'Romantic Road South' begins. Cheltenham has a great deal of charm and interest itself, for example, The Pittville Pump Rooms **1**, Holst Birthplace Museum **2**, and the Cheltenham Art Gallery and Museum **3**. The romantic route is highlighted on the map to show the loveliest villages and countryside.

Traveling anti-clockwise you start at Painswick, with a 15th century church that has 12 bells, the peal of which is one of England's finest. This is the village where Painswick Rococo Garden **4**, can be found. Then through Stroud **9**, to Tetbury **6**, once described as an architectural gem, and on to Cirencester **10**, capital of the Cotswolds, where the second largest city in Roman Britain is buried beneath its modern shopping center. Next, Bibury **7**,

one of the most beautiful of English villages, and below Bibury is Lechlade **11**, where the romantic poet Shelley, (1815) was inspired by the church to write 'A Summer Evening Churchyard'. Finally through the ancient wool town of Burford **12**, to Northleach **8**, returning back to Cheltenham. Take the 'Romantic Road' to the north or choose another trail using the NBCompass.

ℹ Tourist Information

Burford	☎ 01993 823558
Cheltenham	☎ 01242 522878
Cirencester	☎ 01285 654180
Northleach	(summer only)
	☎ 01451 860715
Stroud	☎ 01453 765768

Hotels

🏨 Cheltenham
♛ Cheltenham - Tetbury

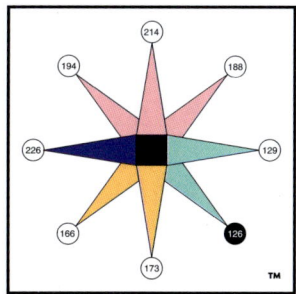

TM

Distance from London

Cheltenham 96 miles

LONDON

1. Pittville Pump Room

In this Grade 2 listed building, (building preservation order) and regency pump rooms, visitors can still 'step back in time' and taste the famous Cheltenham Spa waters. This is the only natural alkaline water in Britain, but be warned, it is salty. Set within the splendid grounds of Pittville Park along with the museum, Cheltenham's 'Gallery of Fashion' traces the history of fashion from 1760 to the present day. 1 mile north from the town center. Closed Tuesdays.

Pittville Pump Room, Pittville Park, Cheltenham, Gloucestershire
☎ 01242 523852

 10-4.30pm

 Cheltenham

A 40

2. Holst Birthplace Museum

This is the Regency Terrace where the famous composer was born in 1874. Gustav Theodore Holst was a British composer of Swedish descent whose compositions include, 'The Planet' suite, 'The Hymn of Jesus', an opera, and 'The Perfect Fool', a choral symphony. He was also outstanding as a teacher. Holst died in 1934. The museum also shows the daily way of life in Victorian and Edwardian times. A five minute walk from the town center. Closed on Sundays and Mondays.

Holst Birthplace Museum, 4 Clarence Road, Cheltenham, Gloucestershire
☎ 01242 524846

 10-4pm

 Cheltenham

A 40

3. Cheltenham Art Gallery

Cheltenham Art Gallery has a world renowned 'Arts and Craft Movement Collection', inspired by William Morris, (English designer and craftsman 1834 -1896) with rare Chinese and English ceramics. There are 300 years of paintings by Dutch and English artists. And you can also discover the social history of elegant Cheltenham, Britain's most complete Regency town. Located just one minute's walk from the town center. Entry is free. Closed on Sundays.

Cheltenham Art Gallery, Clarence Street, Cheltenham, Gloucestershire
☎ 01242 237431

 10-5pm

  Cheltenham

A 40

4. Painswick Rococo Garden

Painswick Rococo Garden was created in the early 18th century. The 6 acre gardens were laid out in a hidden Cotswold combe behind the newly built Painswick House. The Garden combines charming garden structures with winding woodland walks, a large 'Kitchen Garden', herbaceous borders and wonderful vistas of the surrounding Cotswold hills. It typifies the flamboyant nature of the Rococo period of garden design. Closed through December.

Painswick Rococo Garden, The Stables, Painswick House, Painswick, Gloucestershire GL6 6TH
☎ 01452 813204

 11-5pm

 Gloucester

A 46   A 4073
www.beta.co.uk/painswick

5. Cotswold Country Tours

A luxurious way to see the Cotswolds countryside in the sublime comfort of a Rolls Royce Silver Spirit. You are advised to book, so please ask wherever you are staying, and you will be collected from there to see this beautiful part of England, or even Stratford-upon-Avon or Oxford. Please be sure to give your NBC Card number, and receive 10% off the published prices, payment is accepted by £ cash, or US travelers checks. Members of the Institute of Advanced Motorists.

Cotswold Country Tours, The Coach House, Upper Swell, Stow-on-the-Wold, Gloucs
☎ 01451 870550   Ⓕ 01451 870550

🕐 8-8pm

% 10%

Moreton-in-Marsh

Ⓐ 429

6. The House of Cheese

Although tiny, this award-winning specialist shop is one of the best retailers of cheese in the UK, and offers a different experience from supermarkets by selling the very best cheeses from small country makers, and importing fresh French cheeses. House of Cheese hold a Royal warrant for supplying H.R.H. the Prince of Wales. They also stock Duchy Original products from his nearby farm and country home. If the weather is good, buy from the selection of over 120 cheeses and picnic in the beautiful countryside. Located in the town center.

The House of Cheese, Church Street, Tetbury, Gloucestershire
☎ 01666 502865

 P

🕐 9-5.30pm

% 10%

CC Am Ex Visa

Kemble   Cheltenham

Ⓐ 433

7. Bibury Trout Farm

In the beautiful Cotswolds village of Bibury you will find this working trout farm, open to visitors and selling fresh and smoked trout, which is considered as one of the better fish in Britain. With the opportunity to discover the techniques and 'how trout farming works', this will prove an interesting stop to make. Open from 10am on Sunday. On the B4425 between Cirencester and Burford.

Bibury Trout Farm, Bibury, Cirencester, Gloucestershire
☎ 01285 740215

  P

🕐 9-5pm

Kemble   Cheltenham

Ⓑ 4425

8. World of Mechanical Music

Keith Harding's World of Mechanical Music is a living museum of various kinds of self-playing musical instruments that were the pride and joy of past generations. The only kind of entertainment available in the home before regular radio broadcasting began in 1924. The instruments are presented as a continuous live entertainment, and they are all put into first class working order at these world famous workshops. The quality of the working exhibits at this attraction is remarkable.

World of Mechanical Music, The Oak House, High Street, Northleach, Gloucestershire
☎ 01451 860181

 P

🕐 10-6pm

 Cheltenham

Ⓐ 40/429

Heart of England

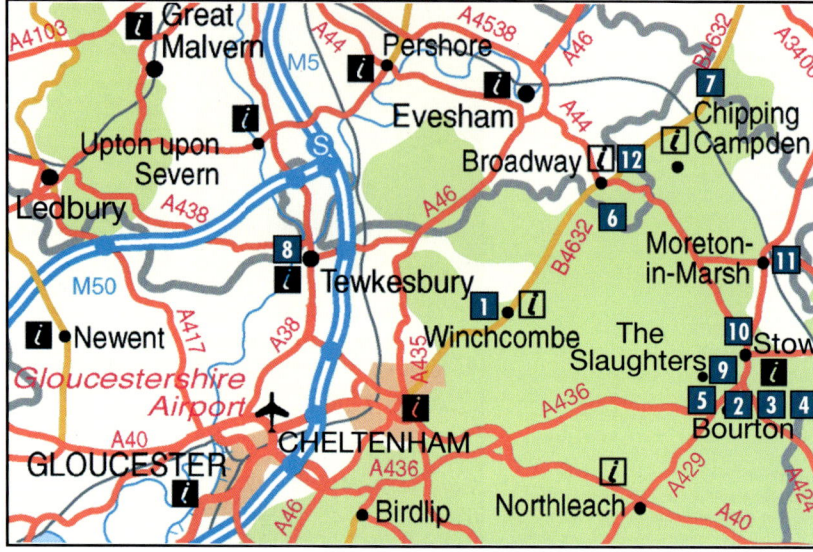

Cotswolds 'Romantic Road to the North'

Starting in Cheltenham the route is anti-clockwise on the map. Begin by traveling to Sudeley Castle **1**, at Winchcombe, and then continue to Bourton-on-the-Water. Bourton is one of the focal points of the Cotswolds where the River Windrush flows along the main street. In this town there are many attractions, the Motor Museum **2**, the Model Village **3**, and the Perfumery Exhibition **4**. Nearby are the picturesque villages of Lower Slaughter **5**, and Upper Slaughter **9**, from where you will arrive at Stow-on-the-Wold **10**, with its many antique shops and Moreton-in-Marsh **11**. From there, to the wonderful Chipping Camden and Hidcote Manor Garden **7**. Next, Broadway **12**, with its antique shops and natural village charm. Penultimately, to Snowshill Manor **6**, where an eccentric craftsman, Charles Wade, restored this 17th century house in which you will find a most unusual selection of objects. Before returning to Cheltenham continue on to

Tewkesbury **8**, which has one of England's finest abbey churches. This lovely town is situated where the rivers Avon and Severn join into one. From here return to Cheltenham. Take the 'Romantic Road South' or continue traveling around Britain with the NBCompass

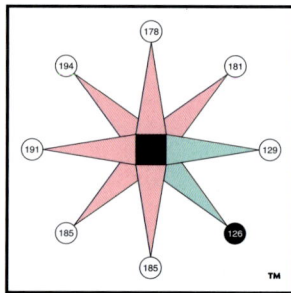 Tourist Information

Cheltenham
☎ 01242 522878
Stow on the Wold
☎ 01451 831082
Winchcombe (summer only)
☎ 01242 602925

GF Bourton on the Water

Hotels

Cheltenham
Cheltenham - Chipping Campden - Stow-on-the-Wold

Distance from London

Cheltenham 96 miles

LONDON

1. Sudeley Castle and Gardens

Winner of the Christies, 'Garden of the Year' award in 1996, this is also one of England's great historic houses. The Royal connections go back a 1,000 years. It was the palace of the sixth wife of Henry VIII, Katherine Parr. The lives of his six wives are summarised as, 'divorced, beheaded, died, divorced, beheaded, survived'. Katherine Parr was the last. Henry VIII, Elizabeth I and Charles I have all stayed here, and there is a wealth of history on show. An impressive collection of masterpieces by Turner, Van Dyck and Reubens, and as mentioned above, the wonderful gardens that surround the castle.

Sudeley Castle and Gardens, Winchcombe , Gloucester GL54 5JD
☎ 01242 602308

 11-5pm

 1 Child Free

Cheltenham

M 5 J11   A 40/46
www.stratford.co.uk/sudeley

2. Cotswold Motor Museum

The home of the loveable 'Brum' as seen on TV worldwide. The Cotswold Motor Museum has beautiful cars and Britain's largest display of advertising signs, toys and pedalcars. Housed in an 18th century watermill this is a unique experience. Having purchased your ticket for the Motor Museum you have free entry to the Village Life Exhibition, which presents an interesting look at period reconstructions and a model of the Old Corn Mill. Open from March to November

Cotswold Motor Museum, Bourton-on-the Water, Gloucester GL54 2BY
☎ 01451 821255

 10-6pm

 %

CC All

Moreton-in-Marsh

A 40/429

3. The Model Village

You will be sure to enjoy visiting the Model Village of the Village in the Cotswolds, and amazingly there's a model village in the model village. Here at the New Inn, Mr C A Morris decided in 1935 to turn the vegetable garden of the inn into something more interesting, and by 1937 the Model Village was completed. Listen at the church and take a look inside. The family have kept the village to this very day and it is carefully maintained by his son Peter and wife Maureen. Please use the voucher in the back of the guide.

The Model Village, Bourton-on-the-Water, near Cheltenham, Glos GL54 2AF
☎ 01451 820467

★ P

 9-6pm

21 Coupon

Moreton-in-Marsh

A 40/429

4. Perfumery Exhibition

This is unique, it's the only exhibition of its kind in Europe. The perfumes are actually manufactured on the premises and the perfumery exhibition includes the origins of perfume, as well as a cinema (movie theater) with 'smells'. There is also a perfume quiz and a perfume garden. This is a sensory experience with a difference and very fascinating. Sundays open from 10 - 5pm.

Perfumery Exhibition, Victoria Street, Bourton-on-the-Water, Gloucestershire GL54 2BU
☎ 01451 820698

★ P

 9-6pm

21

CC MC Visa

Moreton in Marsh

M 40   A 40/429

5. The Old Mill Museum

This 19th century flour mill, with its mighty water wheel, stands on the banks of the River Eye. It is a fascinating stop on the 'Cotswolds Trail' and allows an interesting insight into the original workings of a Victorian flour mill. There is an ice cream parlour and delightful riverside tea rooms. Situated between Bourton-on-the-Water and Stow-in-the-Wold. Please show guide and card.

The Old Mill Museum, Mill Lane, Lower Slaughter, Gloucestershire GL54 2HX
☎ 01451 820052

 10-6pm

 All

⇄ Moreton-in-Marsh

A 40/429

6. Snowshill Manor

A 'picture-perfect' Tudor House with a 17th century façade, best known for Charles Paget Wade's collections of craftsmanship and design, including musical instruments, clocks, toys, bicycles, weavers' tools, spinners' tools and armour. The cottage and small gardens are also on view, the gardens are now organically maintained. Located 3 miles south west of Broadway.

Snowshill Manor, Snowshill, near Broadway, Worcester WR12 7JU
☎ 01386 852410

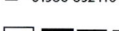 

 Page 91

  Page 66

⇄ Moreton-in-Marsh

A 44

7. Hidcote Manor Garden

One of the most delightful gardens in England, created by the great horticulturist Major Lawrence Johnston. A series of small gardens separated by walls and hedges. Hidcote is famous for rare shrubs, trees, herbaceous borders, 'old' roses and interesting plant species, and is another wonderful experience of the Cotswolds hidden beauty. Last admission l hour before closing. Located 4 miles north east of Chipping Campden.

Hidcote Manor Garden, Hidcote Bartrim, near Chipping Campden GL55 6LR
☎ 01386 438333

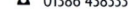

 Page 91

  Page 66

⇄ Chipping Camden  Broadway

B 4632

8. Tewkesbury Abbey

In the lovely town of Tewkesbury on the Rivers Avon and Severn is one of England's finest Norman Abbey churches. The last of the monasteries to be dissolved by Henry VIII, and thanks to the townspeople of that time, who bought it for £453, and continued support from the public, the abbey is still here today. Wonderful stained glass windows and glimpses of history throughout the abbey. The offer applies in the abbey shop, except books, music, food and stamps. Restricted access when services are in progress.

Tewkesbury Abbey, Church Street, Tewkesbury, Gloucestershire
☎ 01684 850959

 7.30-6pm

 % 10% (Shop) Coupon

⇄ Tewkesbury  Cheltenham

M 5 J9   A 38/438

'The Tailor of Gloucester' Beatrix Potter

The House of the Tailor of Gloucester **A1**, was used by Beatrix Potter to illustrate her story of mice who helped a tailor. It is now a shop and small museum devoted to her works. Gloucester has played a significant part in England's history since Roman times when it was called Glevum. The four 'gates' of the medieval city still meet at the central 'Cross' **B1**, (where the Tourist Information Centre is now housed). Gloucester Cathedral **A1**, begun in 1089, replacing an earlier abbey, is one of England's most impressive cathedrals. Around the Norman Cathedral there are still many historic buildings. Visit the Gloucester Folk Museum **A1**, in Westgate Street (free) to look at the local history.

Gloucester Docks, once a busy port, are now better known for the museums, attractions and shops that have moved into the fifteen Victorian warehouses. For example, the fascinating National Waterways Museum **B1**, and the Robert Opie Collection - Museum of Advertising and Packaging **B1**, which looks at the promotion of English household goods from 1870 to the present day. South west of Gloucester is Berkeley Castle **B1**, beside the River Severn, and the Jenner Museum **B1**. It was Edward Jenner who pioneered the

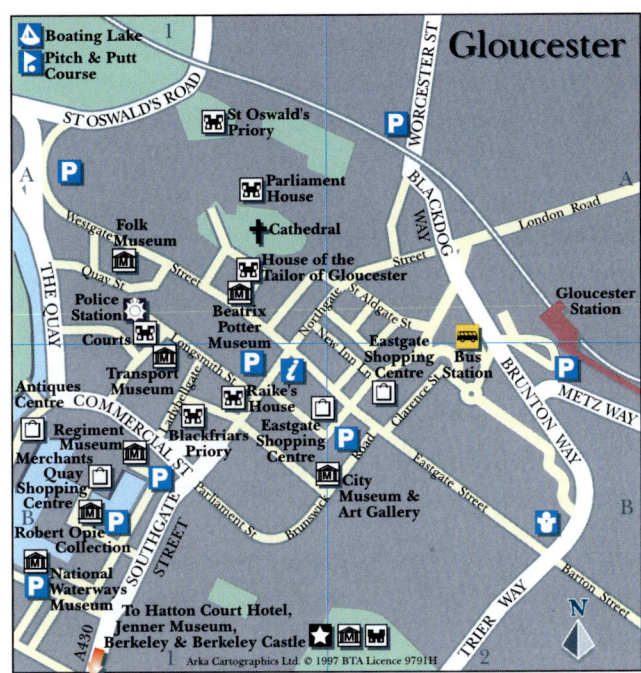

vaccination for smallpox. Choose where to go next with the NBCompass.

i Tourist Information

Gloucester ☎ 01452 421188

Hotels

Cheltenham
Cheltenham

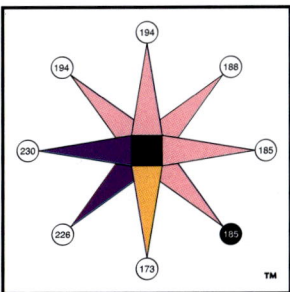

Distance from London

Gloucester 100miles

1. Gloucester Cathedral

Gloucester Cathedral has a tradition of daily worship. Founded in 1089, the architectural style is Norman. In 1216 Henry III was crowned here and Edward II who was murdered in 1327 at Berkeley Castle, (13 miles to the south west) is buried here in a tomb near the high altar. The fan-vaulted cloisters are the earliest surviving in England, and the medieval stained glass window, the largest in Britain, is also spectacular, both have often been copied in other churches. The Bell tower contains the heaviest medieval bell in England. Admission is free, but a donation would be welcome.

Gloucester Cathedral, 17 College Green, Gloucester GL1 2LR
☎ 01452 528095

🕐 7.30-6pm

⇄ ◪ Gloucester

Ⓜ 5 J11   🅰 40

Map ref: A1

2. House of the Tailor of Gloucester

This unique gift shop is situated in the building illustrated as the Tailor's house in Beatrix Potter's famous story of 'The Tailor of Gloucester'. Inside is a treasure trove of books and perfect childrens' gifts. There is also a display of Beatrix Potter's life and work, including first editions and early Peter Rabbit merchandise. A three dimensional automated scene of the mice at work on the mayor's coat can also be seen. Located close to the cathedral.

House of the Tailor of Gloucester, 9 College Court, Gloucester
☎ 01452 422856

🕐 9.30-5.30pm

⇄ ◪ Gloucester

Ⓜ 5 J11   🅰 40

Map ref: A1

3. City Museum and Art Gallery

The museum, built on an excavated part of the Roman wall, has a variety of displays illustrating archaeology, natural history and geology of the area. One of the highlights is the 'Birdlip Mirror', dating from around AD25, it is a fine example of Celtic metalwork, and a unique Norman backgammon set is also displayed. The Art Gallery has paintings by, amongst others, Turner and Gainsborough, and there are also collections of barometers, long case clocks, Staffordshire porcelain and Bristol blue glass as well as lively temporary exhibitions. Admission is free.

City Museum and Art Gallery, Brunswick Road, Gloucester GL1 1HP
☎ 01452 524131

🕐 10-5pm

⇄ ◪ Gloucester

Ⓜ 5 J11   🅰 40

Map ref: B2

4. National Waterways Museum

This award winning museum is on three floors of the listed Victorian Llanthony Warehouse. Explore the rich tapestry of 200 years of inland waterways, through imaginative displays, films, working models and the two quaysides of historic craft. Walk through the replica canal maintenance yard where their blacksmith can often be seen demonstrating his skills. Boat trips available between April and October. Open until 5pm in the Winter. Follow the brown and white signs for Historic Docks.

National Waterways Museum, Llanthony Warehouse, Gloucester Docks, Gloucester
☎ 01452 318054

🕐 10-6pm

 2⃣1⃣

⇄ ◪ Gloucester

Ⓜ 5 J11   🅰 40

Map ref: B1

5. The Robert Opie Collection

The museum is unique, and will be of great interest as it brings to life a fascinating look at Britain, and its social history from 1870 to the present day. What makes it unique is that it does this through old packs, advertisements, newspapers, magazines, toys and games, TV commercials and shop recreations. Notice how the English have advertised and promoted goods in comparison to at home in the US, you may notice some interesting similarities. Located in the Albert Warehouse at the Gloucester Docks. Open at weekends until 6pm.

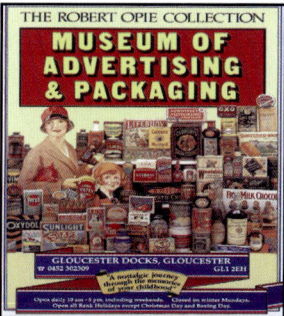

The Robert Opie Collection, Albert Warehouse, Gloucester Docks, GL1 2EH
☎ 01482 302309

 10-5pm

⇄ ⤢ Gloucester

M 5 J11 A 40

Map ref: B1

6. Hatton Court Hotel

This is a classic Cotswolds Country House Hotel with 45 rooms and is a good location for visitors to the area. Set in its own grounds it is ideally placed for visiting Cheltenham 8 miles away to the east, Gloucester 3 miles to the north and around the Cotswolds. Originally built in the 17th century, it is a charming hotel with views across the Severn Valley and Malvern Hills. Own health suite. Please book ahead. English Tourist Board 4 crown recommended.

Hatton Court Hotel, Upton Hill, Upton St Leonards, Gloucester GL4 8DE
☎ 01452 617412 Ⓕ 01452 612945

 24hrs

 20%

⇄ ⤢ Gloucester

M 5 J11 A 40 B 4073

Map ref: B2

7. Berkeley Castle

England's oldest inhabited castle. Since 1153, 24 generations of Berkeleys have transformed a savage Norman Fortress into a truly stately home full of treasures and history. Surrounded by sweeping lawns and Elizabethan terraced gardens, there is also a butterfly farm. It is located on the A38 south of Gloucester. Closed from November until the end of March. Open, Tuesday to Sunday 1-5 in April and May. In June from Tuesday to Saturday 11-5pm and 1-5pm Sundays. July and August open from Monday and September from Tuesday, same hours as June.

Berkeley Castle, Berkeley, Gloucestershire GL13 9BQ
☎ 01453 810332

 11-5pm

 MC Visa

 ⤢ Stroud

M 5 J13/14 A 38

Map ref: B1

8. Jenner Museum

Located just by Berkeley Castle, discover the beautiful home of Edward Jenner who pioneered the vaccination against smallpox 200 years ago. Interestingly, the museum's existence today is largely due to a few kind benefactors. There is a new display on modern immunology, the medical science Jenner founded, and guide books are available. With such a key role in both our histories your visit, and any purchases in the gift shop are also a great help to their continuing work. Follow brown and white signs to museum in Berkeley town center from A38. Tues-Sat 12.30-5.30pm. Sun 1-5.30pm.

Jenner Museum, Church Lane, High Street, Berkeley, Gloucester GL13 9BH
☎ 01453 810631

 12.30-5.30pm

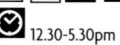

 ⤢ Stroud

M 5 J13/14 A 38

Map ref: B1

Heart of England

Hereford and Worcester 'Elgar and the mighty Cathedral'

In the attractive town of Hereford, visit the 11th century cathedral **1**, which contains the extraordinary 'Mappa Mundi', (1290) showing the Earth as flat. The 'black and white' Old House **2**, is now a museum of local history. Trace the history of cider at HP Bulmer **3**, combined with a visit to the Cider Museum **4**.

From Hereford heading south are Kilpeck Church **5**, stop and enjoy the stunning views at Symonds Yat **17**, and then visit the extraordinary Clearwell Caves **6**, at this point you are on the border of Wales. From here north west, through Ross-on-Wye, to Eastnor Castle **7**. Worcester is only 15 miles from here. Alternatively, if you travel north from Hereford you can visit Burton Court **8**, and Croft Castle **9**, then continue to Ludlow in Shropshire, definitely one of England's most beautiful towns. Ludlow is dominated by the 11th century castle **10**, and from here you can reach Stokesay Castle **11**.
Worcester, whose the focal point is the cathedral **12**, is attractively set on the banks of the River Severn. You can watch how Royal Worcester Porcelain is made at their museum and visitor center **13**. On a musical note, facing the cathedral at the bottom of the High Street stands a statue of Sir Edward

Elgar, (1857 - 1934) and on the edge of Worcester, at Lower Broadheath, is Elgar's Birthplace **15**. North of Worcester, you can follow a stretch of the Severn Valley along 16 miles of picturesque countryside railway **16**.

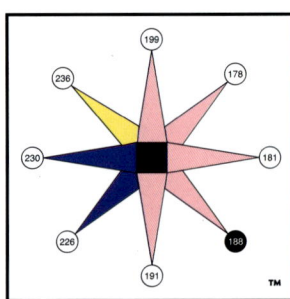

i Tourist Information

Hereford	☎ 01432 268430
Worcester	☎ 01905 726311

Hotels

👑 Malvern Hills - Malvern - Ludlow - Worcester

Distance from London

Hereford 134 miles

LONDON

1. Hereford Cathedral

Hereford Cathedral has stood on the beautiful banks of the River Wye since 676. Its medieval map of the world, the 'Mappa Mundi', is the finest example of its type and can be seen in a new exhibition with models and interactive touch screens. Visit the fascinating Chained Library, in which 1,500 books were tethered together by iron chains as a precaution against theft. NBC Card for free entry to Chained Library. On Sundays open between 11-3.15pm

Hereford Cathedral, 5 College Cloisters, Cathedral Close, Hereford HR1 2NG
☎ 01432 359880

 10-4pm

Hereford

M 50   A 438

2. The Old House, City Museum

The Old House, built in 1621, was originally part of Butcher's Row and is an outstanding example of half-timbered Jacobean domestic architecture. The porch has the Coat of Arms of the Butchers' Guild of London on the doorway. During its history the magnificent timber framed building was used as a saddler's, a hardware store, a fish shop and a bank. The Old House is now a museum of local history containing 17th century furniture on three floors, with four poster beds in the bedrooms. Closed on Mondays.

The Old House, City Museum, High Town, Hereford
☎ 01432 364598

 10-5pm

 Hereford

M 50   A 438

3. HP Bulmer Visitor Centre

The history of cider can be traced back a thousand years or more. Bulmers was founded in Hereford in 1887 by Percy Bulmer, son of a local vicar. Using cider apples from the Rectory orchard and an old cider mill at a neighbouring farm, he produced his first cider and laid the foundations for Bulmers today. Begin at the Bulmers Visitor Centre, in the vaulted cellars beneath the original mill. A short film about the company is followed by a tour to the press hall, fermentation vessels, bottling hall and keg filling plant. The cider museum can be visited separately.

HP Bulmer Visitor Centre, The Cider Mills, Plough Lane, Hereford HR4 0LE
☎ 01432 352000

 Tours 10.30am , 2.15 and 7.30pm

 Hereford

M 50   A 438

4. Museum of Cider

Cider, the apple based alcoholic drink, is most popular in England and France. Here in the heart of Herefordshire discover the heritage of cider making, from growing the apples to making the drinks which also include Cider Brandy, Cider Liqueur and Apple Apéritif. There are often additional events and exhibitions as well as the working distillery. A gift shop and off licence are on site, although if you rather enjoy the experience, cider is available in most pubs. Open daily except 1 Nov to 31 March, Tuesday - Sunday 11-3pm. Located in Hereford off the A438 towards Brecon.

Museum of Cider, 21 Ryelands Street, Hereford HR4 0LW
☎ 01432 354207

 10-5.30pm

 50% entry

 Hereford

M 50   A 438

5. Kilpeck Church

Located 6 miles south west of Hereford is the little hamlet of Kilpeck with its Norman church, built in 1135. The background to the carvings and decorations, (some of the best examples in England) is quite fascinating, and certainly unique. During the 12th century, Oliver de Merlemond made a pilgrimage from Hereford to Spain. Impressed by several churches he saw, he brought French masons over to recreate the style of carvings. Hence the church has many lustful figures showing their genitals, and tail-biting dragons. Not what you would normally associate with a religious building.

Kilpeck Church, Kilpeck, nr Hereford

 7.30-6pm

 Hereford

 465

6. Clearwell Caves

Located approximately 20 miles south of Hereford, Clearwell Caves are the Royal Forest of Deanís mining heritage. Stout footwear is recommended as you wander through nine large caverns, with miles of passageways leading past frozen waterfalls and deep pools. Iron has been mined here since the Iron Age, 2,500 years ago - the story of iron is told here within the caves and whatever the weather outside, the temperature underground is a constant 10°C (50°F). Open from March - October.

Clearwell Caves, nr Coleford, Royal Forest of Dean, Gloucestershire GL16 8JR
☎ 01594 832535

 10-5pm

Monmouth

5/50   48/46   4228

7. Eastnor Castle

This is a splendid Georgian Castle created by many of the age's finest architects and landscapists. It is in a fairytale setting, with a deer park, arboretum and lake. Situated in a vast estate in the Malvern Hills, the interior has tapestries, fine art, armour and furniture. Gothic and Italianate furniture and richly decorated interiors have been restored, to much critical acclaim. Open in July and August, Monday to Friday 11-5pm. September to May, Sundays only, 11-4.30pm.

Eastnor Castle, Eastnor, Ledbury, Herefordshire HR8 1RL
☎ 01531 633160

 11-5pm

MC Visa

 Ledbury

50 J2

8. Burton Court

Built around a 14th century Great Hall, Burton Court offers an insight into a typical squire's (English country gentleman) house. Displayed here is an extensive collection of European and Oriental costumes. You can also find a collection of old natural history specimens, (the most recent in 1918), including animal mounts, as well as some other quite unusual personal collections. Open from April to mid-September. Not open on Mondays, Tuesdays or Fridays. Self pick fruit, (when in season) adds another pleasure.

Burton Court, Eardisland, Leominster, Herefordshire HR6 9DN
☎ 01544 388231

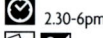 2.30-6pm

Leominster   Hereford

44

9. Croft Castle

Home of the Croft family since Domesday, (with a break of 170 years from 1750). The walls and corner towers date from the 14th and 15th centuries, while the interior is mainly 18th century, when the fine Georgian-Gothic staircase and plasterwork ceilings were added. A splendid avenue of 350 year old Spanish chestnuts runs through the park, and an Iron Age fort, (Croft Ambrey) may be reached by footpath, (an uphill walk of approx. 40 mins). Located 5 miles north west of Leominster.

Croft Castle, nr Leominster, Shropshire HR6 9PW
☎ 01568 780246

  P

 Page 91

 Page 66

 Leominster

A 49 B 4361

10. Ludlow Castle

Ludlow is one of England's most attractive towns, and although there are many visitors to the splendid castle, it is also the picturesque town that makes this an enchanting place to visit. The ruined castle sits on cliffs high above the River Teme. Built in 1086, it was later damaged in the Civil War, and then abandoned in 1689. In the early summer Shakespeare plays are performed within the castle walls in the open air. The castle is rivalled only by the huge 15th century church in Ludlow.

Ludlow Castle, The Square, Ludlow, Shropshire
☎ 01584 873355

 P

 10.30-5pm

 Ludlow

A 49/4117

11. Stokesay Castle

This is probably the finest medieval manor house in England. Situated in the peaceful Shropshire countryside. The castle now forms part of a picturesque group of buildings gathered around a grassy courtyard, with its own splendid timber-framed Jacobean black and yellow gatehouse. The parish church was largely rebuilt in the 17th century but many Norman features remain. Located 7 miles north west of Ludlow.

Stokesay Castle, Craven Arms, Shropshire
☎ 01588 672544

 P

 10-6pm

 Page 67

 Craven Arms 1 mile

A 49

12. Worcester Cathedral

Admission is free to Worcester Cathedral, although a donation is welcome. The cathedral is the architectural highlight of Worcester, it suffered a collapsed tower in 1175 and then a disastrous fire in 1203, before the present structure was started in the 13th century. Overlooking the River Severn and by College Green, the cathedral has a fine position in the city. There are many interesting tombs and carvings to be discovered within and a huge Norman crypt survives from the first cathedral in 1084.

Worcester Cathedral, High Street, Worcesterhire
☎ 01905 722480

  P

 Worcester

M 5 J6/7 A 44

13. Royal Worcester

Royal Worcester was founded in 1751 by Dr John Wall. The company has been in continuous production ever since and received its first Royal Warrant in 1789, granted by King George III. Here you can visit the Dyson Perrins Museum which houses the world's largest collection of Worcester porcelain. The offer is for the fascinating 'Manufactory and Film Show' in the Visitor Centre, where you can see the products being made. Sunday hours are from 11-5pm.

Royal Worcester, Severn Street, Worcester WR1 2NE
☎ 01905 23221

9-5.30pm

 Worcester

M 5 J7   A 44

14. The Commandery

The photograph depicts Charles II on a visit to the Commandery, his Royalist headquarters at the Battle of Worcester in 1651. The Commandery has period rooms offering a glimpse of Tudor and Stuart life, whilst the museum exhibits and audio visual presentation tell the turbulent story of England's Civil War. The museum is close to the Porcelain factory and three minutes from the cathedral. Sundays 1.30-5.30pm.

The Commandery, The Sidbury, Worcester WR1 2HU
☎ 01905 355071

10-5pm

 Worcester

M 5 J7   A 44

15. The Elgar Birthplace Museum

Here you can visit the cottage in which Edward Elgar, probably England's greatest composer, was born. Set in the attractive rural surroundings of Worcestershire from where he drew much of his inspiration, it houses a unique collection of photographs, manuscripts and personal memorabilia of the man and his life. It is closed on Wednesdays. Located 3 miles west of Worcester off the A44.

The Elgar Birthplace Museum, Crown East Lane, Lower Broadheath, Worcester WR2 6RH
☎ 01905 333224

10.30-6pm

 Worcester

M 5 J7   A 44

16. Severn Valley Railway

Take the train from Kidderminster or Bridgnorth through Bewdley, and enjoy a wonderful trip along the Severn Valley Railway to numerous picturesque villages along the River Severn. Covering 16 miles of glorious countryside, trains operate every weekend throughout the year and daily from the end of May to the beginning of October. Kidderminster station is adjacent to the mainline station. The offer is available on the 'Freedom of the Line' ticket and is £1 off each adult, please present your NBC card. *Please check train times by phoning (UK) 0800 600 900 - ask for Severn Valley railway (24hrs).

Severn Valley Railway, The Railway Station, Bewdley, Worcestershire DY12 1BG
☎ 01299 403816

*10.30-5pm

% £1

 Kidderminster

M 5   A 456

www.svr.co.uk

The Industrial Revolution 'Ironbridge

Ironbridge Gorge in Shropshire was the birthplace of the Industrial Revolution and is a 'World Heritage Site'. This is where the first Bridge of Iron was built, across the River Severn in 1777-1779, by Abraham Darby III. It all began in 1709, when Abraham Darby I pioneered the use of inexpensive coke, rather than charcoal, to smelt iron ore. The use of iron in transport, (wheels and rails) engineering, (steam engines, ships and locomotives) and construction, made this one of the world's greatest iron making centers. Then came the industrial decline of the 20th century which practically silenced Ironbridge.

Today it has been restored with a number of fascinating museums relating to that period in history. Set along the wooded banks of the Severn, you would hardly associate the surroundings with those of today's 'industrial sights'. The best place to start is at the Ironbridge Visitor Centre **B1**, where you can pick up a free guide with detailed attraction information. Around Ironbridge, visit Rowley's House, and Shrewsbury Castle **A1/2**, the Royal Air Force Museum to the east **A2**, and the not inconsiderable remains of the romantic 11th century Wenlock Priory **B1**. The NBCompass provides a selection of further places to visit in the surrounding area.

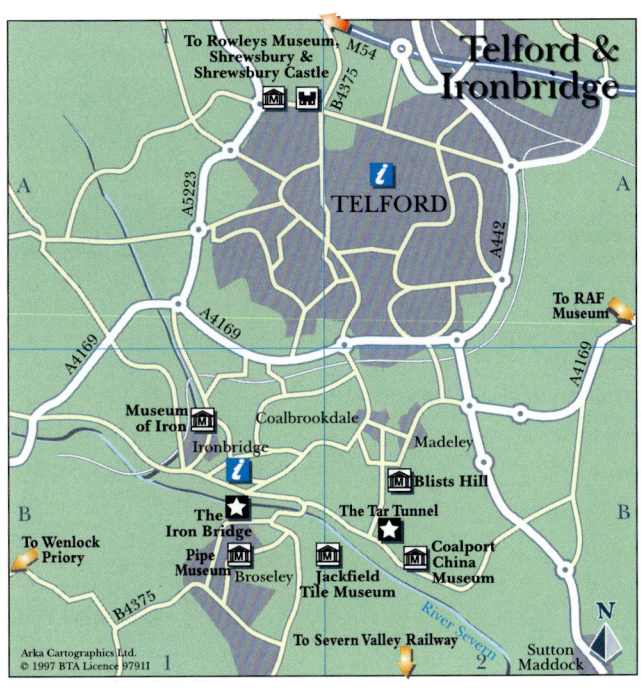

Tourist Information

Ironbridge   ☎ 01952 432166

Hotels

Ironbridge

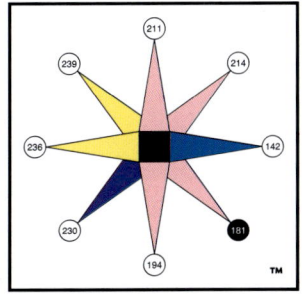

Distance from London

Ironbridge 152miles

1. Visitor Centre, Ironbridge

This center has a spectacular 40ft model of the Gorge as it was in 1796. There are displays of the way the River is managed now, compared to the time of the early Industrial Revolution. It is interesting to see and understand the methods by which the modern western world takes for granted fresh water at the turn of a tap. Nearby, the Merrythought Teddy Bear shop is one of the more recent industries. Purchase a passport to all of the five museums at the Visitor Centre, and you will receive a Souvenir Guide (worth £1.99).

Ironbridge Visitor Centre, Ironbridge, Telford, Shropshire TF8 7AW
☎ 01952 432166

  P

 10-5pm

 Guidebook

 Telford

M 54 J4

Map ref: B1

2. Museum of Iron, Ironbridge

Coalbrookdale and the Museum of Iron. This is where the remarkable achievements of Abraham Darby I come to life. Visit the Darby furnace, and Rosehill and Dale House, the beautifully restored homes of the Quaker (members of religious, Society of Friends, founded by George Fox in 1648-1650, and devoted to peace principles) ironmasters. Purchase a passport to all of the five museums at the Visitor Centre, and you will receive a Souvenir Guide (worth £1.99).

Ironbridge Museum of Iron, Ironbridge, Telford, Shropshire TF8 7AW
☎ 01952 432166

 P

 10-5pm

 Guidebook

 Telford

M 54 J4

Map ref: B1

3. Ironbridge and Toll House

The Ironbridge and Tollhouse. Here you will be provided with an introduction to the Iron bridge erected in 1779, that spans the River Severn. The Tollhouse, which contains the information center and an exhibition, is the focal point of the whole valley. Purchase a passport to all of the five museums at the Visitor Centre, and you will receive a Souvenir Guide (worth £1.99).

Ironbridge and Toll House, Ironbridge, Telford, Shropshire TF8 7AW
☎ 01952 432166

  P

 10-5pm

 Guidebook

 Telford

M 54 J4

Map ref: B1

4. Blists Hill Victorian Town

Blists Hill Victorian Town. Step back in time to a living community of the 1890is on this 50 acre site. Along gas lit streets of this re-created Victorian town, past railway sidings, yards and pigsties, shops and offices, experience the sights, sounds, tastes and smells. Purchase a passport to all of the five museums at the Visitor Centre, and you will receive a Souvenir Guide (worth £1.99). From there there are two more fascinating museums, The Jackfield Tile Museum and Coalport China Museum. Also, the Tar Tunnel and Pipe Museum, look for the details in your free souvenir guide.

Blists Hill Victorian Town, Ironbridge, Telford, Shropshire TF8 7AW
☎ 01952 432166

 P

 10-5pm

 Guidebook

 Telford

M 54 J4

Map ref: B2

5. Rowley's House

Shrewsbury is an historic town almost enclosed by a great loop of the River Severn, and just near the center in Barker Street is Rowley's House. In AD60 the Romans built a garrison, (fortified) town call Viroconium. Finds from the excavation are displayed here, including a 2nd century decorated silver mirror, in this timber framed 16th century building and adjoining 17th century mansion. Closed on Mondays. Open Sundays from 10-4pm in the Summer only. If you buy a ticket that also includes Clive House, Regimental Museum and castle, it's '2 for 1' at all 3 attractions.

Rowley's House, Barker Street, Shrewsbury, Shropshire SY1 1QH
☎ 01743 358516

🕐 10-5pm

 Shrewsbury

M 54 A 5

Map ref: A2

6. Shrewsbury Castle

Shrewsbury, with its surrounding river is almost an island. The castle of red sandstone was first built in 1083, and guards the entrance to the town and houses the Regimental Museum. Shrewsbury castle was a necessary defense against Saxon and Norman invaders, and having been rebuilt over the centuries, it now houses a regimental museum. The town's medieval wealth as a center of the wool trade can be seen in the attractive timber framed buildings in the High Street and in Fish Street. Closed on Mondays. If you buy a ticket that also includes Clive House and Rowley's House, it's '2 for 1' at all 3 attractions.

Shrewsbury Castle, Castle Street, Shrewsbury, Shropshire
☎ 01743 358516

🕐 10-5pm

 Shrewsbury

M 54 A 5

Map ref: A2

7. Royal Air Force Museum

Britain's largest and best kept collection of Military and Civil Transport Aircraft, including the history of civil aviation heritage in the British Airways Exhibition. You will find World War II aircraft including Spitfire, Hurricane and Mosquito, Research and Development aircraft, a huge missile collection and art galleries with works from the Second World War, 'War Artists Collection', seen for the first time outside London. The approach and central display hall are designed like a runway, complete with landing lights, and floor-to-roof windows give airfield views.

Royal Air Force (Aerospace) Museum, Cosford, Shifnal, Shropshire TF11 8UP
☎ 01902 374872

🕐 10-5pm

  CC All

 Bridgnorth/Telford

M 54 J3 A 41

Map ref: A2

8. Wenlock Priory

The small town of Much Wenlock is peppered with half-timbered buildings. Here, the prime attraction is the romantic ruins of Wenlock Priory, set in an interesting garden full of topiary. There are substantial remains of the early 13th century church and Norman chapter house. Running south west from Much Wenlock is the high scarp of Wenlock edge, which provides a magnificent view. Located 3 miles south west of Ironbridge. From 1st November to 31st March, open only between 10-1pm and 2-4pm, on Wed to Sunday. Otherwise daily from 10-6pm.

Wenlock Priory, Much Wenlock, Shropshire
☎ 01952 727466

🕐 10-6pm

 % Page 67

 Bridgnorth/Telford

M 54 A 5273/458

Map ref: B1

The Walled City of Chester

Once a Roman legionary fortress and naval base named Dewa, it rests on the loop of the River Dee. Chester was re-fortified at the start of the 10th century by the daughter of Alfred the Great, who extended the walls down to the river and created the present 2 mile circuit. The walls are accessible from various points, and provide the best views of the city and its surroundings. Perhaps to start with, glimpse at the past by visiting the Grosvenor Museum (free) **B1,** where you can trace the town's history, with an emphasis on Roman times, or visit the Heritage Centre **B1,** for the town's broader history. Chester is very attractive and is filled with fascinating sights. Highlights include the cathedral **A1,** the richly carved front of Bishop Lloyd's House **A1,** and the Rows along the main streets. The Rows **B1/2,** with their black and white architecture, are unique shopping arcades set on two levels that first appear in the city records for 1331. Katie's Tea Rooms **A/B1,** in Watergate Street is Britain's largest, and is set in one of the oldest buildings. Traveling 3 miles north of Chester you reach Chester Zoo **A1,** and another 3 miles to Cheshire Oaks **A1,** Europe's largest Designer Outlet Village. Ness Gardens **A1,** with its fine views of the Dee Estuary and Welsh Hills, are just 8 miles to

the north west of Chester. The NBCompass points you to North Wales in the west or choose from the other destinations.

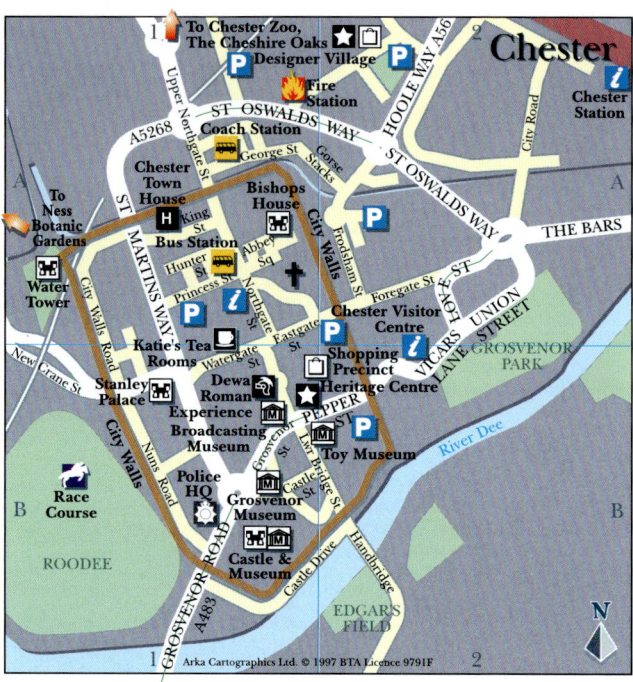

i **Tourist Information**

Chester ☎ 01244 351609

GF Chester

Hotels

Chester

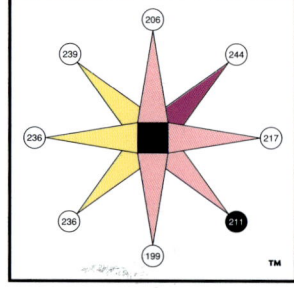

Distance from London

Chester 195miles

Heart of England

1. Chester Visitor Centre

A good place to start your trip around Chester. Admission is free, and a video presentation introduces the history, main features and places of interest. Enjoy the sounds, sights and smells as you stroll round a recreated typical Victorian Chester street. There are also working craft shops and a 'Rows' café.

Chester Visitor Centre, Vicars Lane, Chester
CH1 1QX
☎ 01244 351609

 9-6pm

 Chester

 56/53 A 51

Map ref: A2

2. Chester Heritage Centre

Another ideal introduction to the story of Chester and its unique buildings. The Heritage Centre was once one of the many churches of Chester. Follow the development of the city from prehistoric times to today, and find out why Chester's Rows and Walls were built and when. There is also a brass rubbing section. On Sundays the center is open from 12 to 5pm

Chester Heritage Centre, Bridge Street Row, Chester, Cheshire
☎ 01244 402008

 11-5pm

 Chester

M 56/53 A 51

Map ref: B1

3. Chester Cathedral

A place of worship for over 1,000 years. Parts of the Norman church, begun in 1092, can still be seen in the present building. Discover the finest choir stalls in Britain, with intricate carvings, and the famous 'Cobweb Picture'. There is a beautiful garden and admission to both the church and garden are free. An exhibition of the cathedral's history can also be seen here. A welcome leaflet is available.

Chester Cathedral, St Werburgh Street, Chester, Cheshire
☎ 01244 324756

7-6.30pm

Chester

M 56/53 A 51

Map ref: A1

4. Broadcasting Museum

A fascinating museum that tells the story of British Broadcasting from the early days to satellite TV, using a range of media. Return to the golden days of wireless, discover how your voice or picture goes 'on the air'and what goes on in a television studio. A unique collection of historic equipment, a selection of which you can buy. Sundays 11-4pm. Located next to 'Owen Owen' department store in Bridge Street (Upper Level).

Broadcasting Museum, 42 Bridge Street Row, Chester CH1 1NN
☎ 01244 348468

10-5pm

Chester

M 56/53 A 51

Map ref: B1

5. Dewa Roman Experience

Discover what life was like in Roman Britain. Step aboard a Roman Galley and stroll along reconstructed streets experiencing the sights, sounds and smells of Roman Chester. Explore the Roman fortress in the 10ft deep excavations and handle 'dig' discoveries in the 'finds' room. In the 'hands on' room you have an opportunity to try on some armour.

Dewa Roman Experience, Pierpoint Lane, Bridge Street, Chester
☎ 01244 343407

9-5pm

⇄ ▨ Chester

M 56/53   A 51

Map ref: B1

6. Grosvenor Museum

Admission is free to this interesting museum that takes you back into Chester's past. An introduction to the Roman Fortress of Dewa, its people, army and buildings. Walk through a unique reconstructed Roman graveyard, or visit a period house and Victorian schoolroom. Plus many more exhibitions and galleries. NBC cardholders also receive a 10% discount in the shop. On Sundays the museum is open from 2 - 5pm.

Grosvenor Museum, 27 Grosvenor Street, Chester
☎ 01244 402008

10.30-5pm

 % 10%

⇄ ▨ Chester

M 56/53   A 51

Map ref: B1

7. Chester Toy Museum

This museum houses the biggest collection of 'Matchbox' toys in Europe. It also features old amusement machines and even a 1950's Juke Box. Other interesting items on display are dolls, teddy bears, Meccano and Dinky, Hornby trains, (old toys) and much more besides. The NBC discount is a half price admission. Open every day and great fun.

Chester Toy Museum, 13 a Lower Bridge Street, Chester, Cheshire CH1 1RS
☎ 01244 346297

10-5pm

 % 50% off entry

⇄ ▨ Chester

M 56/53   A 51

Map ref: B2

8. Katies Tea Rooms

A rather special tea room to visit. This is England's biggest and oldest traditional tea rooms. Set in beautiful and historic buildings, 1,000 year old oak beams, wattle and daub, (old building method) walls, and silver service. Soak up the historic atmosphere as you enjoy a meal ,tea or coffee. Offer is a free color poster of the building in 1,300AD as a memento of your visit to this historic tearooms. Located in the center 100 yards along Watergate Street. Open from 10-6pm on Sundays.

Katies Tea Rooms, Watergate Street, Chester CH1 2LA
☎ 01244 400322

9-10pm

 Value £3

⇄ ▨ Chester

M 56/53   A 51

Map ref: A/B1

9. Cheshire Workshops

In the heart of the Cheshire countryside, and overlooked by medieval castles, is the Cheshire Workshops. Candle making is the greatest interest here, and these candle makers demonstrate hand carving, and provide numerous unusual gift ideas. There are also glass sculpture and pyrography, (poker work) showrooms. Located 9 miles south east of Chester. Entry is free. Sunday closing is at 4 pm.

Cheshire Workshops, Burwardsley, nr Chester, Cheshire CH3 9PF
☎ 01829 770401

 10-5pm.

 Chester

M 6/56 A 41/534

Map ref: B2

10. Chester Zoo

Chester Zoo is the UK's largest zoological gardens with over 5,000 animals in 500 species. The animal enclosures are spacious and set in over 100 acres of award winning gardens. There is also a huge tropical house, free-flight aviary, exotic birds and a penguin pool, an overhead railway and water bus. Situated 2 miles north of Chester city center, follow the signs. Open from 10am to 5.30 Summer, and 3.30pm Winter.

Chester Zoo, Upton-by-Chester, Cheshire CH2 1LH
☎ 01244 380280

 10-5pm

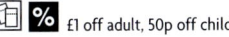 £1 off adult, 50p off child

 Chester

M 56 J15 A 41

Map ref: A1

11. Cheshire Oaks

The Designer Factory Outlet village is at junction 10 of the M53, (Sainsbury's exit). Here you can save up to 50% of the recommended retail prices of famous name goods and clothes. Parking is free. There are 60 stores including names such as Timberland, Levi's, Jaeger and Next, shoes, fashion and books. This is one of Europe's largest designer discount villages. Save hundreds of pounds with the book of special VIP discounts and coupons to be collected at the information desks when presenting the coupon in the back of this guide. Sundays 11-5pm.

Cheshire Oaks, Kinsley Road, Ellesmere Port, Cheshire L65 9JJ
☎ 0151 3567932

10-6pm

% Coupon

Ellesmere Port

M 53 J10

Map ref: A1

12. Ness Botanic Gardens

In 1898, Arthur Kilpin Bulley, a Liverpool cotton broker, founded Ness Gardens by building his house on a gorse-covered sandstone outcrop. He systematically incorporated surrounding fields into what has now become one of the country's leading botanic gardens, a learning garden, with plants from all over the world. On his behalf, pioneering plant collectors scoured the temperate regions of the Far East for alpine and hardy plants that could be cultivated in this climate. The gardens were bequeathed to the University of Liverpool by his daughter in 1948.

Ness Botanic Gardens, Ness, Neston, South Wirral L64 4AY
☎ 0151 353 0123

 9.30-5pm

  Chester

 M 53 J4

Map ref: A1

The Beatles 'Liverpool'

In 1207 King John set up rights for settlers to establish a port on the Mersey River. Chester as the key port was gradually abandoned, and the 'new' village of Liverpool became England's second port. In the 18th century it grew in prominence as a result of trade with America and the West Indies, and with that came great employment and prosperity. By the time Queen Victoria came to the throne Liverpool had become Britain's biggest commercial seaport. In the 1960's The Beatles gave the city a new reputation with the Liverpool sound and the Mersey beat.

Purchase a National Museums and Galleries on Merseyside pass, it is very inexpensive, and will enable you to visit 8 key local attractions, many of which are listed below. A visit to Albert Docks **B1**, encompasses the Beatles Story, Museum of Liverpool Life (NMGM), Tate Gallery, Maritime Museum (NMGM), and nearby Mersey Ferry. Other attractions in the busy center of Liverpool are, the Liverpool Museum (NMGM) and Walker Art Gallery (NMGM) **A2**, the Conservation Centre (NMGM) **A2**, the Cavern Quarter **A/B1**, and the Metropolitan Cathedral **B2**, that has a magnificent interior. Travel south of Liverpool to Speke Hall **B2**, and onto Paul McCartney's house, or across the Mersey, to Port Sunlight and the Lady Lever Art

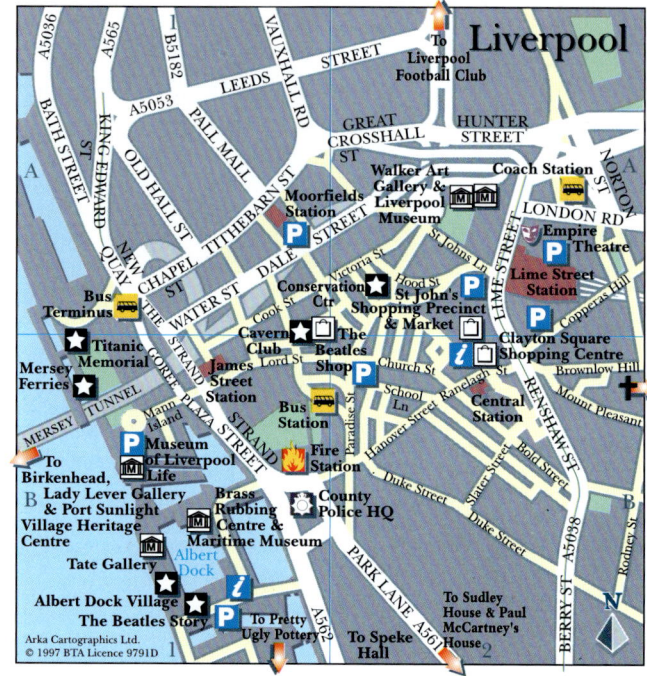

Gallery (NMGM) **B1**. North of the center is Liverpool Football Club **A2**.

_i_ **Tourist Information**

Liverpool, Albert Docks
☎ 0151 708 8854

Liverpool, City Centre
☎ 0151 709 3631

Hotels

Liverpool

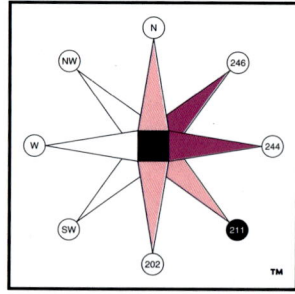

Distance from London

Liverpool 215 miles

1. Beatles Story

The Beatles Story is where you experience the most sensational success story the pop world has ever known, in the city where it all began. Re-live the Fab Four's meteoric rise to fame with this nostalgic story, in an award winning attraction. From Hamburg (in Germany) to the Cavern beat, and board a Yellow Submarine for a Magical Mystery Tour. There's a John Lennon exhibition, numerous photos, and so much more to discover about their lives and influences. The shop is full of Beatles gifts and collectables.

Beatles Story, Britannia Vaults, Albert Docks, Liverpool
☎ 0151 709 1963

10-6pm

 Liverpool/Lime Street
M 62/57

Map ref: B1

2. Tate Gallery

The Tate Gallery, which re-opened in July 1998, has an outstanding national collection of 20th century art. This is one of the best collections of contemporary art outside London. The gallery was converted from its warehouse setting by architect James Stirling. It opened in 1988 as London's first outstation and it is in a fine setting at the Albert Docks. Free entry, although a charge is made for special exhibitions. Closed on Mondays.

Tate Gallery, The Collonades, Albert Docks, Liverpool
☎ 0151 709 0507

10-6pm

Liverpool
M 62/57

Map ref: B1

3. Mersey Ferries

Take a 50 minute cruise with commentary and spectacular waterfront views on Liverpool's famous ferry across the Mersey. The ferries depart daily from Pier Head, Woodside and Seacombe, and you can break your journey at Seacombe Aquarium, (life beneath the Mersey) or at the Woodside restaurant for lunch or afternoon tea. Ferries at Pier Head are signposted from the Albert Docks and city center. From 9am on Saturdays and Sundays.

Mersey Ferries, Victoria Place, Seacombe, Wallasley L44 6QY
☎ 0151 630 1030

730-7pm

 Liverpool
M 62/57   A 41
www.connect.org.uk/merseyworld/ferries
Map ref: B1

4. Beatles Shop

The Beatles Shop, open 'Eight Days a Week', has perhaps the largest selection of Beatles goods, products and collectables. A trip to Liverpool would be incomplete without at least taking a look at what's for sale in this dedicated store. John, Paul, George and Ringo look down from above the shop entrance in Mathew Street. The in-store 'juke box' is full of Beatles singles and costs 10p a record (donated to charity). Please show your NBC card or guide to receive a free Beatles mug when spending over £5.

Beatles Shop, 31 Mathew Street, Liverpool
☎ 0151 236 8066

9.30-5.30pm
 £5+
Liverpool
M 62/57

Map ref: A1

5. The Magical Mystery Tour

The Beatles magical Mystery Tour is a two hour guided tour on a replica of the bus featured in the 'Magical Mystery Tour'. The tour departs each day at 2.20pm at the Albert Docks, and visits former homes, schools and birthplaces of the Beatles, Penny Lane, Strawberry Fields and ending in the world famous Cavern Club (free entry). You will also receive a free souvenir poster and a complimentary drink, or a souvenir from the Cavern Club. Please use the coupon in the back of the guide.

The Magical Mystery Tour, The Cavern Club, 10 Mathew Street, L2 6RE
☎ 0151 236 9091   Ⓕ 0151 236 8081

 £2 Coupon

Liverpool

M 62/57

Map ref: A1

6. The Conservation Centre

Buy the NMGM, (National Museums and Galleries on Merseyside) pass at any of their eight Museums and Galleries*, it's outstanding value. The Conservation Centre has recently won the, 'European Museum of the Year' award. It is the only center for museum conservation in Europe to open its doors to the public. Here you will discover how experts preserve everything, from birds and bugs, to fine oil paintings and furniture. Meet a conservator at work in a live video link, and take part in a hands-on activity or behind the scenes tour.

The Conservation Centre, Whitechapel, Liverpool L1 6HZ
☎ 0151 478 4999

 P

🕐 10-5pm

 % *NMGM

Liverpool

M 62/57
www.merseyworld.com/museums
Map ref: A2

7. Walker Art Gallery

Buy the NMGM, (National Museums and Galleries on Merseyside) pass at any of their eight Museums and Galleries*, it's outstanding value. The Walker Art Gallery, next to the Liverpool Museum, is one of the finest in the North of England, split into six main sections. From 13th century European art, passing through Pre-Raphaelite and Victorian, Impressionist and Post Impressionist to 20th century British, and a superb Sculpture Gallery which contains a priceless collection from the world's leading artists. Sundays 12-5pm.

Walker Art Gallery, William Brown Street, Liverpool L3 8EL
☎ 0151 478 4199

 P

🕐 10-5pm

% *NMGM

Liverpool

M 62/57

www.merseyworld.com/museums
Map ref: A2

8. Speke Hall

One of the most famous half-timbered houses in the country. The Great Hall, Oak Parlour and priest holes evoke Tudor times while the small rooms, some with William Morris wallpapers, show the Victorian desire for privacy and comfort. Fine plasterwork and tapestries, plus a fully equipped Victorian kitchen and servants' hall. The restored garden has spring bulbs, rose garden, rhododendrons, summer border and stream garden; bluebell walks in the ancient Clough Woodland; spectacular views of grounds and the Mersey basin from a high embankment 'the Bund', peaceful walks in wildlife oasis of Stocktons Wood. Located just 8 miles from Liverpool's center.

Speke Hall, The Walk, Liverpool L24 1XD
☎ 0151 427 7231

 P

🕐 Page 91

 Page 66

Liverpool

M 62/57   A 5300

Map ref: B2

9. Paul McCartney's House

The House where Paul McCartney lived is outside the city center, and accessible only by a *local bus from Speke Hall or a taxi from the center. A 1950's terraced house, this is an interest for the really dedicated followers of the Beatles and McCartney. Number 20, Forthlin Road is a modest home with a rose bush and fence at the front, here Lennon and McCartney did much of their practising and early songwriting. Please note that all visitors must reserve in advance.

Paul McCartney's House, 20 Forthlin Road, Liverpool
☎ 0870 900 0256

 Page 91

 Page 66

 Liverpool and Taxi/Local Bus*

M 62/57

Map ref: B2

10. Port Sunlight Heritage Centre

Port Sunlight is a picturesque 19th century garden village just 20 minutes from Liverpool or Chester, built by William Lever, (Unilever) for the workers in his soap factory. At the Heritage Centre, (*entry is only 40-50p) you can learn the history of the village, the factory and its workers. Do visit the Lady Lever Art Gallery, whilst you are here, which contains some extraordinary works of art and 1,800 Wedgwood pieces.

Port Sunlight Heritage Centre, 95 Greendale Road, Port Sunlight, Wirral L62 4XE
☎ 0151 644 6466

  P

 10-4pm

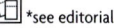 *see editorial

 Port Sunlight   Birkenhead

M 53 J4

Map ref: B1

11. Pretty Ugly Pottery

The Pretty Ugly Pottery Experience is a tour, (given by a pretty ugly tour guide) which will show you the processes involved in creating the famous Pretty Ugly Pottery. The process keeps alive the ancient art of hand thrown pottery, turning clay into a crafted mug. You can make one yourself and either collect it a few days later or have it sent to you, a unique experience! Alternatively, watch the craftsmen and women at work using skills that are thousands of years old, and then buy one from the gift shop. Offer is 2 for 1 on the tour.

Pretty Ugly Pottery, Mariners Wharf, Queens Dock, Liverpool
☎ 0151 707 1000

 P

 10-5pm

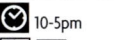 Tour

 Liverpool

M 6/62

Map ref: B1

12. Liverpool Football Club Museum & Tour

This successful football club has just got better! Their new interactive museum is now open. All the cups, trophies, medals, rare memorabilia, shirts of the famous stars, two unique films and a real penalty shooting range. You can take a unique 'behind-the-scenes' tour of 'Fortress Anfield' with a chance to see the 'Home' dressing room and even sit in the Managers seat, this combines to make the attraction quite an experience. Open every day, but no tours (*must be booked in advance) on match days.

Liverpool Football Club Museum & Tour, Anfield Road, Liverpool L4 0TH
☎ 0151 260 6677

 P

 10-5pm

 Liverpool

M 62/57

Map ref: A2

for more fascinating days out on Merseyside

the NMGM **eight** pass

NATIONAL MUSEUMS AND GALLERIES ON MERSEYSIDE

**buy an eight pass
and visit again and again
the National Museums & Galleries
on Merseyside**

You can buy your
'eight pass' from any of the
eight NMGM attractions.
To find out more telephone 0151 207 0001.

**value for money –
for a full 12 months**

Heart of England

'15th to the 21st Century' in Cheshire

The peaceful villages of Cheshire hold many delights, some influenced by the Industrial Revolution, others influencing the future and today's world. Starting at Arley Hall **1**, and traveling onto the two stately homes at Tatton Park **2**. Continuing east, Quarry Bank Mill, (founded in 1784) at Styal **3**, is a wonderfully restored cotton mill and living museum, it is enormous, and was one of Britain's biggest producers by the 1840's. The mill owner and workers were housed in Styal, and many of their houses remain.

Macclesfield, is a former silk center, and the history of silk is told at the Silk Museum **4**. Jodrell Bank **5**, is where you enter the 21st century. The big surprise is the 250ft Radio Telescope dish towering above such beautiful surroundings. Dropping south, there are the gardens of Biddulph Grange **6**, and the delightful Little Moreton Hall **7**, with its amazing black timbers and white plaster it was built in the 15th century within a moat. At this point you are just north of 'The Potteries' at Stoke-on-Trent, or you can visit Stapeley Water Gardens **8**, and the elegant town of Nantwich. Towns ending in '-

wich' were salt towns and their story is told at Northwich, in the Salt Museum **9**.

Tourist Information

Nantwich   ☎ 01270 610983

Hotels

nr Macclesfield - Nantwich

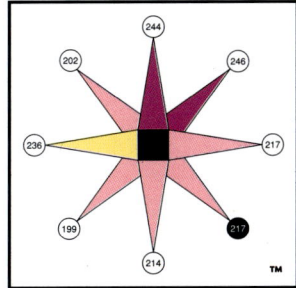

Distance from London

Nantwich 175miles

1. Arley Hall and Gardens

Arley Hall, with its ancient history, extensive gardens and parkland, has been owned and run by the same family for more than 500 years. The original hall was built in 1468, and the present hall and chapel were built between 1832 and 1845 in the Victorian Jacobean style. There is fine plasterwork, paintings, porcelain and a magnificent library. The gardens are delightful. The grounds, gardens and chapel are closed on Mondays. The hall is open May to August 11-5pm on Tuesdays and Sundays.

Arley Hall, Arley, near Northwich, Cheshire
☎ 01565 777353

 11-5pm

 Knutsford

M 6/56

2. Tatton Park

One of the most complete historic estates in England that is open to visitors. The early 19th-century Wyatt house, set within a landscaped deer park, contains the Egerton family collection of pictures, books, china, glass, silver and specially commissioned Gillow furniture; servants'rooms and cellars depict life 'downstairs'. The theme of grandeur extends into the gardens, features include a spectacular Japanese garden, Italian garden, orangery, fernery, rose garden and pinetum. Located 15 miles south of Manchester. *The offer applies only to the Explorer Ticket.

Tatton Park, Knutsford, Cheshire WA16 6QN
☎ 01565 654822

 Page 91

 % *20% Page 66

 Knutsford

 6 J19 A 556

3. Quarry Bank Mill & Styal Country Park

A Georgian cotton mill, built in 1784 by Samuel Greg, an early pioneer of the factory system. Still in working order, it gives an insight into the evolution of the cotton textile industry and early industrial revolution. The restored Apprentice House provides a glimpse into the life of the pauper apprentice children who did menial tasks at the mill. The mill is powered by a magnificent 50 ton waterwheel. During 1997 a project to restore steam power using an 1840's beam engine took place. The engine and new displays are installed in the original engine house. Extra charge for special events. Located 10 miles south of Manchester.

Quarry Bank Mill &Styal Country Park, Wilmslow, Cheshire SK9 4LA
☎ 01625 527468

 Page 91

  Page 66

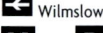 Wilmslow Manchester

 56 B 5166

4. Silk Museum and Paradise Mill

Macclesfield Silk Museum presents the fascinating story of silk, linking Macclesfield to China and the Far East. There is a colourful audio visual programme, exhibitions, models and room settings. The offer is combined with Paradise Mill, just a short distance away, where Jacquard silk handlooms have been restored and are used for demonstrations. The museum was a working silk mill until 1981. The Silk Museum is open from 11-5 each day except Sundays 1-5pm, and Paradise Mill is open Tuesday - Sunday 1-5pm.

Silk Museum and Paradise Mill, Roe Street, Macclesfield, Cheshire SK7 6MD
☎ 01625 613210

 11-5pm

 Macclesfield

 6 J17   523

Heart of England

5. Jodrell Bank

This science center, planetarium and arboretum, (garden of trees) is one of the Cheshire highlights. The 250ft Radio Telescope stands as a prominent landmark, it provides a unique and dramatic hi-tech scientific backdrop. At the feet of the telescope stands the Science Centre, Planetarium and beautiful Arboretum. The exhibition contains interactive displays on astronomy, energy and the environment, and tours the wonders of the sky at night. Offer doesn't include English Bank Holidays. Open from 23rd March to 22nd October. Situated on the A535.

Jodreii Bank, Lower Withington, Near Macclesfield, Cheshire SK11 9DL
☎ 01477 571339

10.30-5.30pm

CC Visa

Holmes Chapel   Macclesfield

M 6 J18   A 535

6. Biddulph Grange Garden

An exciting and rare survival of a High Victorian garden, acquired by the National Trust in 1988 and focus of an extensive restoration project. Conceived by James Bateman, the 15 acres are divided into a number of smaller gardens designed to house specimens from his extensive and wide ranging plant collection. An Egyptian Court, Chinese Pagoda, Joss House, Bridge and Pinetum, together with many other settings, all combine to make the garden a miniature tour of the world. Located 6 miles north of Stoke-on-Trent.

Biddulph Grange Garden, Biddulph Grange, Biddulph, Stoke-on-Trent ST8 7SD
☎ 01782 517999

Page 91

Page 66

Congleton

M 6 J15/17   A 500/527

7. Little Moreton Hall

Begun in 1450 and completed in 1580 Little Moreton is regarded as the finest example of a timber-framed moated manor house in the country. The drunkenly reeling south front opens onto a cobbled courtyard and the main body of the Hall. The Chapel, Elizabethan Long Gallery, Great Hall, wall paintings and Knot Garden are of particular interest. Location for Granada TV's 1996 adaptation of Daniel Defoe's novel Moll Flanders. There are optional, and free guided tours (50 minutes) at regular intervals throughout the afternoon. Located 4 miles south west of Congleton.

Little Moreton Hall, Congleton, Cheshire CW12 4SD
☎ 01260 272018

Page 91

Page 66

Congleton   Leek

M 6 J16/17   A 34

8. Stapeley Water Gardens

This is the world's largest water garden center, and has over 60 acres of gardens, lakes and fountains. The 'Palms Tropical Oasis' is a glass house paradise of waterfalls, fountains, exotic palm trees and flowering plants. See piranhas, sharks, reptiles, huge koi carp, monkeys, parrots and macaws. There is also a National Collection of over 200 Water Lilies. Open on Sundays from 11-5pm.

Stapeley Water Gardens, London Road, Nantwich, Cheshire
☎ 01270 623868

9-6pm

Nantwich

M 6   A 51/529

The Potteries 'Stoke-on-Trent'

In 1910 a group of six towns, Tunstall, Burslem, Hanley, Stoke-on-Trent, Fenton and Longton, came together under one inclusive name, Stoke-upon-Trent (The Potteries). When visiting this area, its capital and main shopping location is Hanley, with Stoke railway station 1 mile south. When planning your visit, the locations of the various towns should be considered as they are quite spread apart. The best local transport is the Wedgwood Express, this is linked to the Rail service from London (pick up a leaflet from the Tourist Information Centre **A2**). The key potteries starting from the north and ending in the south are Royal Doulton at Burslem **A1**, tour, shop and museum. The Potteries Museum at Hanley **A1**. Bridgewater Factory Shop at Hanley **A2**. Spode at Stoke **A1**, tour, shop and museum. Gladstone at Longton **B2**, museum. Wedgwood at Barlaston **B2** (and further south) tour, shop, museum. There are numerous factory shops along the routes, but please keep in mind that 'first' wares cost the same as London or anywhere else in England, the bargains are for the 'seconds', (which are not quite perfect) or if you can buy something that is not available in the US. The Wedgwood Express Bus service, (highly recommended) runs from the city center around the

Potteries, and a day pass allows you to hop on and hop off as you like. Discover more with the NBCompass.

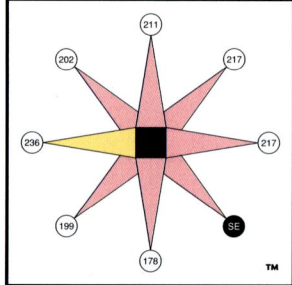

i Tourist Information

Stoke on Trent ☎ 01782 284600

🚌 Wedgwood Express

Hotels

STAKIS HOTELS Stoke-on-Trent

Stoke-on-Trent

Distance from London

Stoke 165miles

1. Royal Doulton Visitor Centre

Opened in May 1996, the center has been officially named the 'Home of the Royal Doulton Figure'. With over 1,500 figures on display, a museum and movie theater tell the story of Royal Doulton. There is a demonstration area where you can see the craftsmen and women at work, and you can even try making a pottery flower. Guided tours are available, (90 minutes) but should be booked in advance. There is a restaurant and two shops selling reduced price tableware and giftware. Open Sundays 10-4pm. Please show the NBC Card and Guide.

Royal Doulton Visitor Centre, Nile Street, Burslem, Stoke on Trent, Staffs
☎ 01782 292434

 9.30-5pm

 £1 off entry

 Stoke

M 6 J 16　**A** 500/50　**B** 5051

Map ref: A1

2. Moorcroft

It was in 1928 that Queen Mary appointed W Moorcroft, Potters to Her Majesty the Queen. The pottery has just celebrated its centenary year 1897-1997, and the company is still supplying Liberty of London and Shreve & Co. of San Francisco in the USA. The methods of production are much the same today as they were many years ago with their brilliance of color. The museum displays some remarkable pieces as well as taking you through the history of the company. Tours, (at 11am) take approximately 1 hour and there is a small charge. Admission is free.

Moorcroft, Sandbach Road, Burslem, Stoke-on-Trent
☎ 01782 207943

 P

 10-5pm

 Stoke

M 6 J15　**A** 53

www.moorcroft.com
Map ref: A1

3. Potteries Museum

The Potteries Museum houses the world's largest collection of Staffordshire ceramics. Formerly the City Museum and Art Gallery, the museum offers an opportunity to look at the history, and background to the famous and unique 'Potteries'region of Stoke-on-Trent, that is made up of six towns. The museum is in Hanley, (the city center) which is north of Stoke-on-Trent. Tours are available. Sundays 2-5pm.

Potteries Museum, Bethesda Street, Hanley, Stoke-on-Trent
☎ 01782 202173

 **P**

10-5pm

Stoke

M 6 J 15

Map ref: A1

4. Bridgewater Potteries

In 1984 Emma Bridgewater (born Cambridge and educated at Oxford) set up Bridgewater to produce beautiful and traditionally made English earthenware. The blend with contemporary designs, makes this a fabulous collection of pottery, both exciting and individual. The pieces recall the charm of period farmhouse kitchens with original patterns and themes, that are applied using hand decorating. For an exciting present or for your own use, this is unique but practical. Offer applies in the factory shop.

Bridgewater Potteries, Eastwood Works, Lichfield Street, Hanley, Stoke-on-Trent ST1 3EJ
☎ 01782 201328

  P

 9.30-4.30pm

 5% (Shop)

 Stoke

M 6 J15　**A** 50

Map ref: A2

5. Spode

Over the past 200 years Spode has become one of the most famous ceramics names in the world, here you have the opportunity to visit the pottery. This is the oldest pottery, that is still on its original site, in the UK. The ceramics are very collectable and the visitor center has live demonstrations, crafts, tours and an excellent factory shop. Located near the Stoke-on-Trent railway station. Offer applies to the Visitor Centre. Open on Sundays 10 - 4pm.

Spode, Church Street, Stoke-on-Trent, Staffordshire ST4 1BX
☎ 01782 744011

 9-5pm

 Stoke

M 6 J15/16

Map ref: A1

6. Wedgwood Visitor Centre

Wedgwood Visitor Centre is where you can discover and experience the unique creation of Wedgwood ceramics. Watch potters and decorators, try your hand at these skills, and then take a trip to the 'living museum' to see the history of Wedgwood since 1759 to the modern times. Here, there are hundreds of rare and beautiful pieces. Take the Wedgwood Express Bus service to or from here (it takes you around the Potteries). Wedgwood is located in Barlaston, south of Stoke-upon-Trent. Saturday 10-5pm, Sunday 10-4pm.

Wedgwood Visitor Centre, Barlaston, Stoke-on-Trent ST12 9ES
☎ 01782 282120

 9-5pm
 % 10% (Shop)
 Stoke

M 6 J15   A 34
www.wedgwood.co.uk
Map ref: B2

7. Gladstone Working Pottery Museum

With its cobbled yard and impressive giant bottle kilns, (ovens) Gladstone Pottery perfectly captures the city's atmospheric past. It is the only complete Victorian Pottery factory that is preserved from an era of coal fired Bottle Ovens. Here you may see demonstrations of traditional pottery techniques. Situated in Longton on the A50, 3 miles south east of Stoke station.

Gladstone Working Pottery Museum, Uttoxeter Road, Longton, Stoke-on-Trent, Staffs ST3 1PQ
☎ 01782 319232

 10-5pm.
 Stoke

M 6 J15

Map ref: B2

8. Aynsley China

The company was founded in 1775, and has a long tradition of making fine bone china that is sold across the world. Aynsley are best known for their fine bone china giftware and tableware. Located in Longton close to the Gladstone Pottery, the Aynsley factory shop has an excellent range of 'seconds' and discontinued lines available at much reduced prices. Open Sunday 11-4pm.

Aynsley China, Sutherland Road, Longton, Stoke-on-Trent
☎ 01782 599499

 9-5.30pm

 Stoke

M 6 J15   A 500

Map ref: B2

'Jane Austen's and the Peak District

Derby, is the home of Royal Crown Derby **1**, and has the county's only cathedral. Located in the southern part of Derbyshire, the region has a unique custom of Well Dressing (water worship) between May and September, when Wells and attractive water sources are 'dressed', with pictures made from natural growing things. From Derby, car enthusiasts can travel a short distance to Donington **3**, others can experience a number of literary connections.

Continue up to the Derwent Valley Centre **4**, to uncover the area's Industrial Heritage, or to Wingfield Manor **5**, and Matlock, where The Red House Stables Carriage Museum **6**, provides many stagecoaches, horses, and carriages used in films such as 'Jane Eyre' and 'Pride and Prejudice'. From there to Bakewell, (well known for Bakewell tart) and Haddon Hall **7**, where Jane Austen stayed whilst writing 'Pride and Prejudice'.

Nearby, one of Britain's most impressive stately homes is Chatsworth House **8**.

Continuing north is Hathersage **9**, where Charlotte Bronte spent two weeks at the vicarage in 1895, and renamed the village 'Morton' in her novel Jane Eyre. Travel west to the gracious spa town of Buxton **10**, 1,000ft up in the Peak District, home to an historic Opera House, and an

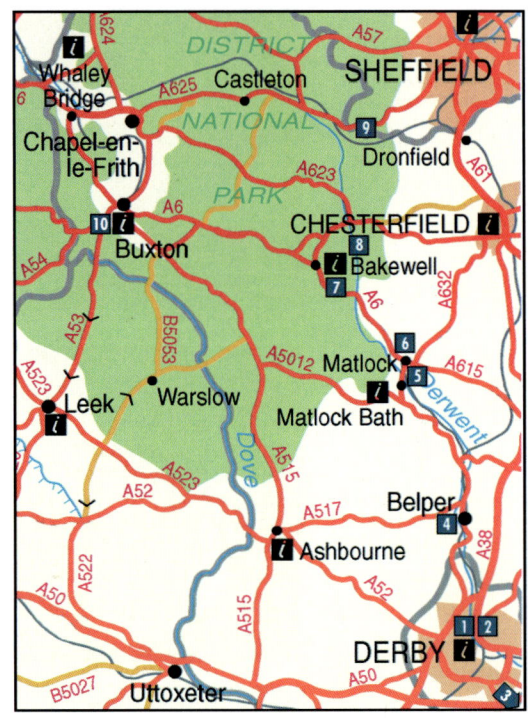

excellent base for breathtaking walks. The NBCompass highlights the surrounding experiences.

i Tourist Information

Bakewell	☎ 01629 813227
Buxton	☎ 01298 25106
Derby	☎ 01332 255802
Matlock	☎ 01629 55082

👑 Hotels

nr Ashbourne - Buxton - Derby - Hathersage

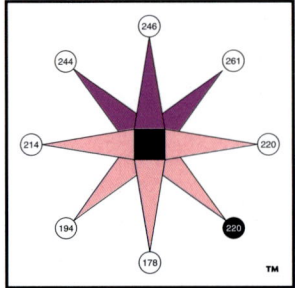

Distance from London

Derby 126miles

1. Royal Crown Derby

Home of Royal Crown Derby pottery, here you can discover how it's produced. This is a fascinating exhibition, away from the usual hustle and bustle of the Potteries in nearby Stoke-on-Trent, where many of the most celebrated ceramics manufacturers are now based. The shop has both new and 'seconds' for sale. Tours run twice a day in the summer weekdays, it is advisable to book. No children allowed under 10 years old. Generally open from 10am to 4pm, but closed for lunch 12.30-2pm Monday to Friday.

Royal Crown Derby, Osmaston Road, Derby
☎ 01332 712800

  P

 10-4pm

Derby

M 1 J25   **A** 52

www.royal-crown-derby.co.uk

2. Derby Industrial Museum

The Silk Mill, in which the museum is located, was built between 1717 and 1721. It was the prototype for Britain's first modern factory, and a model for subsequent factory development. It displays an introduction to Derby and its industrial history. There are sections on mining, quarrying, railway and general engineering, and the manufacture of bricks and stoneware. The museum is famous for its collection of Rolls-Royce aero engines. Closed on Sunday .

Derby Industrial Museum, The Silk Mill, off Full Street, Derby DE1 3AR
☎ 01332 255308

  P

 10-5pm

 Derby

M 1 J25   **A** 52

3. Donington Grand Prix Collection

A priceless array of cars, depicting the story and development of the racing car. Among the collection you will find cars produced by the BRM marque, together with Maserati, the diminutive Austin Seven racers, and the famous Ferrari and Bugatti marques. Then there are world championship cars driven by the likes of Jim Clark, Jackie Stewart, and Nigel Mansell's Williams. The museum has five halls filled with an enviable collection that is sure to delight any racing enthusiast.

Donington Grand Prix Collection, Donington Park, Castle Donington, Derbyshire DE74 2RP
☎ 01332 811027

 P

 10-5pm

  Derby

M 1 J23a   **A** 453

4. Derwent Valley Visitor Centre

Derwent Valley Visitor Centre is situated in Belper North Mill, and is a former cotton spinning mill which was constructed in 1803, and is regarded as one of the world's most important industrial buildings. The reason is that it is the first completely fireproof building remaining in the world today. The mill contains heritage, spinning and cotton winding exhibitions. Florence Nightingale, (1820-1910) was raised in nearby Lea Village, (see also, the Florence Nightingale Museum in London). Open from 1-5pm Thursday to Sunday.

Derwent Valley Visitor Centre, Belper North Mill, Bridgefoot, Belper DE56 1YD
☎ 01773 841485

 P

 1-5pm

 % 50p off entry

 Belper

A 6/517

5. Wingfield Manor

This huge, ruined country mansion was built in the mid 15th century. Mary Queen of Scots was imprisoned here in 1569. Though unoccupied since the late 1770's, the Gothic 'Great Hall 'and 'High Tower' are a testament to its heyday. It has been used in the film 'Jane Eyre'. Located 17 miles north of Derby. Open Wednesday to Sunday.

Wingfield Manor, Wingfield, Derbyshire
☎ 01773 832060

   P

🕐 12-5pm

 % Page 67

⇄ 🖊 Alfreton 4 miles

M 1 J28 **A** 38 **B** 5035

6. Red House Stables

One of the finest collections of original horse-drawn vehicles and equipment. Here you can see the many horses and carriages that are used in film and television productions including, 'Pride and Prejudice', 'Jane Eyre', 'Sense and Sensibility' and many more. There are trips by horse and carriage that can be arranged but booking is recommended. Located 1 mile north of Matlock off the A6. Weekends 10-4pm.

Red House Stables, Old Road, Derby Dale, Matlock, Derby DE4 2ER
☎ 01629 733583

  P

🕐 10-5pm

 🗓

⇄ 🖊 Matlock

M 1 J28/29

7. Haddon Hall

Built over 600 years ago, and overlooking the River Wye this rambling and quintessentially English medieval castle with its terraced gardens has escaped the ravages of time. Used on location for Zefirelli's film of 'Jane Eyre' and the birthplace of Haddon Hall Minton china, it really should enchant you. Haddon is 2 miles south of Bakewell on the A6.

Haddon Hall, Bakewell, Derbyshire DE45 1LA
☎ 01629 812855

  P

🕐 11-5pm

 🗓

⇄ Chesterfield 🖊 Derby

M 1 J30 **A** 6

8. Chatsworth

Chatsworth is one of England's finest houses. Although the offer is for the gardens, the house should certainly be visited, (look out for the painting of a violin hanging on a door in the music room). The gardens contain spectacular fountains, ponds and a canal, a giant rockery, rose gardens and a maze. Recent additions include a 'Cottage and Kitchen' garden. Offer is one adult at child rate with one full paying adult, garden entry only. Open mid March to the end October. *Ask for a 'Treasure Houses' discount leaflet, to receive discounts and free guides at their other 9 properties in the guide.

Chatsworth, Bakewell, Derbyshire DE45 1PP
☎ 01246 582204

 P

🕐 11-5pm

 % *Treasure Houses

CC All

⇄ Chesterfield 🖊 Bakewell

M 1 J29 **A** 6

Robin Hood Country

The name, Nottingham is most associated with the evil Sheriff, lace making and the writer, D.H. Lawrence (1885-1930). The Sheriff may be fictional but Nottingham Castle **1**, built on top of the 128ft rock above the city, is not. Today the town is well known for its broad industrial base with firms such as Boots, (the pharmacists) and Raleigh, (bicycles). Visit theTales of Robin Hood **2**, Galleries of Justice **3**, Caves **4**, Museum of Costume **5**, and as the city has long been famous for its lace, the Lace Centre **6**.

On the edge of Nottingham visit Thrumpton Hall **13**, (2 for 1 with your NBC card) or travel north west to Eastwood **7**, the birthplace of D.H. Lawrence, and the home of the poet Lord Byron, (1778-1824) at Newstead Abbey **8**. Traveling east from here, you'll arrive at the unique Upton Hall Watch and Clock Museum **9**, and Newark Castle **10**. The Sherwood Forest Visitor Centre **11**, and the World of Robin Hood **12**, are 18 miles from Nottingham's center. This is where the legendary Robin Hood lived, 'took from the rich to give to the poor', and poached venison from the forests of the King, with the resultant fights against the evil Sheriff of Nottingham. There's more to discover with the NBCompass.

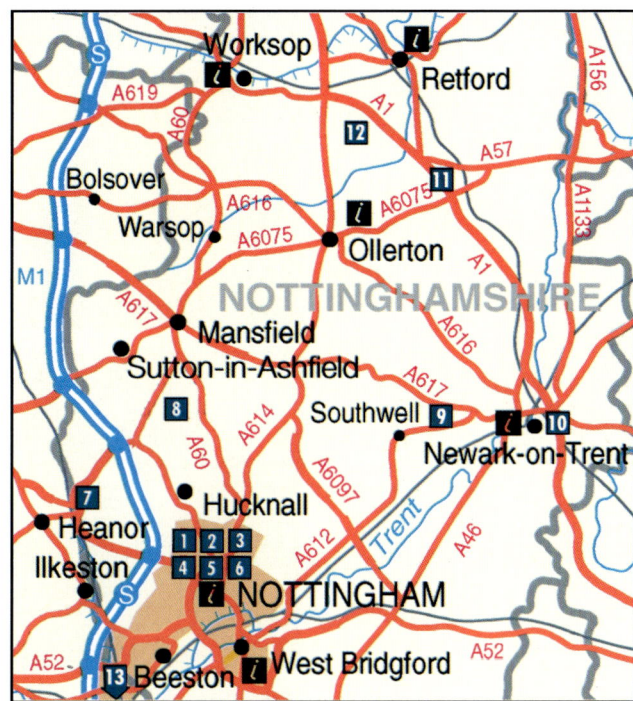

i **Tourist Information**
Nottingham ☎ 0115 915 5330

Hotels

STAKIS HOTELS Nottingham

👑 Nottingham

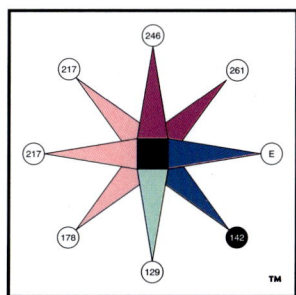

Distance from London

Nottingham 126 miles ➡

1. Nottingham Castle

Nottingham Castle, the museum and art gallery are one of the most visited attractions in the region. The exhibitions are lively and set in a magnificent Ducal mansion, the location has some spectacular views of the city, made famous by its 'Sheriff' and the tales of Robin Hood. Located in the city center and open daily, *entry is free Monday to Friday, but a small charge is made at weekends.

Nottingham Castle, Castle Gate, Nottingham NG1 6EL
☎ 0115 915 3700

 10-5pm

 *Mon-Fri

Nottingham

M 1 J26

2. The Tales of Robin Hood

Travel back in time in the company of the world's favorite outlaw, Robin Hood. At the Tales of Robin Hood you will be given an experience of medieval adventure in sight, sound and smell. Escape from the evil Sheriff of Nottingham and flee to Sherwood Forest in the unique adventure cars. Follow the tourism signs to Nottingham City Centre for Maid Marian Way.

The Tales of Robin Hood, 30-38 Maid Marian Way, Nottingham NG1 6GF
☎ 0115 948 3284

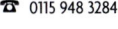

 10-6pm

Nottingham

 M 1 J26

3. Galleries of Justice

Located in the magnificent, grade2 listed, Shire Hall, this award-winning museum takes you through more than 250 years of crime, punishment and law, on a unique, historic site. Witness the splendour of the magnificent Victorian courtroom and interact with the warders of the old county gaol (jail, slammer). New in 1998, the Police Galleries and the Crime and Punishment Galleries, an arresting experience! New in 1999, the Discovery Galleries. Closed on Mondays. Please use the coupon in the back of the guide.

Galleries of Justice, Shire Hall, High Pavement, Lace Market, Nottingham NG1 1HN
☎ 0115 952 0555

 10-5pm

Coupon

 Nottingham

 M 1 J26 A 52

4. The Caves of Nottingham

Guided by an informative audio-tape, (English, French, German and Spanish) visitors can explore a 700 year old man-made cave system which lies beneath a modern day shopping center. The caves were previously used as dwelling places, storage rooms and pub cellars before their most recent use as air raid shelters during the Second World War. The system also features England's only remaining underground medieval tannery, and Victorian slum remains. The caves open 1 hour later on Sundays.

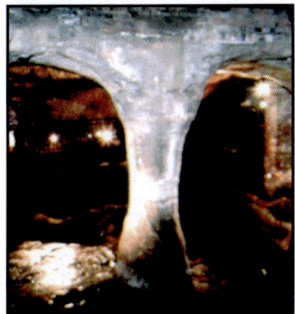

The Caves of Nottingham, Drury Walk, Broadmarsh Centre, Nottingham NG1 7LS
☎ 0115 924 1424

 P

 10-4.15pm

Nottingham

 M 1 J26 A 52

5. The Museum of Costume & Textiles

The museum is located in a row of elegant late 17th and 18th century houses, near to the Gatehouse and Robin Hood Statue. The majority of the costume is middle class, although there are examples of haute-couture and working class. This would be expected for, the middle class save their clothes, the upper class pass them on, and the working class wear them out. Apart from the superb collection of costume, (in chronological order) and accessories, the finest collection of machine made lace in the country can be found here. Closed on Monday and Tuesday.

The Museum of Costume & Textiles, 51 Castle Gate, Nottingham NG1 6AF
☎ 0115 915 3500

 10-4pm

 Nottingham
M 1 J26 A 52

6. The Lace Centre

Nottingham has long been famous for its exquisite lace and the Lace Centre, a medieval 14th century house, is filled to capacity. There are demonstrations of lacemaking on Thursdays from 2-4pm between April and October and knowledgeable staff who will be pleased to answer any questions you may have at any time. Admission is free and the center is located below the castle wall opposite the Robin Hood statue.

The Lace Centre Castle Road, Seven's Building, Nottingham NG1 6AA
☎ 0115 941 3539

 10-5pm

Nottingham
M 1 J26 A 52

7. D.H. Lawrence Birthplace Museum

DH Lawrence, (1885-1930) was an influential English poet and novelist who was born in Nottinghamshire, the son of a miner. His works include, 'Sons and Lovers', 'Women in Love', and Lady Chatterley's Lover'. The house at 8a Victoria Street has been restored and furnished to the style of a miner's home in 1885, when the Lawrence family lived there. A video presentation tells of his early life. Eastwood, where the museum is located, is 7 miles north west of Nottingham.

D.H. Lawrence Birthplace Museum, 8a Victoria Street, Eastwood, Nottingham
☎ 01773 763312

 10-5pm

 Nottingham
M 1 J26 A 610

8. Newstead Abbey

Newstead Abbey is a beautiful historic house set in extensive gardens and parklands. Once the home of the romantic poet Lord Byron, (1788-1824) his own apartments and many splendid 19th century rooms have been restored, together with important collections of manuscripts and poems, and first editions of his work. Located 12 miles north of Nottingham on the A60, Mansfield Road. The grounds are open all year and the house from April 1st to 30th September. Offer includes house and grounds.

Newstead Abbey, Linby, Nottingham NG15 8GE
☎ 01623 793557

 9-5pm

Nottingham
M 1 J27 A 60

9. Upton Hall Clock & Watch Museum

The British Horological Institute at Upton Hall, is in a Grade 2 listed, (British preservation order) late Georgian Country House with Victorian renovations. Home of the Institute, a professional body formed to look after the training of watch and clock makers. See the collection of clocks, watches and artifacts (made by human workmanship). To check the exact time in Britain you can telephone a speaking clock, (dial 123) this is known as TIM and the original is here. There's a connection to the Royal Observatory in Greenwich. On the A612 in the village of Upton. Afternoons only April to mid August.

Upton Hall Clock & Watch Museum, Upton Hall, Upton, Newark NG23 5TE
☎ 01636 813795

 1.30-5.30pm

CC MC Visa

⇄ Newark ⇗ Nottingham

A 612

10. Newark Castle

The historic ruins date back to the early 12th century. Newark was of strategic importance during the Civil War, when it withstood three sieges by Parliamentarians before the castle was ordered to be partially destroyed. The remaining Norman gatehouse is considered to be a fine example. King John is said to have died at Newark castle, and in the adjoining Gilstrap Centre, the 'Newark Story' exhibition presents the fascinating history of the castle.

Newark Castle, Gilstrap Centre, Castlegate, Newark NG24 1BG
☎ 01636 78962

 10-5pm

⇄ Newark ⇗ Nottingham

M 1 A 1/46

11. Sherwood Forest Visitor Centre

The forest that provided cover for Robin Hood and his Merry Men. Actually, of the vast area of oak and silver birch, very little was actually forest during the time of Robin Hood. The Visitor Centre is in Sherwood Forest County Park at Edinstowe, 18 miles north of Nottingham city, off the A614. It stands near the Major Oak, (known as Robin Hood's tree) and there is an exhibition of life-size models of Robin, and the other outlaws. The center has as much information as is known about Robin, the Merry Men and Maid Marian, who he is said to have married. Little John's grave can be seen at Hathersage.

Sherwood Forest Visitor Centre, Edwinstowe, Mansfield, Nottinghamshire
☎ 01623 823202

 9.30-4.30

⇄ ⇗ Mansfield

M 1 A 614/616

12. World of Robin Hood

Visitors are taken back in time to the 12th century, where a costumed guide takes you into Robin Hood's medieval England. This attraction is designed to be an adventure into a Sherwood Forest and Nottingham castle experience, through armouries, dungeons and into the Banqueting Hall, then out into the streets to see craftsmen and how people lived. There are other attractions such as the World of Owls and the Fairytale World of Robin Hood. Located 5 miles east of Sherwood Forest.

World of Robin Hood, Haughton Farm Haughton, nr Retford, DN22 8DZ
☎ 01623 860210

 10.30-5pm

CC MC Visa

⇄ ⇗ Retford

A 1

SOUTH AND MID WALES. Cardiff is Wales' capital city and the youngest capital city in Europe, located, where most of the population live, in the south east of the region. The Welsh national flag is a red dragon on a white and green field. The national emblem is a 'leek', national sport, rugby and perhaps the most familiar symbols are the 'welsh lovespoon', Laura Ashley and the superb Welsh male voice choirs.

Sometimes referred to as one of Britain's best kept secrets, it is a land of mountains and green hills on the western coast of Britain. Wales is quite compact, being no more than 200 miles from north to south.

The south and mid Wales region developed coal mines and ironworks in the valleys through the 18th and 19th centuries, which since the decline in the coal industry, has changed the face of the area. Heading about 25 miles north of Cardiff, in South Glamorgan are the Brecon Beacons, (a 520 sq mile National Park). This is where rural Wales begins, small country towns and sheep farms on the hills, forestry plantations and lakes inhabited by a sparse population. Continuing further north into Powys, there's a cluster of enchanting old spa towns, and to the north west, hills merge into the great moorlands beyond, and rise to the Cambrian Mountains and out to the coast. About 20% of the population speak Welsh, but you will find most people speak English and all the signs are also in English.

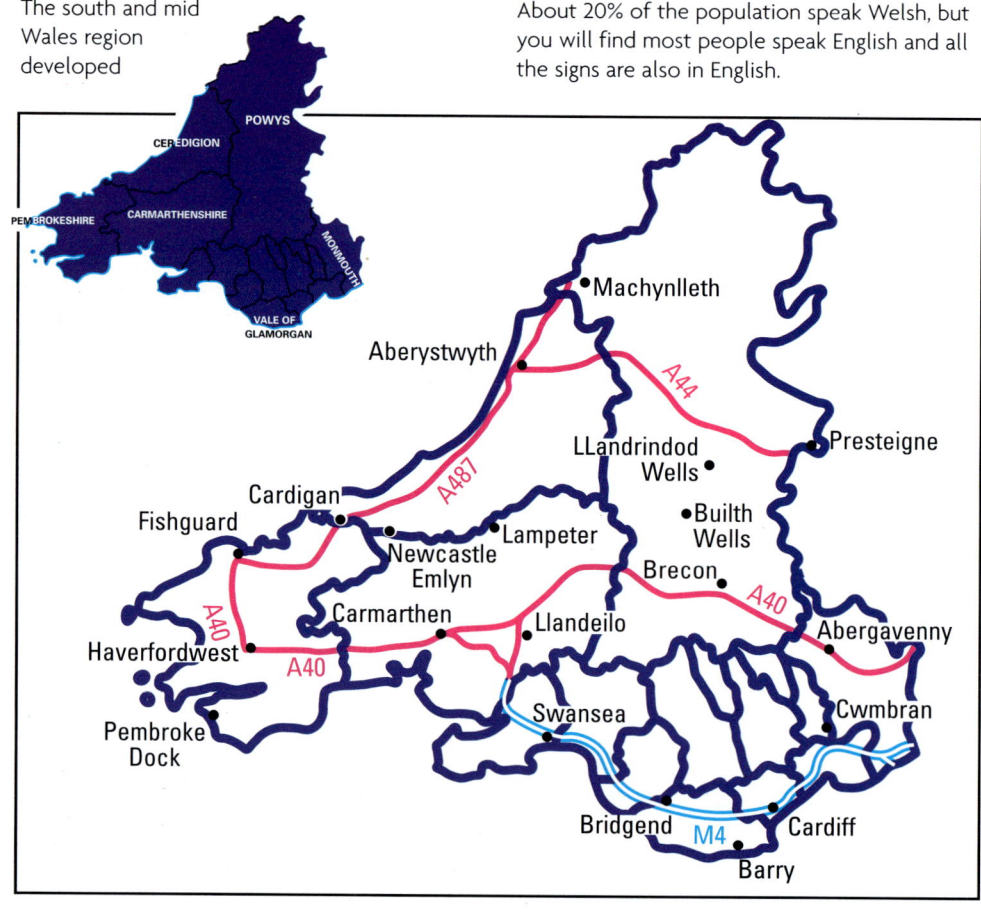

Access/Getting Around

From London

 By Road

(page ref. 36,37)

The M25 London Orbital Motorway links the M4 in the west, to the M40 and A41 joining the A40/A44 to south and mid Wales, to the M1/M6/M54 and M5/A5 in the north west for North Wales.

By Rail

(page ref. 94,95)

A network of railway lines criss-cross the whole area but the faster services are those leading to and from Paddington station to South Wales and Euston station to North Wales.

By Coach

(page ref. 96,97)

Coaches run frequently from London Victoria to most key towns in Wales including, Cardiff and Brecon.

By Air

Cardiff airport is the modern airport, just 12 miles from Cardiff center.

Powis Castle & Garden

Trail List and Page No.s

Castell Coch

Cardiff
'Capital of Wales'

Cardiff, the capital of Wales is a historic city, and is only 2 hours by train from London. The fairy-tale Cardiff Castle **1**, rebuilt between 1867 and 1875 with the wealth of the Marquess of Bute, (reputedly the richest man in Britain at that time) is most extraordinary. Cardiff was the world's principal coal port at the start of the 20th century, profiting from its rail links with the south Wales mines but is now split into two focal points. First of these is the center, with its wonderful architecture and attractions such as the Lovespoon Gallery **2**, by the castle, National Museum and Gallery **3**, and City Hall. Second, to the south of the center, is the Bay Area which is continuing to be developed. Start at the Visitor Centre **4**, and on your walk around visit Techniquest **5**, a hands-on Science Museum. There is a choice of two spendid houses, Tredegar **6**, to the east, or after a stop for some local history, at the Museum of Welsh Life **7**, visit Dyffryn House **8**. To the north of Cardiff, two spectacular castles, the fairy-tale Castell Coch **9**, and Caerphilly Castle **10**, with its own 'leaning tower'. Finally, experience life as a coalminer at Big Pit **12**, located 28 miles from the city center. To London, north or mid Wales, or another choice from the NBCompass.

ℹ Tourist Information

Cardiff	☎ 01222 227281
Caerphilly	☎ 01222 880011

GF Cardiff

Hotels

Cardiff
Newport
Cardiff - Newport

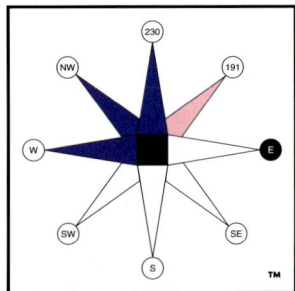

Distance from London

Cardiff 150 miles

LONDON

1. Cardiff Castle

The twelve sided castle was founded in the 12th century. In 1766 the 3rd Marquess of Bute, whose family owned the castle, employed the 'eccentric' but gifted architect, William Burges, to create an ornate mansion, rich in medieval images and romantic detail. The same collaboration was involved in the creation of the 'fairy tale' Castell Coch north of Cardiff. This architectural style amazes and delights visitors. Some of the many highlights are the Clock Tower, Roof Garden, Library, Summer Smoking Room, Octagon Tower and the Banqueting Hall.

Cardiff Castle, Castle Street, Cardiff CF1 2RB
☎ 01222 822083

 10-6pm

 Cardiff
M 4 J30

2. Castle Welsh Crafts, Lovespoon Gallery

Castle Welsh Crafts and Lovespoon Gallery offer you the gifts and crafts that symbolise Wales. Hand carved Welsh Lovespoons, miner's lamps, pottery, coal sculptures and numerous 'Welsh' items under one roof. Located opposite Cardiff castle. The offer applies to both the Welsh Craft Centre and the Lovespoon Gallery. Interestingly, there are tour guides available at, 1 Castle Street (Leisurelink Visitor Services). Do pop in and inquire. The shop and gallery are closed on Sundays.

Castle Welsh Crafts (Lovespoon Gallery),
1 Castle Street, Cardiff CF1 2BS
☎ 01222 343038

 9.30-5.30pm
% 10%
 All
 Cardiff
M 4 J30

3. National Museum and Gallery

This is a good introduction to Wales as the emphasis at the museum is on the story of Wales from the earliest times. The galleries illustrate Welsh geology, plants and animals, (you can see the largest leatherback turtle ever discovered) as well as the story of man, his work and his art. The art collection is of international standing, and includes many French and Post-Impressionist works by painters including Monet, Renoir, Cézanne and Pissarro. Learn about mining, and iron, steel and tinplate manufacturing in Wales. The modern industries include oil-refining and electricity. Closed Mondays.

National Museum and Gallery, Cathays Park, Cardiff CF1 3NP
☎ 01222 397951

 10-5pm

 Cardiff
M 4 J30

4. Cardiff Bay Visitor Centre

The Cardiff Bay Visitor Centre is an important exhibition for the future of Cardiff. The award winning 'Tube' sets out the vision for Cardiff Bay in an exciting futuristic exhibition. Reuniting the city center with its waterfront, the Bay development aims to regenerate 2,700 acres, creating a superb maritime city. Tour the center and enjoy a large screen presentation, the unique large scale model and panoramic views of the Bay. From October to April open to 5pm. Follow the brown and white signs to the Bay Area.

Cardiff Bay Visitor Centre, Cardiff Bay, Cardiff
☎ 01222 463833

 9.30-7.30pm

  Cardiff
 4 J33

5. Techniquest

Located in the spectacular Cardiff Bay redevelopment area, this is an exciting hands-on Science Discovery Centre. Create your own shadow in color, film your own animation, launch a hot air balloon, even see the stars by day. An amazing 160 interactive exhibits and a Planetarium, with a state of the art 100 seat Science Theater, Discovery Room, make this an educational and fun place to visit. Follow the brown and white signs to the Bay Area.

Techniquest, Stuart Street, Cardiff CF1 6BW
☎ 01222 475475

 9.30-4.30pm

Cardiff

M 4 J33

6. Tredegar House and Park

Tredegar House is one of the wonders of Wales' 17th century architecture. For over five hundred years had been the ancestral home of the Morgans, later Lord Tredegar. The property affords the opportunity for an intriguing look at both state rooms, and 'below stairs' in thirty restored rooms. Uncover the Morgan stories and mysteries on a 'Victorian Family' tour. The parkland has carriage rides, boating, self trail walks, formal gardens and craft workshops. Located just 20 minutes from the center of Cardiff. Open daily in August, summer from Wednesday to Sunday, please check other times.

Tredegar House and Park, Coedkernew, Newport NP1 9YW
☎ 01633 815880

 11.15-4.15pm

 % £1 off

Newport

M 4 J28 A 48

7. The Museum of Welsh Life

Experience Wales and its culture by visiting this open air Museum of Welsh Life. Here you can discover over 500 years of Culture brought to life through a variety of authentic buildings set within 100 acre parklands. Watch the craftsmen demonstrate their skills and see the display of Welsh Crafts. Located just 4 miles west of Cardiff city center off the A4232 at St Fagan's, follow the signs.

The Museum of Welsh Life, St Fagans, Cardiff CF5 6XB
☎ 01222 573500

 10-5pm

CC Visa MC

Cardiff

M 4 J33 A 4232

8. Dyffryn Gardens

Originally known as the 'Manor of Worelton', the Dyffryn estate was lived in for over 400 years. In fact, some say the ghost of Admiral Sir Thomas Button, the most famous family member, still haunts the grounds! The landscaped gardens are amongst the finest in Wales, designed by Thomas Mowson in 1910, they consist of 12 separate themes. Examples include, the Mediterranean, Physic, Theater and Pompeii Gardens, as well as an arboretum, broad sweeping lawns and a lily canal. The Glasshouse Range, contain large collections of tropical and temperate plants. From October to March open Wednesday to Sunday. Located 5 miles west of Cardiff.

Dyffryn Gardens, St Nicholas, Cardiff CF5 6SU
☎ 01222 593328

   H P

 10-5.30pm

Cardiff

M 4 J33 A 48

9. Castell Coch

Cadw - Welsh Historic Monuments, have many magnificent properties in their care, purchase a 3 or 7 day Explorer Pass (see page 233) at any of these properties, and get unlimited entry to any Cadw properties that you wish to visit whilst in Wales. Castell Coch is an enchanting castle, and a combination of Victorian Gothic fantasy and timeless fairytale. Its rounded towers and conical turrets peep through the trees on the hills of north Cardiff. The fantasy continues inside the castle with breathtaking painted walls and ceilings, this is a 'must see' creation by the brilliant architect William Burges for the extremely rich third Lord Bute.

Castell Coch, near Cardiff, Wales
☎ 01222 810101

 9.30-6.30

 % Page 233

 Cardiff

 4 J32 470

10. Caerphilly Castle

Cadw - Welsh Historic Monuments, have many magnificent properties in their care, purchase a 3 or 7 day Explorer Pass (see page 233) at any of these properties, and get unlimited entry to any Cadw properties that you wish to visit whilst in Wales. Caerphilly Castle. This vast fortress is one of the greatest surviving castles of the medieval western world. The huge 30 acre site is equalled in size among British castles at Windsor and Dover. The construction work was done between 1268 and 1271, and 30 acres of the valley was flooded to create a lake, the fortress was then set on three artificial islands.

Caerphilly Castle, near Cardiff, Wales
☎ 01222 883143

 9.30-6.30

% Page 233

 Cardiff

A 468/470/469

11. John Hughes Grogg Shop

The Grogg shop, (grogg ,spirit and water) is famous throughout the sporting and particularly rugby world for its unique handmade figures. The shop, a former pub, is a haven for visiting teams, and the ceilings and walls are covered in signed jerseys and memorabilia. The business, father and son, make the figures on the premises. Sunday closed. Free gift on spend over £20.

John Hughes Grogg Shop, Broadway, Pontypridd, Mid Glamorgan
☎ 01443 405001

 9-5pm

 Pontypridd

 4 J32  470

12. Big Pit

The only colliery in Wales offering real underground tours of the mines, 300ft below the hillside, by experienced miners. This was a former working colliery, and on the surface, there are now houses exhibitions, displays, a café and a gift shop. The underground tours take about an hour, and it is advisable to wear sturdy shoes, miner's lamps provided! The tour is not suitable for children under 5 years old. Signposted from the M4 J 25/26.

Big Pit, Blaenafon, Torfaen, South Wales NP4 9XP
☎ 01495 790311

★  P

9.30-5pm

Newport

M 4 J 25/26 A 465

Laura Ashley's Wales

Laura Ashley grew up in Wales, and the plants and colors of the countryside are reflected in her fabric designs. Llangoed Hall **2**, is owned by Sir Bernard Ashley, founder of the Laura Ashley empire, a beautiful hotel, stay or perhaps stop for tea on your travels through Wales. Between Llangoed Hall and Llandrindod Wells is the Cambrian Woollen Mills **3**, where tweeds and woollens have been used to complement Laura Ashley's collections. Llandrindod Wells, is a pretty Victorian Spa Town. You can still taste the sulphur or magnesium 'waters' at the Pump Rooms in Rock Park, the taste is quite unpleasant, but is believed to have healing qualities. A fascinating Cycle Museum **4**, has been created at the Automobile Palace. Continue north stopping at Elan Valley **10**, it has a series of awe inspiring great dams, set amongst beautiful countryside, this is a good area for walks, riding and picnicking. It is next, at Rhayader, that you will find Welsh Royal Crystal **5**, and if you wish to stay on the Laura Ashley theme head north west to Machynlleth **9**, where she had her first shop. To see one of the most wonderful castles in Wales, travel north east through Newtown on to Welshpool where you will find Powis Castle and Gardens **6**. Local history and canal trips can be included whilst you are at Welshpool **7,8**.

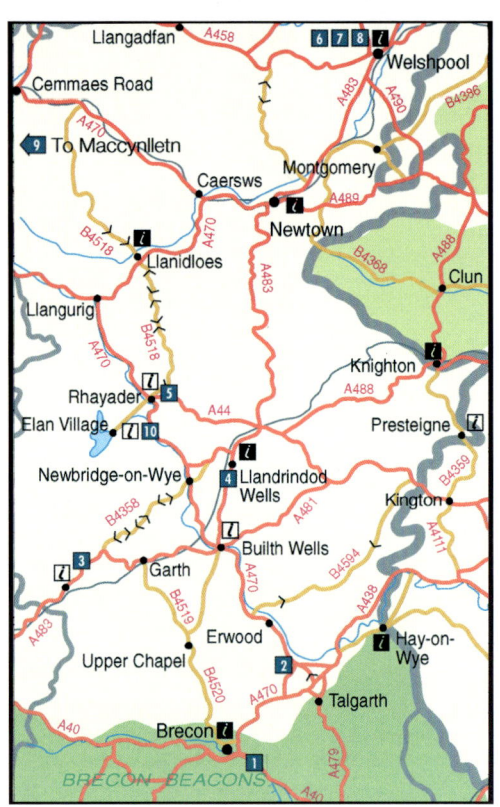

Tourist Information

Brecon ☎ 01874 622485
Llandrindod Wells
☎ 01597 822600

Hotels
Llandrindod Wells

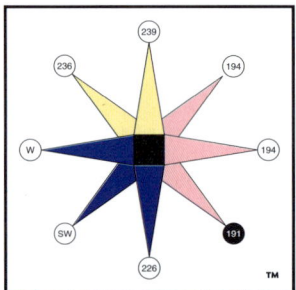

Distance from London

Brecon 175miles

1. Peterstone Court Hotel

Located on the banks of the River Usk, just 4 miles outside the old Market town of Brecon in the Brecon Beacons National Park, Peterstone, once the property of Lord Glanusk, is a carefully restored Georgian Manor house, on a site that goes back to the time of William the Conqueror. An idyllic base from which to explore the many towns and attractions on offer in the Park, or if you don't want to move, fishing from the bottom of the garden, a small health club, a snooker table and enviable views. NBC's guest's will be given automatic upgrade. Please quote NBC guests when booking.

Peterstone Court Hotel, Llanhamlach, Brecon, Powys LD3 7YB
☎ 01874 665387 Ⓕ 01874 665376

🕐 24hrs

% 10%

cc All

⇄ Abergavenny 25 miles Brecon

A 40

2. Llangoed Hall

Llangoed Hall is a magnificent Country House hotel, situated on the banks of the River Wye and surrounded by 17 acres of gardens and parkland. It is owned by Sir Bernard Ashley, founder of the 'Laura Ashley' empire. The 23 room hotel has been decorated with many of the Ashley family antiques, personal items, and Sir Bernard's private art collection of 18th and 19th century works. Afternoon tea is served between 3.30-5pm, reserve for dinner, or to stay at this highly commended hotel (a top commendation by the Welsh Tourist Board). Located north east of Brecon. No children allowed.

Llangoed Hall, Llyswen, Brecon, Powys LD3 0YP
☎ 01874 754525 Ⓕ 01874 754545

🕐 24 hrs

⇄ Brecon

A 470

3. Cambrian Woollen Mills

Wool was a major product from the 13th century onwards and by 1310 some 10 million fleeces were exported every year. The Black Death which swept Britain in 1348 put manual workers in short supply and much land was grassed over for sheep. Today this working woollen mill enables you to take a guided tour of the factory and experience the process and methods used for wool production in the present day. Offer applies to the museum. A483 just north of Llanwrtyd Wells. Closed on Sundays.

Cambrian Woollen Mills, Llanwrtyd Wells, Powys
☎ 01591 610211

🕐 9.30-4.30pm

⇄ Llanwrtyd Wells Brecon

A 483

4. Cycle Museum

In the spa town of Llandrindod Wells, the UK's number 1 cycle museum has been re-created in the delightful old building that had previously housed a magnificent collection of 160 cycles, and related objects many years ago after the bicycle was invented in 1865. The collection is both fascinating and unique. You can discover how the bicycle evolved, and as the cycle developed, how the various accessories were introduced (such as cycle lamps before batteries!). In nearby Spa Road, which leads to the Rock Spa where the waters can be tried, there is a sweetshop, 'The Candyman' that sells jars of traditional old fashioned sweets.

Cycle Museum, Automobile Palace, Llandrindod Wells, Powys LD1 5DL
☎ 01597 825531

🕐 10-5pm

 Coupon

⇄ Llandrindod Wells

A 44/483

5. Welsh Royal Crystal

See the Welsh Masters of fire and glass at work and enjoy a tour of the manufacturing process of lead crystal tableware and gifts. See glass blowing, cutting and decoration of the glass shape and final polishing. Welsh Royal Crystal melts glass containing a lead content in excess of 30% (known as full lead crystal) which is considered the best quality glass from which crystal products are made. The shop stocks their products at very affordable prices. On the A44 North West of Llandrindod Wells towards Rhayader.

Welsh Royal Crystal, 5 Brynberth Industrial Estate, Rhayader, Powys LD6 5EN
☎ 01597 811005

 9-4.30pm

 % Free Entry

CC All

 Llandrindod Wells

A 44/470

6. Powis Castle & Garden

The world famous garden, overhung with enormous clipped yews, shelters rare and tender plants. Laid out under the influence of Italian and French styles, the garden retains its original lead statues, an orangery and an aviary on the terraces. In the 18th century an informal woodland wilderness was created on the opposing ridge. Perched on a rock above the garden terraces, the medieval castle contains one of the finest collections of plants in Wales. It was originally built c.1200 by Welsh princes and was subsequently adapted and embellished by generations of Herbert's and Clive's, who furnished the castle with a wealth of fine paintings and furniture. Wednesdays.

Powis Castle & Garden, Welshpool SY21 8RF
☎ 01938 554338

    P

 Page 91

 Page 66

 Welshpool

A 490/483

7. Powysland Museum

Situated rather attractively by the canal, the museum depicts the history of Montgomeryshire with archaeological and historical collections. Housed in an old restored warehouse in the attractive market town of Welshpool, near the beautiful Powis Castle. There are often new and varied temporary exhibitions. Just 5 minutes walk from the station and town center. Closed between 1-2pm, and on Wednesdays.

Powysland Museum, The Canal Wharf, Welshpool, Powys SY21 7AQ
☎ 01938 554656

  P

 11-5pm

 % 50p off entry

 Welshpool

A 5/458

8. Montgomery Canal Cruises

Located close to the Powysland Museum, this is a unique experience. You may either choose to hire (rent) a canal boat for a day or longer, or take a daily boat trip. The canal takes you along a very scenic route, and there is also an opportunity to take a 4 course meal on a relaxing two hour cruise. The canal system is remarkable, and was once used for transporting goods.

Montgomery Canal Cruises, Severn Street Wharf, Welshpool, Powys SY21 7AQ
☎ 01938 553271

  P

 Telephone for details

 % 10%

 Welshpool

M 54   A 5/458

CAERNARFON CASTLE

CASTELL COCH

TINTERN ABBEY

PLAS MAWR

Discover some of the finest historic attractions in the World.

Wales has a rich and varied history which can be experienced by visiting the magnificent sites in the care of Cadw: Welsh Historic Monuments.

North Wales features the four World Heritage Listed Sites of Caernarfon, Harlech, Conwy and Beaumaris, South Wales abounds with the unexpected, including the Victorian Gothic fantasy of Castell Coch, and Caerphilly Castle, one of Europe's greatest surviving medieval fortresses.

To the west, among the spectacular coastlines and rugged hills of west Wales are the Bishop's Palaces at Lamphey and St David's.

ADW

North Wales

NORTH WALES IS DOMINATED by Snowdonia National Park and Snowdon, which at 3,560ft is the highest mountain in Wales. Snowdonia is made up of steep mountains and valleys, mountain lakes, moors and estuaries. It is here that in the past, slate, copper and gold where mined, and you will be able enjoy journeys through beautiful countryside on railways that once serviced this influential industry. Traveling through Wales, you will notice hills and coastlines dotted with castles, built by Welsh Princes to defend against the invading English. This is a heart of Welsh language and culture, although not many of the Welsh place names are as long as: Llanfairpwllgwyngyllgogerychwyrndrobwllllantisi liogogogoch, a Victorian railway station in the village with the longest, nestling on the Isle of Anglesey in the north west.

There are a number of contrasting and exciting places to visit, from the summer home of the Liddell's, (Alice Liddell - Alice in Wonderland) at Llandudno in Gwynedd, and next door, the fairy tale town of Conwy. Further west brings you to Anglesey from where Dublin, Ireland's capital, is accessible. Dropping south west, famous castles such as Caernarfon, where Prince Charles was given office as the Prince of Wales in 1969, and Harlech, with a sheer drop to the sea on one side. The amazing fantasy-Italianate Portmeirion Village, home to the famous Portmeirion flowered pottery, is opposite Porthmadog. Many of these regions and their castles are World Heritage Sites and designated areas of 'Outstanding Natural Beauty'. The magic and enchantment of Wales is in abundance in the north and just waiting for you to fall under its spell.

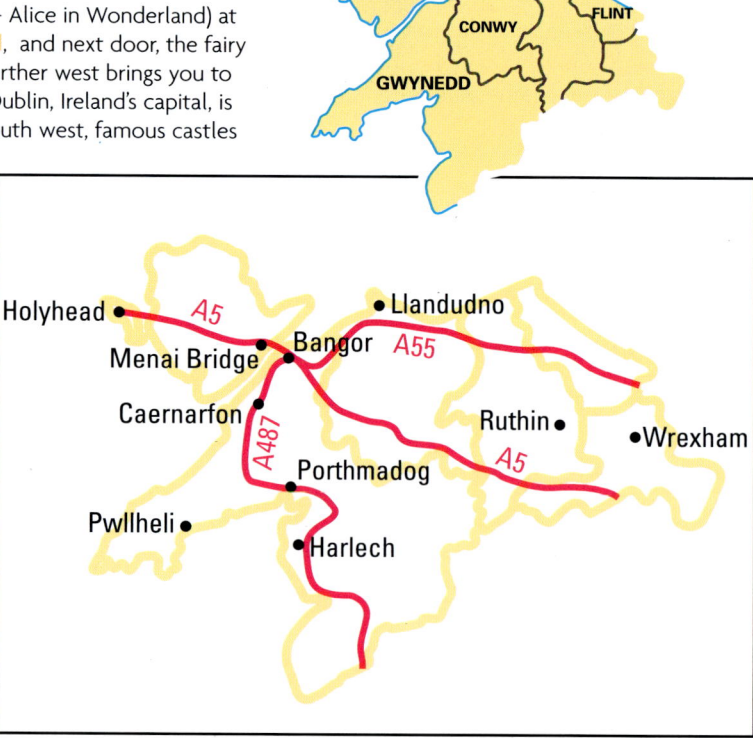

North Wales

Access/Getting Around

From London

By Road

(page ref. 36,37)

The M25 London Orbital Motorway links the M4 in the west, to the M40 and A41 joining the A40/A44 south and mid Wales, to the M1/M6/M54 and M5/A5 in the north west for north Wales.

By Rail

(page ref. 94,95)

A network of railway lines criss-cross the whole area but the faster services are those leading to and from Paddington station to south Wales and Euston station to north Wales.

By Coach

(page ref. 96,97)

Coaches run frequently from London Victoria to most key towns in Wales including, Welshpool and Bangor.

By Air

Cardiff Airport is the modern Airport, just 12 miles from Cardiff center. Manchester Intl. to the east.

Conwy suspension bridge

Trail List and Page No's

- Royal Wales 'A World Heritage'   **236**
- Alice in Wonderland and Conwy Castle   **239**

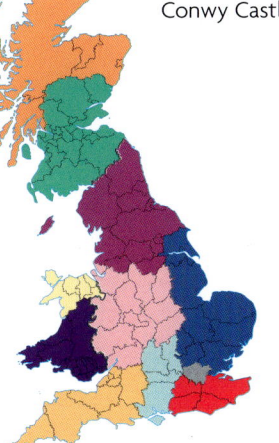

Bodnant Garden

North Wales

Royal Wales 'A World Heritage'

Henry VIII and the Tudor dynasty dating from 1485, originated from Anglesey in north west Wales, where it later became a tradition that the eldest son of the reigning monarch be crowned 'Prince of Wales', when he came of age. It is also a tradition for monarchs of Britain to wear, 'Welsh Gold' wedding rings.

Starting from Harlech Castle **1**, journey to Portmeirion **3**, the extraordinary home of the famous ceramics. Nearby, you can experience the captivating scenery on the Ffestiniog Railway **4**. If you are in this area in the first week of July, head 37 miles east to Llangollen **9**, for the Eisteddfod International Festival of singing, music and dance. It attracts performers from nearly 50 countries including America. Otherwise, travel north to the Snowdon Mountain Railway **5**, which takes you up the 3,500 ft mountain, and to Wales' most personal industry at the Welsh Slate Museum **6**. On the edge of Anglesey is Caernarfon Castle **7**, where Prince Charles was invested. Crossing into Anglesey, is the longest named village, abbreviated to 'Llanfair PG' by the locals, and Beaumaris Castle **8**, with its 16 towers. In the north west at Holyhead, is where Irish ferries travel to and from Ireland.

i Tourist Information

Caernarfon ☎ 01286 672232
Llanfair PG ☎ 01248 713177

Hotels

Criccieth - Llanfairpwll - Llangollen

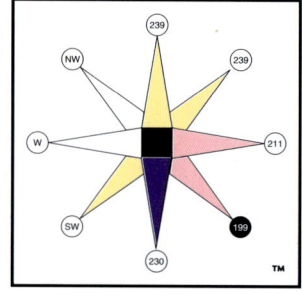

Distance from London

Caernarfon 248miles

LONDON

North Wales

1. Harlech Castle

Cadw - Welsh Historic Monuments, have many magnificent properties in their care, purchase a 3 or 7 day Explorer Pass (see page 233) at any of these properties, and get unlimited entry to any Cadw properties that you wish to visit whilst in Wales. Harlech Castle was the work of King Edward I and represents a high point in medieval castle building. As with so many of King Edward I castles it was designed by the brilliant castle architect James of St George. It was raised between 1283 and 1290 on the towering rock above Tremadog bay, and naturally protected on three sides by cliffs. It is a World Heritage Listed site.

Harlech Castle, Harlech, Gwynedd, Wales
☎ 01766 780552

  P

 9.30-6.30pm

 % Page 233

 Harlech Pwllheli

A 496

2. Hotel Maes-y-Neuadd

The reason for suggesting a stop at this historic manor house, apart from the fact that the hotel has been awarded the highest rating by the Welsh Tourist Board, is the ideal location for exploring the area. Set in Snowdonia National Park, it is close to Harlech Castle, Portmeirion, and the enchanting Ffestiniog Railway's 14 miles route to the 'slate capital'. Offer applies to Room and Breakfast rates, but please reserve in advance, most major credit cards are accepted. Located less than a mile off the B4573 between Harlech and Talsarnau.

Hotel Maes-y-Neuadd, Talsarnau, nr Harlech, Gwynedd LL47 6YA
☎ 01766 780200 Ⓕ 01766 780211

H ★ ✕ P

 24 hrs

% 25%

 All

 Harlech Pwllheli

B 4573

3. Portmeirion Village

Portmeirion, a private Village created by Clough William-Ellis. Here he fulfilled a childhood dream where astonishing Italianate buildings may seem rather out of place in the Welsh landscape, but for that reason, are more outstanding. The 'Village' was used in the Sixties British cult series 'The Prisoner'. The Ship Shop sells Portmeirion's famous pottery. In the evenings the village is closed to the public If you stay there awhile, be sure to reserve if you wish to lunch at the Portmeirion Hotel, (UK) telephone 01766 770228.

Portmeirion Village, Caernarfonshire, Glynedd
☎ 01766 770228

★ ✕ H P

 9-5pm

 All

 Minffordd  Bangor

A 487

4. Ffestiniog Railway

Established in 1832, this is the world's oldest passenger carrying narrow gauge railway. Built to carry slate from the mines in the mountains of Blaenau Ffestiniog, to the coastal town and former port of Porthmadog. The 14 mile line travels through spectacular scenery within the Snowdonia National Park, running past waterfalls, lakes and mountains, through thick forest, river valleys and tranquil pastures. Many attractions in the area can be reached by the railway. 10 departures a day during the summer, and trains run at weekends in the winter (weather permitting). Free travel for each child under 16, with a full paying adult.

Ffestiniog Railway, Porthmadog, Caernarfonshire
☎ 01766 512340

★   P

 Portmadog & Blaenau Ffestiniog

A 487

5. Snowdon Mountain Railway

Britain's only public rack and pinion railway, its 5 mile route runs from Llanberis to the summit of Snowdon, the highest mountain in England and Wales. Trains run daily (weather permitting) from March 15 to 1 November. The highest section of the track is open from May to October. Located just 8 miles from the A5/55 North Wales Expressway. Offer is second ticket at half price with one full paying adult (*not available during July and August).

Snowdon Mountain Railway, Llanberis, Caernarfon, Gwynedd LL55 4TY
☎ 01286 870223

 % *Discount
⇄ Bangor ⬚ Caernarfon
A 5/55 4086

6. Welsh Slate Museum

This was one of the largest slate quarries in Britain. With a museum and excellent commentary, it is a fascinating look at the history of the area. The buildings were reputedly designed on the pattern of a British army fort in India. The machinery in the workshops was powered by a waterwheel 60ft in diameter, which has now been restored and is working again. Open March to October 10 to 5pm, 10 to 4pm other times.

Welsh Slate Museum, Gilfach Ddu, Llanberis, Gwynedd LL55 4TY
☎ 01286 870630

 10-5pm

 Bangor
A 55/4086

7. Caernarfon Castle

Cadw - Welsh Historic Monuments, have many magnificent properties in their care, purchase a 3 or 7 day Explorer Pass (see page 233) at any of these properties, and get unlimited entry to any Cadw properties that you wish to visit whilst in Wales. Caernarfon Castle. The setting for the investiture of H.R.H Prince Charles as Prince of Wales, and perhaps the most famous and impressive castle in Wales. A World Heritage Listed site, the castle is complemented by the interesting exhibitions in many of its towers.

Caernarfon Castle, Caernarfon, Gwynedd, North Wales
☎ 01286 677617

 9.30-6.30
 % Page 233
 Bangor ⬚ Caernarfon
A 487 B 4366

8. Beaumaris Castle

Cadw - Welsh Historic Monuments, have many magnificent properties in their care, purchase a 3 or 7 day Explorer Pass (see page 233) at any of these properties, and get unlimited entry to any Cadw properties that you wish to visit whilst in Wales. Beaumaris Castle, (beau mareys - beautiful marsh) was the last and largest castle to be built by England's King Edward I to contain Wales. It is a perfectly symmetrical stronghold midway by sea between Conwy and Caernarfon, that was never quite completed as the King became distracted and funds and supplies faltered. It is a World Heritage Listed site.

Beaumaris Castle, Anglesey, Gwynedd, North Wales
☎ 01248 810361

 9.30-6.30
 % Page 233
 Bangor
A 5/545

'Alice in Wonderland' and Conwy Castle

Alice Pleasance Liddell was the real girl about whom Lewis Carroll, (real name, Charles Dodgson) wrote his imaginative books, 'Alice in Wonderland', and 'Through the Looking-Glass'. As a child she would visit Llandudno with her parents, and it was thought Lewis Carroll met her there and made up the stories to entertain her, 'Alice in Wonderland' was the result of one such visit. Llandudno is perfect for walking around, and the Rabbit Hole **A1**, is a must. The Gogarth Abbey Hotel was once the Liddell family home, and a light afternoon meal can be enjoyed there if you make an appointment, also visit the Great Ormes Head **A1**, by taking Britain's longest cable car with some spectacular views of Snowdonia.

The fairy-tale castle of Conwy **B1**, is within this walled city, perhaps the best preserved example of a fortified town in Britain. Conwy is reached over three bridges and again is easy to walk around. It has the Smallest House **B1**, on the quayside, measuring just 10ft high by 6ft wide. Visit also, Aberconwy House **B1**, and the gardens at Bodnant **B2**, 4 miles to the south of Conwy, again with stunning views of Snowdonia from the terraces. Discover more with the NBCompass.

Tourist Information

Conwy	☎ 01492 592248
Llandudno	☎ 01492 876413

GF Conwy and Llandudno

Hotels

Llandudno

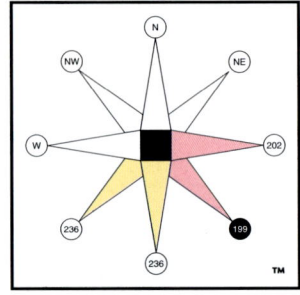

Distance from London

Conwy 242 miles

1. Alice in Wonderland Centre

A visit to Llandudno where the real Alice spent the summers of her childhood, is incomplete without a visit to 'Alice's Adventures in Wonderland' For those who enjoyed this classical story, here is a magical experience of the world of Lewis Carroll's Alice down a Rabbit Hole. Walk through a warren of beautiful life size scenes, many of the models are animated and designed in the authentic style of the book. Super gift shop and there is a recorded narration available. Just north of Llandudno station in Trinity Square.

Alice in Wonderland Centre, 3/4 Trinity Square, Llandudno
☎ 01492 860082

  P

 10-5pm

 All

⇄ Llandudno

A 55/470

Map ref: A1

2. Conwy Castle

Cadw - Welsh Historic Monuments, have many magnificent properties in their care, purchase a 3 or 7 day Explorer Pass (see page 233) at any of these properties, and get unlimited entry to any Cadw properties that you wish to visit whilst in Wales. Conwy Castle set within the walled city of Conwy is one of the most picturesque of Welsh Castles, and a masterpiece of medieval architecture. There are 21 towers, and this castle was built in an astonishing four and a half years between 1283 and 1287. Here remains one of the most complete fortified towns and castles in Britain. It is a World Heritage Listed site.

Conwy Castle, Conwy, North Wales
☎ 01492 592358

  P

 9.30-6.30

 % Page 233

⇄ Conwy

A 55 B 5106

Map ref: B1

3. Aberconwy House

Dating from the 14th century, this is the only medieval merchant's house in Conwy to have survived the turbulent history of this walled town for nearly six centuries. Furnished rooms and an audio visual presentation show daily life from different periods in its history. The house has limited electric lighting and therefore is dark on dull days.

Castle Street, Conwy LL32 8AY
☎ 01492 592246

  P

 Page 91

 Page 66

⇄ Conwy

A 55

Map ref: B1

4. The Smallest House in Great Britain

This was a fisherman's house and is the smallest house in Great Britain. The last inhabitant was 6ft 2 inches tall and left the house in 1900. There is a commentary available, and do purchase postcard of the house, (it's not to scale !) entry is only 50p. The house is 6ft wide and 10ft high. Perhaps the quickest and certainly most unique attraction of all that you may visit. Open until 9pm in July and August.

The Smallest House in Great Britain, The Quay, Conwy LL32 8BB
Ⓕ 01492 593484

 10-4pm

⇄ Conwy

A 55

Map ref: B1

5. Conwy Butterfly Jungle

Conwy Butterfly Jungle has hundreds of exotic tropical butterflies from jungles around the world. They fly freely around you in 700 sq. yds of beautiful tropical gardens. A visually dazzling experience, educational and a superb photo opportunity. Situated just 300 yards walk from the town or quay into the park, there is also a fishpool, tropical birds and a jungle spring at the exhibition.

Conwy Butterfly Jungle, Bodlondeb Park, Conwy LL32 8DY
☎ 01492 593149

🕐 10-5.30pm

Conwy 1 mile

A 55/470

Map ref: A1

6. Conwy Suspension Bridge

Designed and built by Thomas Telford, the famous engineer, this elegant suspension bridge was completed in 1826: it replaced the ferry, previously the only means of crossing the river. The toll-keeper's house has recently been restored and furnished as it would have been a century ago. Located just 100yds from Conwy town center. Adjacent to Conwy Castle.

Conwy Suspension Bridge, Conwy, LL32 8LD
☎ 01492 573282

 P

🕐 Page 91

 Page 66

 Conwy

A 55

Map ref: B1

7. Bodnant Garden

The garden at Bodnant is one of the finest in the world, and is situated above the River Conwy looking across the valley towards the Snowdon Range. The garden is in two parts. The upper part around the house, (the private residence of Lord and Lady Aberconway) consists of the Terrace Gardens as well as informal lawns shaded by trees. The lower portion, known as 'The Dell' is formed by the valley of the River Hiraethlyn, a tributary of the Conwy, and contains the pinetum and wild garden. Located 8 miles south of Llandudno.

Bodnant Garden, Tal-y-Cafn, Colwyn Bay LL28 5RE
☎ 01492 650460

 P

🕐 Page 91

 Page 66

 Llandudno

A 55/470

Map ref: B2

8. Rhyl Sea Life Centre

Immediately you set foot into Rhyl Sea Life Centre, you feel as if you have stepped beneath the waves in this excellent themed center. Take a stroll through the shallows and on into the depths through the underwater tunnel. Kingdom of the Seahorse. Learn about the historic captive breeding programme and join in the project to re-introduce these endangered creatures to British waters.

Rhyl Sea Life Centre, East Parade, Rhyl, Denbighshire LL188 3AF
☎ 01745 344660

 P

🕐 10-5pm

 Coupon

Rhyl

A 55/548

Map ref: A2

THE NORTH OF ENGLAND has been host to many famous literary figures. As you will discover, it is hardly surprising when it encompasses areas like the Lake District, in Cumbria, of which John Constable, (the famous landscape painter) had said, 'is the finest scenery that ever was', then stretches across to the south east, and passing through Brontë Country, to York, in Yorkshire.

The Lake District is Poet's Country, with numerous lakes and fells, and is actually quite small at about a 28 mile radius. The best way to take in its beauty is by walking. Four of its peaks are higher than 3,200 ft with the Pennines dominating the eastern region. Carlisle, the largest town, to the north and bordering Scotland, is a good base for exploring Hadrian's Wall, (a defensive wall across the northernmost

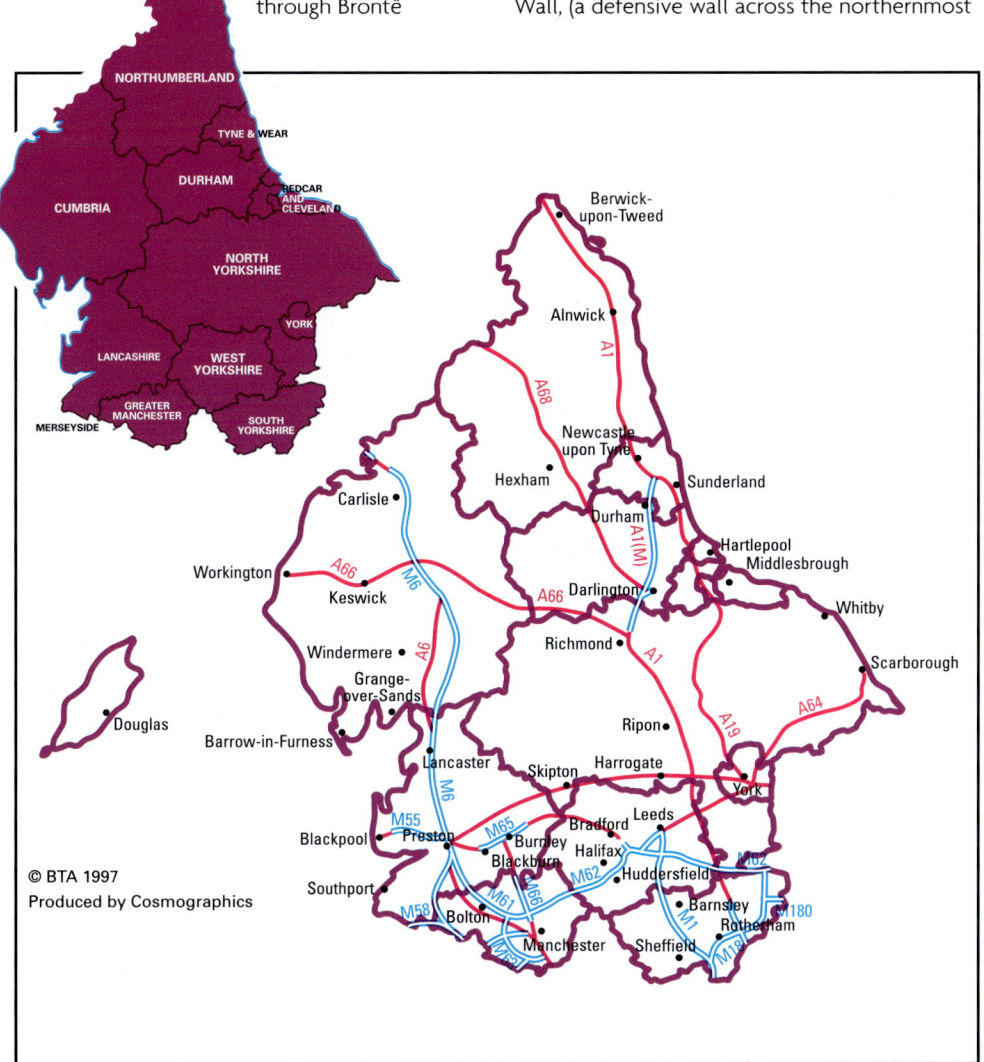

© BTA 1997
Produced by Cosmographics

boundary of the Roman Empire, AD 122 and 73 miles long). The region's weather is quite often rain and mist, so be well prepared.

To the south of Cumbria is Lancashire, with its mixture of seaside, wild country and industry. Amongst its portfolio of attractions are Blackpool, (the largest vacation resort in Europe) and by contrast the fine county town of Lancaster. Manchester was known to the Romans, who built a fort here in AD 79, and by the 14th century had established itself on a flourishing woollen trade. With the industrial revolution, and the building of the Manchester Ship Canal in the 18th century, the world's cotton capital became a major inland port. As with many of the industrial cities of that time, Manchester has had to work hard at rebuilding and redeveloping the city, and has met with a great deal of success in achieving this aim.

Yorkshire, is divided into West Yorkshire, South, East and North Yorkshire, the north borders Cumbria in the west. West Yorkshire has the literary shrine of Haworth, home of the Brontë's, a countryside of bleak Pennine moorlands dotted with farms. The walled city of York in North Yorkshire is their most visited city. Yorkshire, made up of wild hills, moors, valleys and open spaces, is generally unspoilt but still has its share of industrial towns. There are many splendid homes and castles to be seen in this area of England, that provide visitors with inspiration and excitement.

East of Cumbria, is Durham to the south, and Northumberland borders Scotland. Panoramic views from empty hills, and the National Park hide the area's past conflicts, from the Roman occupation to the battles between England and Scotland.

Trail List and Page No.s

Access/Getting Around

From London

By Road

(page ref. 36,37)
The M25 London Orbital Motorway links the M40 in the west and M1 to the north west with the M6 and A1(M) to the north.

By Rail

(page ref. 94,95)
A network of railway lines criss-cross the whole area but the faster services are those leading to and from London Euston to the Lake District, Cumbria and Kings Cross to Yorkshire.

By Coach

(page ref. 96,97)
Coaches run frequently from London Victoria to most key towns in Cumbria, Yorkshire and the north of England including, Leeds, York, Skipton, Kendal, Keswick and Carlisle.

By Air

Manchester Airport (there is a railway service direct to Windermere, Lake District) and Leeds/Bradford Airport for Yorkshire.

Culture meets Cool 'Manchester'

Manchester, 'Gateway to the North', offers a fusion of traditional and cutting edge art and culture, with fascinating museums. A large number of museums and places of interest can be visited around Deansgate, a key road in the center. Listing a few from north to south, the unusually proportioned Manchester Cathedral, John Rylands Library, where an important collection of historical documents and Bibles in over 300 languages can be seen, and the Abraham Lincoln Statue. Then a cluster to the east, close to the river and opposite the G-Mex Exhibition Centre, Granada Studios Tour **1**, the Museum of Science and Industry, Air and Space Gallery, and the Peoples History Museum, recounting the struggles of the working class people through the industrial revolution. You will be delighted by the outstanding Victorian architecture that can still be seen as you walk around. Manchester is famous for its legendary music, club scenes and nightlife, eat out at Chinatown or dine, drink and dance in Manchester's Gay Village, there is a music scene here that feeds the city 24 hours a day. To get the inside story on 'what's on and where' it's best to pick up a copy of the listing magazine 'City Life', an excellent guide.
The city is quite walkable,

(although you should try the tram system). Other recommended places to see and things to do are the Whitworth Art Gallery **2**, the Gallery of Costume **3**, and 6 miles to the south west of the city center, Bramall Hall **4**.

ℹ️ Tourist Information
Manchester   ☎ 0161 234 3157

Hotels
🛡️ Manchester
👑 nr Manchester

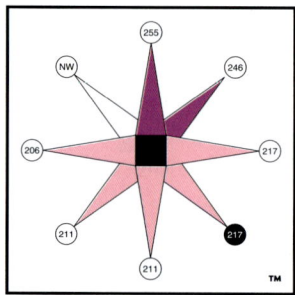

Distance from London

Manchester 202miles

1. Granada Studios

Before visiting Granada Studios you can pick up a £5 discount coupon at the local *Tourist Information Centres. Granada Studios, situated just outside city center Manchester, is Europe's largest TV and Film park. The admission price includes a 50 minute backstage tour, where you can take a peek behind the TV screen and learn about the tricks of the trade. There are numerous rides and attractions including the House of Commons live comedy debate, Motion Master Cinema, the UFO zone and Sooty Show (a popular childrens' glove puppet show). Arrive early if you want to see and experience everything. Last entry at 3pm - closed on Mondays.

Granada Studios,
Water Street, Manchester M60 9EA
☎ 0161 832 4999 (24hrs)

 9.45-5pm

 % * Tourist Information Centre

Manchester

M 56/62/602

2. Gallery of English Costume

Housed in a splendid Georgian Mansion, the Gallery houses one of the most comprehensive costume collections in Britain. The displays focus on the changing styles of everyday fashion and accessories, and covers over 400 years. Of particular interest are the special exhibitions 'Fashion since the Sixties', (1960 to the present day) and 'New Woman, New Look', the development of women's fashion from 1890 to the 1950's. The photo opposite is of a 1743 Wedding Dress with quilted silk petticoat. Closed on Mondays. From Nov - Feb open until 4pm.

Gallery of English Costume, Platt Hall, Rusholme, Manchester M14 5LL
☎ 0161 224 5217

 10-5.30pm

Manchester

M 56/66 A 34

3. The Whitworth Gallery

The Whitworth Gallery is the home to internationally-famous collections of British watercolours, textiles, and wallpapers as well as an impressive range of prints, drawings, modern paintings and sculpture. The Gallery received Designated Status from the Government in recognition of its outstanding collections. Displays from the collections are changed regularly alongside a program of exhibitions and events in the galleries and Sculpture Court. With a host of talks, tours, concerts and workshops, this is a great place to visit. There's an award winning Bistro and a bookshop. Sunday 2-5pm.

The Whitworth Gallery, The University of Manchester, Oxford Road, Manchester M15 6ER
☎ 0161 275 7452

 10-5pm

Manchester

M 56/66 A 34

www.whitworth.man.ac.uk

4. Bramall Hall

This magical black and white timber framed Tudor house was the home of Charles Nevill, cotton industrialist. Dating back to the 14th century it was remodelled by Nevill in Victiorian times. Journeying through the house will afford you glimpses into the hall's fascinating history. Beautiful Tudor rooms with spectacular plaster ceilings, a 16th century embroidered table carpet, wall paintings, fine architecture, and furniture and paintings from different periods. Open from 11am on Sundays.

Bramall Hall, Bramhall Park, Bramhall, Cheshire SK7 3NX
☎ 0161 485 3708

 1-5pm

 Bramhall/Cheadle Hulme

M 60/63 J1/22 A 5102

Brontë
'The Surrounding Cities'

The three main cities that are to the east of the Brontë's home in Haworth are Bradford, Leeds and Halifax, all of which, (as did Haworth) prospered and grew through the wool trade, in the mid 19th century. Today these busy, light industrial cities, are attracting new culture and recreational use.

Leeds offers a thriving cultural scene and has some fascinating museums, for example the Royal Armouries **1**, City Art Gallery **2**, Henry Moore Institute **3**, and the Thackray Medical Museum **4**. Temple Newsam House **5**, is 3 miles away to the south east, and the spectacular mansion, Harewood House **6**, is 7 miles north of Leeds.

Halifax has many 19th century buildings that owe their existence to wealthy cloth traders, here you can visit the award winning Eureka Museum **7**.

Bradford, home to the superb National Museum of Photography, Film and Television **8**, also has the only Museum of Colour in Britain **9**. Bradford (due to the large number of immigrants who previously worked in the mills) has a huge number of good Indian restaurants, born out of their enterprise as the textile industry declined. Three miles north of Bradford, is a fascinating model factory village, Saltaire **10**, that was built by Sir Titus Salt, (who

made a fortune from weaving) for housing, education and the recreation of his workers. The old mill, 1853 Gallery now houses work by the contemporary painter David Hockney, born in Bradford in 1937.

i Tourist Information

Bradford	☎ 01274 753678
Halifax	☎ 01422 368725
Leeds	☎ 0113 242 5242

Hotels

STAKIS HOTELS Bradford - Leeds

Monk Fryston - Wakefield

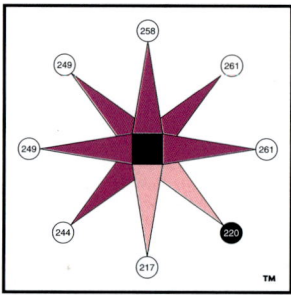

Distance from London

Leeds 195miles

1. Royal Armouries Museum

The museum is quite spectacular with displays and live demonstrations, interactive games and thousands of exhibits from a world famous collection. From the Tower of London, it tells the story of arms and armour around the world, in battle, sport, self defense and fashion. There are often new exhibitions, events, and the museum's use of film, music and poetry is excellent. Please use the coupon at the back of the NBC guide. Closed November to April on Mondays.

Royal Armouries Museum, Armouries Drive, Leeds SL10 1LT
☎ 0113 220 1999

 10-5pm
 Coupon MC Visa
 Leeds
M 1/6 J21

www.armouries.org.uk

2. City Art Gallery

The Art Gallery houses prints and drawings, including a fine collection of British Romantic watercolors, and modern sculpture. The sculpture collection is strong in works by Henry Moore, (1898-1986) who was the son of a Yorkshire coalminer, and Epstein. The Henry Moore Institute next door is also free admission, and is devoted to the display, study and research of sculpture. There are important collections of 20th century British paintings, and of late 19th and early 20th century French paintings. Open 10-4pm on Saturday and 2-5pm Sunday.

City Art Gallery, The Headrow, Leeds, Yorkshire
☎ 0113 247 8248

 10-6pm

Leeds
M 1/62

www.leeds.gov.uk

3. Henry Moore Institute

In an award winning granite faced building, the Henry Moore Institute is devoted to the exhibition, study and promotion of sculpture. Henry Moore was a student of Leeds College of Art. There is no permanent exhibition but four galleries house the exhibits and there is a study center and audio visual facility Located in the center of Leeds next to the City Art Gallery, it is approximately 10 minutes walk from Leeds City station. Visitors can receive a free poster of their choice. Open until 9pm on Wednesdays.

Henry Moore Institute, 74 The Headrow, Leeds LS1 3AA
☎ 0113 234 3158

 10-5.30pm

 Leeds
M 1/62

4. Thackray Medical Museum

This award winning museum brings the history of medicine to life. Discover how medicine has developed from leech tubes to keyhole surgery and laser treatments. You can choose a character, then visit the Victorian healers from a 'quack' to a doctor, and find out who survives their treatment! In the interactive Bodyworks Gallery, there's an opportunity to explore the body and a reconstructed 'Victorian Street' enables you to take a walk back in time. Great fun for young and old alike. Closed on Mondays.

Thackray Medical Museum, Beckett Street, Leeds LS9 7LN
☎ 0113 244 4343

 10-5.30pm

 Leeds

M 1/62

5. Temple Newsam House

Built around 1500, Temple Newsam was the birthplace of Lord Darnley, husband of Mary Queen of Scots. It became the home of the Ingram family until it was sold to Leeds City Council in 1922. It contains a magnificent collection of paintings, Chippendale furniture, silver and ceramics. The 1,200 acre park was laid out by Capability Brown and has a Home farm and Rare Breeds herd. Located 4 miles east of Leeds. On Sundays open from 1-5pm, last entry is at 4.15 daily. The entry fee is just £2.

Temple Newsam House ,Temple Newsam House, Leeds LS15 0AE
☎ 0113 264 7321

 10-5pm

 Leeds
M 62 J30   A 63

6. Harewood House

One of England's architectural masterpieces, this should not be missed. Family home of the Lascelles for over 200 years, it was designed by John Carr of York, the breathtaking interiors are by Robert Adam, furniture made especially by Thomas Chippendale, and with the gardens, designed by Capability Brown, it is a spectacular combination. The Terrace Gallery is nationally acclaimed and shows a wide range of contemporary works. Open daily from 15th March to 26th October. Grounds and gardens from 10am, house from 11am. A61, 6 miles north of Leeds. *Ask for a 'Treasure Houses' discount leaflet, to receive discounts and free guides at their other 9 properties in the guide.

Harewood House, Harewood, Leeds LS17 9LQ
☎ 0113 288 6331

 10-6pm
  * Treasure Houses
 MC Visa
 Leeds 7 miles
M 1   A 1/61

7. Eureka Museum

Although the museum was designed especially for children between 3 to 12 years, that should not put off adults, it's great fun! Eureka opens up a fascinating world of hands-on exploration, where over 400 exhibits let you touch, talkback, and smell as well as look and discover so much more about yourself and the world around. Adjacent to Halifax railway station.

Eureka Museum, Discovery Road, Halifax, West Yorkshire HK1 2NE
☎ 01422 330069

  P
 10-5pm
 £1 off
 Halifax
M 62 J24

8. National Museum of Photography, Film and TV

This fascinating and innovative museum, (relaunched in Spring 1999) houses the three types of media that have transformed the 20th century. Journey through six floors of highly interactive displays and don't miss Britain's largest cinema experience - IMAX, alongside the unique Pictureville Cinema, showing the best of world cinema. Other new galleries include digital imaging, news, animation, light and magic, special exhibitions of major shows and artists, a public-access archive and research center. *There is a charge for IMAX, Pictureville and the ride simulator. Closed on Mondays.

National Museum of Photography, Film and Television, Pictureville, Bradford, West Yorkshire BD1 1NQ
☎ 01274 727488

 10-6pm
  *See text
 Bradford
M 606/62   A 650/647

www.nmsi.ac.uk/mmpft/

Haworth 'Home of the Brontës'

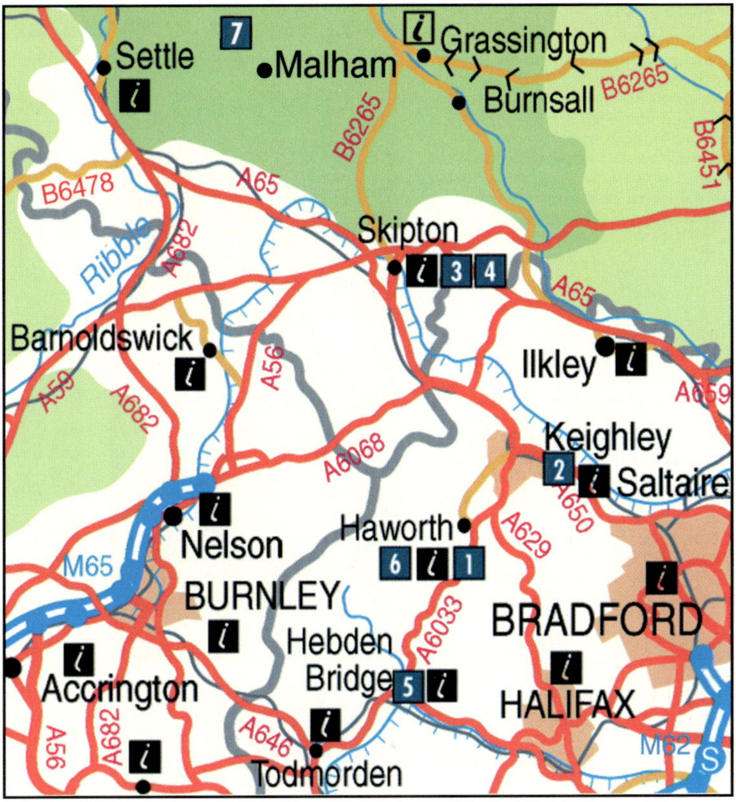

Anne Brontë wrote two novels, 'The Tenant of Wildfell Hall' and 'Agnes Grey', Charlotte wrote 'Jane Eyre', 'Villette' and 'Shirley', and Emily wrote 'Wuthering Heights'. The Brontë Parsonage Museum **1**, is where they lived from 1820-1861, (it has been slightly extended since). It remains decorated as it was during the 1850's. Both Charlotte and Emily are buried under the family vault in the Church of St Michael. When visiting the Parsonage, imagine how bleak it would have been during their lifetime, when the trees and landscape would not have been so developed as they are today. On the edge of Haworth is Hebden Bridge **5**, where the houses seem to be invisibly supported as they cling to the valley. Penistone Hill Country Park **6**, has fine views and is good for walks into 'Brontë Country', for example, the Brontë waterfalls.

Also, do explore the area around Haworth, there are some wonderful places to visit, for example to the north, one of England's best-preserved medieval castles, Skipton Castle **3**. Above Skipton are the Yorkshire Dales, prime walking country with rural villages among meandering river valleys, and Malham Cove **7**, that has a gigantic natural amphitheatre.

i Tourist Information

Haworth	☎ 01535 642329
Skipton	☎ 01756 792809

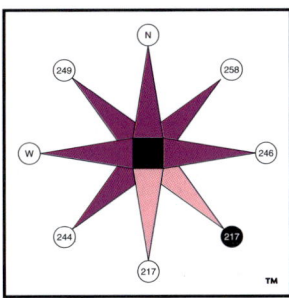

Distance from London

Skipton 225 miles

---

1. Brontë Parsonage Museum

Home to the Reverend Patrick Brontë and his family from 1820-1861, Charlotte, Emily, Anne and their brother Branwell. The rooms are decorated in the early 19th century style and arranged as they were in Brontës day, with original furnishings and paintings. A large number of books, manuscripts, drawings and personal possessions relating to the family are also on display, together with a permanent exhibition of their 'family history'. The original house has been extended slightly to accommodate the exhibitions. Open 11 - 4.30pm October to January and closed mid-January to mid-February.

Brontë Parsonage Museum, Haworth, Keighley, West Yorkshire
☎ 01535 642323

 10-5pm

 Keighley

A 629/6033

2. Keighley and Worth Valley Railway

To reach Haworth, home of the Brontë family, the Victorian Keighley and Worth Valley Railway is the privately run service that will get you there from York or Leeds , with 5 to 7 trains running per day. It stops at Oakworth station, where parts of a well loved British film, 'The Railway Children' were filmed. At the end of the line is the railway museum at Oxenhope. The stops are as follows, Keighley - Ingrow - Damems - Oakworth - Haworth - Oxenhope. A special offer is available upon production of a BritRail Pass.

Keighley and Worth Valley Railway, Keighley, West Yorkshire
☎ 01535 647777

 BritRail Pass

 Keighley

A 629

3. Skipton Castle

Skipton, Sceptone, or 'Sheeptown', was a settlement long before the Normans arrived and built the castle. Two massive stone Towers guard the entrance to this superb 900 year old moated fortress with the peaceful Conduit Court at its center. It boasts a 50ft long banqueting hall with walls decorated with seashells. It is, without doubt, one of the most complete and well preserved medieval castles in England. There are illustrated tour sheets. Offer applies to gift and souvenir shop. Open from 12 noon Sundays. Situated in the center of Skipton, A629 from Haworth.

Skipton Castle, Skipton, North Yorkshire BD23 1AQ
☎ 01756 792442

10-6pm

 % 10% in shop    MC Visa

 Skipton

M 62 J24 **A** 629

www.skiptoncastle.co.uk

4. Wright Whisky Co.

Established in 1982, next to Skipton Castle in the Old Smithy, (founded in 1673). The shop is an 'Aladdin's Cave' with an extraordinary range of malt whiskies, (150) together with over 900 wines from around the world. Bob Wright has also dedicated his adjoining building to related products, such as glasses, books and thermometers. Offer is a free whisky tasting, please show your NBC card or guide. There is no obligation to purchase. Closed Sundays.

Wright Whisky Co., Raikes Road, Skipton, North Yorkshire
☎ 01756 700886

 9-6pm

 MC Visa

 Skipton

M 62 **A** 629

Wordsworth and Beatrix Potter 'Lake District'

The Lake District boasts two of the best known literary connections, William Wordsworth, (1770 - 1850) who spent most of his life here, and Beatrix Potter, (1866 - 1943) who moved here in 1906. But it has also enjoyed the company of Charlotte Brontë, the romantic poet Shelley, (1792 - 1822) the poet Tennyson, (1809 - 1892) and John Ruskin, (1819 - 1900). It is ideal walking country with endless scenic views, but let us focus on the main attractions. With so many places to visit perhaps start in the south and head north along lakes Windermere and Coniston to Grasmere.

Beginning on the Windermere side are, the Beatrix Potter Attraction **1**, the unique Windermere Steamboat Museum **2,** and Windermere Lake Cruises **3**, or Mountain Goat Tours **4**, for local tours. Then traveling anti-clockwise, take the picturesque railway **6**, and visit the Aquarium of the Lakes at Lakeside **7**. On the west side of Lake Windermere is Grizedale Forest Park, and Ruskins House at Brantwood **8**. Nearby, Hill Top **9**, (Beatrix Potter) and the Beatrix Potter Gallery **10**. Finally, Rydal Mount **11**, (Wordsworth) Dove Cottage and the Wordsworth Museum **12**. For attractions in the surrounding area see the trail

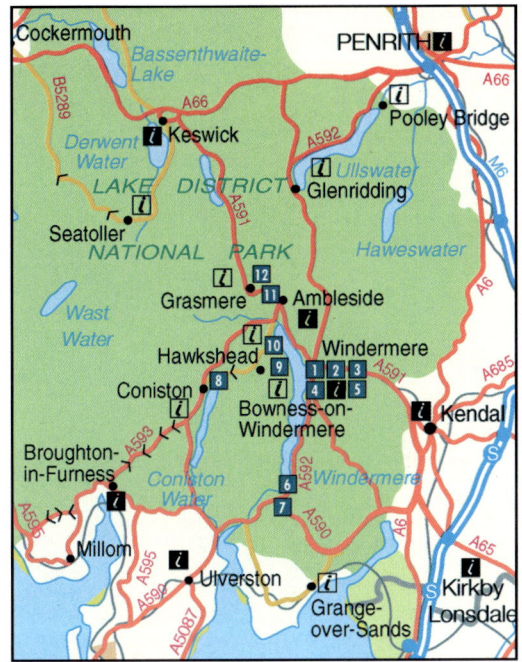

etitled, 'Around the Lakes and Hadrian's Wall'. The NBCompass will guide you on to another selection.

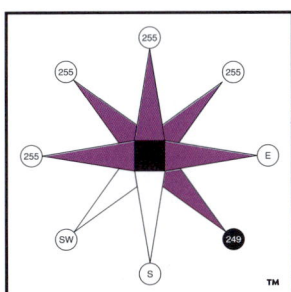 Tourist Information

Ambleside	☎	015394 32582
Bowness	☎	015394 42895
Grasmere	☎	015394 35245
Windermere	☎	015394 46499

Mountain Goat Tours

Hotels

Grasmere

STAKIS HOTELS Keswick

Ambleside - Bowness-on-Windermere - Grasmere - Keswick - Windermere

Distance from London

Kendal 264miles

1. Beatrix Potter Attraction

Discover the wonderful world of Beatrix Potter in this award winning attraction. An informative commentary and guide on the life of Beatrix Potter and her work is available. Visit many of the characters from her books, see films and video that describe her, and how many of the tales came to be written. You can also sit and enjoy tea in these enchanting surroundings. This 'attraction' should not be confused with the 'Beatrix Potter Gallery', as described later in this section. Offer is one child free with each paying adult.

Beatrix Potter Attraction, The Old Laundry, Crag Bow, Bowness-on-Windermere, Cumbria LA23 3BT
☎ 015394 88444

 10-6.30pm

CC Visa MC

 Windermere

M 6 J36 A 5074

2. Windermere Steamboat Co.

In its spectacular lakeside setting, the Windermere Steamboat Museum houses a remarkable collection of 35 steam, sail and motor boats in excellent condition, and offers you the opportunity to take a trip on board one of these fine boats, (weather permitting) during the summer. There is even a steamboat trip where you can take afternoon tea on the lake, quite an experience. The museum also contains the houseboat used in Arthur Ransome's childrens' story, 'Swallows and Amazons'. Located just north of Bowness on the A592.

Windermere Steamboat Co. Rayrigg Road, Bowness-on-Windermere
LA23 1BN
☎ 015394 45565

 10-5pm

 % 10%

 Windermere

M 6 J36 A 5074

3. Windermere Lake Cruises

An excellent way to take a trip around Lake Windermere, on an historic steamboat. Start the cruise at Ambleside, Bowness or Lakeside, and a break in the journey is permitted, if time allows, to visit the Aquarium of the Lakes, or Lakeside and Haverthwaite Steam Railway. Offer applies to the 'Freedom of the Lake' cruise, and tickets are valid for 24 hours from time of issue. The 21 mile journey around the lake takes approximately 3 hours. Please present the coupon at the back of the guide.

Windermere Lake Cruises, Lakeside, Ulverston, Cumbria LA12 8AS
☎ 015395 31188   (F) 015395 31947

 % £ 1 off Coupon

 Windermere

M 6 J36 A 590/592

4. Mountain Goat Tours

One of the best ways to get around and see the Lake District is on the popular full or half day, small coach Mountain Goat Tours, which offer choices to suit everyone, and they are very good at providing details to help you choose. Reserve and depart at the Tourist Information Centres in Windermere, Waterhead and Ambleside (King Street). There is even a tour up to Hadrian's Wall (ask for the Keswick Tour). To reserve in advance Fax, (+ 44) 15394 45164. Tours daily from 8am.

Mountain Goat Tours, Victoria Street, Windermere, Cumbria
LA23 1AD
☎ 015394 45161   (F) 015394 45164

% 10%

CC MC Visa

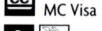 Windermere

M 6 J36 A 591

5. Peter Rabbit and Friends

Peter Rabbit and Friends, the shop that takes you into a World of Gifts, that feature Peter Rabbit and all the Beatrix Potters characters. There are wonderful clothes for children to enjoy, and there are beautiful gifts for all ages. Exclusive Royal Albert figurines, silver spoons, tableware, Wedgwood plates, books, rugs, jewellery and numerous items for children's rooms. A mail order catalogue is also available. There are shops in other NBC Trails that also have this special offer, so look for them throughout the guide. Open Sunday 11-6pm. Also at 4 Crescent Road, Windermere.

Peter Rabbit and Friends, Stock Lane, Grasmere, Cumbria LA22 9ST
☎ 015394 88968

 P

 9-5.30pm

 10%

 All

 Windermere

A 591

6. Lakeside & Haverthwaite Railway

n the picturesque Lake District, these hard working steam locomotives haul the trains on this remarkable steeply graded railway.. Fortunately the comfortable coaches ensure a pleasant and stunning journey past lakes and river scenery. You can also connect with Windermere Lake Cruises at Lakeside. The offer applies to the train only. Check timetable at Lakeside, trains run daily, 22nd March to 6th April, and 3rd May to 2nd November. Signposted from M6.

Lakeside & Haverthwaite Railway, Haverthwaite Station, Ulverston, Cumbria LA12 8Al
☎ 015395 31594

 P

 Windermere

M 6 J 36

7. Aquarium of the Lakes

This new indoor Visitor Centre is now open at Lakeside, The Aquarium of the Lakes, it is open throughout the year. The exhibition features the largest collection of freshwater fish in England. Over 30 fascinating displays on the weird and wonderful aquatic life of the Lake District. Displays include cascading waterfalls, a riverbank at night, a walk through an underwater tunnel surrounded by live fish and water creatures, a walk along a recreated lake bed, an AquaQuest water lab and a chance to meet rays and British sharks from Morecambe Bay.

Aquarium of the Lakes, Lakeside, Newby Bridge, Cumbria LA12 8AS
☎ 015395 30153

 P

 9-6pm

 MC Visa

 Windermere

M 6 J 36   **A** 590

8. Ruskins House

Brantwood was the former home of the eminent Victorian, John Ruskin, poet, artist, critic and social reformer. A video presentation tells of his life. As well as displays of his water colors and personal memorabilia in surroundings that are much as he left them, there are continual exhibitions by local artists housed here. There are also regular theater events and readings, plus a book and crafts shop. Situated on the east shore of Coniston Water in a fine Lakeland estate. Open in the winter, Wednesdays to Sundays from 11-4pm.

Ruskins House, Brantwood, Coniston, Cumbria LA21 8AD
☎ 015394 41396

 P

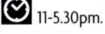 11-5.30pm.

 All

 Windemere

 6 J 36   **A** 590

9. Hill Top

Beatrix Potter wrote many of her famous childrens' stories in this little 17th-century house, and traditional cottage garden; the house still contains her furniture and china. A selection of her original illustrations is displayed at the Beatrix Potter Gallery, Hawkshead. Hill Top is a very small house and only a limited number of visitors can be admitted at any one time. During the busiest periods this may give rise to long delays and some visitors may not gain admission at all. Please help to preserve Hill Top by avoiding peak times, particularly mornings in school holidays (closed Thur and Fri except Good Friday , a public holiday).

Hill Top, Near Sawrey, Ambleside LA22 OLF
☎ 015394 36269

🕐 Page 91

Page 66

⇄ ✎ Windermere

M 6 J35

10. Beatrix Potter Gallery

An annually changing exhibition of original illustrations from the childrens' stories. One of the many historic buildings in this picturesque village, this was once the office of the author's husband, the solicitor William Heel, and the interior remains largely unaltered since his day. Open from 28th March to 2nd November. Closed on Fridays and Saturdays. Admission is by timed ticket. During the busiest periods this may give rise to long delays and some visitors may not gain admission at all. Located in the square at Hawkshead.

Beatrix Potter Gallery, Main Street, Hawkshead LA22 ONS
☎ 015394 36355

🕐 Page 91

Page 66

⇄ ✎ Windermere

M 6 J 36   A 591   B 5286

11. Rydal Mount and Gardens

In the heart of the Lake District, between Ambleside and Grasmere, you will find glorious views over Lake Windermere. The house, which now belongs to descendants of the great poet, retains a lived-in, family atmosphere and has seen little change since Wordsworth and his family came to live here in 1813. This is the house, in which William Wordsworth lived for 37 years, it contains portraits, personal possessions and first editions of his poets work. Wordsworth was a keen landscape gardener and the 4 acre garden remains very much as he designed it. Keep your ticket for a 15% discount at Wordsworth's House (NT).

Rydal Mount and Gardens, Ambleside, Lake District, Cumbria
☎ 015394 33002

🕐 9.30-5pm

21 % Wordsworth's House

⇄ ✎ Windermere

M 6 J 36   A 591

12. Dove Cottage and Wordsworth Museum

Dove Cottage was William Wordsworth's home from 1799 to 1808, he moved here when he was 19. The award winning museum displays the Wordsworth Trust's unique collections of manuscripts, books and paintings interpreting the life and work of Wordsworth, his family and circle. Headphone sets enable you to hear the poems read aloud. The garden, 'a little nook of mountain-ground', is open when the weather permits. Closed in January. Keep your ticket for a 15% discount at Wordsworth's House (NT).

Dove Cottage and Wordsworth Museum, Grasmere, Cumbria LA22 9SH
☎ 015394 35544

🕐 9.30-5.30pm

21 % Wordsworth's House

⇄ ✎ Windermere

M 6 J 36   A 591
www.@dovecott.demon.co.uk

Around the Lakes and Hadrian's Wall

Explore around the Lakes, and discover what inspired the many great poets, artists and writers who spent weeks, months, and sometimes years of their lives admiring these romantic landscapes. Guiding you through this area, and highlighting some of the many attractions, the first stop is Kendal **9**, a busy market town, and the southern gateway to the Lake District, (also well known for Kendal Mint Cake). If you travel clockwise around the lakes and coastline, your first stop is Sizergh Castle **10**, next Levens Hall **1**, and then Holker Hall **11**, at Cartmel, a village with one of the area's finest churches, the 12th century Priory. The Laurel and Hardy Museum, where Stan Laurel was born in 1890, is at Ulverston **2**. Heading up the coast, the scenic miniature Ravenglass and Eskdale Railway **3**, takes you to or from the 13th century Muncaster Castle **4**.

To get to Hadrian's Wall, stay on the coastal road through Sellafield **5**, Maryport **6**, and Cockermouth **7**, where Wordsworth was born in a house on the High Street. From here a long straight Roman road leads to Carlisle **8**, near the border with Scotland. Visit the outposts of Hadrian's Wall along to Birdoswald Roman Fort at Gilsland **12**. If you prefer the mountains and scenery, where Wordsworth wandered, visit Ullswater **13**, for a walk around the 'most beautiful' of all Cumbria's lakes. Finally, Keswick **14**, and the interesting museums

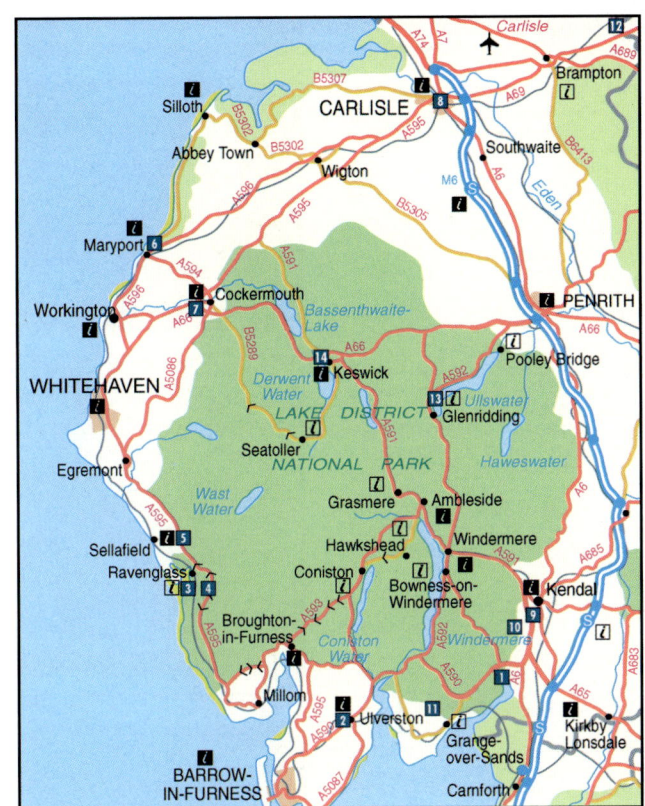

there, 'Beatrix Potter', 'Cars of the Stars', and 'Pencils'.

ℹ️ Tourist Information

Carlisle	☎ 01228 512444
Kendal	☎ 01539 725758

Maryport ☎ 01900 813738

Hotels

see also, 'Beatrix Potter Trail'

Carlisle - Kendal - Ullswater

Distance from London

Carlisle 304miles

1. Levens Hall

Levens Hall, originally built in 1250 around the peel tower, is mainly an Elizabethan House with superb plasterwork and carved woodwork. It is most famous for the Topiary Gardens, laid out in 1694, with cones, corkscrews, pyramids and numerous wonderful shapes, that remain largely unchanged to this day. The offer applies to the gardens, open from 10am. Closed Fridays and Saturdays. Situated 5 miles south of Kendal.

Levens Hall, Kendal, Cumbria LA8 OPD
☎ 015395 60321

 12-5pm

 Coupon

 Kendal

 6 J36 590

2. Laurel and Hardy Museum

The Museum contains the largest collection of material relating to the inspirational American comedians, Stan Laurel and Oliver Hardy. Heroes of the era of the silent screen, visitors will be amused to see some of the eighty Laurel and Hardy films that are held in the museum. Letters, photographs, press cuttings and personal possessions are also on display. The museum is just 5 minutes walk from Ulverston station, or on the A590.

Laurel and Hardy Museum, 4c Upper Brook Street, Ulverston, Cumbria LA12 7BH
☎ 01229 582292

 10-4.30pm

 MC Visa

 Ulverston

 6 J36 590

3. Ravenglass and Eskdale Railway

This is a most beautiful train journey on England's oldest narrow gauge railway, (38cm/15") that runs for seven and a half miles from the old Roman port of Ravenglass to the Eskdale Valley. The trains are hauled by either steam or diesel locomotives. Be sure to visit Muncaster Castle and Mill, the offer is £1 off an adult return, please show your NBC card/guide. The train runs daily from March 22nd to November 2nd. Ravenglass main line station adjoins the Ravenglass and Eskdale station.

Ravenglass and Eskdale Railway, Ravenglass, Cumbria CA18 1SW
☎ 01229 717171

 9-6pm

 £1

 MC Visa

 Ravenglass

 6 J 36 590/595

4. Muncaster Castle

The richly furnished home of the Pennington family since 1208. This impressive historic castle is set in splendid woodland gardens with superb views of the Lakeland fells (stretch of moorland). There is an Owl Centre with talks and displays. To enjoy the spectacular scenery that surrounds you throughout this region take the Ravenglass & Eskdale Railway. Muncaster Castle is at Ravenglass and is open from 12.30-4pm from April to October. Closed on Saturdays.

Muncaster Castle, Ravenglass, Cumbria CA18 1RQ
☎ 01229 717614

 12.30-4pm

 AmEx MC Visa

 Ravenglass

 595

5. Sellafield Visitors Centre

With the increased use of Nuclear Fuel throughout the world, Sellafield is a Visitor Centre that wishes to guide you into the 21st century and let you get behind the scenes to answer any questions or misconceptions you may have. A total of 10 'hands on' interactive zones explain the fascinating world of British Nuclear Fuels. You can take a tour of the Sellafield site, and it makes an interesting educational stop along the west coast to or from Hadrian's Wall or west from the Lake District.

Sellafield Visitors Centre, Sellafield, Seascale, Cumbria CA20 1PG
☎ 019467 76510

  10-6pm

 Sellafield Whitehaven
M 6 J36 **A** 590/595

6. The Senhouse Roman Museum

A museum on the site of finds from the Roman Fort of Maryport. Mainly sculptures and altars, giving an interesting glimpse at the lives of people 1,800 years ago. The collection is housed in a late 19th century Naval Battery on the cliff top, adding a fine view of Solway Firth. No photographs please. From Maryport follow signs to the north edge of town. Open from April to June and October, 10-5pm except Mondays and Wednesday. November to March, open Friday to Sunday 10.30-4pm. July to Sept 10-5pm every day.

The Senhouse Roman Museum, The Battery, Sea Brows, Maryport, Cumbria CA15 6JD
☎ 01900 816168

 P
 10-5pm

 Maryport Carlisle
M 6 J41 **A** 596

7. Wordsworth House

The house where William Wordsworth was born in 1770. This typical north country gentleman's Georgian town house was built in 1745. Seven rooms are furnished in 18th century style, with some personal effects of the poet; his childhood garden, with terraced walk, leads down to the Derwent. 25 minute video display in the old stables, last showing of video at 4pm. In the local church, (Wordsworth's father is buried in the churchyard) you will find a stained-glass window in memory of the poet. Upon presentation of your ticket from Dove Cottage or Rydal Mount - receive 15% discount off entry.

Wordsworth House, Main Street, Cockermouth, CA13 9RX
☎ 01900 824805

 P
 Page 91
 % See text Page 66
 Penrith / Cockermouth
M 6 J40 **A** 66

8. Tullie House Museum

This award winning museum and art gallery has displays and interactive exhibits telling the turbulent history of Carlisle. There are important collections relating to the prehistoric and Roman periods in Cumbria, the Roman items coming mainly from Hadrian's Wall. There are some excellent examples of 18th and 19th century English porcelain also on display. Follow signs from the railway station in the town towards the castle. Sundays from 12am.

Tullie House Museum, Castle Street, Carlisle, Cumbria CA3 8TP
☎ 01228 534781

 P
 10-5pm

 Citadel 1 mile Carlisle
 M 6 J42/43 **A** 6/69

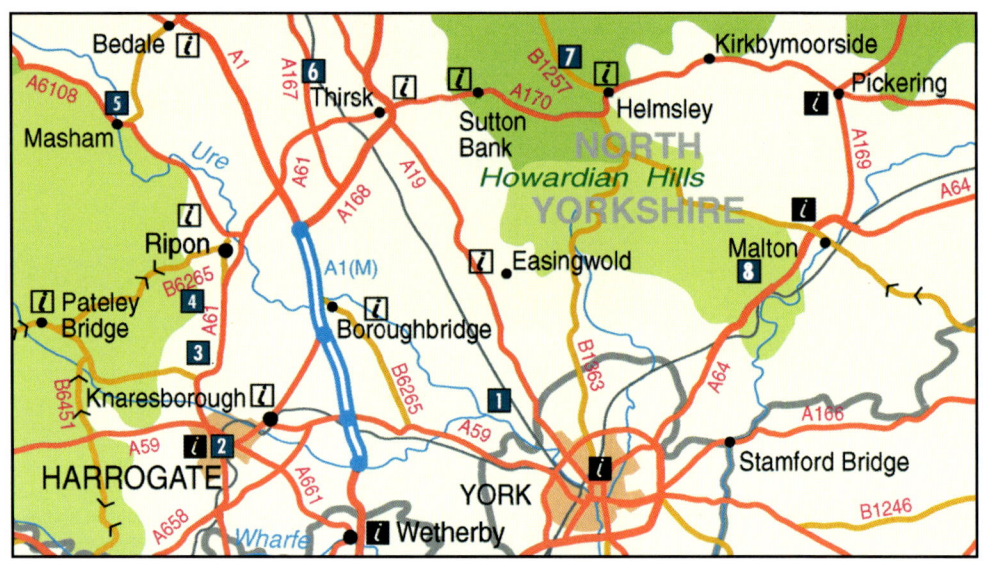

Beyond the Walls of 'York'

The county of Yorkshire has many unrivalled Gothic abbeys, castles, magnificent country manor houses, and gardens from each period in England's history. Taking a clockwise journey around York, many of those can be seen here. On the outskirts is Beningbrough Hall **1**. At Harrogate, Harlow Carr Botanical Garden **2**, and next Ripley Castle **3**, in the village that was remodelled into a typical French style in 1827, (although the Yorkshire character prevails). Fountains Abbey and nearby Studley Royal **4**, are the grand romantic ruins of a 12th century abbey, (the largest monastic ruin in Britain) with neighbouring 18th century Georgian gardens. At Masham, the Black Sheep Brewery **5**, offers you a

diversion to see how English beer is made. Continue your journey onto the period showpiece, Sion Hill Hall **6**, near Thirsk. At Rievaulx Abbey **7**, discover a beautiful and well preserved ruin set in the peaceful surrounds of the River Rye Valley. Finally, Castle Howard **8**, 15 miles north east of York, in its dramatic setting of lakes, fountains and extensive gardens, is undoubtedly one

of the finest residences in Yorkshire.

ⓘ Tourist Information
York   ☎ 01904 621756

Hotels
STAKIS HOTELS York

Harrogate - Helmsley - Ripon - York

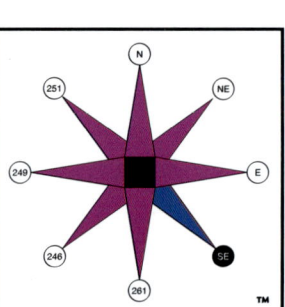

Distance from London

York 206 miles →

1. Beningbrough Hall

Built around 1716, this imposing house sits on a slight rise above the water meadows of the River Ouse. The Great Hall, which is two storeys high, is particularly impressive, and there is exquisite woodcarving, a cantilevered oak staircase, furniture and porcelain. The house is furnished in period style and the fully equipped Victorian laundry gives a fascinating insight into the drudgery of servants' lives at that time. Located 8 miles north west of York. Closed on Thursdays, please check opening times if visiting between November and April.

Beningbrough Hall, Shipton-by-Beningbrough, York, North Yorkshire YO6 1DD
☎ 01904 470666

 11-5pm

 Page 66

 York

 19

2. Harlow Carr Botanical Gardens

Harlow Carr Botanical Gardens form the headquarters of the Northern Horticultural Society; one of the most prestigious gardens in the north of England. Rock, heather, winter and foliage gardens, flower, vegetable and fruit trails, one of the longest streamside plantings in the country, a woodland, arboretum, wild flower meadow together with national plant collections, including rhubarb, make up the 68 acre gardens. Please use the coupon in the back of the guide. Located on the B6162, Otley Road.

Harlow Carr Botanical Gardens, Crag Lane, Harrogate, North Yorkshire HG3 1QB
☎ 01423 565418

 9.30-6pm

 Coupon

 Harrogate

A 1/61   B 6162

3. Ripley Castle

Ripley is one of Britain's last surviving Estate villages. Home of the Ingilby family since the 1320's, Ripley Castle stands at the heart of a delightful Estate with lakes, deer park, kitchen gardens and hot houses. The 15th century tower contains a waggon roof, one of only three remaining in England, a secret Priests' Hole, and memorabilia from the battle of Marston Moor. This contrasts strongly with the elegance of the Georgian wing which has fine chandeliers, furniture and family portraits. The castle overlooks magnificent Capability Brown designed gardens and woodlands. Offer does not apply on special event days.

Ripley Castle, Ripley, Harrogate, North Yorkshire HG3 3AY
☎ 01423 770152

 10-5pm

Harrogate

A 1/61   B 6165

www.ripleycastle.co.uk

4. Fountains Abbey & Studley Royal Water Gardens

One of the most remarkable sites in Europe, sheltered in a secluded valley. A World Heritage Site, it encompasses the spectacular ruin of a 12th century Cistercian abbey, an Elizabethan mansion, and one of the best surviving examples of a Georgian green water garden. Elegant ornamental lakes, avenues, temples and cascades provide a succession of unforgettable eye-catching vistas in an atmosphere of peace and tranquillity. St Mary's Church, built by William Burges in the 19th century, provides a dramatic focal point to the medieval deer park with over 600 deer. Located 4 miles west of Ripon.

Fountains Abbey & Studley Royal Water Gardens, Fountains, Ripon HG4 3DY
☎ 01765 601005

 Page 91

 Page 66

 Harrogate

A 1   B 6265

5. Black Sheep Brewery Visitor Centre

Black Sheep Brewery is a traditional working brewery owned by Masham's famous Theakston family who've been brewing fine ales for five generations. Discover the process of creating traditional English ale by taking a tour of the brewhouse and fermenting rooms and also watching their video presentation. Tours are at, 11, 12.30, 2, 3, and 4pm and take approximately 1 hour (making a reservation is advised). You will then be able to try their ales at the Bistro which is open until 11pm.

Black Sheep Brewery Visitor Centre, Wellgarth, Masham, Yorkshire HG4 4EN
☎ 01765 689227

🕐 10-5.30pm

⇄ Ripon

A 1 /6108

6. Sion Hill Hall

An Edwardian Country Mansion with 20 room settings, from Butler's Pantry to Master Bedroom, depicting past times, and with members of staff in period costume, this makes this an unusual and delightful place to visit. A diverse collection of furniture, paintings, clocks, porcelain, costume and dolls form just some of the display. An added value is that the NBC offer also applies to the birds of prey and conservation center in the Victorian walled garden, where there are flying demonstrations each day. Open March to October. Hall closed Mondays and Tuesdays. Off the A167 near Thirsk.

Sion Hill Hall, Kirby Wiske, Thirsk, North Yorkshire YO7 4EU
☎ 01845 587206

🕐 12.30-5pm

⇄ ⇗ Thirsk

A 1/167

7. Rievaulx Abbey

Everywhere peace, and everywhere serenity. One of the most atmospheric of all the ruined medieval abbeys of the North. Twelve Clairvaulx monks came to Rievaulx, as part of the missionary effort in 1132, and from these modest beginnings sprang one of the wealthiest monasteries of medieval England.

Rievaulx Abbey, Helmsley, North Yorkshire
☎ 01439 798228

🕐 10-6pm

 % Page 67

 ⇗ Thirsk

A 170 **B** 1257

8. Castle Howard

Designed by Sir John Vanbrugh, Castle Howard is still owned and lived in by the Howard family. It is a very grand palace, (the largest house in the north of England) with some exceptional architectural designs. Highlights include the Great Hall with its magnificent columns, wall paintings, and the circular gallery. Also the Long Gallery, Antique Passage, and the Chapel. There is a beautiful garden and parkland. Castle Howard was used as the location for a television version of Evelyn Waugh's novel, 'Brideshead Revisited'. *Ask for a 'Treasure Houses' discount leaflet, to receive discounts and free guides at their other 9 properties in the guide

Castle Howard, Near Malton, York YO6 7DA
☎ 01653 648444

🕐 11-4.30pm

 *Treasure Houses

 Malton 🚗

 64

York 'The Eternal City'

There are few of England's cities that are as steeped in history as York. So much of this history has been retained that it is like experiencing a living museum. York began in Roman times as Eboracum, to Anglo Saxon times as Eoforwic, and Viking times as Jorvik. It is still encircled by its 13th and 14th century walls, (3 miles) with four gates and has as its centerpiece, York Minster **A2**, England's largest medieval church.

Over Lendal Bridge and the River Ouse, pick up a Yorkboat Tour **A1**, or on Museum Street, turn left to the Multangular Tower, Yorkshire Museum and York Gallery. Clockwise from here are the spectacular York Minster, and the Treasurer's House **A2**. Towards the center around Stonegate is Twelfth Century House, (the oldest in the city) and the 'Shambles' for some unique shops.

Between Clifford Street, Tower Street, and the river Foss, are the Jorvik Viking Centre, Fairfax House, the York Castle Museum, York Dungeon and Cliffords Tower. Coney Street **A2**, leads you back to the Lendal Bridge, and the National Railway Museum **A1**, or continue to explore the city at your own pace. There are a number of choices when continuing with the use of the NBCompass.

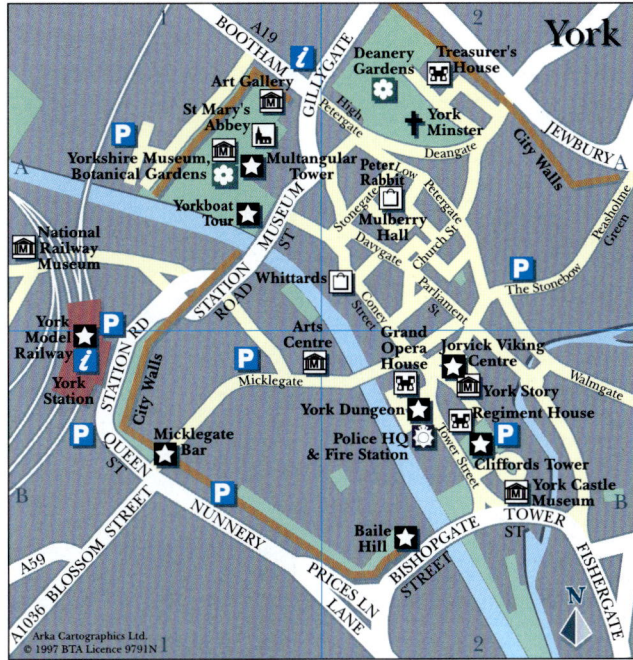

i Tourist Information

York   ☎ 01904 621756

GF York

Hotels

STAKIS HOTELS York

Ⓦ York

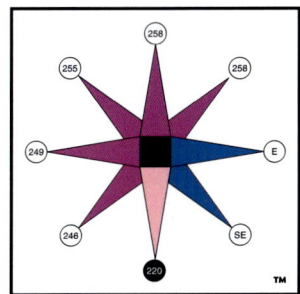

Distance from London

York 206 miles ➡

1. York Minster

One of the great cathedrals of the world, with origins tracing back to the 7th century, but the current building dates from the 13th century. The stained glass windows are magnificent, and the largest collection in Britain. Entry to the cathedral is free, as are the conducted tours, but a donation is requested. Some parts of the cathedral require a small payment. Other highlights include the Chapter House, Central Tower, and the Choir Screen, but the size and beauty of the whole cathedral is breathtaking.

York Minster, Deangate, York
☎ 01904 622774

 7-7pm

 York
M 62 A 1/64

Map ref: A2

2. Yorkboat Guided River Trips

Yorkboat are operated by the White Rose Line, Yorkshire's leading cruise operator. Cruises sail every day from February to the end of November, and whether it's a summer's day, damp or dreary you will be comfortable and entertained during the 1 hour trips. See where Saxons fought Vikings, where monks entertained their guests and witches were ducked during the Middle Ages. There's also a floodlit 'Evening Cruise' or alternatively the 'Ghost Cruise', both between April and October. Located 3 mins over Lendal Bridge.

Yorkboat Guided River Trips, The Boatyard, Lendal Bridge, York YO1 7DP
☎ 01904 628324

 From 10.30am

 York
A 1/64

Map Ref: A2

3. Treasurer's House

York's 'hidden treasure'. Set in the tranquil shade of York's magnificent Minster, this elegant 17th and 18th century house has much earlier origins and boasts links as far back as the Romans. It contains a medieval-style hall with half-timbered gallery, and fine Georgian features, including exquisite decorated plasterwork, panelling and elaborate fireplaces. The house also has the dubious distinction of being home to the oldest ghost in England! Closed on Sundays.

Treasurer's House, Minster Yard, York, North Yorkshire YO1 2JD
☎ 01904 624247

 10.30-5pm
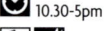 Page 66
 York
A 1/64

Map Ref: A2

4. York Dungeon

Whatever everyday life was really like for our forefathers, one thing is for certain, their history and ours is full of the most grisly punishments and unbelievably evil villains. York Dungeon has become renowned for its scenes of medieval torture and execution, providing both education as well as entertainment.. Two great attractions are the real story of Dick Turpin, and the tale behind the recent sighting of a ghostly Roman legion

York Dungeon, 12 Clifford Street, York YO1 1RD
☎ 01904 632599

 10-5pm
 Coupon
 York
A 1/64

Map ref: B2

5. Cliffords Tower

Standing high on a mound in the city of York, Clifford's Tower is one of the pair of castles built by William the Conqueror after his victory in 1066. York was often the seat of government in the 13th and 14th centuries, so the castle would have been magnificently appointed. Today the tower stands as a symbol of the mighty medieval English kings.

Cliffords Tower, Tower Street, York
☎ 01904 646940

🕐 9.30-6pm

% Page 67

York 1 mile

A 1/64

Map ref: B2

6. Yorkshire Museum

Part of York's Roman city wall runs through the Museum Gardens, where you can see a wide range of animals and plants. At the heart of the museum lies the majestic ruin of the medieval St Mary's Abbey. In the museum you can look at the intricately carved sculptures, and wander through the reconstructed Abbey archway as early music plays softly. A short film offers greater insight into medieval life and the greater religious houses of Yorkshire. The museum holds some of Britain's most important archaeological treasures.

Yorkshire Museum, Museum Gardens, York YO1 2DR
☎ 01904 629745

🕐 10-5pm

York

A 1/64

Map ref: A1

7. York Castle Museum

The museum is in two 18th century prisons, built on the site of York Castle. There are displays of armour, weapons, (especially swords) musical instruments, toys and dolls. The collection of costume and accessories is one of the best in Britain. A fabulous reconstruction of a Victorian York Street, Kirkgate, with its courts and alleys is fascinating, and contains a number of old shop fronts and other buildings from York, and Yorkshire, rescued from destruction during the 1930's.

York Castle Museum, The Eye of York, York YO1 1RY
☎ 01904 653611

🕐 9.30-6.30pm

York

A 1/64

Map Ref B2

8. Jorvik Viking Centre

Deep beneath the streets of York the spirit of Vikings lives on. Take a journey back 1,000 years to an accurate reconstruction of the Viking city of Jorvik, complete with sounds and smells evocative of the time. Visited by over ten million people. Jorvik Viking Centre, Britain's journey through time. Located in central York in the Coppergate shopping center. Last admission November to March is 3.30pm.

Jorvik Viking Centre, Coppergate, York YO1 1NT
☎ 01904 643211

🕐 9-5.30pm

York

A 1/64

Map ref: B2

9. National Railway Museum

Your ticket for the National Railway Museum will take you on a spectacular journey through the life and history of the railways. The museum has a superb collection of Royal Carriages, engines, trains, paintings and photographs, supported by special exhibitions. This is a celebration of the transport revolution that swept the world. Located just behind York station, 5 minutes walk, west from the city center. Please use the coupon in the back of this guide.

National Railway Museum, Leeman Road, York YO2 4XJ
☎ 01904 621261

 10-6pm

 £1.60 off. Coupon

 York

 1/64

Map ref: A1

10. Peter Rabbit & Friends

Peter Rabbit and Friends, the shop that takes you into a World of Gifts, that feature Peter Rabbit and all the Beatrix Potters characters. There are wonderful clothes for children to enjoy, and there are beautiful gifts for all ages. Exclusive Royal Albert figurines, silver spoons, tableware, Wedgwood plates, books, rugs, jewellery and numerous items for children's rooms. A mail order catalogue is also available. There are shops in other NBC trails that also have this special offer, so look for them throughout the guide. Open Sunday 11-6pm.

Peter Rabbit & Friends, 47 Stonegate, York
☎ 01904 638411

 9-5.30pm

 10%

 AmEx MC Visa

 York

Map ref: A2

11. Mulberry Hall

Mulberry Hall is one of the world's leading independent fine china and crystal specialists, carrying a wide range of Europe's finest products, including Herend, Meissen, Wedgwood and Baccarat. They offer excellent personal service, attention to detail, and can send even the most fragile goods with confidence to the US, or any part of the world. Situated between York Minster and Betty's Tea Shop. The gift is a Herend Porcelain Basket on spend over £100. Please show the guide as well. Closed Sundays.

Mulberry Hall, Stonegate, York YO1 2AW
☎ 01904 620736

9.30-6pm

 All

York

Map ref: A2

12. Whittard of Chelsea

Whittard of Chelsea have been a specialist tea merchants since 1886. The store sells pure, single estate traditional and exotic large leaf teas as well as tea, gifts and associated china. Look out for other Whittard of Chelsea shops throughout the guide. Offer applies to loose leaf teas and gift sets only. Sundays open from 12-5pm. An ideal English gift.

Whittard of Chelsea, 46 Parliament Street, York
☎ 01904 653505

9.30-6pm

10%

MC Visa AmEx

 York

Map ref: A2

HISTORIC  SCOTLAND

UNLOCK 5,000 YEARS OF HISTORY

WHY buy a ticket at every castle when a Scottish Explorer Ticket will give you unlimited access to all Historic Scotland attractions?

WHY only visit castles when Historic Scotland sites cover 5,000 years and range from mysterious stone circles through country houses to Royal Palaces and Abbeys?

WHY wait until your vacation ends before realising how much an Explorer Ticket can save?

HISTORIC SCOTLAND look after many of Scotland's top heritage attractions, including Edinburgh and Stirling Castles, as well as Urquhart Castle in the shores of Loch Ness.

To receive a 10% discount on the Scottish Explorer Ticket (a 7 day ticket costs just £12.50*) simply present your NBC Card at any of our attractions.

Photo far left
Dunstaffnage
Left *Edinburgh Castle*

AND SAVE MONEY WITH THE HISTORIC SCOTLAND EXPLORER PASS

For further information about **HISTORIC SCOTLAND** telephone:- + 44 131 668 8800
or write to us at:-
HISTORIC SCOTLAND
Longmore House
Salisbury Place
Edinburgh
Scotland
EH9 1SH

*Prices were correct at time of going to press and are subject to change without notice

265

THE LOWLANDS OF SCOTLAND, in terms of industry, commerce and wealth, have traditionally been the most prosperous. This can be illustrated by the antics of the legendary Rob Roy (1671-1734) who came from the Highlands, and raided the richer Lowland properties to feed his clan, earning him a similar reputation to England's Robin Hood. Other famous names help you to imagine the beauty and variety within the region, names such as Robert Burns, (poetry) Sir Walter Scott, (literature) James Watt, (inventor of the steam engine) and Charles Rennie Mackintosh, (Glasgow's most celebrated designer). Dumfries and Galloway is blessed with a mild climate, gardens, farmland, wooded valleys and winding rivers, which merge into moorland, forests, hills and mountains. The Border Region where the land borders England, continues to be scattered with castles reminding us of many hundreds of years of past conflicts. Contrastingly to that history, it is an area of tranquil villages, bustling textile towns and varied scenery. In the center, Lothian and Strathclyde, is where you find Edinburgh, the striking capital city of Scotland, with its magnificent castle. Glasgow, Scotland's second capital, is to the west, both of these main cities are rich in heritage and culture. Continuing north east through lochs and glens, (narrow valleys) to the unspoilt coastline, where you reach places like St Andrews, the world famous, 'Home of Golf' in Fife The

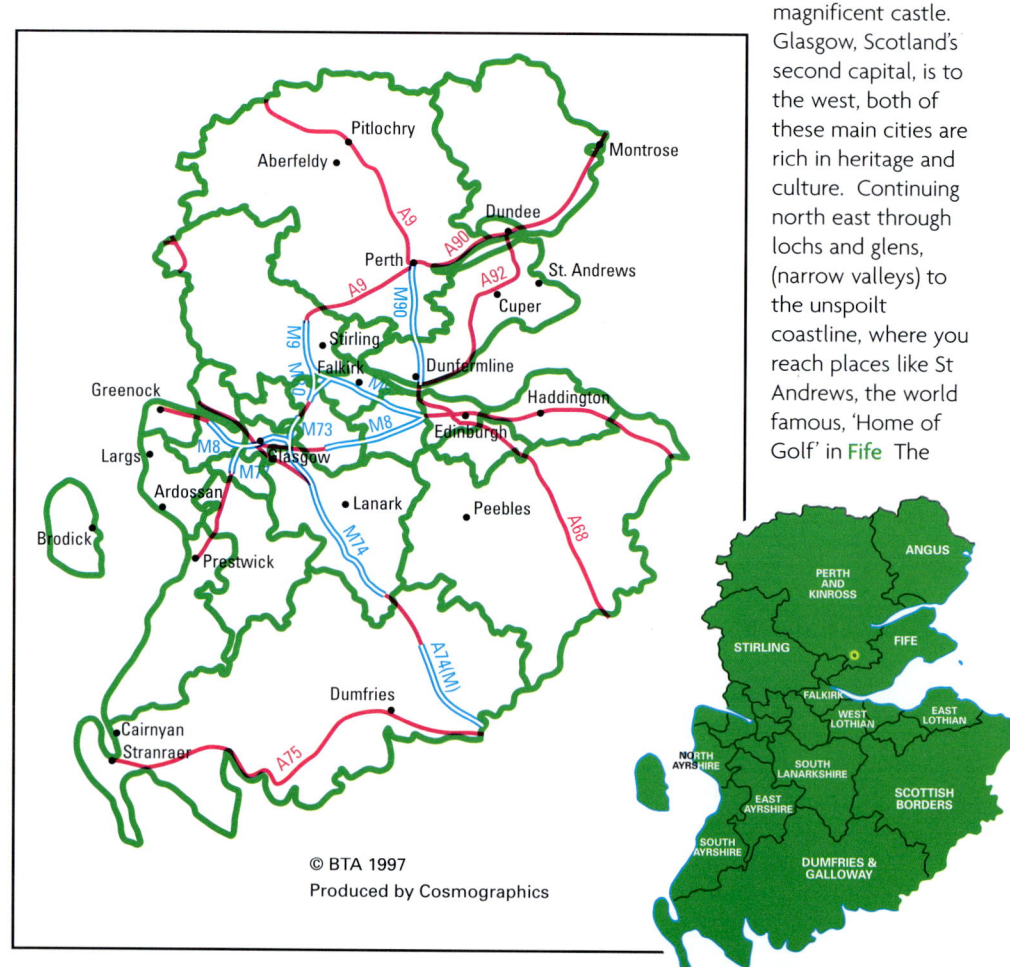

© BTA 1997
Produced by Cosmographics

North Sea borders the region on three sides, and above that, past fields of raspberries and strawberries, are the ancient cities of Perth and Dundee.

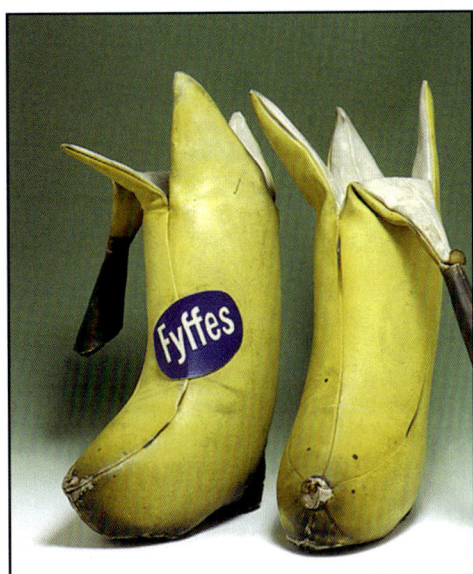

Peoples Palace

Trail List and Page No's
- Edinburgh 'Scotland's Capital City'   **268**
- Glasgow 'Scotland's Second Capital'   **272**

Access/Getting Around

From London
By Road
(page ref. 36,37)
The M25 London Orbital Motorway links the M1 to the north west and M6/M74 Glasgow with the A1(M) onto Edinburgh and A9 Inverness to the north.

By Rail
(page ref. 94,95)
A network of railway lines criss-cross parts of the area but the faster services are those leading to and from London's Kings Cross and Euston stations. A half hourly ScotRail Shuttle service runs between Edinburgh and Glasgow in just 50 minutes.

By Coach
(page ref. 96,97)
Coaches run frequently from London Victoria to most key towns in Scotland, including, Edinburgh, Glasgow and Stirling.

By Air
Aberdeen, Edinburgh and Glasgow are the key Airports, none being more than 8 miles from their city centers.

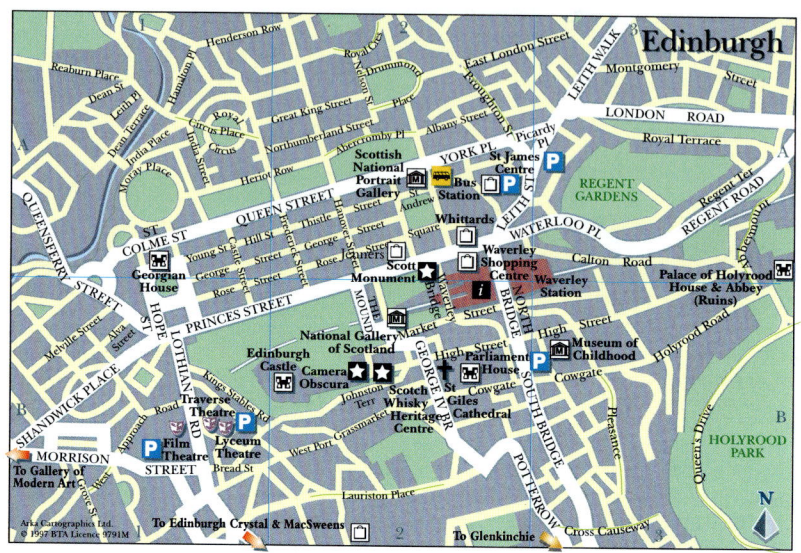

Edinburgh 'Scotland's Capital City'

Edinburgh is set on a series of volcanic rocks, the Old Town runs down from the Castle **B2**, and contrasts with the New, with its elegant Georgian Streets and Squares. Its museums and galleries display the riches of many cultures, and each year it plays host to Britain's largest arts extravaganza, the Edinburgh Festival. Edinburgh falls into two main sightseeing areas, The Royal Mile, (Old) around Edinburgh Castle **B2**, and Princes Street, (**New**) all of which is within walking distance.

Old, starting with the Royal Mile, from Castle Hill to Canongate, includes Edinburgh Castle, the Edinburgh Old Town Weaving Co., (2 for 1 tour, with NBC card), Scotch Whisky Heritage Centre, Camera Obscura, and Parliament House. Mercat Cross marks the city center, and on to the Museum

of Childhood, and the Palace of Holyroodhouse **B3**.

New, from Georgian House in Charlotte Square **A1**, to the many shops along Princes Street. Pass the Floral Clock, to the National Gallery of Scotland **A2**, and the Scott Monument, dedicated to Sir Walter Scott, poet and novelist 1771-1832. There are some real tastes of Scotland around Edinburgh, buy a haggis from MacSweens, or crystal at Edinburgh Crystal **B1**, and for

whisky, the Glenkinchie Distillery **B3**. Stay in Scotland, or back to England with the NBCompass.

ℹ️ Tourist Information

Edinburgh   ☎ 0131 473 3800

GF Edinburgh

Hotels

Edinburgh

STAKIS HOTELS Edinburgh - Edinburgh airport

Edinburgh

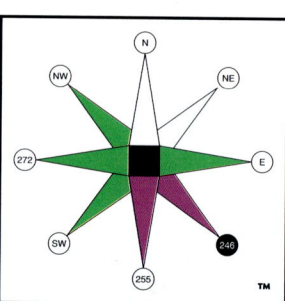

Distance from London

Edinburgh 372miles

1. Edinburgh Castle

Historic Scotland care for over 60 properties in Scotland, and upon presentation of your NBC Card/Guide at any of the properties you will receive a 10% discount on a 7 Day Pass for entry to all of their properties. Edinburgh Castle, a most famous castle that dominates Scotland's capital and gives stunning views of the city and countryside. Within the castle is the highly acclaimed, 'Honours of the Kingdom' exhibition which traces the history of Scotland's Crown Jewels, and culminates in a visit to the Crown Room, housing the Scottish Regalia and Stone of Destiny.

Edinburgh Castle, Castle Hill, The Royal Mile Edinburgh
☎ 0131 225 9846

  P

 9.30 -5pm

 % Page 265

  Edinburgh

M 8   **A** 8/7

Map ref: B2

2. Scotch Whisky Heritage Centre

Beside Edinburgh Castle, this award winning Visitor Centre offers more than a distillery visit. An explanation of the whisky making process and 'Ghostly Blenders' show are followed by a whisky barrel ride. Then a free 'dram' of whisky to try (for adults only). This is a fascinating and lively tour and the center is open 7 days a week.

Scotch Whisky Heritage Centre, 354 Castlehill, The Royal Mile, Edinburgh
☎ 0131 220 0441

★ **P**

 10-5pm

 21 Coupon

 Edinburgh

M 8   **A** 8/7

Map ref: B2

3. Camera Obscura

Next to the castle, enjoy a real time 'bird's eye' view of Edinburgh from high up inside the viewing area of the giant Victorian camera. Watch the goings on of the people below as every 15 minutes a friendly guide explains how it works, and tells the story of Edinburgh with humor and enthusiasm. Also, just outside the camera room, the rooftop terrace looks out across the city. An extraordinary display of holograms can be seen in the rooms leading up to the camera room.

Camera Obscura, Castle Hill, The Royal Mile, Edinburgh EH1 2LZ
☎ 0131 226 3709

★

 9.30-6pm

 21

 Edinburgh

M 8   **A** 8/7

Map ref: B2

4. National Gallery of Scotland

The Gallery is housed in an early 19th century neo-classical building designed by William Playfair. Its collection of works date from the 14th century. There is an outstanding collection of paintings, drawings and prints by great artists from the Renaissance to Post-Impressionism. These include Rembrandt, Vermeer, Turner, Constable, Monet and Van Gogh. The gallery also houses the finest collection of Scottish painting. Sundays 2-5pm.

National Gallery of Scotland, The Mound, Edinburgh EH2 2EL
☎ 0131 624 6200

M **P**

 10-5pm

Edinburgh

M 8   **A** 8/7

Map ref: A2

5. The Scottish National Gallery of Modern Art

The Gallery houses an unrivalled collection of the 20th century, with Scottish art, as well as Dada and Surrealist masterpieces, German expressionism and French Art. The exhibition includes works by Vuillard, Matisse, Picasso, Magritte, Miro, Hockney and Bacon. There is also a Parkland and sculpture garden. Sundays 2-5pm. Look out for their regular special exhibitions.

The Scottish National Gallery of Modern Art, Belford Road, Edinburgh EH4 3DR
☎ 0131 624 6200

 10-5pm

Edinburgh

M 8   A 8/7

Map ref: B1

6. The Scottish National Portrait Gallery

Here you will discover a unique visual history of Scotland, told through the portraits of those who shaped it. Including such luminaries as Mary, Queen of Scots and Robert Burns, right up to Jimmy Shand and Sean Connery. There are many regular exhibitions and changing displays of photography. Sundays 2-5pm

The Scottish National Portrait Gallery, 1 Queen Street, Edinburgh EH2 1JD
☎ 0131 624 6200

 10-5pm

 Edinburgh

M 8   A 8/7

Map ref: A2

7. Museum of Childhood

Founded in 1955, the city's Museum of Childhood, the first ever to be devoted to the history of childhood, is a favorite with children and adults alike. Often described as the 'noisiest museum in the world', five galleries display toys, games and pastimes, babies' items, health and schooldays. There are often also temporary exhibitions. Spend over £3 in the shop and receive a 10% discount. Entrance is free. Audio tour. Located in the Royal Mile and closed on Sundays.

Museum of Childhood, 42 High Street, Edinburgh EH1 1TG
☎ 0131 529 4142

10-5pm

% 10% (£3+)

Edinburgh

M 8   A 8/7

Map ref: B3

8. St. Giles Cathedral

The Gothic exterior is dominated by a 15th century tower, the only part to escape major renovation in the 19th century. The cathedral, situated on the Royal Mile, is known as the High Kirk, (church) of Edinburgh, and the carved pew in the Preston Aisle is used by the Queen when she stays here. Inside the magnificent Thistle Chapel can be seen the rib-vaulted roof and carvings, and the fine organ and stained glass are also wonderful. Admission is free, although a donation would be welcome.

St. Giles Cathedral, High Street, Edinburgh
☎ 0131 225 9442

8-7pm

Edinburgh

M 8   A 8/7

Map ref: B2

9. Palace of Holyrood House

At the opposite end of the Royal Mile to Edinburgh Castle, is the Palace of Holyrood House, the Queen's official residence in Scotland. The present palace was built in 1529 to accommodate James V. In the James V tower, in 1566, Mary Queen of Scots, (1542-1587) saw the murder, by her jealous husband Lord Darnley, of her trusted Italian secretary. Then, in 1567 she was accused of murdering Lord Darnley, and when she married the Earl of Bothwell, (also implicated in the murder) two months later, a rebellion ensued and she lost her crown. Today the public may visit the Royal Apartments and gardens.

Palace of Holyrood House, East end of Royal Mile, Edinburgh
☎ 0131 556 1096

 9.30-5pm

  Edinburgh

M 8   A 8/7

Map ref: A3

10. Macsweens

Haggis, (minced heart, lungs and liver of sheep with suet, fat and oatmeal) is one of Scotland's traditional foods. MacSweens of Edinburgh is a family run business that specialises in making a full range of traditional hand-made haggis to an authentic recipe, from miniature to 'Chieftains' (big!). You can also find many other traditional Scottish foods here, so why not discover the taste of Scotland at their factory shop. Closed at weekends. Perhaps a taxi south from Edinburgh center, or by buses, C70, 81, 87, 62, 64, 65 from the Bridges.

Macsweens, Dryden Road, Bilston Glen, Loanhead, Edinburgh EH20 GL2
☎ 0131 440 2555

  P

 8.30-5pm

% 15%    Visa MC

 Edinburgh

M 8   A 8/7

Map ref: B1

11. Edinburgh Crystal Visitor Centre

Since 1867, Edinburgh Crystal has been developing the art of glassmaking. At Edinburgh Crystal Visitor Centre, you will find a modern factory, making a very traditional product, where the elements of earth, air, fire and water are harnessed to bring to life the natural beauty of crystal. Ancient skills, with constantly evolving new ideas and designs. A warm welcome, fascinating tour and unique opportunity to see craftsmen glassblowing, inscribing delicate patterns and engraving. Located 10 miles south of the city center. From April 1 - Sept 29 at 11am,12 noon ,1 and 2pm ,* a free minibus is available on Waverley Bridge, outside the Acanthus café.

Edinburgh Crystal Visitor Centre, Eastfield, Penicuik, Mid Lothian EH26 8HB
☎ 01968 675128

 9-5pm

 Edinburgh and *Bus

A 701

Map ref: B1

12. Glenkinchie Distillery

A visit to Glenkinchie, home of the Edinburgh malt, involves a short and pleasant drive from the city center into the rolling farmland of East Lothian. Here you can see the distilleries at work, employing the excellent Scottish barley and pure, clear water from the nearby Lammermuir Hills, in the making of a capital malt in every respect. A brand new exhibition of malt whisky is housed in the listed red brick maltings, and you can enjoy a complimentary dram. Open from 12 on Sundays.

Glenkinchie Distillery, Pencaitland, Tranent, East Lothian
☎ 01875 342004

 9.30-5pm

 Edinburgh

A 68/6093

Map ref: B3

Glasgow 'Scotland's Second Capital'

Although often associated with its industrial past, Glasgow now rivals Edinburgh in its new cultural strength. These contrasts are seen throughout the city, which incidentally has its own underground train network. The remarkable benefit to visitors is that an enormous number of the most important museums and galleries in Glasgow can be visited absolutely free, as you will see on the following pages. One of the main influences on the cultural changes that took place in Glasgow was, Charles Rennie Mackintosh, (1868-1928) Glasgow's most celebrated designer. He was instrumental in the development of, 'Art Nouveau' and his works and influence are seen throughout the city.

To soak up the history and culture, start at Glasgow Cathedral **A2**, visit St Mungo Museum of Religious Life and Art, and then Provand's Lordship. The People's Palace **B2**, looks at the work and leisure of the ordinary people of Glasgow, and in the center, take a break at Willow Tea Rooms **A1**, in a Charles Rennie Mackintosh recreation. The main road (M8) south west takes you to the Burrell Collection **B1**, three miles away, but continuing along Sauchiehall Street you reach Kelvingrove Park, the Museum of Transport, and the Hunterian Art Gallery

A1. Edinburgh, Inverness or England with the NBCompass.

i **Tourist Information**

Glasgow ☎ 0141 204 4400

GF Glasgow

Hotels

Glasgow

STAKIS HOTELS Glasgow - Glasgow airport

Glasgow

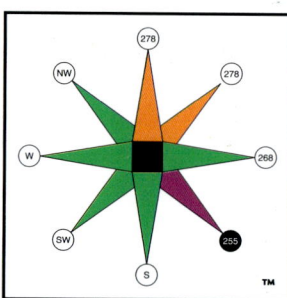

Distance from London

Glasgow 403miles

1. Glasgow Cathedral

Historic Scotland care for over 60 properties in Scotland, and upon presentation of your NBC Card/Guide at any of the properties you will receive a 10% discount on a 7 Day Pass for entry to all of their properties. Glasgow Cathedral is one of the most magnificent buildings of medieval Scotland. It is a rare example of a complete pre-Reformation Scottish cathedral. David I established the medieval diocese in the early 12th century, but the main building wasn't completed until well into the 14th century. Much of the medieval splendour is revealed today.

Glasgow Cathedral, Castle Street, Glasgow
☎ 0141 552 6891

 Daily

  Page 265 'Free'

 Glasgow

M 74 A 74

Map ref: A2

2. St Mungo Museum of Religious Life and Art

Glasgow Museums have ten separate museums, each with its own emphasis and personality. Admission at each museum and gallery is free. St Mungo is the first museum in the world to look at all the major religions together. It has the first authentic Buddhist Zen Garden in Britain which was specially designed and constructed in the courtyard. The Museum also houses, perhaps the most important religious painting, 'Christ of St John of the Cross' by Salvador Dali.

St Mungo Museum of Religious Life and Art, 2 Castle Street, Glasgow G4 0RH
☎ 0141 553 2557

 P

 10-5pm

 Glasgow

M 74

Map ref: A2

3. Provand's Lordship

Glasgow Museums have ten separate museums, each with its own emphasis and personality. Admission at each museum and gallery is free. Provand's Lordship. This is the oldest house in Glasgow, set in the heart of the most ancient part of the city. Dating from 1471, it was originally built as the Manse, (a religious minister's house) for St Nicholas Hospital, and shows period displays including a sweet shop on the ground floor.

Provand's Lordship, 3 Castle Street, Glasgow G4 0RH
☎ 0141 552 8819

 P

 10-5pm

 Glasgow

M 74

Map ref: A2

4. People's Palace

Glasgow Museums have ten separate museums, each with its own emphasis and personality. Admission at each museum and gallery is free. People's Palace. The 'Palace 'was opened in 1898, and has come to represent the spirit and character of Glasgow. Originally showing temporary exhibitions, providing a reading room and hosting concerts, it became the city's social and political history museum in the 1940's, and now brings you up to the present day.

People's Palace, Glasgow Green, Glasgow G40 1AT
☎ 0141 554 0223

 P

 10-5pm

 Glasgow

M 74

Map ref: B2

5. Gallery of Modern Art

Glasgow Museums have ten separate museums, each with its own emphasis and personality. Admission at each museum and gallery is free. The Gallery of Modern Art. This magnificent 18th century landmark building has been refurbished, and designed to show off the works of national and international importance. It comprises of four floors, and the main galleries are named after the four elements, Earth, Fire, Water and Air, highlighting the most exciting and innovative aspects of modern art.

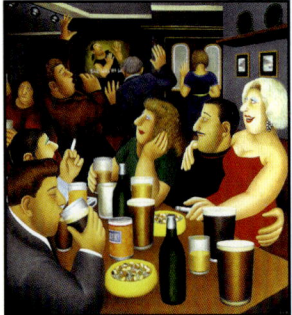

Gallery of Modern Art, Queen Street, Glasgow G1 3AZ
☎ 0141 229 1996

   P

 10-5pm

≢ ⬕ Glasgow

M 74

Map ref: B2

6. Willow Tea Room

A recreation of the original Charles Rennie Mackintosh Tea Room, designed in 1903 for Miss Catherine Cranston. Enjoy a stop here whilst traveling around the city. Choose from English tea, coffee or a light meal and at the same time continue your journey of discovery in the surroundings of Glasgow's best loved designer. Open from 12 - 4.15pm on Sundays. Also at 97 Buchanan Street tea rooms.

Willow Tea Room, 217 Sauchiehall Street, Glasgow G2 3EX
☎ 0141 332 0521

⬕ 9.30-4.30pm

% 10%

≢ ⬕ Glasgow

M 74

Map ref: A1

7. Museum of Transport

Glasgow Museums have ten separate museums, each with its own emphasis and personality. Admission at each museum and gallery is free. Museum of Transport. Amongst its outstanding displays, the museum boasts a reconstruction of a 1938 Glasgow Street, an authentic motor car showroom, movie theater, and a railway station which provides a focal point for the display of Scottish railway locomotives.

Museum of Transport, Kelvin Hall, 1 Bunhouse Road, Glasgow G3 8DP
☎ 0141 305 2600

  P

 10-5pm

≢ ⬕ Glasgow

M 74

Map ref: A1

8. Art Gallery and Museum, Kelvingrove

Glasgow Museums have ten separate museums, each with its own emphasis and personality. Admission at each museum and gallery is free. The Art Gallery and Museum is a magnificent example of late Victorian civic architecture, the imposing red sandstone faç
ade is one of the city's major landmarks. Situated in mature parkland in Glasgow's West End, it houses one of the finest civic art collections in Britain, including works by Rembrandt, Van Gogh and Whistler. It is Scotland's second most visited building.

Art Gallery and Museum, Argyle Street, Glasgow G3 8AG
☎ 0141 649 7151

   P

 10-5pm

≢ ⬕ Glasgow

M 74

Map ref: A1

9. Hunterian Art Gallery and the Mackintosh House

Hunterian Art Gallery houses an internationally renowned collection of paintings, drawings and prints by the Paris-trained American painter James McNeill Whistler, and furniture and drawings by Charles Rennie Mackintosh. Charles Rennie Mackintosh's works are supplemented by a complete reconstruction, and integral part of the gallery of his house at no. 6 Florentine Terrace, where he lived from 1906 to 1914. There are also works by Rembrandt, Chardin, Stubbs, Ramsay, Reynolds, Pissarro, Sisley and Rodin, plus Scottish painting from the 18th century to the present day. Temporary exhibitions and a 'Sculpture Courtyard'. Closed daily between 12.30-1.30.

Hunterian Art Gallery and the Mackintosh House, University of Glasgow, 82 Hill Head St., Glasgow
☎ 0141 330 5431

 P

⏰ 10-5pm

 Glasgow

M 74

Map ref: A1

10. Burrell Collection

Glasgow Museums have ten separate museums, each with its own emphasis and personality. Admission at each museum and gallery is free. This is one of the most important museum buildings of the 20th century. Representing the life's passion of just one man, wealthy Glaswegian shipowner, Sir William Burrell (1861-1958). The award winning collection covers an astounding range, that numbers over 8,000 and is the star of Glasgow's renaissance. Highlights include the tapestries and stained glass.

Burrell Collection, 2060 Pollokshaw Road, Glasgow G43 1AT
☎ 0141 649 7151

 P

⏰ 10-5pm

 Glasgow

M 74

Map ref: B1

11. House for an Art Lover

This is Glasgow's newest visitor attraction, built from the prize-winning designs of Charles Rennie Mackintosh. View the beautifully re-created exhibition rooms and the contemporary exhibition room. The remarkable design of practically every part of the house is quite inspirational, and the house is a popular location for private functions during week days. Please do check that it is open if you are not going at the weekend. A taxi from the city center costs around £6 each way.

House for an Art Lover, Bellahouston Park, Glasgow G41 5BW
☎ 0141 353 4770

 P

⏰ 10-5pm

 Glasgow

M 8 J23/24

Map ref: B1

12. Pollok House

Glasgow Museums have ten separate museums, each with its own emphasis and personality. Admission at each museum and gallery is free. Pollok House. Set in over 300 acres of formal gardens and the peaceful rolling parkland of Pollok Country Park, Pollok House is Glasgow's major surviving example of 18th century domestic architecture. It contains one of the finest collections of Spanish paintings in Britain, with works by El Greco and Goya.

Pollok House, 2060 Pollokshaw Road, Glasgow G3 1AT
☎ 0141 632 0274

 P

⏰ 10-5pm

  Glasgow

M 74

Map ref: B1

Scotland – The Highlands

THE HIGHLANDS OF SCOTLAND had, for over a thousand years, a Celtic society founded on clans. These were broken up by England after 1746, following the defeat of an attempt on the British Crown, led by Bonnie Prince Charlie. Here within these lands is the epitome of Scottish scenery, magnificent mountains and glens, lochs and worn coastlines. Heading north west of Glasgow past Loch Lomond, (Scotland's largest lake, 23 miles) are the west Highlands, where lochs teem with salmon and trout, Golden eagles soar above the steep mountains, and red deer roam the moors.

Inverness is the 'capital' of the Highlands, it is close to Loch Ness, (with the famous monster) and leads to Ben Nevis, (Britain's highest peak, 4,406ft) with its dramatic landscape. The ski slopes of the north, at Aviemore on the Cairngorm Mountains, form the highest land mass in Britain. Pass whisky distilleries, to

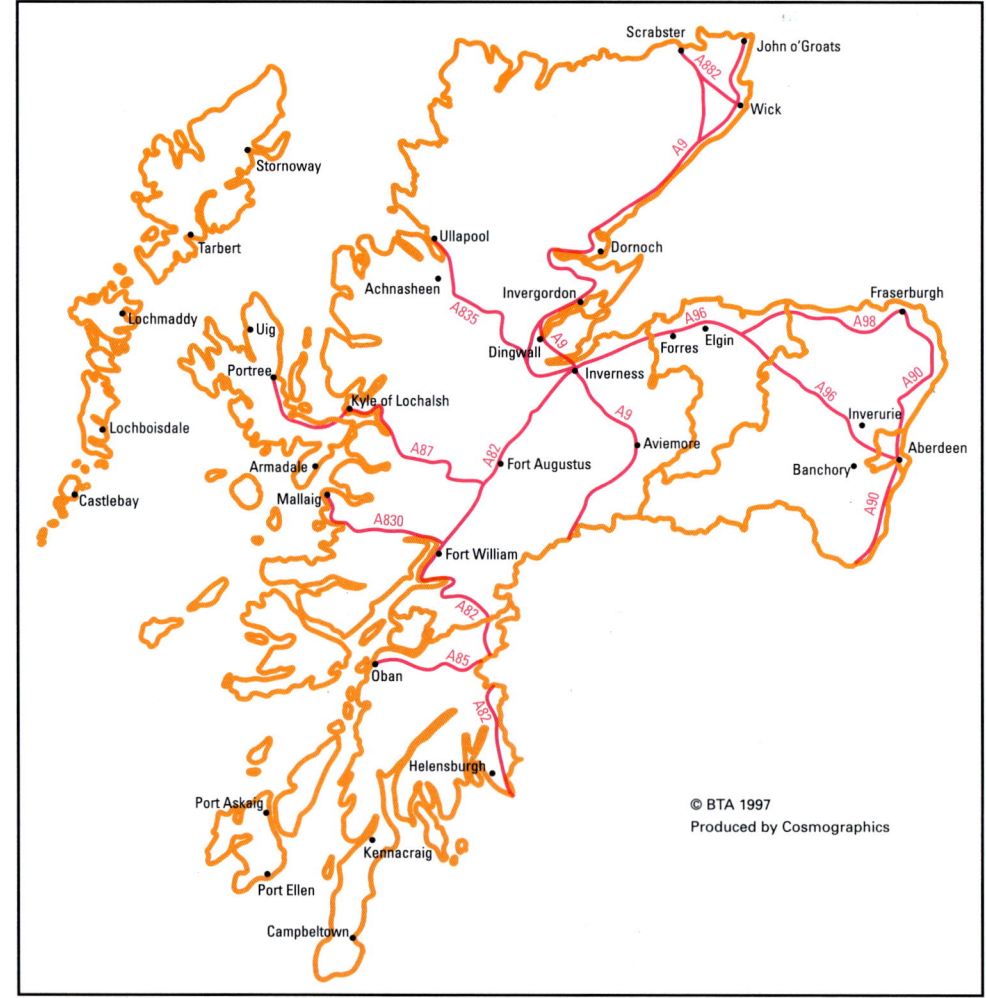

© BTA 1997
Produced by Cosmographics

Aberdeen in the Grampian Region, Scotland's third largest city, often referred to as the 'Granite City'.

Above Inverness, takes you to the rugged sandstone peaks, rising above a landscape of moors, and hundreds more lochs out to the Isle of Skye, a climbers paradise, where you are never more than 5 miles from the sea. John O'Groats, on the far north's lonely coast, claims to be Britain's most northerly village. Those that have journeyed across Britain, have a phrase that suggests the distance they have traveled, 'From Land's End to John O'Groats'. Land's End being Britain's southernmost point, about 875 miles away from here.

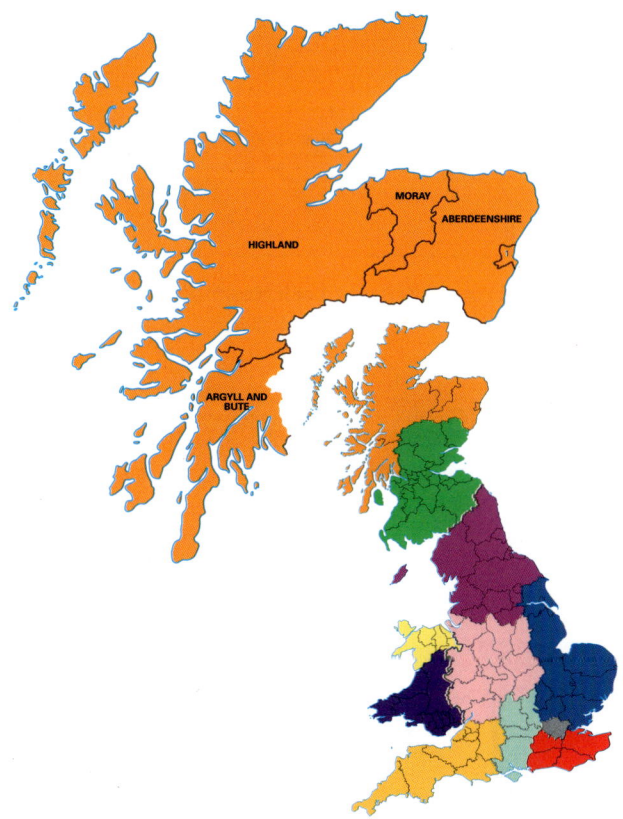

Access/Getting Around

From London
 By Road
(page ref. 36,37)
The M25 London Orbital Motorway links the M1 to the north west and M6/M74 Glasgow with the A1(M) onto Edinburgh and A9 Inverness to the north.

By Rail
(page ref. 94,95)
A network of railway lines criss-cross parts of the area but the faster services are those leading to and from London's Kings Cross and Euston stations. A half hourly ScotRail Shuttle service runs between Edinburgh and Glasgow in just 50 minutes and from either of these stations services to Aberdeen and Inverness.

By Coach
(page ref. 96,97)
Coaches run frequently from London Victoria to most key towns in Scotland including, Inverness, Aberdeen and Dundee.

By Air
Aberdeen, Edinburgh and Glasgow are the key Airports, none being more than 8 miles from their city centers. There is also an Airport at Inverness.

Trail and Page No.
• Loch Ness Monster & Inverness   **278**

'Loch Ness' and Inverness

Loch Ness, famed as the home of the legendary Loch Ness Monster, 'Nessie', is 24 miles long. Inverness is at the northern tip and Fort Augustus at the southern point. Inverness, as the traditional capital of the Highlands is where the route begins. Six miles east of Inverness is Culloden **2**, where on 16 April 1746, Bonnie Prince Charlie's army was slaughtered by Government troops under George II, finally ending hopes of the Scottish (Stuart family) restoration to the British throne.

From Inverness on the west side, Urquhart Castle **3**, to Loch Ness, the Loch Ness Exhibitions **4,5**, and the Bonnie Prince Charlie Centre **6**. Continuing south to Fort Augustus Abbey **7**, in Fort Augustus Village, where six locks, (locks of a canal, as opposed to lochs!) bring the Caledonian Canal into Loch Ness. There is an attractive forest trail that begins 2 miles further on from the village center, at Inchnacardoch. Finally, 25 miles further south is the awesome Ben Nevis, Britain's highest peak, reaching 4,406 ft above sea level. The NBCompass will help you visit

more of Britain, or guide you back to Edinburgh, Glasgow or London.

i Tourist Information

Inverness ☎ 01463 234353
Loch Ness* (Fort Augustus)

Loch Ness* ☎ 01320 366367
GF Inverness

Hotels

STAKIS HOTELS Inverness
Aviemore

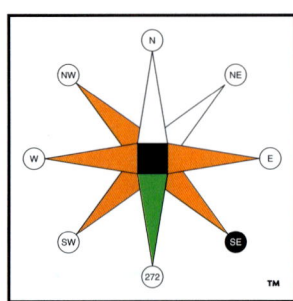

Distance from London

Inverness 526 miles

1. Hector Russell Kilt Maker

Discover the history, culture and tradition inherent in Scotland's national garment, and some of the secrets of how it's made. This is a unique opportunity to see within the world's largest kiltmaker workshop, audio visual displays and demonstrations of the craft, its history and development. Hector Russell have 18 shops throughout Scotland. October until mid May 9-5pm, closed on Sundays. Summer, Sundays open 10-5pm. Located west of the River Ness, Inverness town center.

Hector Russell KIlt Maker, 4-9 Huntly Street, Inverness IV3 5PR
☎ 01463 222781

 9-9pm

 All

Inverness

 9/82

2. Culloden Visitor Centre

Here, on 16th April 1746, the Jacobite army under Bonnie Prince Charlie was slaughtered by Government troops under, 'Butcher Cumberland' George II's younger son, finally ending the hopes of a Stuart restoration to the British throne. On the battlefield site are the memorials and graves. Footpaths now mark the boundaries of the front lines. The visitor center (National Trust for Scotland) has an audio visual presentation.

Culloden Visitor Centre, Culloden, Inverness
☎ 01463 790607

 9-6pm

Inverness

 9 B 9006

3. Urquhart Castle

Historic Scotland care for over 60 properties in Scotland, and upon presentation of your NBC card and guide at any of the properties you will receive a 10% discount on a 7 Day Pass for entry to all of their properties. Urquhart Castle. The remains of one of the largest castles in Scotland dominate a rocky promontory on Loch Ness. Once the site of the residence of a Pictish nobleman. Splendid views up and down Loch Ness.

Urquhart Castle Loch Ness, near Drumnadrochit, Inverness
☎ 01456 450551

 9.30 -5pm

 % Page 265

 Inverness

A 82/831

4. The Official Loch Ness Monster Exhibition

This is the home of the authoritative exhibition on the mysterious phenomenon of Loch Ness. Centered upon a walk through a 40 minute audio visual presentation, the exhibition displays much of the actual equipment used in the exploration of Loch Ness. Ever since the prows of Viking longships bore the sea dragon figure head, Norse and Celtic folklore tells of water horses in Highland Lochs. Located just 15 miles south of Inverness. Opening times vary from September to June, usually 10 - 4pm but please check first.

Loch Ness Visitor Centre, Drumnadrochit, Inverness IV3 6TU
☎ 01456 450573

 9-7.30pm

Inverness

 82

5. Original Loch Ness Visitor Centre

At the Original Loch Ness Visitor Centre you will be able to view facts, and the latest news on the Loch Ness Monster, (Nessie) with the aid of a wide screen Sony Cinema, (movie theater) system. The Loch is 24 miles long and up to 740 ft deep. It is located 14 miles south from Inverness on the A82. This attraction is linked with the Bonnie Prince Charlie Heritage Centre. 1 ticket for both attractions.

Original Loch Ness Visitor Centre, Drumnadrochit, Inverness IV3 6TJ
☎ 01456 450342

 9-9pm

 All
 Inverness
 82

6. Bonnie Prince Charlie Heritage Centre

Having visited the Original Loch Ness Monster Visitor Centre you will receive location details, and free entry, to the educational, Official Bonnie Prince Charlie Heritage Centre. Here you can follow the extraordinary journey of Prince Charles Edward Stuart in 1745. His story looks at the Battle of Culloden, his exile in France and final escape to freedom. Located at Lewiston off the A82.

Bonnie Prince Charlie Heritage Centre, Lewiston, Drumnadrochit, Inverness IV3 6TJ
☎ 01456 450225

 9-9pm
 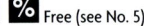 Free (see No. 5)
 Inverness
82

7. Fort Augustus Abbey

This 19th century Benedictine monastery is in a former military fort, housing a unique heritage center, with exhibitions, Loch Ness cruises, shop and accommodation. Situated in the picturesque Fort Augustus. A 'Walkman' commentary on the exhibition is available. Located half way between Inverness and Fort William on the A82 at the junction with B862.

Fort Augustus Abbey, Loch Ness, Inverness PH32 4BD
☎ 01320 366233

 9-6pm

 MC Visa
 Inverness
82   862

8. Inchnacardoch Lodge Hotel

Inchnacardoch Lodge Hotel is a Victorian hunting lodge set in 9 acres overlooking Loch Ness, and just half a mile away from Fort Augustus. An ideal base for exploring Loch Ness. All rooms are en suite (with bathroom). The hotel is non-smoking and has fishing, riding, golf and magnificent walks nearby. The offer is 3 nights stay for the price of 2, in March, April and October, or 4 nights stay for the price of 3 in May, June and September.

Inchnacardoch Lodge Hotel, by Fort Augustus, Inverness
☎ 01320 366258   Ⓕ 01320 366248

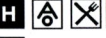
 24hrs

 All
 Inverness
82

1	2	3	4
5	6	7	8
9	10	11	12
13	14	15	16
17	18	19	20
21	22	23	24
25	26	27	28
29	30	31	32
33	34	35	36

Index

Index

Index

Index

Index

Index

Index

London Pride

The Original London Walks

MUSEUM OF THE

MOVING IMAGE

Shakespeare's Globe

Victoria and Albert Museum

MADAME TUSSAUD'S
Coupon no. TOR-164

GUIDE FRIDAY
SAVE £2
on any Guide Friday
town or city tour.
Only one discount per tour.

Not valid in conjunction with any other offer

GUIDE FRIDAY
SAVE £2
on any Guide Friday
town or city tour.
Only one discount per tour.

Not valid in conjunction with any other offer

GUIDE FRIDAY
SAVE £2
on any Guide Friday
town or city tour.
Only one discount per tour.

Not valid in conjunction with any other offer

GUIDE FRIDAY
SAVE £2
on any Guide Friday
town or city tour.
Only one discount per tour.

Not valid in conjunction with any other offer

GUIDE FRIDAY
SAVE £2
on any Guide Friday
town or city tour.
Only one discount per tour.

Not valid in conjunction with any other offer

GUIDE FRIDAY
SAVE £2
on any Guide Friday
town or city tour.
Only one discount per tour.

Not valid in conjunction with any other offer

London Pride
(Sightseeing Tour)
2 tickets for the price of 1

Not valid in conjunction with
any other offer

Ref. I. F.

GUIDE FRIDAY
SAVE £2
on any Guide Friday
town or city tour.
Only one discount per tour.
Not valid in conjunction with any other offer

GUIDE FRIDAY
SAVE £2
on any Guide Friday
town or city tour.
Only one discount per tour.
Not valid in conjunction with any other offer

MOMI
South Bank, Waterloo,
London SE1

£1.50 off adult full admission

Not valid in conjunction with
any other offer (valid until 31/12/2000)

The Original London Walks
£1 Discount
Not valid in conjunction with
any other offer

English Heritage

15% Discount on Visitor Pass

Not valid in conjunction with
any other offer (valid until 31/12/2000)

Madame Tussauds
Marylebone Road, London NW1
Valid for up to 4 people, this coupon allows
a discount of £1 off an Adult, Child or Senior
Citizen ticket for
Madame Tussaud's.

This voucher cannot be exchanged for cash or used in
conjunction with any other offer. Value of free admission
not to exceed value of paid admission.
(valid until 31/12/2000)

Victoria and Albert Museum
£1 off admission

t his voucher cannot be exchanged for cash or used in
conjunction with any other offer. Value of free admission
not to exceed value of paid admission.
(valid until 31/12/2000)

Shakespeare's Globe
New Globe Walk, Bankside,
London SE1

50p off admission
Not valid in conjunction with
any other offer (valid until 31/12/2000)

LONDON
PLANETARIUM
Combined TOR-165

Coupon no. TOR-170

Bateaux London

Catamaran Cruisers

Wimbledon Lawn Tennis Museum

Spaghetti House

Spaghetti House

Spaghetti House

Spaghetti House

Pescatori

Pescatori

Fuego

Vecchia Milano

Rock Circus

1 Piccadilly Circus, London W1

Valid for up to 4 people, this coupon allows a discount of £1 off an Adult, Child, Senior Citizen or Student ticket for Rock Circus

This voucher cannot be exchanged for cash or used in conjunction with any other offer.
Value of free admission not to exceed value of paid admission.(valid until 31/12/2000)

London Brass Rubbing

The Crypt, St Martin in the Fields Church, Trafalgar Square WC2

£1 off any brass rubbing

Not valid in conjunction with any other offer

Madame Tussauds

Marylebone Road, London NW1

Valid for up to 4 people, this coupon allows a discount of £1.50 off an Adult, Child or Senior Citizen combined ticket for
Madame Tussaud's & The London Planetarium

This voucher cannot be exchanged for cash or used in conjunction with any other offer.
Value of free admission not to exceed value of paid admission. (valid until 31/12/2000)

Wimbledon Lawn Tennis Museum

Church Road, Wimbledon, London SW19

£1 off admission

Not valid in conjunction with any other offer

Catamaran Cruisers

Charing Cross Pier, Victoria Embankment, London WC2

10% discount

Not valid in conjunction with any other offer

Bateaux London

Charing Cross Pier, Victoria Embankment, London WC2

10% discount evenings
5% discount lunches

Not valid in conjunction with any other offer

Spaghetti House

30 St Martin's Lane, London WC2

0171 836 1626

Complimentary carafe of House Wine
(Meal for 2 or more)

Not valid in conjunction with any other offer
(valid until 31/12/2000)

Spaghetti House

16 Jermyn Street, London SW1

0171 734 7334

Complimentary carafe of House Wine
(Meal for 2 or more)

Not valid in conjunction with any other offer
(valid until 31/12/2000)

Spaghetti House

74 Duke Street, London W1

0171 629 6097

Complimentary carafe of House Wine
(Meal for 2 or more)

Not valid in conjunction with any other offer
(valid until 31/12/2000)

Pescatori

Dover Street, London W1

0171 493 2652

Complimentary carafe of House Wine
(Meal for 2 or more)

Not valid in conjunction with any other offer
(valid until 31/12/2000)

Pescatori

Charlotte Street, London W1

0171 580 3289

Complimentary carafe of House Wine
(Meal for 2 or more)

Not valid in conjunction with any other offer
(valid until 31/12/2000)

Spaghetti House

77 Knightsbridge, London SW1

0171 235 8141

Complimentary carafe of House Wine
(Meal for 2 or more)

Not valid in conjunction with any other offer
(valid until 31/12/2000)

London Dungeon

28-34 Tooley Street, London SE1

2 tickets for the price of 1

This voucher cannot be exchanged for cash or used in conjunction with any other offer .Value of free admission not to exceed value of paid admission.
(valid until 31/12/2000)

Vecchia Milano

44 Wellbeck Street, London W1

0171 935 2371

Complimentary carafe of House Wine
(Meal for 2 or more)

Not valid in conjunction with any other offer
(valid until 31/12/2000)

Fuego

Pudding Lane, London EC3

0171 929 3366

10% off the total bill

(Meal for 2 or more)

Not valid in conjunction with any other offer
(valid until 31/12/2000)

Warwick Castle

Warwick Castle

Knebworth House

Dungeons of Windsor

The Model Village Bourton - on - the Water

ROYAL ARMOURIES MUSEUM

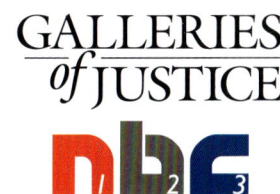

Brighton
Sea Life Centre
Marine Parade, Brighton, Sussex
2 tickets for the price of 1

This voucher cannot be exchanged for
cash or used in conjunction with any other offer. Value of
free admission not to exceed value of paid admission.
(valid until 31/12/2000)

Portsmouth
Sea Life Centre
Clarence Esplanade,
Portsmouth, Hampshire
2 tickets for the price of 1

This voucher cannot be exchanged for
cash or used in conjunction with any other offer. Value of
free admission not to exceed value of paid admission.
(valid until 31/12/2000)

Hunstanton
Sea Life Centre
Southern Promenade,
Hunstanton, Norfolk
2 tickets for the price of 1

This voucher cannot be exchanged for
cash or used in conjunction with any other offer. Value of
free admission not to exceed value of paid admission.
(valid until 31/12/2000)

Warwick Castle
Castle Lane, Warwick
£2 off adult Full admission

This voucher cannot be exchanged for cash or used in
conjunction with any other offer. Value of free admission
not to exceed value of paid admission.
(valid until 31/12/2000)

Hastings
Sea Life Centre
Rock-A-Nore Road,
Hastings, Sussex
2 tickets for the price of 1

This voucher cannot be exchanged for
cash or used in conjunction with any other offer. Value of
free admission not to exceed value of paid admission.
(valid until 31/12/2000)

Rhyl
Sea Life Centre
East Parade
Rhyl. Denbighshire
2 tickets for the price of 1

This voucher cannot be exchanged for
cash or used in conjunction with any other offer. Value of
free admission not to exceed value of paid admission.
(valid until 31/12/2000)

Dungeons of Windsor
30a High Street, Windsor.
Berkshire
2 tickets for the price of one

Not valid in conjunction with any other offer
(valid until 31/12/2000)

Knebworth House
Knebworth, Hertfordshire
2 tickets for the price of one
(not special event days)

Not valid in conjunction with any other offer
(valid until 31/12/2000)

Warwick Castle
Castle Lane, Warwick
£2 off adult Full admission

This voucher cannot be exchanged for cash or used in
conjunction with any other offer. Value of free admission
not to exceed value of paid admission.
(valid until 31/12/2000)

Royal Armouries
Armouries Drive,
Leeds, Yorkshire
2 tickets for the price of 1

Not valid in conjunction with any other offer
(valid until 31/12/2000)

Model Village
Bourton-on-the-Water,
Nr Cheltenham, Glosr
2 tickets for the price of 1

Not valid in conjunction with any other offer
(valid until 31/12/2000)

Woburn Safari Park
Woburn Park, Bedfordshire
One child free with 2 adults
paying full admission prices

Not valid in conjunction with any other offer
(valid until 31/12/2000)

Galleries of Justice
Shire Hall, High Pavement,
Lace Market, Nottingham
2 tickets for the price of 1

This voucher cannot be exchanged for
cash or used in conjunction with any other offer.Value of
free admission not to exceed value of paid admission.
(valid until 31/12/2000)

York Dungeon
12 Clifford Street, York
2 tickets for the price of 1

This voucher cannot be exchanged for
cash or used in conjunction with any other offer.Value of
free admission not to exceed value of paid admission.
(valid until 31/12/2000)

National Seal Sanctuary
Gweek, Cornwall
2 tickets for the price of 1

This voucher cannot be exchanged for
cash or used in conjunction with any other offer.Value of
free admission not to exceed value of paid admission.
(valid until 31/12/2000)

Questionnaire

We would be delighted to receive any comments, suggestions or amendments for incorporation in the next edition. As we constantly strive to improve the guide we would also value your comments on individual attractions, also in the unlikely event of their offer not being honoured do let us know. In the first instance we recommend that you show the participating company the reverse of your NBC Card, and the NBC Guide, should it be requested. If there are any further difficulties please note the name of the company, date of your visit and the difficulty you encountered, in the panel below, and return it to us at the following address:

NBC Ltd. Fulton House
Fulton Road
Wembley Park
Middlesex HA9 0TF
UK.

Thank you for your kind help.

Name of Attraction/Shop
Date Visited
Type of Problem or Difficulty
1.
2.
3.

Name of Attraction/Shop
Date Visited
Type of Problem or Difficulty
1.
2.
3.

Name of Attraction/Shop
Date Visited
Type of Problem or Difficulty
1.
2.
3.

✎Notes

Notes

Please Note (page 67)
English Heritage offer NBC cardholders a 15% discount on Visitor Passes
Please use the special Coupon located in the back of this guide